OXFORD **IB STUDY GUIDES**

W9-BYI-440

Constantine Ziogas

Economics

FOR THE IB DIPLOMA

2nd edition

OXFORD

UNIVERSITY PRESS

OXFORD
UNIVERSITY PRESS

Great Clarendon Street, Oxford OX2 6DP

Oxford University Press is a department of the University of Oxford.
It furthers the University's objective of excellence in research,
scholarship, and education by publishing worldwide in

Oxford   New York

Auckland   Cape Town   Dar es Salaam   Hong Kong   Karachi
Kuala Lumpur   Madrid   Melbourne   Mexico City   Nairobi
New Delhi   Shanghai   Taipei   Toronto

With offices in

Argentina   Austria   Brazil   Chile   Czech Republic   France   Greece
Guatemala   Hungary   Italy   Japan   Poland   Portugal   Singapore
South Korea   Switzerland   Thailand   Turkey   Ukraine   Vietnam

Oxford is a registered trade mark of Oxford University Press
in the UK and in certain other countries

© Constantine H. Ziogas 2012

The moral rights of the author have been asserted

Database right Oxford University Press (maker)

First published 2008

All rights reserved. No part of this publication may be reproduced,
stored in a retrieval system, or transmitted, in any form or by any means,
without the prior permission in writing of Oxford University Press, or as
expressly permitted by law, or under terms agreed with the approprate
reprographics rights organization. Enquiries concerning reproduction
outside the scope of the above should be sent to the Rights Department,
Oxford University Press, at the address above

You must not circulate this book in any other binding or cover
and you must impose this same condition on any acquirer

British Library Cataloguing in Publication Data

Data available

ISBN: 978-0-19-839001-5
10 9 8 7 6 5 4 3 2 1

Printed in Great Britain by Bell & Bain Ltd, Glasgow

Paper used in the production of this book is a natural, recyclable product made from wood grown in
sustainable forests. The manufacturing process conforms to the environmental regulations of the country
of origin

Acknowledgments

The Publisher would like to thank the following for permission to reproduce photograph:
Cover image: Steven Vidler/Eurasia Press/Corbis

Dedication

To my darlings, Daphne, Myrto and Elias

Introduction for the student

- This book has been written specifically for the student studying Higher or Standard Level Economics for the IB Diploma Programme.

- It may be helpful to any student of Introductory Economics, especially in the area of understanding the construction and use of diagrams.

- The study guide is organized in boxes and bullet points, and also includes 'tips' to help your work. Explanations are provided for all points presented.

- The importance of diagrams in Economics in general, and in the IB examination process in particular, cannot be overemphasized. This guide has been written to help you realize that diagrams are not just 'pictures' for you to remember and 'paste' onto your answer sheets, but perfectly logical constructions that once you understand you will never forget.

- Essay-style questions have been included to help you ensure that you have covered all the material.

- All Higher Level material is clearly marked. Section 5 focuses on the mathematical knowledge and skills required by Higher Level students.

- The glossary covers every term found in the syllabus and will be useful to you both for reference and as a revision source.

Constantine H. Ziogas

Contents

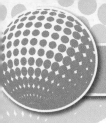

Foundations of economics

Scarcity

Economics as a discipline would not exist without scarcity.

This is the fundamental problem that all societies face. It refers to the excess of human wants over what can actually be produced to fulfill these wants. Human wants are unlimited. On the other hand, the means of fulfilling these human wants are limited because the resources available are limited. As a result, choices have to be made.

For example, society cannot enjoy all the books and all the tables it wants because the number of trees required to produce these two goods is limited. It somehow has to decide how many books and how many tables it wants to produce. If more tables are produced then fewer books will be enjoyed and vice versa. We define as the opportunity cost of a choice, the value of the next best alternative sacrificed. If, for example, by giving (or more correctly, 'allocating') a tree to table production, one extra table is produced but 25 books need to be sacrificed, we say that the opportunity cost of producing one more table is 25 books.

Resources (factors of production)

Resources are also referred to as factors of production. They include all inputs used in the production of a good or service. They are typically separated into the following four categories.

- **Land and raw materials (natural resources)**

  These are inputs into production that are provided by nature, for example agricultural and non-agricultural land, forests, pastures, mineral deposits, oil, natural gas, lakes and rivers. The world's land area and raw materials are limited. Some resources, such as oil and coal deposits, are non-renewable: if they are used now, they will not be available in the future. Other resources, for example forests (timber) and the stock of fish, are renewable.

- **Labour (human resources)**

  Labour includes all forms of human input, both physical and mental, into current production. The labour force is, at any point in time, limited both in number and in skills. The total number of people available for work is referred to as the labour force or working population.

- **Capital**

  Physical capital includes manufactured resources; in other words, goods used to produce other goods. The world has a limited stock of capital (limited supply of factories, machines, tools and other equipment). Note that the meaning of capital in economics is different from that used in ordinary speech where people refer to money as capital.

- **Entrepreneurship**

  Entrepreneurship is related but not identical to management. When a new venture is being considered, risks exist. They involve the unknown future. Someone must assess these risks and make judgments about whether or not to undertake them. The people who do so are called entrepreneurs. Entrepreneurship refers to the willingness and ability of certain individuals to take risks and to mobilize the remaining factors of production.

Related concepts

In addition to the idea of physical capital already mentioned, it is useful to include natural capital and human capital.

- **Natural capital**

  Natural capital can be thought of as natural resources which may be improved upon or may be depleted. Thinking in terms of natural capital can easily accommodate another related concept, sustainability, which refers to the idea of preserving and even increasing or improving upon the available stock of natural resources.

- **Human capital**

  Labour may also be improved upon, in that the labour force may become more productive. The term human capital refers to the education, training and skills embodied in the labour force of a country. Even if the size of the labour force of an economy is constant over time, the stock of human capital may increase.

Other useful introductory terms

Social sciences: disciplines that systematically study human behaviour from different perspectives. Economics, psychology, anthropology, political science, sociology and history are all considered social sciences.

Models: simplified and often simplistic representations of reality. They are constructed to study a phenomenon and through it explain past observations and perhaps predict future ones. Evaluating the appropriateness or usefulness of a specific model is not easy.

Normative economic statements: value judgments, opinions and statements that cannot be falsified or proven right or wrong; statements that cannot be tested against fact (data). Examples are: 'Inflation is rising too fast' or 'Income distribution is not fair'. Key phrases in normative statements include 'ought to be', 'should be', 'too much', 'too little', 'is fair', 'is unfair', and so on.

Positive economic statements: statements that can be falsified or proven, at least in principle, right or wrong. They can be tested against facts (data), for example: 'A minimum wage policy will increase unemployment among unskilled workers.'

Economic goods: goods and services that require scarce resources to be sacrificed in order for them to be produced.

Free goods: in contrast to economic goods, free goods have a zero opportunity cost of production. (There are very few real-world examples, perhaps sea water and air.) Note that goods available at a zero price are not free in the economist's sense if scarce resources have been used up to produce them.

Competitive market: a market where there are very many small firms, the good is homogeneous (it is considered identical across firms by consumers) and nothing prevents a new firm from entering the market or an existing firm from exiting.

Ceteris paribus: a Latin phrase that means 'all other things remaining constant'.

Rationality: in economics rationality is taken to imply purposeful behaviour and, more specifically, utility-maximizing consumers and profit-maximizing firms.

The fundamental questions of economics

Three fundamental questions

Scarcity necessitates choice. As a result all societies, independently of their level of economic development or the economic system adopted, must answer the following three questions.

- **What** (which goods and services) will be produced and in what quantities?
- **How** will each good or service be produced (using, for example, a labour-intensive or capital-intensive technology)?
- **For whom** will goods and services be produced? (How will income be distributed?)

Countries develop their own set of institutions that answer these three questions. How these institutions do this depends on the economic system the country has adopted. An economic system can be broadly defined as the institutional framework within which economic activity takes place. It is easy to distinguish two extreme cases but in the real world there are many variations. The two extremes are market economies and command economies, and between these extremes are mixed economies.

- A **market economy** is one where households and firms, each acting in their own self-interest and through their interaction in markets, provide answers to the three questions.
- A **command economy** is one where the state provides the answers.
- A **mixed economy** is one where both markets and the state provide the answers.

Central to the idea of a market economy is the concept of a market. A market should be thought as a mechanism that can provide answers to the three fundamental questions. For example, the market can determine:

- whether this good or that good will be produced and in what quantities
- which production technology a firm should use to produce a good or a service
- how much income the owner of each factor of production will earn.

Economics is the study of markets: their successes and their failures. Questions of resource allocation are investigated in economics. Taking the example given earlier, economics investigates how many workers and how many trees will be allocated to the production of tables, and how many workers and how many trees will be allocated to the production of books. Given a set of resources (that is, a specific amount of labour and trees) there are various possible allocations. Each allocation leads to some amount of tables and some amount of books produced and consumed. Not all of these allocations are best for society. Economics studies the allocations that result from the operation of the market mechanism and then examines whether they answer the three fundamental questions in the best possible way or not. Sometimes we will see that the market as a mechanism succeeds and results in the best possible answers for society to these questions. Many other times, the market as a mechanism fails. When it fails it automatically creates a role for the government to step in and attempt to correct the market failure. However, as we will see, there is no *a priori* guarantee that the answers that governments provide are necessarily better as government failure is also possible.

The production possibilities curve

The production possibilities curve (PPC) – also referred to as the production possibilities frontier (PPF) – is the first economic model we will study. Through it, a number of important economic concepts will be illustrated and become clear. For example, the model provides us with a visual account of scarcity, attainable and unattainable choices, opportunity cost, efficiency and growth.

A PPC refers to an economy with a fixed amount of resources, characterized by a given level of technology as well as some institutional framework, and producing only two goods. A PPC shows for every amount produced of good X, the maximum amount of good Y that this economy can produce if it fully utilizes its limited resources using the available technology. For example, referring to Figure 0.1, if the economy decides to produce X1 units of good X then it can produce Y1 units of good Y at the most, (assuming that it fully utilizes its limited resources with the available technology). A PPC is a technological relationship and it provides no information about choices. It shows what an economy can do, not what it chooses to do.

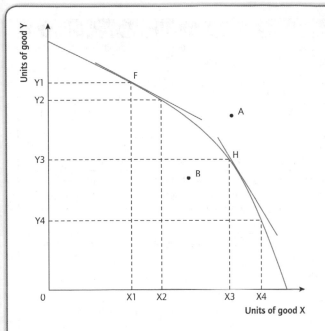

Figure 0.1 The PPC

The existence of a PPC reflects scarcity: the limited resources available constrain any economy in producing only some combinations of output. Combinations of output represented by points outside a PPC (such as point A in Figure 0.1) are **unattainable** given the amount of resources available and the current level of technology. Points inside the PPC (such as point B in Figure 0.1) show **attainable but inefficient** output combinations in the sense that available resources are not fully utilized, for example there is unemployment. Points on the PPC (such as points F and H) show **attainable and efficient** combinations as there is no waste of scarce resources and it is not possible to produce more of one good without sacrificing some of the other.

The negative slope of the PPC reflects that, in order to produce more of one good, resources have to be diverted away from the production of the other good so that less of the other good can now be produced: there is an opportunity cost involved in producing an extra unit of a good. This opportunity cost is the amount of the other good that has to be sacrificed. The opportunity cost of producing X1X2 extra units of good X is equal to the Y1Y2 units of good Y that need to be sacrificed. The opportunity cost of producing X3X4 extra units of X is equal to Y3Y4 units of good Y that need to be sacrificed.

As scarce resources are not equally well suited for the production of all goods (because resources tend to be specialized), the opportunity cost of producing more and more units of a good increases: ever-increasing amounts of good Y need to be sacrificed to produce more and more units of good X. This is why the PPC is bowed towards the origin. The slope (the tangent at each point, such as at points F and H) becomes steeper and steeper, reflecting that the opportunity cost of producing more of good X is increasing. Producing X3X4 more units of good X is costlier than producing X1X2 more units of X because resources much better suited for the production of good Y must now be diverted to the production of good X. If, on the other hand, resources were perfectly substitutable then the PPC would be a negatively sloped straight line reflecting constant opportunity costs.

Growth of an economy can be shown through an outward shift of the PPC. It implies that combinations of output that were initially unattainable can now be produced. For such an outward shift to occur, more or better resources should become available and/or technology should improve. It can be argued that adopting a better institutional framework will also contribute to growth.

> **TIP**
> Make sure that the PPC you draw touches the two axes and is not 'floating' in mid air. Draw it bowed (concave) towards the origin unless you are using it to illustrate constant opportunity costs. Also note that the axes may be labelled 'consumption goods' and 'capital goods' to illustrate the opportunity cost of investment. In this case, the opportunity cost of producing more capital goods (that is, the opportunity cost of investment) is the sacrifice of current levels of consumption.

Unemployment implies the existence of (labour) resources that are not utilized. The economy is producing some combination of output represented by a point located inside its PPC. It follows that if unemployment increases then the new point will lie somewhere closer to the origin as fewer units of at least one of the two goods will be produced. Conversely, if unemployment decreases there is no shift in the PPC as the labour factor of production has not increased. The economy will just move from some combination inside its PPC to another combination closer to the curve itself (that is, to any point located to the northeast of the original point).

Explanation	
Points outside the PPC	These are unattainable combinations of output: more or better resources and/or improved technology would be necessary to produce such combinations.
Points on the PPC	These are attainable and efficient combinations as there is no waste of scarce resources.
Points inside the PPC	These are attainable but inefficient combinations as scarce resources are not being used, so they are wasted.

What the PPC can illustrate	
Scarcity	The existence of the PPC illustrates scarcity. If scarcity did not exist then all points in the 'goods space' created when drawing our two axes would be attainable – this is obviously unrealistic.
Choice	Once the PPC is constructed, a society can choose any combination of output (point) on it, or, if society's preferences or priorities change, move from one combination to another one along the curve.
Efficiency	Efficiency is shown at all points on the PPC, as each reflects full use of available resources given the available technology without any waste.
Inefficiency	Inefficiency is shown at all points inside the PPC, as given the amount produced of one of the two goods, more of the other could be produced. This implies wasted (idle or unemployed) resources and so inefficiency.
Opportunity cost	Movement from one point on the PPC to another implies that more of one of the two goods is produced but less of the other. So the extra amount produced of one good comes at a cost: this cost is the amount sacrificed of the other good. The opportunity cost of producing more units of the good on the horizontal axis is given by the slope of the PPC.
Constant opportunity cost	A linear PPC reflects constant opportunity costs: producing more and more units of one good always requires the same amount of the other good to be sacrificed.
Increasing opportunity cost	A concave (bowed in towards the origin) PPC shows increasing opportunity cost, as to produce equal extra units of one good, increasing amounts of the other good have to be sacrificed.
Growth	An outward shift of the PPC reflects growth as combinations of output previously unattainable become attainable.

Central themes

- **How much of a role should markets have and how much of a role should government have?**

  Markets can be considered as a mechanism leading to some allocation of scarce resources. There is no guarantee that the market outcome is the best outcome from society's point of view. For example, markets may lead to too much pollution, or not enough libraries; they may lead to unacceptably high rates of unemployment or to inadequate health care for lower-income households; they may lead to excessively risky lending practices by financial institutions or to not enough basic scientific research. On the other hand, even if there is a role for the government to play, can we guarantee that intervention will improve matters? What is the extent and the type of intervention that is necessary? At what cost?

- **What is sustainability and why has it emerged as such an important concept?**

  The concept is closely but not exclusively related to the environmental effects of current patterns of production and resource allocation. The World Development Report 2010 states:

  > 'Development that is socially, economically and environmentally sustainable is a challenge, even without global warming. Economic growth is needed, but growth alone is not enough if it does not reduce poverty and increase the equality of opportunity. And failing to safeguard the environment eventually threatens economic and social achievements.'

These points are not new. They only repeat what still is, after more than 20 years, perhaps the most widely used definition of sustainable development: 'Development that meets the needs of the present without compromising the ability of future generations to meet their own needs.'

- **Given scarcity, should we only care about efficiency or should equity also be a goal?**

  Is there perhaps a trade-off between these two goals? What do we mean in economics by the term 'efficiency'? What does 'equity' mean? There has been much debate on whether policies that promote equity hurt or also promote efficiency. Does the answer depend on the types of policy that are employed to ensure equity?

- **If an economy grows, is there economic development?**

  Is there perhaps too much attention being paid to how fast an economy grows? When does economic growth lead to development? Can there be development without growth? To what extent can one confidently claim that an advanced economy is a developed economy? Should we focus on country totals or should we pay closer attention to variations within a country?

1.1 Competitive markets: demand and supply

Microeconomics is concerned with the individual parts of the economy. It is concerned with the demand and supply of particular goods, services and resources. In other words, it focuses on individual markets.

Markets

A market can be defined as an institution which permits interaction between buyers and sellers. It can also be considered a mechanism that determines which goods and services will be produced in an economy and so how scarce resources will be allocated.

Several different types of market exist beyond product markets where goods and services are being exchanged. Factors of production are traded in factor markets. The labour market is an example of a factor market. The stock market, the bond market and the foreign exchange market are examples of financial markets.

The interaction of consumers and producers (firms) in product markets determine the market price of each product. Changes in market conditions therefore result in changes in market prices. These set off a chain of events leading to more or less of the good being produced and so to a new allocation of scarce resources.

To analyse how markets function we need to examine the behaviour of consumers and of producers.

Demand: the behaviour of consumers

The demand for a good summarizes the behaviour of buyers in a market. It is the relationship between various possible prices and the corresponding quantities that consumers are willing and able to purchase per time period, ceteris paribus. Ceteris paribus means that all other factors affecting demand are assumed constant.

This relationship between price per unit and quantity demanded per period of time is inverse (negative), meaning that if the price increases then quantity demanded will decrease as consumers will be willing and able to buy less per period.

The inverse relationship between price and quantity demanded is referred to as the law of demand. The law of demand states that if the price of a good rises then quantity demanded per period will fall, ceteris paribus.

A demand curve shows this inverse relationship between the price per unit of a good and the quantity of the good demanded per period. Price per unit is measured on the vertical axis; quantity demanded per period is measured on the horizontal axis.

A demand curve may refer to an individual consumer or to the market. The market demand curve is the horizontal summation of all the individual demand curves. This means that at each price we add the quantities demanded by each individual. So if a market consists of Joey and Ross, and at a price of €2.00 Joey is willing and able to buy five lattes per week while Ross is willing and able to buy seven lattes per week, then at the price of €2.00 the market demand is 12 lattes per week.

For example, in Figure 1.1.1, if the price per unit is P1 then consumers will be willing and able to buy Q1 units per period, whereas if the price increased to P2 per unit then consumers will be willing and able to buy Q2 units per period, ceteris paribus.

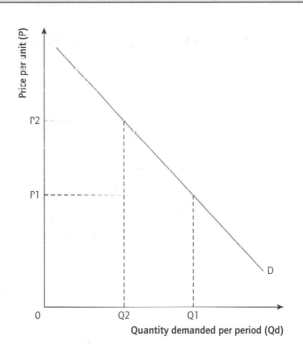

Figure 1.1.1 A typical market demand curve

Goals of typical consumers

Consumers' utility is the satisfaction derived from consuming a good or a bundle of goods. Typical consumers will try to maximize their utility: this means that they will choose the bundle of goods which maximizes their satisfaction and which they can afford, given their income and the prices they face in the market.

Why do we expect the law of demand to hold?	
The substitution effect	If the price of X increases then all other goods automatically become relatively cheaper so consumers will tend to substitute other goods for X
The income effect	If the price of X increases then purchasing power of consumers decreases and they will be able to afford less of X

TIP A typical demand curve can be drawn as a straight line using a ruler or drawn slightly curved and it may or may not touch the axes. What matters when drawing a typical demand curve is that it is negatively sloped.

Other factors affecting demand ('shift' factors)

- Changes in consumers' income may affect demand. For example, if income increases then demand for most goods is expected to increase, so the demand curve is expected to shift to the right. This is the case of 'normal' goods.

For some goods, typically lower-quality goods, an increase in income will lead to a decrease in demand and a shift of the demand curve to the left. This is the case of 'inferior' goods.

The same good may behave as a normal good in one society or market and as an inferior good in another. For example, in a country with a generally low-income population, an increase in income may lead to an increase in the demand for used cars, whereas in another country where people have higher incomes, a further increase in income levels may lead to a decrease in the demand for used cars.

A good is a normal good if:	A good is an inferior good if:
an increase in income leads to an increase in its demand or, more generally, if income and demand change in the same direction	an increase in income leads to a decrease in its demand or, more generally, if income and demand change in opposite directions

- Changes in the price of other related goods will have an impact on demand. First let's consider a change in the price of **complements**. Two goods are considered complements if they are often consumed together. For example, for many people coffee and sugar are complements because they

drink their coffee with sugar. We expect that if the price of coffee increases then the demand for sugar may decrease. More generally, if goods X and Y are considered as strong complements then an increase in the price of good Y will lead to a decrease in the demand for good X. Demand for X will shift to the left.

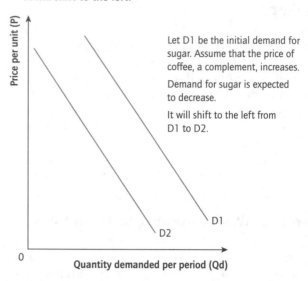

Let D1 be the initial demand for sugar. Assume that the price of coffee, a complement, increases.

Demand for sugar is expected to decrease.

It will shift to the left from D1 to D2.

Figure 1.1.3 The effect of an increase in the price of a complement

There may also be changes in the price of **substitutes**. Two goods are considered substitutes if they are in competitive consumption and consumers typically buy one or the other as the goods satisfy the same need or want. Examples are coffee and tea or Pepsi Cola and Coca Cola. If a supermarket increases the price of Pepsi Cola then it is expected that the demand for Coca Cola will increase. More generally, if good X and good Y are considered close substitutes then an increase in the price of good Y will lead to an increase in the demand for X. Demand for X will shift to the right.

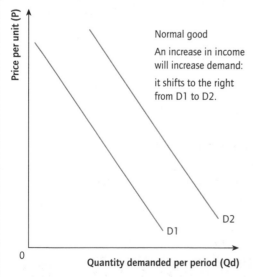

Normal good

An increase in income will increase demand:

it shifts to the right from D1 to D2.

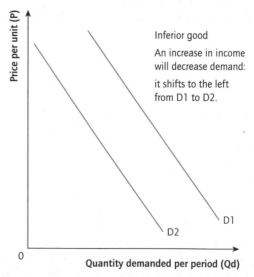

Inferior good

An increase in income will decrease demand:

it shifts to the left from D1 to D2.

Figure 1.1.2 The effect of an increase in income on a normal good and on an inferior good

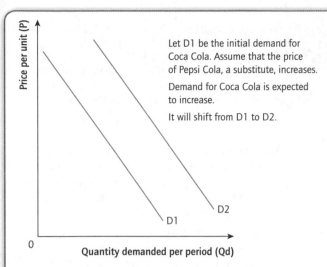

Let D1 be the initial demand for Coca Cola. Assume that the price of Pepsi Cola, a substitute, increases.

Demand for Coca Cola is expected to increase.

It will shift from D1 to D2.

Figure 1.1.4 The effect of an increase in the price of a substitute

Be careful, though, when analysing demand in this way. To take another example, let's assume that salmonella-tainted chicken is found in the supermarkets of a particular country. Demand for chicken will collapse and so will its price. What do you expect to happen to the demand for fish if fish is considered a safe substitute?

■ Changes in tastes affect demand. The more desirable people find a good, the more they will demand it. Tastes are affected by advertising, by fashion, by observing other consumers, by considerations of health, etc.

■ Changes in the size of the market (the number of consumers) will have an effect. As the size of a market increases, demand for most products will tend to rise and vice versa.

■ Changes in the age distribution of the population affect the pattern of demand. A well-known example refers to an ageing population (where the average age is rising) where demand for false teeth rises and demand for chewing gum drops.

■ Expectations of changes in market prices or in income will have an effect. For example, if people expect that the price of a good will rise in the future, they are likely to buy more of it now before prices go up (shifting the current demand curve to the right).

Shifts of demand versus movements along a demand curve

Many students make mistakes over this because they do not get into the habit of distinguishing between demand and quantity demanded. Demand changes (and on a diagram the demand curve shifts) when any determinant other than the price of the good changes. For example, a change in income will change demand and shift the demand curve to the right or to the left. Quantity demanded changes when the price of the good changes and results in a movement along the demand curve. For example, if the price of a good increases it is quantity demanded that decreases. Demand and its graphical representation are not affected. There is only a movement along the demand curve.

> **TIP** Avoid saying or writing that the demand curve shifts 'up' or 'down'. Using these terms very often leads to mistakes. Instead use the expression 'the demand curve shifts to the right' if you are describing an increase in demand and 'the demand curve shifts to the left' if you are describing a decrease in demand.

We have a:	movement along the demand curve	→	If the price of the good changes $\Delta(P)$
	shift of the demand curve	→	if any of the other factors affecting demand changes $\Delta(Y, Ps, Pc, T)$ (where Y denotes income, Ps stands for price of substitutes, Pc stands for price and T stands for tastes)

Supply: the behaviour of producers

The supply of a good summarizes the behaviour of producers (or firms) in a market. It is the relationship between various possible prices and the corresponding quantities that firms are willing to offer per period, ceteris paribus. Ceteris paribus means that all other factors affecting supply are assumed constant.

The relationship between price per unit and quantity supplied per period is direct (positive), meaning that at higher prices producers will be willing to offer more per period.

This positive relationship between price per unit and quantity supplied per period of time is often referred to as the law of supply. The law of supply states that if the price of a product increases then quantity supplied per period is expected to increase.

A supply curve shows the direct relationship between the price per unit of a good and the quantity supplied per period. It is typically upward sloping. Price per unit is measured on the vertical axis and quantity supplied per period on the horizontal axis.

A supply curve may refer to an individual firm or to the market. The market supply curve is the horizontal summation of the supply curves of an individual firm. This means that at each price we add the quantities supplied by each firm. So, if a market consists of 100 identical firms and each is willing to offer 200 units per month at the price of $5.00, then the market supply will be 20,000 units per month priced at $5.00 per unit.

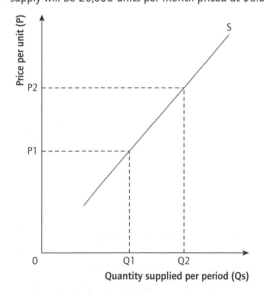

Figure 1.1.5 A typical market supply curve

In Figure 1.1.5, if the price is P1 then producers will be willing to offer Q1 units per period, whereas if the price increased to P2 per unit then producers will be willing to offer Q2 units per period.

Why do we expect the law of supply to hold?	
A simplistic but acceptable explanation is:	because at a higher price, a firm's profit margin is greater, inducing it to offer more units per period
or, perhaps, more correctly:	
a theoretically sound explanation is:	because if it becomes costlier for the firm to produce more and more units per period of time using existing capacity, then it will be willing to do so only at a higher per unit price

Other factors affecting supply ('shift' factors)

- Changes in the cost of factors of production affect supply. If input prices increase (for example, if the wages paid to labour increase or the price of a raw material used in the production of the good increases) then, ceteris paribus, supply is expected to decrease. So the supply curve is expected to shift to the left. At each price, firms will be willing to offer less, or they will be willing to offer each unit at a higher price than before.

Figure 1.1.6 illustrates the effect of an increase in the wages paid. Assume that the original supply curve is S1. In the left-hand side diagram, before an increase in wages paid, firms were willing to offer Q1 units per period at price P. If wages paid increase then, as a result of the increased costs of production, firms will be willing to offer only Q2 units per period at price P. The same holds for all prices so supply decreases, shifting to the left to S2. In the right-hand side diagram firms were willing to offer Q units per period at price P1 per unit before an increase in wages. After wages increase, firms will be willing to offer Q units only at the higher price P2. The same holds for all units so supply decreases, shifting left to S2.

TIP It should be clear at this point why it is a better idea to describe increases in supply as a shift of the supply curve to the right and decreases in supply as a shift to the left. If you draw a supply curve and you shift it 'up' you will realize that now at each price the firms are willing to offer less and not more.

- Changes to technology affect supply. Improved technology allows firms to offer more units of the good at the same price, increasing supply and shifting the supply curve to the right. Improved technology decreases the cost of producing each extra unit of the good.

- Changes in productivity affect supply. Productivity is defined as output per unit of input, so labour productivity would be output per worker. If, for example, those in the labour force become more experienced, better trained and/or healthier then labour productivity will increase. If labour productivity increases then, ceteris paribus, firms will be willing to offer more units at each price, increasing supply and shifting the supply curve to the right. An increase in labour productivity implies decreased production costs.

TIP If wages increase by 5% and at the same time labour productivity increases by 5%, then costs per unit of output are the same, so supply will neither increase nor decrease. If wages increase by 15% while labour productivity increases by only 5%, then production costs will have increased, so supply will decrease and the supply curve will shift to the left.

- Changes in government policy affect supply. Indirect taxes and subsidies affect the cost of producing an extra unit of a good. An indirect tax is a payment to the government by firms per unit of output produced, whereas a subsidy is a payment to firms by the government per unit of output produced. An indirect tax will increase production costs and lead to a decrease in supply and a shift of the supply curve to the left, whereas a subsidy will decrease production

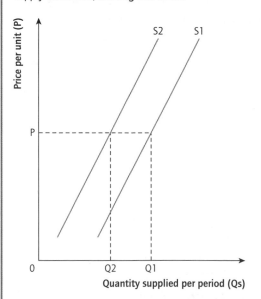

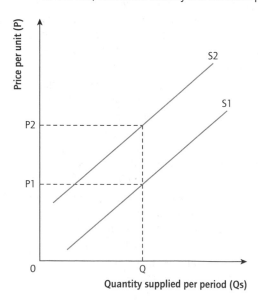

Figure 1.1.6 The effect on market supply of an increase in wages paid

costs and lead to an increase in supply and a shift of the supply curve to the right.

The supply decision is predominantly affected by changes in production costs.	
Production costs can change if: the price of an input changes	If the wages paid decrease, production costs will decrease and supply will increase, shifting the supply curve to the right (and vice versa)
technology changes	If technology improves, production costs will decrease and supply will increase, shifting the supply curve to the right (and vice versa)
productivity changes	If productivity increases, production costs will decrease and supply will increase, shifting the supply curve to the right (and vice versa)
an indirect tax is imposed or eliminated	If an indirect tax is eliminated, production costs will decrease and supply will increase, shifting the supply curve to the right (and vice versa)
a subsidy is granted or eliminated	If a subsidy is granted, production costs will decrease and supply will increase, shifting the supply curve to the right (and vice versa)

- A change in the price of a good that is jointly supplied will have an effect on supply. This is best understood through an example. If a firm produces mutton it is jointly producing wool. If the price of mutton increases in the market this firm will have an incentive to increase the quantity supplied of mutton, but at the same time the supply of wool will increase and its supply curve will shift to the right.

- A change in the price of a good in competitive supply will have an effect. This is also best understood through an example. Assume a farmer with a fixed amount of land uses it to produce lemons and oranges. If the price of oranges increases then this farmer will have the incentive to increase the quantity supplied of oranges so the supply of lemons will decrease, shifting that supply curve to the left.

- Changes in the size of the market (the number of firms) affect supply. As more firms join a market, for example, supply will tend to increase, shifting the supply curve to the right.

- Changes in expectations affect supply. For example, the expectation that the price will be higher in the future may cause supply of a good to decrease now, shifting its supply curve to the left.

- Changes in other factors can be significant. For obvious reasons, weather conditions affect the supply of farm products. Floods in Australia, a heat wave in Russia or drought in Brazil will adversely affect the world supply of wheat,

 TIP Supply curves may be drawn as straight lines or curved; they may or may not start from the vertical (or horizontal) axis. Typically, they are upward sloping.

decreasing it and shifting its supply curve to the left. A major accident, a terrorist act or a war may affect the supply of oil.

Shifts of supply versus movements along a supply curve

Many students make mistakes over this because they do not get into the habit of distinguishing between supply and quantity supplied. Supply changes (and on a diagram the supply curve shifts) when any determinant other than the price of the good changes, just as in the case of demand. For example, a change in the price of a raw material will change supply and shift the supply curve to the right or to the left. Quantity supplied changes when the price of the good changes and results in a movement along the supply curve. For example, if the price of a good increases then it is quantity supplied that increases. Supply and its graphical representation will not be affected. There is only a movement along the supply curve.

		movement along the supply curve	if the price of the good changes $\Delta(P)$
We have a:		shift of the supply curve	if any of the other factors affecting supply changes $\Delta(Pf, Tech, Prod, Pj, Pc, Tx, Sub, etc.)$ (where Pf denotes price of factors like labour, Tech stands for technology, Prod for productivity, Pj for prices of jointly produced goods, Pc for goods in competitive supply, Tx for indirect taxes, Sub for subsidies)

Equilibrium

Price and output determination in a competitive market

The price at which a good will be sold in a competitive market will be determined by the interaction between consumers and producers; in other words, by the interaction of demand and supply.

If at some price there is excess supply (if quantity supplied per period exceeds quantity demanded) then the price will tend to drop. If at some price there is excess demand (if quantity demanded per period exceeds quantity supplied) then the price will tend to rise.

It follows that there will be no tendency for the price to change if there is neither excess supply nor excess demand in the market. This requires that quantity demanded per period at that price is equal to quantity supplied. This price is the equilibrium price and the corresponding quantity is the equilibrium quantity.

A price is an equilibrium price if quantity demanded is equal to quantity supplied, so there is neither excess demand nor excess supply.

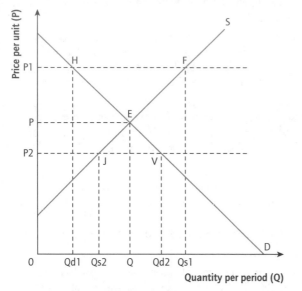

We say that the market 'clears' or that the market is in equilibrium.

Figure 1.1.7 The determination of equilibrium price in a competitive market

Referring to Figure 1.1.7, we can answer the following questions.

■ Could P1 be the equilibrium price?

At P1 consumers are willing to buy Qd1 units per period while firms are willing to offer Qs1 units per period. Quantity supplied per period is greater than quantity demanded. There is excess supply equal to Qs1 − Qd1 = HF units per period which will create pressure for the price to fall. Since excess supply creates a tendency for the market price to fall, it follows that P1 is not an equilibrium price.

■ Could P2 be the equilibrium price?

At P2 consumers are willing to buy Qd2 units per period while firms are willing to offer Qs2 units per period. Quantity demanded per period is greater than quantity supplied. There is excess demand equal to 0Qd2 − 0Qs2 = JV units per period which will create pressure for the price to rise. Since excess demand creates a tendency for the market price to increase, it follows that P2 is not an equilibrium price.

Quantity demanded per period is equal to quantity supplied only at price P. At P there is neither excess demand nor excess supply so the market 'clears'. Price OP is therefore the equilibrium price. It is found at the intersection E of the demand and the supply curves.

Changes in equilibrium

Changes in demand conditions

If a factor affecting demand changes, then demand will increase or decrease (and on a diagram the demand curve will shift to the right or to the left). A new equilibrium will result, as at the original equilibrium either excess demand or excess supply will now exist.

Demand increases

These are the effects if demand increases.

■ The demand curve shifts to the right.

■ At the original equilibrium price there will be excess demand.

■ As excess demand exists there will be a tendency for the price to rise.

■ Assuming typical demand and supply curves, a higher equilibrium price and a greater quantity is expected.

In Figure 1.1.8, equilibrium is initially at price P1 and quantity Q1. If demand increases from D1 to D2 then, at the original equilibrium price P1, there will be excess demand equal to FH as quantity demanded (Q′) exceeds quantity supplied (Q1). Excess demand in the market creates pressure on the price to increase until a new equilibrium is established at P2 and Q2.

Demand decreases

These are the effects if demand decreases.

■ The demand curve shifts to the left.

■ At the original equilibrium price there will be excess supply.

■ As excess supply exists there will be a tendency for the price to decrease.

■ Assuming typical demand and supply curves, a lower equilibrium price and a smaller equilibrium quantity is expected.

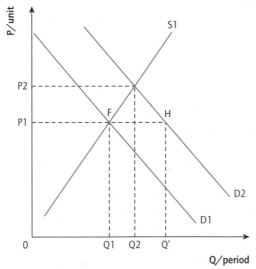

Figure 1.1.8 Effect of an increase in demand on market equilibrium

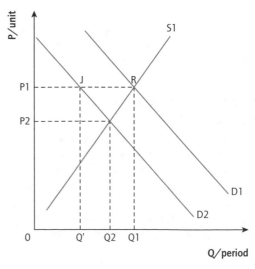

Figure 1.1.9 Effect of a decrease in demand on market equilibrium

In Figure 1.1.9, equilibrium is initially at price P1 and quantity Q1. If demand increases from D1 to D2 then, at the original equilibrium price P1, there will be excess supply equal to JR as quantity supplied (Q1) exceeds quantity demanded (Q'). Excess supply in the market creates pressure on the price to decrease until a new equilibrium is established at P2 and Q2.

If a factor affecting supply changes, then supply will increase or decrease (and on a diagram the supply curve will shift to the right or to the left). A new equilibrium will result as at the original equilibrium either excess demand or excess supply will now exist.

Supply increases
These are the effects if supply increases.

- The supply curve shifts to the right.
- At the original equilibrium price there will be excess supply.
- As excess supply exists there will be a tendency for the price to decrease.
- Assuming typical demand and supply curves, a lower equilibrium price and a greater quantity is expected.

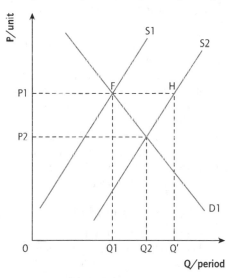

Figure 1.1.10 Effect of an increase in supply on market equilibrium

In Figure 1.1.10, equilibrium is initially at price P1 and quantity Q1. If supply increases from S1 to S2 then, at the original equilibrium price P1, there will be excess supply equal to FH as quantity supplied (Q') exceeds quantity demanded (Q1). Excess supply in the market creates pressure on the price to decrease until a new equilibrium is established at P2 and Q2.

Supply decreases
These are the effects if supply decreases.

- The supply curve shifts to the left.
- At the original equilibrium price there will be excess demand.
- As excess demand exists there will be a tendency for the price to increase.

- Assuming typical demand and supply curves, a higher equilibrium price and a lower quantity is expected.

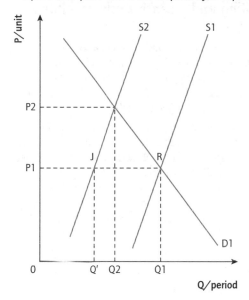

Figure 1.1.11 Effect of a decrease in supply on market equilibrium

In Figure 1.1.11, equilibrium is initially at price P1 and quantity Q1. If supply decreases from S1 to S2 then, at the original equilibrium price P1, there will be excess demand equal to JR as quantity demanded (Q1) exceeds quantity supplied (Q'). Excess demand in the market creates pressure on the price to increase until a new equilibrium is established at P2 and Q2.

Keep in mind that:
excess demand leads to an increase in price
excess supply leads to a decrease in price
also:
an increase in demand increases both equilibrium price and quantity
a decrease in demand decreases both equilibrium price and quantity
but:
an increase in supply increases equilibrium quantity but decreases price
a decrease in supply decreases equilibrium quantity but increases price

Both demand and supply change
If both demand and supply conditions in a market change, it does not matter which one of the two effects is handled first. Either the effect on equilibrium price or the effect on equilibrium quantity will be indeterminate unless you know either diagrammatically — or, algebraically (HL only) — by how much demand and supply changed. For example, if both demand and supply increase and their curves shift to the right, you know for sure that the equilibrium quantity will be greater but the effect on equilibrium price is uncertain.

The role of the price mechanism

The signalling and incentive role of relative price changes

Assume that, for a particular good, demand and supply conditions are such that the equilibrium price P1 and the equilibrium quantity Q1 are determined, as illustrated in Figure 1.1.12. Q1 units of the good are produced, with some scarce resources allocated to its production.

Assume now that preferences in society change and that, for example, demand for the good increases (a symmetric analysis holds for a decrease in demand). Now Q′ units are demanded but only Q1 are supplied. Why and how will more of this good be produced, and so additional scarce resources allocated to and employed in its production? What mechanisms will happen to guarantee that the changed preferences of society will be satisfied?

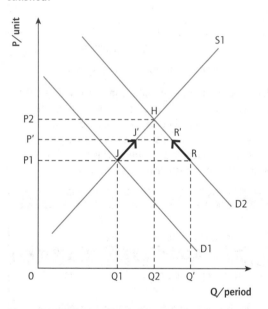

Figure 1.1.12 The signalling and incentive function of relative price changes

The answer lies in the fact that an increase in demand will automatically lead to excess demand, and so a tendency for the market price to increase. This increase in market price is visible to both producers and consumers and each group will act in its own self-interest. The increase in market price has signalling power as it contains information that more of the good is wanted and it also provides an incentive to firms to react to that information and offer more of the good per period.

In Figure 1.1.12, quantity supplied increases along the supply curve as price increases from P to P′. We say that there is an extension of supply from point J to point J′. At the same time, some consumers will be dropping out of the market or cutting back on their purchases as the increase in price leads to a decrease in quantity demanded along the new demand curve D2. There is a contraction of demand from point R to point R′. As long as excess demand exists, the price will continue to rise until price P2 is reached. Price P2 is the new equilibrium price where more units of the good (Q2 units) are produced and consumed. Since more units of this good are produced, it implies that more scarce resources are channelled into its production.

The process leading to more of the good being produced and so more resources being channelled into its production has come about without the government or any other entity intervening. Producers and consumers acting in their own self-interest and responding only to changes in relative prices adjust their behaviour and are responsible for the new outcome. It is as if an invisible hand guides their behaviour. We will see later that this outcome is also the best from society's point of view, but we must also realize that this analysis rests on some very restrictive assumptions that often do not hold.

The rationing function of free market prices

We have seen that prices have a signalling and incentive role in a market economy. They also have a rationing function. If a market is free then whoever is willing and able to pay the market-determined price will end up with the good.

Changes in consumer preferences lead to changes in relative prices which have **signalling power** and **change incentives** of market participants	
If demand increases, excess demand results, so	price increases, leading to an **extension** of supply along the original supply curve and a **contraction** in demand along the new demand curve
If demand decreases, excess supply results, so	price decreases, leading to a **contraction** of supply along the original supply curve and an **extension** of demand along the new demand curve
It follows that the consumer is sovereign in a free competitive market. The change in price (or, as P. Samuelson wrote, a consumer 'voting with their dollars') induces changes in the quantity produced and in the allocation of scarce resources.	

Market efficiency

Consumer surplus

You may be willing to pay $1.00 for a cold soft drink at the beach but it could be that the price is only 75 cents. You will obviously buy it for 75 cents (as it is worth more to you than the price you have to pay). We say that you gained a consumer surplus of 25 cents. For the sake of the argument, assume that a second unit is worth 90 cents to you. You would also buy this second unit as it is worth more to you than the market price you have to pay. The consumer surplus you gained from the second unit is 15 cents. The consumer surplus from consuming both units is therefore equal to 40 cents. You were willing to pay at the most $1.90 for the two units (as much as they were worth to you) and you ended up paying only $1.50.

More generally, we define consumer surplus as the difference between how much consumers are willing and able at the most to pay for some amount of a good, and what they actually end up paying. To be able to identify the consumer surplus on a diagram, it is necessary and useful to realize that a demand curve (and a supply curve) can be read vertically.

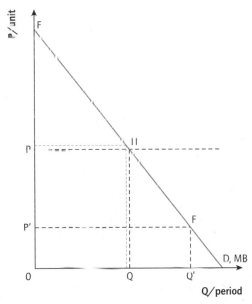

Figure 1.1.13 Consumer surplus

For each Q in a demand diagram, the vertical distance to the curve illustrates how much that specific unit is worth, at the most, to consumers. Unit Q in Figure 1.1.13 is worth P dollars (or distance QH) to consumers as they would be willing to pay P dollars at the most to buy it, not a cent more. If the price was even slightly higher (say at the level of the grey dotted line), then they would not have been willing to buy that last unit Q. Equivalently, unit Q' is worth P' to consumers (or distance Q'F) as that is the most they would be willing to pay to acquire it. The vertical distance to a demand curve measures the marginal benefit (MB) enjoyed from that unit.

If it happens that the price in the market is P dollars then consumers will buy all units up until (at the limit) unit Q, as each of these units is worth more to them than the market price would require them to pay. They would not buy any units past unit Q. For example, they would not buy unit Q' as it is worth P' dollars (or distance Q'F) to them (this is as much as they

would be willing to pay for it at the most) and the price (what they would be forced to pay) is higher, at P dollars.

It follows that Q units are worth area (0QHF) to consumers as that is the amount they would have been willing to pay to enjoy all these units. Given a market price of P dollars, they will end up paying area (0QHP) to enjoy Q units, or the price per unit times the quantity consumed. Consumer surplus is therefore area (PHF), the difference between area (0QHF) and area (0QHP).

On a diagram, consumer surplus is the area below the demand curve and above the price line for the units of the good consumed.

Producer surplus

A firm may be willing to offer a unit of a good for $2.00. If the market price for the unit is $3.00 then it will certainly decide to offer it. We say that the firm benefited from a producer surplus of $1.00. Assume that it would have been willing to offer the next unit if the price was at least $2.20. Since the market price is $3.00 it would also offer this unit, gaining from it a producer surplus of 80 cents. The producer surplus it gained from offering both these units is $1.80 as it required at least $4.20 to be willing to offer them and it ended up earning $6.00 from them.

More generally, we define producer surplus as the difference between what firms earn from selling some amount of a good and the minimum they would require to be willing to offer this amount. To be able to identify the producer surplus on a diagram, it is necessary and useful to realize that a supply curve can be read vertically.

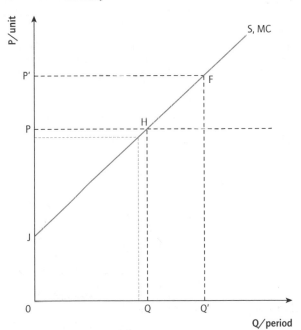

Figure 1.1.14 Producer surplus

For each Q in a supply diagram, the vertical distance to the curve illustrates the minimum a firm requires to be willing to offer that specific unit. This would be nothing but the cost of producing that extra unit. A firm would never accept anything less to be willing to offer an extra unit. The minimum it would accept is the cost of producing it. Later you will realize that the supply curve is nothing but the marginal cost (MC) curve of the firm.

So, for a firm to be willing to offer unit Q in Figure 1.1.14, the lowest price required is P dollars (or distance QH), not a cent less. If the price was even slightly less (say at the level of the grey dotted line), then the firm would not have been willing to offer that last unit Q. It would be willing to offer fewer units per period but not unit Q. Equivalently, for the firm to be willing to offer unit Q' the least payment required is P' (or distance Q'F).

If it so happens that the market price is P dollars per unit, then firms will be willing to offer per period all units up until and including unit Q. They would not be willing to offer unit Q' as they would require more (P' or distance Q'F) than they would get from the market.

It follows that the minimum firms would require to be willing to offer Q units is area (OQHJ), which is the sum of all vertical distances up until unit Q. Given a market price of P dollars per unit, firms will actually earn area (OQHP) by selling Q units or the price per unit (P) times the quantity offered (Q). So, producer surplus is area (JHP), the difference between area (OQHP) and area (OQHJ).

> **On a diagram, producer surplus is the area above the supply curve and below the price line for the units of the good produced and sold.**

Social or community surplus

Social or community surplus is defined as the sum of the consumer surplus and the producer surplus. It is a measure of welfare.

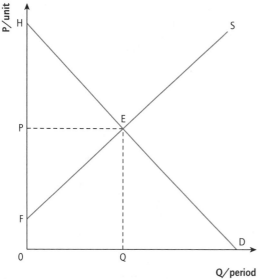

Figure 1.1.15 Social or community surplus

In Figure 1.1.15, given a market price P and an equilibrium quantity Q, consumer surplus is equal to area (FEP) while producer surplus is area (HEP). Given the definition of social surplus it follows that it is equal to area (FEH).

Allocative efficiency

The following question arises: Given supply and demand conditions for a good in a market, what is the optimal amount produced and consumed of this good from society's point of view? It would make sense for society to want all units of a good that are worth more than what they would cost to produce.

Do we have a measure of what each extra unit of a good is worth to society? Can we determine the extra benefit (the marginal benefit) that society enjoys from each extra unit of the good consumed? Yes, we can. It is how much at the most consumers would be willing to pay to enjoy it. This is the vertical distance from each Q to the demand curve.

Do we have a measure of what is the cost to society of producing each extra unit of a good? Yes, we do. It is the lowest amount that firms would be willing to accept to offer each extra unit of a good. This is the vertical distance from each Q to the supply curve, or the marginal cost (MC) of producing each extra unit.

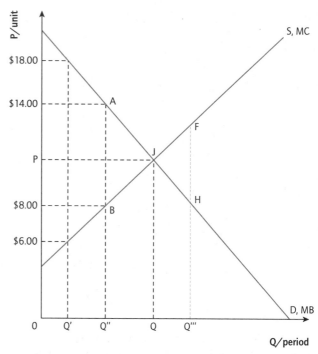

Figure 1.1.16 Allocative efficiency: where for the last Q produced, P = MC and social surplus is maximized

We say that allocative efficiency has been achieved and that scarce resources have been allocated in the best possible way if the optimal amount is produced from society's point of view. If neither too much nor too little of a good is produced and consumed then just the right amount of labour and capital are employed in its production.

In Figure 1.1.16, the optimal amount of the good from society's point of view is Q units. Society would like to enjoy all units up until and including unit Q. For the last unit Q produced, P = MC, or, more generally, marginal benefit (MB) is equal to marginal cost (MC).

Condition for allocative efficiency: the price (or marginal benefit) must be equal to marginal cost (that is, P (= MB) = MC) for the last unit produced.

It is easy to understand why. Referring to Figure 1.1.16, society would want unit Q' to be produced as it is worth $18.00 to consumers (this is the most they would have been willing to pay for it) which is more than the $6.00 it would cost firms to produce (as the minimum firms would be willing to accept to offer that unit is $6.00). We could say that if the market did indeed produce that unit, society would gain a surplus of $12.00 from unit Q'. Similarly for unit Q", as it is worth more ($14.00) than it would cost to produce ($8.00); society would gain a surplus of $6.00 from unit Q". The same argument holds up until and including unit Q which is worth to consumers as much as it would cost to produce it; that is, P (= MB) = MC.

What about unit Q'''? Society would not want that unit produced as this would mean that scarce resources would not be properly used. Why? Because that unit is worth to consumers less than it would cost to produce it. If unit QQ''' were produced, society would have lost surplus from its production equal to FH. It would have lost surplus equal to area (JHF) from the production of all units QQ'''.

What if only Q" units were produced and for some reason units Q"Q were not produced and enjoyed by society? Then society would have lost the surplus represented by the area (ABJ) as all units up until unit Q are worth more than they would have cost to produce.

If, by producing either less or more than Q units, a portion of social surplus is lost, it follows that by producing exactly Q units per period, social surplus is maximized.

Summary

If, for the last unit produced, P (= MB) = MC, then allocative efficiency is achieved and social surplus is maximized.

1.2 Elasticity

In general, elasticity is defined as the responsiveness of some economic variable when another economic variable changes.

Price elasticity of demand

Definition	The responsiveness of quantity demanded to a change in price
Referred to as	PED
Measure	The percentage change in quantity demanded divided by the percentage change in price:

$$PED = \frac{\%\Delta Q_d}{\%\Delta QP}$$

The above can be rewritten as:

$$PED = \frac{\frac{\Delta Q}{Q_1}}{\frac{\Delta P}{P_1}} \text{ or } \left(\frac{\Delta Q}{\Delta P}\right) \times \left(\frac{P1}{Q1}\right)$$

PED is therefore the **ratio of the changes** of two variables (price and quantity demanded) that move in opposite directions. If the price of the good goes up, then the quantity demanded goes down and vice versa. This implies that if the denominator has a plus sign (the price increased) then the numerator will have a negative sign (the quantity demanded will have decreased).

As a result, the mathematical value of PED in calculations is always a negative number. Note though that the minus sign is typically ignored and the value of PED is treated as if it were a positive number.

Ranges of PED

- If PED > 1 we say that demand is price **elastic**. It means that the percentage change in quantity demanded is larger than the percentage change in price, or that a small change in price leads to a **proportionately** greater change in quantity demanded.

- If $0 <$ PED < 1 we say that demand is price **inelastic**. It means that the percentage change in quantity demanded is smaller than the percentage change in price, or that a small change in price leads to a **proportionately** smaller change in quantity demanded.

- If PED $= 1$ we say that demand is **unit elastic**. It means that the percentage change in quantity demanded is equal to the percentage change in price, or that a small change in price leads to a **proportionately** equal change in quantity demanded.

- If PED $\rightarrow \infty$ we say that demand is **infinitely elastic**. It means that a small change in price leads to an infinitely large change in quantity demanded.

- If PED $= 0$ we say that demand is **perfectly inelastic**. It means that a change in price leads to no change in quantity demanded.

Values are:	Terms used are:	Given a change in P:
PED > 1	price elastic demand	%ΔQ is larger
$0 <$ PED < 1	price inelastic demand	%ΔQ is smaller
PED $= 1$	unitary price elastic demand	%ΔQ is equal
PED $\rightarrow \infty$	infinitely price elastic demand	%ΔQ is infinite
PED $= 0$	perfectly price inelastic demand	%ΔQ is zero

Calculating PED between two points on a demand curve

Assume that the price of a good increases from $12.00 to $18.00 and, as a result, quantity demanded decreases from 200,000 units a week to 180,000 units a week. What is the PED for this good equal to?

To answer such a question it is best to construct a small table where the initial price is denoted P1 and the initial quantity demanded Q1 so that mistakes are avoided:

P1 = $12.00	Q1 = 200,000
P2 = $18.00	Q2 = 180,000

The percentage change in quantity is $\frac{(180,000 - 200,000)}{200,000}$ $= \frac{-20,000}{200,000} = -0.10 \text{ or } -10\%$

The percentage change in price is $\frac{(18 - 12)}{12} = \frac{6}{12} = 0.5$ or $+ 50\%$

So, PED $= \frac{-10\%}{+50\%} = -0.2$ and, ignoring the minus sign, PED $= 0.2$. Demand is price inelastic.

PED varies along a typical demand curve

Close inspection of the PED formula reveals that PED is not the same as the slope of the demand curve:

$$PED = \left(\frac{\Delta Q}{\Delta P}\right) \times \left(\frac{P1}{Q1}\right)$$

It is the product of two terms. The first term $\left(\frac{\Delta Q}{\Delta P}\right)$ is the slope of the demand function (or the inverse of the demand curve as illustrated in a graph) which is a constant if the function is linear (that is, the demand is a straight line). The second term $\left(\frac{P1}{Q1}\right)$ varies continuously along a demand curve (see Figure 1.2.1).

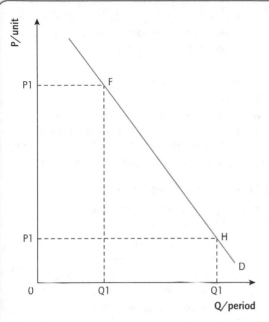

Figure 1.2.1 PED varies continuously even along a linear demand

Referring to Figure 1.2.1, if the initial price P1 is at point F, the ratio $\left(\dfrac{P1}{Q1}\right)$ is bigger than if the initial price P1 was at point H.

It follows that even along a linear, negatively sloped demand curve, price elasticity varies continuously.

Figure 1.2.3 shows that as point A is approached, PED tends to infinity as Q1 tends to zero, while at point B price elasticity is zero as P1 is zero.

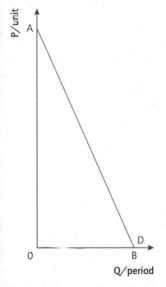

Figure 1.2.2 PED takes on all values from ∞ to zero

It can be shown that at the midpoint M of a linear demand curve, price elasticity is equal to 1. Referring to Figure 1.2.3:

- within line segment AM, corresponding to prices higher than Pm within the segment APm, demand is price elastic (PED > 1)
- within line segment MB, corresponding to prices lower than Pm within the segment PmB, demand is price inelastic (0 < PED < 1)

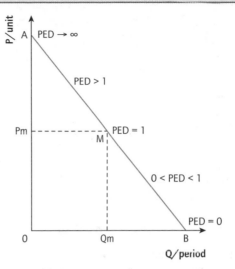

Figure 1.2.3 PED along a negatively sloped linear demand curve

It makes sense. Responsiveness to a price change (that is, PED) will be higher, the higher the initial price of the good, so the more expensive it is.

> **TIP**
> A common mistake is to consider that PED for a linear demand curve that is at 45 degrees to the axes is constant and equal to 1. The slope of such a curve is 1 but, as explained, slope is **not** elasticity.

Demand curves with constant PED

The case of a perfectly inelastic demand curve: PED = 0
In this case the demand curve is vertical at some quantity. Any change in price will lead to no change in quantity demanded.

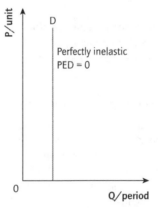

Figure 1.2.4 Perfectly inelastic demand curve (PED = 0)

The perfectly inelastic demand curve (PED = 0) is often used to describe the case of highly addictive goods such as drugs, or to describe the individual demand for pharmaceutical products for which no substitutes exist.

The case of a perfectly elastic demand curve: PED → ∞
In this case the demand curve is horizontal at some price. It is used to describe the demand that a perfectly competitive firm faces. Such a firm is so tiny in size compared with the market that it can sell any amount at the going market price. It is as if it is facing a perfectly elastic demand at the market price.

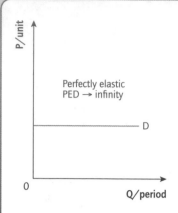

Figure 1.2.5 Perfectly price elastic demand curve (PED → ∞)

The case of a unitary elastic demand curve: PED = 1

The demand curve in this case is asymptotic to both axes (that is, it never touches either axis). The demand curve is a rectangular hyperbola.

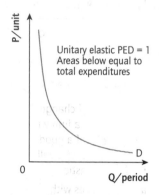

Figure 1.2.6 Unitary elastic demand curve (PED = 1)

All areas below this curve represent the revenues of firms and are equal in size. In other words, in a unitary elastic demand curve, a change in price does not change firms' total revenues.

Relationship between PED and total revenues

What will happen to firms' revenues (and hence to consumer expenditures) if there is a change in price? The answer depends on PED. Total revenues (TR) a firm collects are the product of the price per unit times the quantity sold (TR = PQ). It is not the same as profits, which are the difference between the TR collected and the total costs (TC) incurred.

Consider the three possible cases.

Case 1: A change in price when PED > 1 (demand is price elastic).

A change in price leads to a change in the **opposite** direction in quantity demanded. When demand is price elastic, quantity demanded changes **proportionately** more than price, so the change in quantity has a bigger effect on revenues than does the change in price. So, if demand is elastic, total expenditure changes in the same direction as quantity demanded. If P rises then Q **falls** proportionately more, so TR will **fall**. But if P falls, then Q **rises** proportionately more, so TR will **rise**.

Case 2: A change in price when 0 < PED < 1 (demand is price inelastic).

In this case, price rises **proportionately** more than quantity. The change in price has a bigger effect on TR than the

change in quantity does. TR change in the same direction as price. If P rises then Q falls proportionately less, so TR will **rise**. But if P **falls**, Q rises proportionately less, so TR will **fall**.

Case 3: A change in price when PED = 1 (demand is unitary elastic).

In this case, price and quantity change in exactly the same proportion. The demand curve is a rectangular hyperbola. A change in price will have no effect on TR. If we plot TR against Q, the function will be a straight line parallel to the horizontal axis.

PED and the shape of the TR curve

It follows from the above that there is a close relationship between PED and the shape of the TR curve a firm faces.

Focusing on Figure 1.2.7a, which illustrates the typical, linear, negatively sloped demand curve, we realize that at zero quantity (point at the origin), TR are zero and at a zero price (point H) TR are also zero. As price decreases (thinking of 'walking down' the price axis) from point F to Pm, quantity demanded increases from 0 to Qm. Since demand for that price range is price elastic, the resulting increase in quantity demanded is proportionately greater, so TR rise.

Skipping the midpoint price Pm, if price continues to decrease past Pm all the way down to zero, quantity demanded increases from Qm to H. Since demand is now price inelastic, the resulting increase in quantity demanded is proportionately smaller, so TR decrease.

Having established that TR rise all the way to midpoint Qm and then, right after Qm, they decrease, it necessarily follows that at Qm they are at a maximum. So, right below the midpoint of the linear demand curve where PED = 1, TR are maximized.

> **HL** Define marginal revenue (MR) as the extra revenue from selling one more unit of output. MR is the change in TR because of a change in Q, so it is the slope of the TR curve. At Qm, where TR are at their maximum, it follows that MR is zero. If demand is a negatively sloped line then MR has double the slope. In Figure 1.2.8a therefore it will go through output Qm.

Focusing now on Figure 1.2.7b, which illustrates a unitary elastic demand curve, we realize that any change in price will lead to a percentagewise equal change in the opposite direction of quantity demanded, so that TR remain constant. In the bottom part of Figure 1.2.7b, the TR curve is drawn as a straight line parallel to the quantity axis, illustrating that TR do not change as output varies.

Lastly, Figure 1.2.7c illustrates the case of a perfectly elastic demand curve. This would be the case of a firm which could sell all it wants at the price P', say, for example, £3.00 per unit. It follows that the TR curve is a rising straight line starting from the origin as the revenues from one unit sold will be £3.00, the revenues from two units sold will be £6.00, the revenues from three units sold will be £9.00, and so on. It will become clear that for a firm to be able to sell as much as it wants at the same price, two conditions must apply. The firm must be tiny compared to the market in which it operates. In addition, it must sell a good that consumers consider identical to the good sold by all the other firms in the same market.

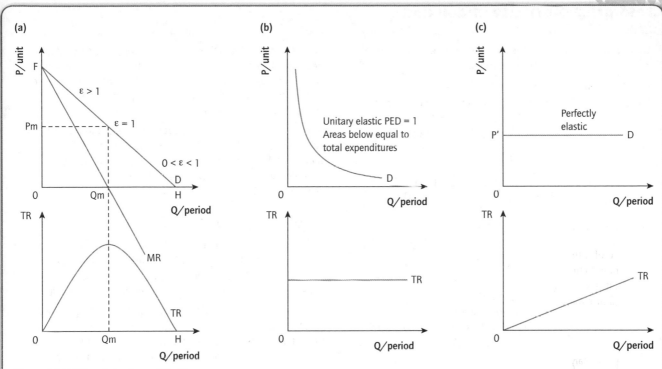

Figure 1.2.7 PED and the shape of the TR curve

Determinants of PED

- The number and closeness of available substitutes affect PED. The more substitutes there are for a good, and the closer these are, the more easily people will switch to these alternatives when the price of the good rises; the greater therefore will be the PED. Also think of how broadly or narrowly the good is defined. One example is Pepsi Cola versus soft drinks. The broader the definition, the fewer the substitutes available to the consumer, so the more price inelastic the demand is expected to be when small price changes are made.

- The proportion of income spent on the good is relevant. The higher the proportion of income spent on a good, the more consumers will be forced to lower consumption when its price rises (the bigger the income effect will be) and the more price elastic the demand will be. If we spend a small proportion of our income on a good (if it is 'insignificant'), then a change in price will not affect our spending behaviour; demand will be price inelastic.

- The time period involved affects PED. When the price of a product rises it takes some time for people to find alternatives and adjust their consumption patterns. It follows that the longer the time period after a price change, the more price elastic the demand is likely to be.

- PED can be determined by whether consumers consider the good or service a necessity. If they do, a change in its price will tend to affect it less than a price change affects other products.

- In some cases, PED depends upon the nature of the good, for example whether or not it is addictive. Demand for addictive products, such as cigarettes and alcoholic drinks, is relatively price inelastic. This has profound implications on governments' decisions to impose tax on such products.

TIP Students often confuse the factors affecting the demand for a product with the factors affecting the PED for a product.

Applications of PED

- PED permits a firm to predict the direction of change of its revenues given a price change. For example, a firm wishing to increase its revenues will lower the price of a good if demand for it is thought to be price elastic and it will increase the price if its demand is price inelastic.

- PED enables comparison of **quantity** changes with **monetary** (price) changes.

- PED allows a government to estimate the size of the necessary tax required to decrease consumption of 'demerit' goods, such as cigarettes or alcoholic drinks.

HL
- PED permits a firm to employ price discrimination. The higher price will be charged in the market with the relatively inelastic demand.

- PED helps a firm determine what proportion of an indirect tax can be passed on to the consumer.

- PED permits the government to determine the incidence of an indirect tax.

- PED helps a government predict the effect of currency devaluation on the trade balance of the country.

PED of primary commodities versus manufactured products

Primary products include food and non-food products. They include agricultural as well as non-agricultural products (those provided by nature, such as timber and minerals). In general, these products do not have close substitutes. Manufactured goods, on the other hand, are subject to extensive product differentiation as producers desperately try to gain an advantage over competitors. Apples, oranges, peaches and kiwi fruit may be considered substitutes for consumers, but they are not as close substitutes as different brands of laptops, DVD players or cell phones, for example. It follows that, in general, PED for commodities is lower than that for manufactured products.

Cross-price elasticity of demand

Definition	The responsiveness of demand for one good (x) to a change in the price of another good (y)
Referred to as	XED (sometimes XPE or CPE)
Measure	The percentage change in the quantity demanded of good x divided by the percentage change in the price of good y:

$$\text{XED} = \frac{\%\Delta Q_x}{\%\Delta \Delta_y} = \left(\frac{\frac{\Delta Q_x}{Q_x^1}}{\frac{\Delta P_y}{P_y^1}}\right) = \left(\frac{\Delta Q_x}{\Delta P_y}\right) \times \left(\frac{P_y^1}{Q_x^1}\right)$$

Here, the sign determines how we interpret XED for a product:

- If XED > 0 then the two goods x and y are substitutes, meaning that they are in competitive demand: if one becomes more expensive then consumers will switch to the other.
- If XED < 0 then the two goods x and y are complements, meaning that they are jointly demanded: if one becomes more expensive and people buy it less, they will also buy less of the other one.
- If XED $= 0$ then the two goods x and y are unrelated.
- It follows that the further away from zero XED is, the **stronger** the relationship between the goods. Conversely, the closer (absolutely) to zero XED is, the weaker the relationship between the two goods.

Figure 1.2.8a illustrates the case of substitutes in which XED is positive. If the price of coffee increases from P1 to P2 then we expect that the quantity of tea demanded per period will increase from Q1 to Q2 as some consumers will switch from drinking the now more expensive coffee and will drink tea instead. Note that **this is not a demand curve** as on one axis we have the price per unit of one good and on the other the quantity demanded per period of another good.

Figure 1.2.8b illustrates the case of complements in which XED is negative. If the price of coffee increases from P1 to P2 then we expect that the quantity of sugar demanded per period will

decrease from Q1 to Q2, as some will consumers will stop or decrease their coffee consumption, leading to less demand for sugar per period. Again, **this is not a demand curve** as on one axis we have the price per unit of one good and on the other the quantity demanded per period of another.

If instead of a positively or negatively sloped line we had a vertical line, it would illustrate the case of two totally unrelated products where XED is zero. For example, if the price of cheesecake rises or falls we expect the demand for iPhones to remain unaffected.

Applications of XED

XED is used by policy makers to delineate (describe) markets. It helps to know the size of XED of different products, for example to decide whether muffins and eggs should be considered as belonging in the same market as breakfast cereal.

Firms can use XED to guide their pricing policy changes. Assume that the price of a substitute product decreases, for example. If firms producing the good do not react, demand for it will probably decrease. Or, if a complement becomes pricier then, assuming no reaction, its producer should expect demand for it to contract.

Calculating XED

Assume that the price of good A increases from \$150.00 to \$180.00 and, as a result, quantity demanded for good B increases from 1.8 million units a week to 2.52 million units a week. What is the PED for good B when there are changes in the price of good A? How are these goods related?

Applying the formula for XED:

$$\text{XED} = \frac{\%\Delta Q_B}{\%\Delta \Delta_A} = \left(\frac{\Delta Q_B}{\Delta P_A}\right) \times \left(\frac{P_A^1}{Q_B^1}\right) = \left(\frac{(2.52 - 1.8)}{180 - 150}\right) \times \left(\frac{150}{1.8}\right)$$

$$= \left(\frac{0.72}{30}\right) \times \left(\frac{150}{1.8}\right) = \frac{108}{54} = +2$$

Since XED is a positive value we conclude that A and B are considered as substitutes.

(a)

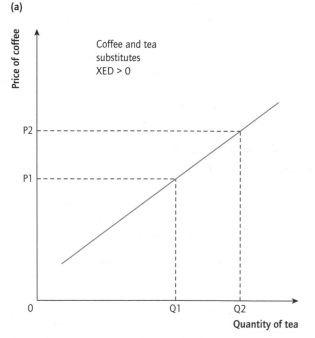

(b)

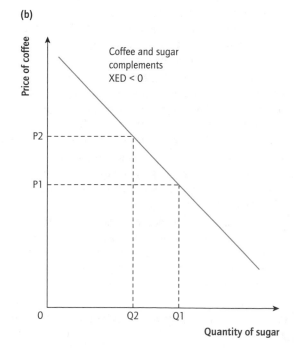

Figure 1.2.8 Substitutes (XED > 0) and complements (XED < 0)

Income elasticity of demand

Definition	The responsiveness of demand when consumer income changes
Referred to as	YED
Measure	The percentage change in quantity demanded divided by the percentage change in income:

$$YED = \frac{\%\Delta Q_d}{\%\Delta Y}$$

This can be rewritten as:

$$YED = \frac{\frac{\Delta Q}{Q_1}}{\frac{\Delta Y}{Y_1}}, \text{ or } \left(\frac{\Delta Q}{\Delta Y}\right) \times \left(\frac{Y_1}{Q_1}\right)$$

Since YED is the ratio of the percentage changes in demand and income levels, it follows that if both changes are positive (plus sign) or if both are negative (minus sign) then YED is a positive number. For example, if an increase in income leads to more of a good being demanded or a drop in income leads to less being demanded, then YED is a positive number. If one change is positive (plus sign) and the other is negative (minus sign), then YED is a negative number. For example, if an increase in income leads to a decrease in quantity demanded, or a decrease in income leads to an increase in quantity demanded, then YED is a negative number.

We can distinguish between normal and inferior goods based on whether YED is positive or negative.

- If YED > 0 the good is a **normal** good since demand increases (decreases) as consumer income increases (decreases): both income and demand change in the same direction.

- If YED < 0 the good is an **inferior** good since demand decreases (increases) as consumer income increases (decreases): income and demand change in opposite directions.

Focusing on normal goods, we can state the following.

- If YED > 1 then the percentage change in demand is greater than the percentage change in income. We say that demand is income elastic, as a rise in income leads to a faster rise (a **proportionately** greater increase) in demand. Luxury goods (as well as most services) are usually considered income elastic. For example, demand for plastic surgery, spa therapy or haute couture clothing is income elastic in many markets.

- If 0 < YED < 1 then the percentage change in demand is smaller than the percentage change in income. We say that demand is income inelastic as a rise in income leads to a slower rise (a **proportionately** smaller increase) in demand. Basic goods (every day goods or 'staple' goods) are usually income inelastic. For example, demand for many food products is income inelastic.

- If YED = 0 then demand for the good is not affected by a change in income. Income may increase or decrease but demand for the good remains the same.

- If YED = 1 then the percentage change in income is equal to the percentage change in quantity demanded: a 5%

increase in income leads to a 5% increase in quantity demanded, for example.

We can use this diagram as a summary.

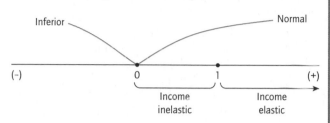

Using a graph to illustrate YED

There are two ways to illustrate YED on a graph. The easy but rather imprecise way is to use a typical demand curve diagram. If YED is positive and so the good is normal, then an increase in income will increase demand and shift the demand curve to the right, while a decrease in income will decrease demand and shift the curve to the left. If YED is negative and so the good is inferior, then an increase in income will decrease demand and shift the demand curve to the left, while a decrease in income will increase demand and shift the curve to the right.

Within this framework, illustrating the case of an income elastic good and an income inelastic good can be a problem. It may be acceptable to illustrate the income elastic case with a big shift to the right of the demand curve if income increases and with a tiny shift to the right if demand is income inelastic.

A better way to illustrate YED is by using an Engel curve, which is just a graph with income on the vertical axis and quantity demanded on the horizontal axis. If the curve is positively sloped then YED is positive and the good is normal. If the slope is negative then YED is negative and the good is inferior. If the curve is vertical then YED is zero. All three cases are illustrated in Figure 1.2.9.

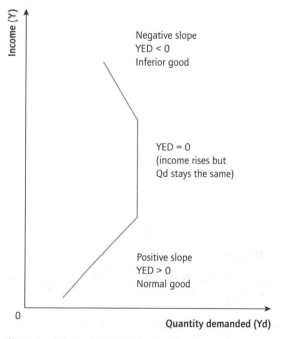

Figure 1.2.9 Illustrating YED through an Engel curve

It is possible to illustrate the cases of products with income elastic and income inelastic demand as well as the case where YED = 1.

To illustrate a product with income elastic demand, draw a straight line Engel curve that cuts the vertical axis, as illustrated in Figure 1.2.10.

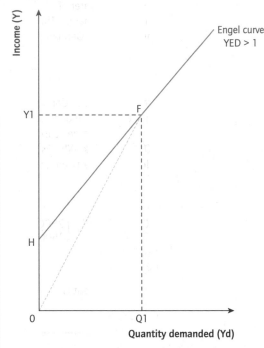

Figure 1.2.10 Income elastic demand (YED > 1)

To illustrate a product with income inelastic demand, draw a straight line Engel curve that cuts the horizontal axis, as illustrated in Figure 1.2.11.

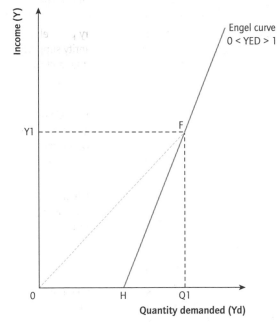

Figure 1.2.11 Income inelastic demand (0 < YED < 1)

To illustrate a product with YED equal to 1, draw a straight line Engel curve that goes through the origin, as illustrated in Figure 1.2.12.

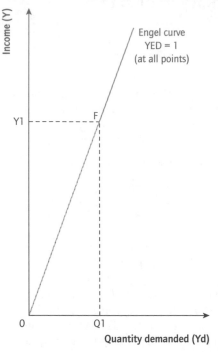

Figure 1.2.12 YED curve (YED = 1)

Optional material

If you are curious why the above results occur, here is an easy proof. Let's rearrange the YED formula as:

$$YED = \left(\frac{\Delta Q}{\Delta Y}\right) \times \left(\frac{Y_1}{Q_1}\right) = \left(\frac{Y_1}{Q_1}\right) \div \left(\frac{\Delta Y}{\Delta Q}\right)$$

So, we have expressed YED as a ratio. The numerator $\left(\frac{Y_1}{Q_1}\right)$ is the slope of the 'ray' (OF). The denominator is the slope of the Engel curve itself. So:

$$YED = \frac{\text{(slope of the ray OF)}}{\text{(slope of the Engel curve itself)}}$$

To check whether YED is greater than, equal to or smaller than 1, you just have to compare the two slopes. In Figure 1.2.10 the slope of the 'ray' is steeper so YED is greater than 1. In Figure 1.2.11 the slope of the 'ray' is flatter so 0 < YED < 1. In Figure 1.2.12 the two slopes coincide so YED = 1.

TIP Some industries are considered cyclical and some acyclical as a result of their YED. Overall economic activity, and therefore incomes, fluctuate and this fluctuation is known as the trade or business cycle. Short-run fluctuations significantly affect auto sales, furniture sales and housing; these industries are referred to as cyclical. Sales of food products in supermarkets are not affected as much by short-run fluctuations; this sector of the food industry is considered acyclical.

Applications of YED

Firms would like to know whether demand for their product is highly income elastic or moderately income inelastic to help them better plan their investments. If an economy is growing and incomes are increasing fast, then firms producing highly income elastic products may have to invest now in expanding their capacity to be able to meet the increased demand. Conversely, farmers growing, say, potatoes may think of switching to kiwi fruit or to agro-tourism, which have a higher YED.

A government may also be interested in knowing YED in various sectors to plan ahead regarding training for displaced workers. The economic significance and viability of income inelastic sectors will shrink in the long run so some workers in these sectors may lose their jobs and will need re-training. In this sense, a growing economy may suffer from increased (structural) unemployment and move away from full employment. Also, as sectors producing highly income elastic products, for example services, will grow fast, employment needs will also grow fast. This means that governments should plan ahead regarding changes in school curricula and vocational schools, so as to avoid employment bottlenecks.

Related to the above is the idea that the so-called sectoral composition of output of an economy changes through time as a result of differing YEDs. Many food products have a low YED once a certain threshold level of income is reached. Any further increases in income are mostly spent on products from the manufacturing sector, for example cars, appliances and furniture, which carry a higher YED. Luxury items and services are considered to have an even higher YED so once households have attained a certain standard of living, further increases in discretionary income are spent mostly on vacations, spa treatments, expensive clothing and expensive cars. In this way the relative size of the primary sector and later of manufacturing shrinks while that of services expands. This is the case for many but not for all countries, with Germany and Australia being notable examples.

Calculating YED

Assume that per capita income in the prefecture of Corinth increases from €25,000 per annum to €33,750 and, as a result, quantity demanded for fatty ground meat decreases from 15,000 kg per week to 14,250 kg per week. What is the YED for fatty ground meat? Is the demand for fatty ground meat in the area of a normal good?

Apply the formula for YED:

$$YED = \left(\frac{\Delta Q}{\Delta Y}\right) \times \left(\frac{Y_1}{Q_1}\right) = \left(\frac{14250 - 15000}{33750 - 25000}\right) \times \left(\frac{25000}{15000}\right)$$

$$\frac{-750}{8750} \times \frac{25}{15} = \frac{-18750}{131250} = -0.14$$

Since YED has a negative value, fatty ground meat is considered an inferior product in that area.

Price elasticity of supply

Definition	The responsiveness of quantity supplied when the price of the good changes
Referred to as	PES
Measure	The percentage change in quantity supplied divided by the percentage change in price:

$$PES = \frac{\%\Delta Q_s}{\%\Delta P}$$

The above can be rewritten as:

$$PES = \frac{\frac{\Delta Q_s}{Q_1}}{\frac{\Delta P}{P_1}}, \text{ or } \left(\frac{\Delta Q_s}{\Delta P}\right) \times \left(\frac{P_1}{Q_1}\right)$$

The sign of PES is positive since supply curves typically have a positive slope (firms offer more of a good per period at a higher price).

Ranges of PES

- If PES > 1 we say that supply is price **elastic**. It means that the percentage change in quantity supplied is greater than the percentage change in price, or that a change in price leads to a proportionately greater change in quantity supplied.
- If 0 < PES < 1 then we say that supply is price **inelastic**. It means that the percentage change in quantity supplied is smaller than the percentage change in price, or that a change in price leads to a proportionately smaller change in quantity supplied.
- If PES = 1 then we say that supply is **unitary price elastic**. It means that the percentage change in quantity supplied is equal to the percentage change in price, or that a change in price leads to a proportionately equal change in quantity supplied.
- If PES → ∞ then we say that supply is **perfectly elastic**. It means that a small change in price leads to an infinitely large change in quantity supplied. Effectively, this means that the firm is willing to offer as much as the market demands at the same, current price.
- If PES = 0 then we say that supply is **perfectly inelastic**. It means that a change in price leads to no change in the quantity supplied. Price changes have no effect on the amount offered per time period.

Using graphs to illustrate PES

PES can be illustrated using linear supply curves. Bearing in mind that a vertical supply curve (see Figure 1.2.13) is perfectly inelastic, implying that a change in price has no effect on quantity supplied (PES = 0), while a horizontal supply curve (see Figure 1.2.14) is perfectly elastic (PES → ∞), it is easy to remember that as supply 'flattens' around some price it becomes more price elastic.

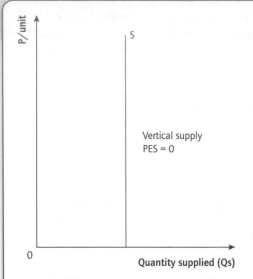

Figure 1.2.13 Perfectly inelastic supply curve (PES = 0)

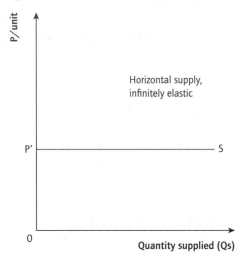

Figure 1.2.14 Perfectly elastic supply curve (PES → ∞)

What matters is whether the linear supply cuts the horizontal axis, the vertical axis or goes through the origin. If the supply curve cuts the horizontal axis (independently of its slope) then is price inelastic, as in Figure 1.2.15.

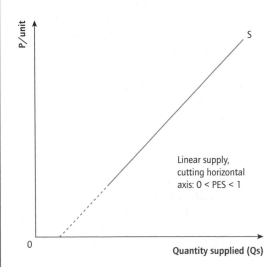

Figure 1.2.15 Price inelastic supply (0 < PES < 1)

If the linear supply cuts the vertical axis (independently of its slope) then it is price elastic, as in Figure 1.2.16.

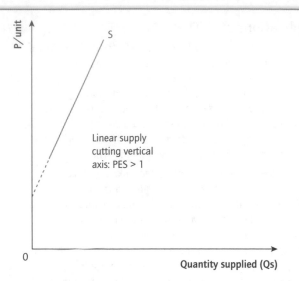

Figure 1.2.16 PES curve (PES > 1)

Lastly, if the linear supply goes through the origin then PES is equal to 1 at all points, as illustrated in Figure 1.2.17.

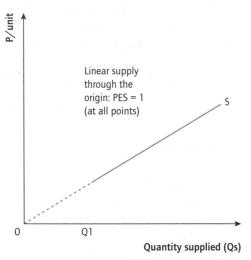

Figure 1.2.17 PES = 1 at all points

Optional material

To convince yourself why the intercept of a linear supply curve determines whether PES is smaller than, equal to or greater than 1, use the same logic presented earlier for YED.

Determinants of PES

- The time period determines PES. In economics, time is distinguished into the momentary period (or market period), the short run and the long run. The distinction is based on the extent to which adjustments can be made. In the momentary (or market) period no adjustments are possible. In the short run some, but not all, adjustments are possible. In the long run all adjustments are possible.

The above definitions become more specific when applied to the theory of production. The momentary period is when all factors of production are considered fixed. The firm is operating in the short run when some, but not all, factors of production are considered fixed. In the long run all factors of production are considered variable (no fixed factors exist).

It follows that in the momentary run, supply is perfectly inelastic (vertical). If demand for the product increases, quantity supplied remains unchanged. The increased demand will be expressed only as a higher price. Supply is not at all responsive. In the short run the increased demand will be partially expressed as an increase in quantity supplied and partially as an increase in price. In the long run, when all factors are variable and the firm can even increase its scale of operations (its size), output could expand even more. So, in the long run, supply is typically expected to be more price elastic than in the short run.

Figure 1.2.18 illustrates the effect of time on the PES of a good. The longer the time period, the greater the PES is expected to be. In the momentary run it is vertical so that the PES is zero, while in the long run it may even be perfectly elastic with firms willing to offer more at the same price P' (although this would require that cost conditions do not change).

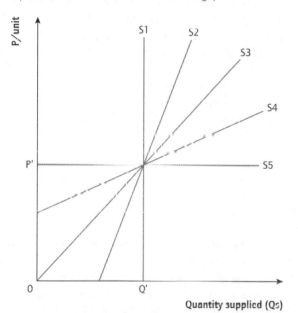

Figure 1.2.18 The effect of time on PES

- Excess (sometimes referred to as unused) capacity is a determining factor of PES. The further below full capacity a firm is operating, the greater the PES is expected to be.

- Whether the firm employs mostly skilled or mostly unskilled labour is significant. Expanding output in a production process that predominantly relies on highly skilled labour may be more difficult than if mostly unskilled workers are required.

- Whether long or short time lags characterize the production process is also relevant. The longer the time lags involved, the longer it takes for supply to adjust to new demand conditions. Agricultural products are characterized by long time lags so supply is often considered perfectly inelastic in the short run.

- The speed by which costs rise as output expands needs consideration. Firms will be encouraged to expand output

by more per time period to lower the additional (marginal) cost of doing so.

- Another determinant of PES is whether it is possible to store the good. If it is possible to store stocks then it may be possible to meet an increase in demand by releasing stocks, so firms can be more responsive in their supply than if their goods are perishable or no stocks are held.

- Mobility of labour is relevant. If, for example, labour is occupationally or geographically immobile then it will be more difficult to meet an increase in the demand for a product than if labour is mobile between occupations or regions.

Applications of PES

PES determines the extent to which an increase in demand will affect the price and/or quantity of the good in a market. The more price inelastic supply is, the greater the increase in price given an increase in demand; the more elastic supply is, the greater the impact of an increase in demand on quantity.

Primary agricultural commodities, for example wheat and corn, are characterized by low PES as their production is subject to long time lags. Think, for example, of a producer planting at a particular time but harvesting six months later. Non-agricultural primary products, such as metals and minerals, are also characterized by low PES because of the associated steep extraction costs. On the other hand, products from the manufacturing sector are characterized by higher PES because given a production plant, the extra costs of producing additional units are typically low.

> **TIP** If you are asked to draw the short-run supply curve for a farm product, for example wheat or coffee, draw it as a vertical line (PES = 0). This also applies if you are asked to draw the supply curve for a concert, a tennis game or the rooms offered by a hotel. The short-run supply curve for each example is also vertical as there is limited, if any, ability to change the 'quantity' offered (of seats or of rooms) per time period following a change in demand.

Calculating PES

Assume that the price of a particular good increases from €16.00 per unit to €18.40 and, as a result, quantity supplied increases from 28,000 units per year to 28,840 units per year. What is the PES for this good?

Apply the formula for PES:

$$\text{PES} = \left(\frac{\Delta Q_s}{\Delta P}\right) \times \left(\frac{P_1}{Q_1}\right) = \left(\frac{28{,}840 - 28{,}000}{18.40 - 16.00}\right) \times \left(\frac{16.00}{28{,}000}\right)$$
$$= \frac{840}{2.40} \times \frac{16}{28{,}000} = \frac{13{,}440}{67{,}200} = +0.2$$

Supply is price inelastic.

1.3 Government intervention

Indirect taxation

Taxes can be categorized as direct or indirect taxes. Indirect taxes are taxes on goods and services and can be imposed on a specific or an ad valorem basis. Specific or unit taxes are a fixed amount per unit of the good produced or consumed. For example, a tax of 100 Indian Rupees per unit of a good is a specific tax. Ad valorem taxes are a percentage of the price and so of consumer expenditures. Value added tax (VAT) is an example of an ad valorem tax which is expressed as a percentage, say 23%, of the price of the good.

Governments impose indirect taxes for a variety of reasons. Typical reasons include revenue collection or an attempt to decrease the consumption of goods. Governments need revenues to finance their expenditures and indirect taxation is one source of revenue. Some goods are considered harmful and governments often try to limit their consumption; examples include cigarettes, alcoholic drinks and petrol (gasoline). Another reason for governments imposing taxes is that they wish to switch expenditures away from imports towards domestically produced goods. One way of doing this is by imposing taxes (known as tariffs) on imports.

Illustrating indirect tax on a diagram

An indirect tax can be considered as an additional cost of production. As such it will tend to decrease the supply of a firm, shifting the supply curve left on a diagram. If we recall that a supply curve can also be read vertically and that it reflects the extra (marginal) cost of producing an extra unit, then it should be clear that an indirect tax will increase this extra cost, shifting the supply curve vertically upwards by the amount of the tax.

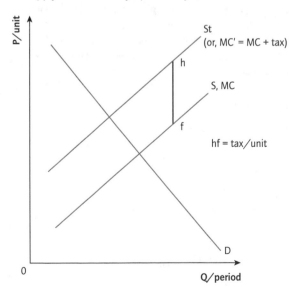

Figure 1.3.1 A specific indirect tax

In Figure 1.3.1 a market is illustrated with a demand curve D and a supply curve S. The supply curve is also the marginal cost (MC) curve. Assume a specific tax equal to hf dollars per unit. Supply will shift vertically upwards to St by distance hf. Alternatively, you may think of MC increasing by hf dollars per unit so that the new MC curve (MC′) is equal to the initial one (MC) plus the tax.

Consequences of a specific indirect tax

Assuming typical demand and supply curves, an indirect tax will make the good more expensive, will decrease the amount consumed and produced and will create revenues for the government. Producers will be earning lower revenues both on a per unit basis and as a total. Consumer spending on the good may increase or decrease, depending on PED.

More specifically, and referring to Figure 1.3.2, the following occurs.

- The market price rises from P to Pc per unit while the equilibrium quantity decreases from Q to Q′ per period. Output and consumption of the good therefore shrink.

- Producers earn only Pp (= hf) per unit sold, so their new average revenue is less than the original, pre-tax price and average revenue P.

- The total revenues the producers collect decrease from area (0QeP) to area (0Q′fPp). Consumer expenditures may increase, decrease or stay the same, depending on the PED between point e and point h, as there is a movement along the demand curve following the shift in supply. Since the price consumers pay increases, their expenditures on the good will increase if demand is price inelastic.

- The government collects tax revenues equal to area (PpfhPc). This area is found by multiplying the tax per unit (fh) by the number of units sold (line segment 0Q′, which is equal to segment Ppf).

- Resources are misallocated and a welfare loss equal to area (feh) results, unless the tax is imposed to limit production of a polluting industry or to curtail consumption of a harmful good, such as cigarettes.

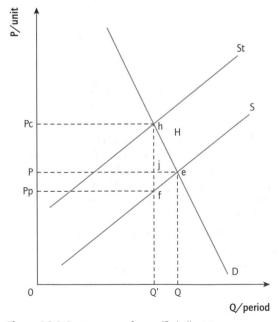

Figure 1.3.2 Consequences of a specific indirect tax

Consequences of an indirect tax, assuming typical demand and supply conditions	
The market price consumers pay	increases
The equilibrium quantity	decreases
The net tax price producers earn (average revenue collected)	decreases
Total revenues producers collect	decrease
Total expenditures consumers make	depends on PED
Social welfare	decreases (but see last bullet above)
Government revenues	increase

Tax incidence

Tax incidence refers to who pays what proportion of a tax. For example, if after a $10.00 tax is imposed on a good its market price increases by $9.00, then the incidence on consumers was $9.00, while the incidence on producers was $3.00 (or 9/12 and 3/12 respectively).

Figure 1.3.2 reveals that the market price did not increase by the full amount of the indirect tax imposed. The size of the tax is line segment fh (the vertical distance between the pre-tax and the post-tax supply curves) while market price increased only by segment hj. It follows that the incidence of this tax is on both consumers and producers: consumers and producers share the tax. Tax incidence on consumers is line segment jh (= PPc) whereas tax incidence on producers is line segment jf (= PPp).

Tax incidence depends on PES and PED. The following relationship holds:

$$\frac{(\% \text{ of tax incidence on consumers})}{(\% \text{ of tax incidence on producers})} = \frac{PES}{PED}$$

To remember the relationship just keep in mind that if incidence on consumers is in the numerator then PED is in the denominator.

Bearing in mind that the two percentages on the left fraction must add up to 100%, the interpretation of the above is straightforward.

- Market price will rise more and hence the consumers' share of the tax will be larger, the less elastic is demand and the more elastic is supply.
- Market price will rise less and hence the producers' share will be larger, the more elastic is demand and the less elastic is supply.
- Equilibrium quantity will decrease less, the more inelastic demand and supply are (the more vertical around the initial pre-tax equilibrium point).

It follows that tax revenue for the government increases as elasticities decrease.

It is argued that a tax is often fully paid by consumers. How can that be the case if the law of demand has almost universal applicability? The answer is that such cases are a result of firms very often being able to supply greater quantities per period at the same price — later we will refer to this as 'constant returns to scale' — that is, facing horizontal (perfectly elastic) supply curves.

It is a common mistake to claim that if demand is price inelastic then the incidence of an indirect tax falls mostly upon consumers. If PES happens to be lower than PED then it is producers and not consumers who will pay a bigger proportion of the tax. So if, for example, PED = 0.8 (price inelastic) while PES = 0.2, then the incidence on consumers will be smaller (consumers will pay 20% of the tax and producers will pay 80% of the tax).

If:	then:	in other words:
PES > PED	tax incidence on consumers is bigger than on producers	% of tax on consumers > % of tax on producers
PES = PED	tax incidence is split between consumers and producers	% of tax on consumers = % of tax on producers
PES < PED	tax incidence on producers is bigger than on consumers	% of tax on consumers < % of tax on producers
PES = 0	producers are burdened by the full amount of the tax	there is 100% of tax on producers and 0% on consumers
PED = 0	consumers are burdened by the full amount of the tax	there is 100% of tax on consumers and 0% on producers
PES → ∞	consumers are burdened by the full amount of the tax	there is 100% of tax on consumers and 0% on producers
PED → ∞	producers are burdened by the full amount of the tax	there is 100% of tax on producers and 0% on consumers

Analysis of an ad valorem (percentage) tax

What if the tax is an ad valorem (a percentage) tax? Such a tax is analysed in the same way as a specific tax except that the shift of supply is not parallel but the 'wedge' (vertical distance) widens at higher prices. Otherwise, the effects are identical to those of a specific tax.

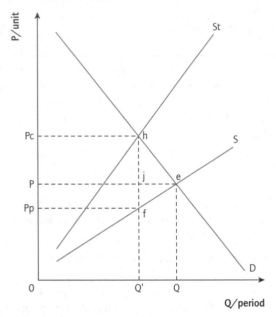

Figure 1.3.3 Effects of an ad valorem (percentage) indirect tax, for example VAT

Figure 1.3.3 illustrates an ad valorem (percentage) tax. Initially, market demand and market supply are at D and S respectively with P the initial market price and Q the initial quantity bought and sold per period. Let an ad valorem (percentage) tax be imposed, say, VAT at 23%.

The dollar amount of the tax at each possible price is not constant anymore. This is why the vertical distance between the original supply curve S and the post-tax supply curve St grows as price increases. The 'wedge' at each output level becomes bigger and bigger.

The effects of this are that:

■ market price that consumers will pay rises to Pc

■ the average revenue collected by firms decreases from P to Pp

■ equilibrium quantity decreases from Q units to Q' units.

Total revenues collected by firms equal area (0Q'fPp). Consumers spend area (0Q'hPc), of which tax revenues collected by the government equal area (PjhPc).

Assuming that the tax was not imposed to limit production of a polluting industry or consumption of a harmful good, a welfare loss equal to area (feh) and resource misallocation results.

Subsidies

A subsidy is defined as a per unit payment to firms by the government aimed at lowering their costs and the market price, and at increasing production, consumption and firms' revenues. Its analysis is symmetrical to that of an indirect tax as once a subsidy is granted the government is paying (and not getting paid) a per unit amount of money to firms. Production costs are lower by the amount of the subsidy so supply shifts vertically downward by that amount (the marginal cost of producing each unit of output is now lower).

Governments grant subsidies for a variety of reasons. Typically, they are granted when for some reason it is considered desirable to make a particular good cheaper so that its consumption increases and it becomes accessible to lower-income households. This includes many health-care and education-related products. Or governments may wish to expand output and consumption of products that are environmentally friendlier. Often governments grant subsidies to farmers to increase their income because of certain characteristics of the agricultural sector. Or it could be that a subsidy is used to make a particular good more competitive and attractive abroad so that it penetrates foreign markets, or to limit imports of competing goods from abroad.

In Figure 1.3.4 the initial demand and supply conditions are represented by curves D and S. The new supply following the granting of the subsidy is at S(sub). The vertical distance hf is equal to the subsidy per unit and represents the decrease in costs each firm enjoys once the subsidy is granted. If you remember that the supply curve also represents marginal cost (MC) then the new supply curve S(sub) is MC' = (MC − subsidy).

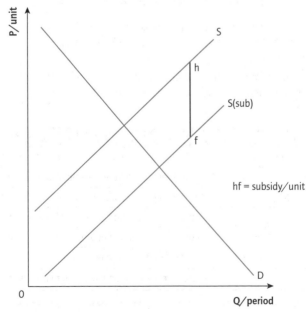

Figure 1.3.4 A subsidy

Consequences of a subsidy

Assuming typical demand and supply curves, a subsidy will make the good cheaper, will increase the amount consumed and produced and will cost the government money. Producers will earn more revenues both on a per unit basis and as a total. Consumer spending on the good may increase, decrease or remain the same, depending on PED.

More specifically, focusing on Figure 1.3.5, the market price consumers pay decreases from P to Pc while the equilibrium quantity increases from Q to Q'. Output and consumption of the good therefore increase.

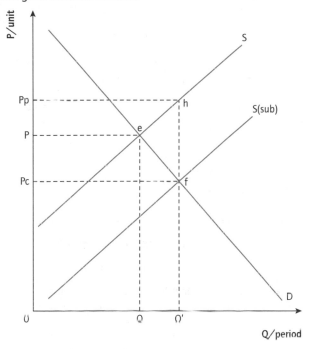

Figure 1.3.5 Consequences of a subsidy

To identify the new average revenue collected by producers you need to be extra careful as it is a common source of students'

errors. First, locate the new equilibrium quantity (Q' in Figure 1.3.5). From point Q' draw a line up all the way to the initial supply curve S. This is line Q'h. The producers earn whatever consumers are paying (Q'f = Pc) **plus** the subsidy per unit fh that the government pays. They therefore earn Q'f + fh, which is equal to Q'h or Pp.

The government spends in total area (fhPpPc), which is found by multiplying the subsidy fh by the quantity produced and consumed Q' (or = Pcf).

Both producers and consumers of a product benefit from a subsidy. Consumers pay a lower price while producers earn more per unit. If the subsidy is not granted to encourage consumption of goods that the government considers beneficial to society, a welfare loss results — here equal to area (feh) — and there is resource misallocation.

Consequences of a subsidy, assuming typical demand and supply conditions	
The market price consumers pay	decreases
The equilibrium quantity	increases
The average revenue collected by producers	increases
Total revenues collected by producers	increase
Total consumer expenditures	depends on PED
Social welfare	decreases (but see above)
Government expenditures	increase

Price controls

Price controls refer to cases where for some reason the government considers the market-determined (equilibrium) price unsatisfactory and, as a result, intervenes and sets the price either below or above it.

Maximum price (price ceiling)

An authority, usually the government, sets a maximum price (also referred to as a price ceiling) if it considers the market-determined price is too high. It is a maximum price in the sense that it is the highest price sellers can legally charge. The price on its own would rise higher towards its equilibrium level but the government creates a ceiling, restricting the price to the desired level. For a maximum price to make any sense it therefore has to be set below the market price.

The aim of setting a price ceiling is to protect the buyers of the product. As such it is set on 'sensitive' products that mostly lower-income households buy. Typically, price ceilings are set on food products and petrol (gasoline), as well as in the rental housing market in the form of rent controls.

In Figure 1.3.6 the government (or another authority) has set the maximum price at P'. Firms will be willing to offer Q1 units per period whereas consumers will be willing and able to purchase Q2 units per period. So, a shortage results equal to Q1Q2 units per period (or equal to hf).

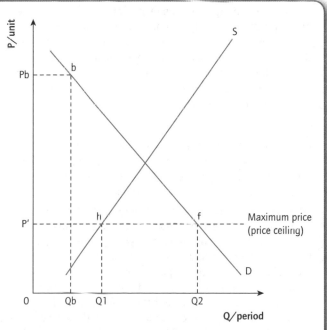

Figure 1.3.6 Maximum price (price ceiling)

The price P' cannot perform its rationing function anymore: individuals may be willing and able to pay the price but it is not certain that they will end up with the good as a shortage exists.

A different rationing mechanism is needed. These are some alternative rationing mechanisms.

- Rationing can be on the basis of 'first come, first served'. This is likely to lead to queues developing as people will rush to buy the price-controlled good before supplies are exhausted. Firms may adopt waiting lists.

- Rationing can be based on sellers' preferences. The product may be allocated on the basis of who the consumer is. Is the consumer a regular? Is the consumer attractive? Is the consumer 'important'? If the answer is 'yes' then the consumer will get the good. In this case the market is not impersonal anymore (which is a major advantage of free markets) but becomes personal. Discrimination may result.

- The product could be allocated on a random basis, for example by ballot, as was the case for the 2006 FIFA World Cup tickets.

- Coupons could be used to ration the good. This alternative has been used in times of war.

A major problem with maximum prices is the likely emergence of parallel ('black' or shadow) markets. Consumers, unable to buy in legal markets, may well be prepared to pay a much higher price. Figure 1.3.6 includes consumers willing to pay price Pb to acquire unit Qb. The willingness to pay, measured by the vertical distance from the horizontal axis to the demand curve, is greater than the maximum price for all produced (and so available) units up to Q1.

In the long run additional costs may emerge. The quality of certain products may worsen as producers may be tempted to use cheaper inputs. Also, if other non-price controlled products can be produced using the same inputs then supply may further shrink, making shortages more severe.

To minimize shortages and the related problems, a government may attempt to encourage supply (that is, attempt to shift the supply curve to the right on the diagram). It might do this through various means, for example it may draw on stocks, assume direct production of the good or grant subsidies or tax relief to producers. Alternatively, governments may attempt to reduce demand. For example, it may encourage production of more and cheaper substitutes.

Consequences on stakeholders: the case of rent control

Figure 1.3.7 is used to illustrate the consequences of a price ceiling on the various stakeholders. The case where rents are controlled in a city is used as an example.

Given demand D and supply S for rental units in a city the equilibrium rent would be at Re with Qe units supplied and demanded. Assume now that city authorities decide that rents for a 'typical' unit cannot exceed R'. Landlords (property owners) are forced to rent their houses or apartments at a lower 'price'. Rents are controlled at the level R' (a price ceiling). At that rent only Q' units are offered for rent while Q2 units are demanded. A shortage of houses and apartments for rent results equal to Q2 − Q1 (that is, line segment Q2Q1). The shortage is directly related to the size of the difference between Re and R'.

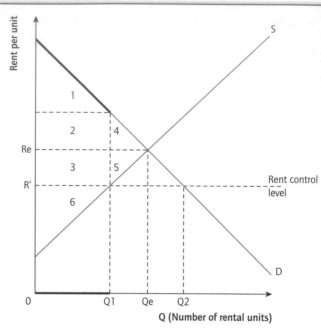

Figure 1.3.7 Rent control as an application of price ceilings

Since rent R' is not a competitive free-market determined rent, it cannot perform its rationing role. Being willing and able to pay rent R' will not guarantee that everyone looking for rented housing will find it. Landlords have to use other rationing mechanisms, the most popular being 'first come, first served'. Landlords also have the power to discriminate against any group they may not like to rent their property to, for example couples with young children or with pets, younger people or immigrants. This could create a parallel ('black' or shadow) market, where landlords may extract 'under the table' payments from tenants over and above the maximum legal rent, or where landlords ask for large down payments.

Are tenants better off or worse off?

Tenants lucky enough to find housing at the lower rent are better off, even though landlords may decide not to maintain the property. Tenants who would have been able to find rented housing at rent Re and who as a result of the shortage are left homeless are definitely worse off. Tenants who are discriminated against or who end up paying significantly more as a result of the shortage are also worse off.

Are landlords better off?

In general, landlords are worse off as they rent out fewer units at a lower rent. Some may be better off if they take the risk to rent at an illegal higher rate and they do not face any consequences. Often, many are forced to leave the market (for example by selling their property) or they may be forced to witness a long-term deterioration of the value of their property if they cannot afford maintenance.

Welfare analysis

Applying welfare analysis to this policy issue will shed light on its consequences to stakeholders.

Before the rent control was imposed, equilibrium rent was at Re and the equilibrium quantity of rental units was Qe. Consumer surplus is equal to area (1 + 2 + 4) and producer surplus is equal to area (3 + 5 + 6). Social (or community) welfare (or surplus) is therefore equal to area (1 + 2 + 4 + 3 + 5 + 6).

After the rent control is imposed consumer surplus changes to area (1 + 2 + 3). Consumers (tenants who find rented housing) pay a lower rent but the quantity of rental units is now only Q1. Remember that consumer surplus is the area below the demand curve and above the price for the number of units bought. Producer surplus has changed to area (6). It is the area above the supply curve and below the price for the number of units 'sold' (in this case, rented out).

What are the changes?

Landlords ('sellers') are unambiguously worse off as they have lost area (5) as well as area (3) which has been transferred to tenants ('buyers') who enjoy the quantity available at a lower rent. Tenants ('buyers') lose area (4) as units Q1Qe are not available anymore. However, they gain area (3) as they pay only R' for the rental units available. Social welfare decreased by area (4 + 5) so now there is allocative inefficiency in the market for rented housing. Landlords ('sellers') are worse off as their surplus has shrunk (assuming they do not receive illegal higher payments). Tenants who as a result of the rent control were not able to find a rental unit are worse off as they have lost area (4), but tenants who were lucky enough to find a rental unit at the lower rent R' are better off as they gain area (3). The effect of such a policy on lower-income households is ambiguous.

Lastly, since there is no guarantee that the apartment units 0Q1 were rented to the tenants who valued these the most, it could be that the social welfare loss is actually bigger than area (4 + 5).

> **TIP** Remember that, even though its seems counterintuitive, a maximum price must be drawn **below** the equilibrium level.
>
> The shortage created is not an area but the distance between the quantity demanded and the quantity supplied at the set price.
>
> It is best to use linear demand and supply curves.

Minimum price (price floor)

An authority, usually the government, sets a minimum price (also referred to as a price floor or, sometimes, price support) if it considers the market determined price is too low. A minimum price is set above the market-determined price and the aim is to protect producers. In order for a minimum price to be effective it must be set above the equilibrium price. In Figure 1.3.8 the competitive free-market equilibrium price would have been at Pe, resulting in an equilibrium quantity Qe. The government considers this price too low and sets the price higher at P'. P' is a minimum price.

Typically, minimum prices are encountered in agricultural markets where governments set a price floor to protect farmers' income.

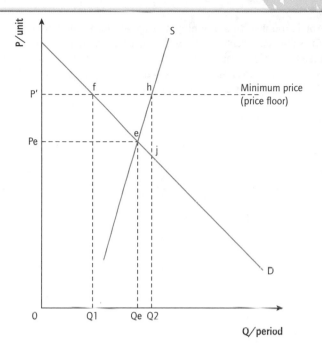

Figure 1.3.8 Minimum price (price floor)

Impact on market outcomes

In Figure 1.3.8 at the price P' firms (in this case farmers) are willing to offer Q2 units per period whereas buyers are willing and able to buy only Q1 units per period. Assuming competitive markets, a surplus results equal to Q2 − Q1 units per period. This is equal to line segment Q1Q2 (or fh).

The government is forced to buy the resulting surplus as otherwise the price would collapse. The surplus must be bought at the promised price P' so government spends area (Q1Q2hf) which is the price it pays, P', times the quantity it must buy, Q_1Q_2.

Consumers are worse off as they enjoy less of the product at a higher price per unit. Producers are better off as their revenues are higher. Without the minimum price their revenues would be equal to area (0QeePe), whereas with the minimum price their revenues are area (0Q2hP'). Government expenditures increase (or government spending in other areas has to decrease). If spending rises then tax payers eventually bear the burden of this policy, as they pay for it in the form of increased taxes. An incentive to overproduce is created, resulting in resource misallocation. For example, too much land will be allocated to the production of one particular farm product. Units QeQ2 are valued by consumers less (see the vertical distance to the demand curve) than it costs to produce them (see the vertical distance to the supply curve). These units are now produced so a welfare loss equal to area (ejh) results.

> **TIP** Remember that, even though it seems counterintuitive, a minimum price must be drawn **above** the equilibrium level: the government creates a floor so that the price does not drop below the desired level.
>
> The resulting surplus is not an area but a distance (a line segment) at the set price.
>
> Draw the supply curve rather steep so that the resulting surplus is not unrealistically large. It is best to use linear demand and supply curves.

Application: setting a minimum wage in the labour market
The same analytical framework can be employed to describe the effects of minimum wage legislation. In Figure 1.3.9 the vertical axis measures the money wage rate (W) per worker and the horizontal axis depicts the number of workers (L).

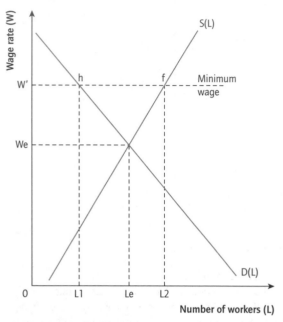

Figure 1.3.9 Minimum wage policy

Firms demand labour to produce the goods and services they produce. The demand for labour is a 'derived' demand. It is negatively sloped as at higher wage rates firms will try to substitute capital for labour. Workers offer their labour services to the labour market. The supply of labour is upward sloping as at higher wage rates the opportunity cost of leisure increases (it becomes more expensive for someone to sit outside the labour market) so more individuals will substitute work for leisure. If the labour market is competitive then the equilibrium wage rate will be at We with Le individuals employed.

If the government now considers that the market determined wage rate We is too low and decides to set a minimum wage at W', then firms at W' will want to hire fewer individuals than the number of individuals willing to offer their labour services. At the higher wage rate W' that the government sets, L2 individuals are looking for a job while firms will hire only L1 workers. The excess supply (surplus) of labour L1L2 (or line segment hf) represents unemployment.

A minimum-wage policy will benefit some workers: those who will end up with a job at W' instead of We. It will typically create unemployment (L1L2) though, and will especially hurt the workers who would have had a job without this policy but are now left without one, namely individuals L1Le.

Maximum price (price ceiling)		Minimum price (price floor)	
Aim:	to protect vulnerable consumer groups	**Aim:**	to protect vulnerable producers, typically farmers
Price is set:	below market-determined price	**Price is set:**	above market-determined price
Results in:	a shortage	**Results in:**	a surplus
	a situation where price cannot perform its rationing role so new rationing mechanisms of the good are needed, for example 'first come, first served', sellers' preferences, random rationing or rationing through use of coupons		government being forced to buy the surplus and having to destroy it, store it or sell it abroad at a lower price (known as dumping)
	the possibility of parallel ('black' or shadow) markets forming		either in taxpayers being burdened by the cost of the policy or in the sacrifice of some other government project
	worse quality and wider shortages in the long run		
Impact on consumers is:	some are better off and some are worse off	**Impact on consumers is:**	they are worse off as they enjoy less at a higher price
Impact on sellers is:	they are worse off as they sell less at a lower price	**Impact on sellers is:**	they are better off as they sell more at a higher price
Impact on welfare is:	inefficiency and welfare loss	**Impact on welfare is:**	inefficiency and welfare loss
Example applications are:	food price controls	**Example applications are:**	price support for farmers
	rent control		minimum-wage policy

Free markets: successes and failures

The fundamental economic problem that all societies face is scarcity: limited resources versus unlimited wants. This necessitates choices (decisions about which goods will be produced and in what quantities). How will scarce resources be allocated? In a market economy, the answer is given by the market (the price) mechanism. The interaction of demand and supply, with consumers aiming to maximize utility and firms trying to maximize profits, determines how much of each good will be produced and consumed. Relative price changes coordinate economic activity as if an invisible hand exists. Relative price changes provide the signals and the incentives for producers and consumers to change their behaviour.

If markets are free and competitive then the outcome is socially efficient. Allocative efficiency is achieved, as just the right amount of the good from society's point of view is produced and consumed. In the real world the necessary conditions to arrive at the socially efficient outcome are not often present. Here are some cases in which market forces may fail.

Case 1: The case of externalities

In many circumstances, the costs and benefits of economic activity are paid for or enjoyed by third parties outside the market. In such cases either more or less than the socially optimal amount is produced and consumed.

Case 2: The case of public goods

The characteristics of certain goods are such that consumers have the incentive to hide their true preferences. This may lead to collapse of the market as profit-oriented firms will not have the incentive to produce and offer these goods. Note that the case of public goods may be considered as a special kind of externality.

Case 3: The existence of monopoly power

Markets are often not competitive as firms may possess significant monopoly power. When monopoly power is present, less than the socially optimal amount of the good will be produced and consumed so fewer than optimal resources will be employed in its production.

Case 4: The case where information is asymmetric

If buyers and sellers share different sets of information then this may also lead to market failure. Certain types of informational failures also involve an externality aspect.

We should note here that the underlying income distribution in a country may be very unfair. Since market demand for any good reflects not just willingness to buy a good but also the ability to do so, households with a severe income constraint, living, say, below the absolute poverty line, may not 'exist' even in markets where the most basic products, such as food, are bought and sold. Paraphrasing Samuelson's famous expression, these households do not have any dollars to vote with. It follows that even if the resulting output mix is considered as allocative efficiency, it may still be socially undesirable.

Externalities as a source of market failure

An externality is present if an economic activity (production or consumption) imposes costs on, or creates benefits for, third parties for which they do not get compensated for, or do not pay for, respectively. Equivalently, an externality exists whenever there is a divergence between private and social costs of production or between private and social benefits of consumption. Externalities are also referred to as spillover effects.

An externality leads to a market failure as either more or less than the socially optimal amount is produced or consumed. Market forces alone fail to lead to an efficient resource allocation.

Externalities may arise in the production process, where they are known as production externalities, or in the consumption process, in which case they are known as consumption externalities. If they impose costs on third parties they are considered negative externalities. In contrast, if they create benefits they are considered positive externalities.

Relevant terms and definitions
Marginal private costs (MPC)
MPC are defined as the costs of producing an extra unit of output. They include wages, costs of raw materials and other costs that a firm takes into consideration in its decision making regarding production. It follows that the supply curve reflects the MPC of a (competitive) firm.

Marginal social costs (MSC)
These are defined as the costs of producing an extra unit of output that are borne by society. They reflect the value of **all** resources that are sacrificed in the specific production process. This means that they include not just the labour and other resources that are sacrificed, the costs of which are taken into consideration by the firm, but also include any external costs that are not taken into consideration by firms in the form of, say, pollution. In this case the MSC of production exceed the MPC and should be drawn above the MPC (the supply) curve. This would be the case of a negative production externality. If, though, a **production** process creates benefits for a third party (say, another firm) then the MSC curve lies below the MPC (the supply) curve as there is an **external production benefit** involved in the process.

Marginal private benefits (MPB)
MPB are defined as the benefits the individual enjoys from the consumption of an extra unit of a good. The willingness of a

consumer to pay for an extra unit is determined by the extra benefits he or she enjoys from consuming that extra unit. The demand curve reflects the MPB enjoyed from consuming extra units of a good.

Marginal social benefits (MSB)

These are the benefits that society enjoys from each extra unit consumed. MSB include the private benefits enjoyed by the individual but in addition any benefits others may enjoy as a result (external benefits). It follows that the MSB curve lies above the MPB (the demand) curve. If, though, individuals' consumption imposes a cost on others then the MSC curve will lie below the MPB (the demand) curve as there is an external cost of consumption generated by the process.

Four types of externalities

The four types of externalities are illustrated in Figures 1.4.1a through to 1.4.1d.

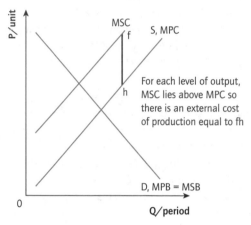

Figure 1.4.1a Negative production externality

Figure 1.4.1a illustrates the case of a firm in the cement industry emitting pollutants into the atmosphere. Demand, which always reflects the MPB of buyers, is identical to MSB as no external effects in the consumption of cement are assumed. Supply of cement reflects the MPC of cement manufacturers (that is, the costs they pay, such as for wages, energy and materials). Since the production process entails external costs in the form of pollution, it follows that society sacrifices in the production of cement more than the firms consider. Society sacrifices environmental assets because of the pollution. The MSC of cement production are therefore bigger than the MPC by the amount of the external costs created. Note that there is no shift involved as many students incorrectly claim: the two curves, MPC and MSC, reflect different information.

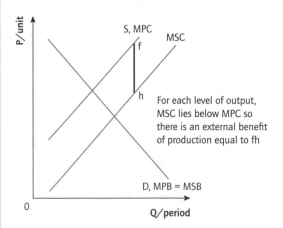

Figure 1.4.1b Positive production externality

In Figure 1.4.1b we are looking at the case of beekeepers producing honey and located next to apple orchards. Bees help in the pollination of apple flowers, allowing more effective transfer of pollen and so increased chances of producing apples as well as greater genetic variation of apple plants. Demand, which always reflects the MPB of buyers of honey, is identical to MSB as no external effects in the consumption of honey are assumed. Supply of honey reflects the MPC of honey producers (that is, the costs they pay, such as for labour and bees). Since the honey producers' production process entails external benefits to apple growers in the form of pollination, it follows that the social costs of honey production are lower than the private costs the beekeepers consider. The MSC of honey production are therefore lower than the MPC by the amount of the external benefit created.

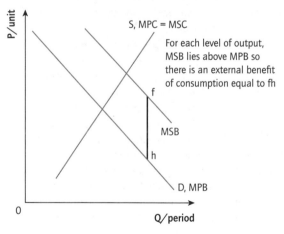

Figure 1.4.1c Positive consumption externality

Figure 1.4.1c illustrates the market for flu vaccinations. If a student visits a doctor and gets vaccinated against flu it is not only the student who benefits but also that person's classmates, teachers and others. The supply of vaccines always reflects the MPC of producers of vaccines (pharmaceutical corporations). They are identical to MSC as no external effects in the production process of vaccines are assumed. Demand for vaccines reflects the MPB of those who are vaccinated. Since their vaccination creates external benefits to others around them in the form of a lower probability that those others will catch flu, it follows that the social benefits of vaccine consumption are greater than the private benefits that individuals take into account in deciding whether to have a vaccination or not. The MSB of vaccines are therefore greater than the MPB by the amount of the external benefit created.

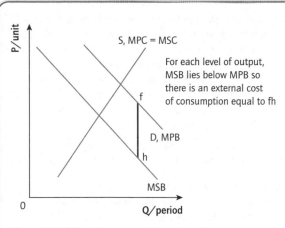

Figure 1.4.1d Negative consumption externality

Figure 1.4.1d relates to alcohol consumption. Assume it illustrates the market for vodka. When people consume alcohol there is always the risk of increased violence, of drunk driving, of lower productivity at work and other negative effects. These are all external costs of drinking. The supply of vodka always reflects the MPC of vodka producers. The MPC are identical to the MSC as no external effects in the production process itself are assumed. Demand for vodka reflects the MPB of those who consume the product. Since consumption of alcohol often creates external costs to others in the form of violence, accidents, lost productivity at work, and so on, it follows that the social benefits of vodka consumption are lower than the private benefits that individuals enjoy when deciding whether to consume alcohol or not. The MSB of alcoholic beverages are therefore less than the MPB by the amount of the external costs created.

Demand:		Supply:	
always reflects the MPB enjoyed by consumers: when drawing the demand curve instead of simply labelling it D, label it D, MPB.		always reflects the MPC paid by firms: when drawing the supply curve instead of simply labelling it S, label it S, MPC.	
If there is no externality in consumption then the benefits enjoyed by society are not any different from the benefits enjoyed by the individuals consuming the good, so label the demand curve D, MPB = MSB.		If there is no externality in production then the costs imposed on society are not any different from the costs paid by the firms producing the good, so label the supply curve S, MPC = MSC.	
If, though, there is an externality in consumption then one of two cases applies:		If, though, there is an externality in production then one of two cases applies:	
if there is an external benefit then the MSB curve lies above the D, MPB curve	If there is an external cost then the MSB curve lies below the D, MPB curve	If there is an external cost then the MSC curve lies above the S, MPC curve	If there is an external benefit then the MSC curve lies below the S, MPC curve
(positive consumption externality)	(negative consumption externality)	(negative production externality)	(positive production externality)

Impact of production and consumption externalities

Impact of a negative production externality

Production externalities arise on the production side so we focus on the market supply in the diagram. The demand curve reflects both the MPB and the MSB involved. The (competitive) market outcome is always determined at the intersection of market demand and market supply.

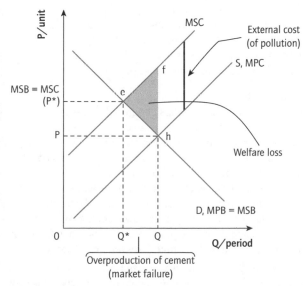

Figure 1.4.2 Negative production externality

Refer to Figure 1.4.2. The market will lead to Q units of cement produced at a market price of P per unit. The socially optimal level of cement output is less at Q*. Why? Because at Q* the MSB are equal to the MSC. For all units past Q* the marginal costs incurred by society exceed the marginal benefits enjoyed by society, so units Q*Q should not have been produced from society's point of view. There is overproduction of cement, which is the market failure in this case. Area (efh) represents the welfare loss as a result of the market failure. Too much cement is produced at too low a price.

Impact of a positive production externality

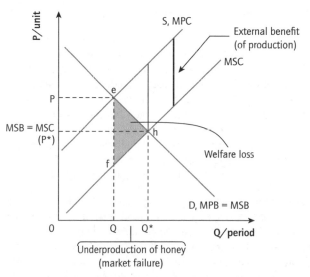

Figure 1.4.3 Positive production externality

Assume that Figure 1.4.3 illustrates the market for honey. The demand curve reflects both the MPB and the MSB that the consumption of honey creates. The (competitive) market outcome is determined at the intersection of market demand and market supply so that Q units of honey will be produced at a market price of P per unit.

The socially optimal level of honey output is more at Q*. Why? Because at Q* the MSB are equal to the MSC. For all units past unit Q the marginal benefits enjoyed by society exceed the marginal costs incurred by society, so units QQ* should have been produced from society's point of view. The market leads to underproduction of honey, which is the market failure in this case. Area (efh) represents the welfare loss as a result of the market failure. Not enough honey is produced from society's point of view.

Research and development (R&D) activities are considered a significant example of a positive production externality as the funder of the R&D programme often captures only part of the returns generated.

Impact of a positive consumption externality

Figure 1.4.4 illustrates the market for flu vaccinations. The supply curve reflects the MPC as well as the MSC of producing vaccines. The (competitive) market equilibrium is determined at the intersection of the market demand and the market supply so that Q vaccines will be produced and consumed at a market price P per unit.

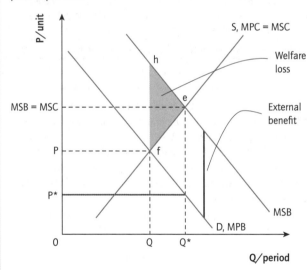

Figure 1.4.4 Market for flu vaccinations

The socially optimal level of production and consumption is more at Q*. Why? Because at Q* the MSB are equal to the MSC. For all units past Q the marginal benefits enjoyed by society exceed the marginal costs of production incurred by society. Units QQ* should therefore have been produced and consumed from society's point of view but they are not: market forces lead to underconsumption and underprovision of vaccines and this is the market failure in this case. Area (efh) represents the welfare loss as a result of the market failure. Not enough vaccines are consumed from society's point of view.

Merit goods

Merit goods are a special class of goods that are defined either in terms of externalities generated and/or in terms of informational failures involved. If the consumption of a good creates very significant positive externalities then it is referred to as a merit good. Education and health care are prime

examples. Alternatively, merit goods can be defined as goods that government would like all members of society to consume in adequate quantities independently of their income or even their preferences. Individuals may not be aware of the benefits arising from the consumption of the good because of lack of information or myopic behaviour (resisting change). This is why education is compulsory in many countries up to at least a certain level. Note the paternalistic role of the state in this case.

Analysis of merit goods is preferably but not necessarily conducted within the positive consumption externality framework.

Impact of a negative consumption externality

Figure 1.4.5 illustrates the market for vodka (but could represent the market for alcoholic drinks in general). The externality arises when vodka is consumed. The supply curve of vodka reflects the MPC as well as the MSC of producing vodka. The (competitive) market equilibrium is determined at the intersection of the market demand and the market supply so Q units of vodka will be produced and consumed at a market determined price P per unit.

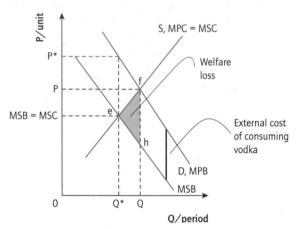

Figure 1.4.5 Market for vodka

The socially optimal level of vodka consumption and production is less at Q*. Why? Because at Q* the MSB are equal to the MSC. For all units past unit Q* the marginal benefits to society of consuming vodka are less than the marginal costs to society of producing it. Units Q*Q should therefore not have been produced and consumed from society's point of view but they are: market forces lead to overconsumption and overprovision of vodka and this is the market failure in this case. Area (efh) represents the welfare loss as a result of the market failure. Too much vodka is consumed from society's point of view.

Demerit goods

Demerit goods are a special class of goods that are defined either in terms of externalities generated and/or in terms of informational failures involved. If the consumption of a good creates very significant negative externalities then the product is referred to as a demerit good. Alcoholic drinks and tobacco products are good examples. Alternatively, demerit goods can be defined as goods of which governments would like to limit consumption. Individuals may not be aware of the costs arising from the consumption of the good because of lack of information or myopic behaviour and the state takes a paternalistic role.

Analysis of demerit goods is preferably but not necessarily conducted within the negative consumption externality framework.

Solutions to externality-related issues

Negative production externalities

Market-based solutions

Indirect taxation

The pioneering work recommending government intervention in the case of polluting firms is attributed to Pigou (1920) when he proposed the imposition of an indirect tax equal to the size of the external cost generated by the firm. The indirect tax would in principle internalize the externality in the sense that it would raise the firm's production costs to the level of the social costs created by its activity. This would induce the firm to limit output of whatever it produced to the socially optimal level. The principle underlying this solution is referred to as the 'polluter pays principle' and the tax is also known as a Pigovian tax or carbon tax.

Figure 1.4.6 illustrates the effect of imposing a Pigovian tax on a polluting firm in the cement industry.

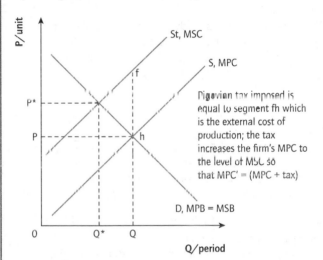

Pigovian tax imposed is equal to segment fh which is the external cost of production; the tax increases the firm's MPC to the level of MSC so that MPC' = (MPC + tax)

Figure 1.4.6 Effect of a Pigovian tax

The government estimates the size of the pollution (external) costs the firms create and imposes a tax equal to that amount. The tax will increase the production costs to the level of the MSC, forcing the firms to internalize the externality. Given the new supply curve St, the market price will rise to P* so that only Q* units of cement will be produced and consumed, the socially optimal level.

Estimating the size of the external cost and of the necessary tax is a difficult task. Many of the costs extend well into the future. In addition, even if the tax leads to the optimal rate of output Q*, the size of the total level of pollution generated by the activity (which is equal to the area between the MSC and the MPC curves for output up to Q*) is dependent on the PED for the good. If demand is very price inelastic, the total pollution generated may be still unacceptably high given all other pollution-generating activities in the economy. An additional issue is that the effects of polluting activities extend beyond national borders but taxation does not. The Dutch government cannot tax a Chinese company.

Assigning and enforcing property rights over assets

After the idea of a Pigovian tax was introduced many economists argued that individuals, without any government intervention, could correct problems arising from externalities through bargaining and a system of bribes and compensations that would make all parties involved better off. The basic idea is that if there is an opportunity to achieve an improved situation, private agents (people and firms) will have the incentive to make agreements that would lead to the improvement. A hotel owner could bargain and agree with a polluting firm nearby that the hotel will pay that firm a certain amount of money per year in exchange for the firm reducing pollutants to a pre-specified level. Both businesses could benefit, for example:

- if the agreement allows the hotel owner to charge higher rates that will cover the payments made to the polluting firm
- if these payments are greater than the lost profit experienced by the firm because of the lower level of production.

For bargaining to be an option there must be a set of well-defined and enforced property rights over an asset and there must be no transaction costs involved, for example the contractual agreement must not be costly to negotiate. The Coase theorem (1960) shows that if there are no transaction costs and if property rights are well defined and enforced, independently of their initial allocation, private parties will have the incentive to negotiate and reach an improved solution if a possible one exists. Typically though, transaction costs are very high and make this kind of bargaining impossible. In addition, it is exceedingly difficult or impossible to define property rights on certain assets, such as the atmosphere or the sea. This issue is closely related to the topic of common access resources (discussed later).

Tradable (or marketable) pollution permits ('cap and trade' schemes)

These are licenses for a specific amount of pollution that the government allocates to polluting firms and that are tradable in the open market. This creates an incentive system as cleaner firms which find it cheaper to lower their level of pollution will have an incentive to sell unused permits to older and dirtier firms that find it costly to lower pollution levels. Under such a scheme, pollution permits are scarce and a market is created for the right to pollute. After all trading is completed, a new allocation of permits will emerge. The total pollution the permits allow will be equal to the target level of total pollution and the loss of output will be smaller than if the government had assigned the same maximum level of emissions for all firms.

A problem of such schemes is that the maximum acceptable level of pollution is difficult to determine. In addition, the initial allocation of permits to firms (or countries) is controversial, while monitoring compliance of firms is costly.

Command and control solutions

Often it is not possible or not effective to rely on changing market signals. Governments resort to direct regulation. Governments can directly regulate output of polluting firms, the prices they can set, where they can or cannot locate, and the type of machines, filters and fuel they can use, for example. In many cases direct regulation may be the only realistic and cost-effective solution but it may also lead to costly and inefficient outcomes.

Advertising (or banning of advertising), moral persuasion or education
This is a different set of solutions whereby the government attempts to change the preferences and practices of consumers and of firms by increasing their awareness of the external costs of certain activities they undertake. By making school children aware of the benefits of recycling today the government aims at creating citizens who will make better choices about such issues in future. When polluting firms are exposed, the bad publicity they receive may force them to alter their practices.

Positive production externalities

Market-based solutions

Granting a subsidy
Granting a subsidy will decrease the costs of production associated with the activity generating the externality and so induce a greater output level. The problem is that it is difficult to estimate properly the size of the external benefits generated and so the correct size of the subsidy.

Assigning intellectual property rights
Intellectual property rights, such as patents, are designed to permit a firm, for example a pharmaceutical corporation, to capture most of the returns generated from its R&D activity. In this way the firm will be willing to invest more in R&D as it will be able to capture most of the benefits. On the other hand, patents create temporary monopoly and so high prices.

Mergers
If the beekeeper and the apple grower in the earlier example merge and become one firm then the positive spillover effects of both activities will be internalized (that is, they will be taken into account in the decisions of the new firm).

Command and control solutions

Direct regulation
Basic research is often publicly funded and is undertaken in research institutions such as universities etc. The spillover benefits are considered so significant that it would be against society's welfare to grant patents to private firms.

Positive consumption externalities (merit goods)

Market-based solutions

Granting a subsidy
The government can estimate the size of the external benefit created and grant a subsidy equal in size that would lower production costs and therefore price. The lower price will induce higher levels of consumption which could equal the socially optimal level, as illustrated in Figure 1.4.7.

The subsidy increases supply of the good (for example vaccinations) to S(sub). The market price will consequently drop to P*. Consumers will be willing to consume Q* at the lower price P* which is equal to the socially optimal level of consumption. Again, estimating the proper size of the subsidy is not an easy task.

Command and control solutions

Legislation and direct provision
When a government considers that the external benefits are very significant to the economy and that any positive price may be prohibitively high for some, very poor, members of society it often directly provides the good or the service free at point of delivery. In many countries this is the case with state education, or with national health-care systems and public hospitals. In many developing countries the tax revenues governments collect may be insufficient to finance free education and health care and this is one of the areas where aid may prove instrumental. Also, many governments make education compulsory up to a certain age. Vaccination to immunize young children is also compulsory in many countries.

Advertising and moral persuasion
A government may resort to advertising the benefits from consumption and use of such goods in an attempt to increase demand (shift the demand curve to the right) to the level of the MSB curve.

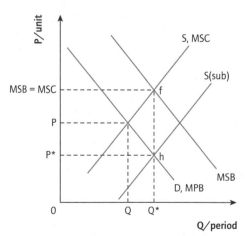

A subsidy equal to the external benefit of consumption (segment fh) would increase supply to S(sub) and lower price to P*, inducing a higher level of consumption equal to the socially optimal level Q*

Figure 1.4.7 The impact of a subsidy in the case of positive spillover effects (merit goods)

Negative consumption externalities (demerit goods)

Market-based solutions

Imposing indirect taxes
An indirect tax equal to the external costs of consumption will decrease supply and so increase the price of the good. The higher price will induce a lower level of consumption. If the size of the tax is correct, the socially optimal level of consumption may be achieved. Figure 1.4.8 illustrates the case.

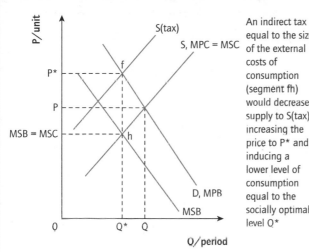

An indirect tax equal to the size of the external costs of consumption (segment fh) would decrease supply to S(tax) increasing the price to P* and inducing a lower level of consumption equal to the socially optimal level Q*

Figure 1.4.8 The impact of an indirect tax in the case of negative spillover effects (demerit goods)

The specific tax fh will decrease supply to S(tax). As a result, the market price of the good will increase to P*. The higher price will lead to a decrease in the quantity consumed to Q*, the socially optimal level of consumption. Several issues arise with such a solution. Again, the optimal tax is difficult to determine. Let's take the examples of drinking and smoking. Alcohol and tobacco are addictive so demand is quite price inelastic. This means that if the goal is to curtail consumption a very high tax will be needed. However, not all consumers are the same. Demand by higher-income individuals will even more price inelastic so their consumption may not be affected at all. On the other hand, a chain of substitutions may start for many poorer addicted individuals who may switch to lower-priced and lower-quality substitutes. Consumption may therefore not decrease as expected and even worse health-related problems may result.

Command and control solutions

Direct regulation
Often governments directly regulate consumption of demerit goods and the behaviour of those who consume them. For example, smoking may be prohibited inside buildings and cigarettes and alcohol may only be sold to people above a certain age.

Advertising and moral persuasion
Governments use advertising to inform the public about the risks of smoking and drinking. The goal is to decrease demand for and consumption of such goods.

Public goods as a case of market failure

A good is considered a public good if it is characterized by the following two properties.

- It is non-excludable. This means that if the good becomes available to even one consumer it automatically becomes available to all. No one can be excluded from consuming it.

- Consumption of the good is non-rival (or non-diminishable). This means that each individual's consumption of the good does not decrease the amount available for all others.

Non-excludability leads to individuals hiding their true preferences and behaving as free-riders because they know that they can enjoy the good without having to pay for it once it becomes available for others. Non-rivalry in consumption implies that the marginal cost of an extra user is zero.

The externality aspect of public goods becomes apparent by realizing that if someone provides or maintains a public good, even at a cost, he or she cannot prevent others from enjoying the benefits. So if the private benefits of providing a public good are small compared to the social benefits and the private costs are larger than the private benefits, then the good will not be supplied at all.

More generally, public goods are a case of market failure because private profit-oriented firms will not have the incentive to produce and offer such goods and services through the market. The market mechanism fails. Even though there may be sufficient demand for such a good, it will not be offered.

Few examples of pure public goods exist. A lighthouse, national defence and traffic lights are typical examples. If a lighthouse is built and maintained on some island no fisherman can be excluded from its benefits. If the lighthouse is 'used' by one boat the amount of its service available to other boats is the same (the marginal cost of one more boat using the service is zero).

Law and order in a town and price stability in an economy are somewhat different examples but they satisfy both criteria of public goods and their implications are interesting. For example, if it is safe for Megan to walk at night in a city then, probably, it is safe for others. Also, if she walks safely there is no less safety available for others. If price stability exists for one then it exists for all economic agents. Similarly, if one benefits from its existence then law and order can even be extended to imply a functional institutional framework, which is especially important for a developing economy and only a government can provide it.

A different example of a pure public good is broadcast television and radio. Both public good properties are satisfied. A broadcast television programme is normally available to any household with a television (a private, separate good). Also, if one person watches the programme there is no less of it available for others to watch. Interestingly, television and radio broadcasting, despite its public good features, is produced and offered by private, for profit companies. This is possible because broadcasters are not selling the programmes but the advertising time, which is both excludable and rival.

Global warming can and should be thought of as perhaps the most significant externality-related example of a pure public 'bad'. Greenhouse gas (GHG) emissions destroy natural capital (for example coastal regions) and are also considered responsible for lower agricultural productivity. Firms emitting greenhouse gases (or even countries which tolerate GHG emissions) impose huge costs from their production activity that are borne by the whole world (external costs). At the same time, global warming imposes costs from which no one can be excluded and if one suffers GHG-related costs, these do not diminish and all the rest suffer the same costs. Conversely, the (clean) atmosphere can be viewed as a pure public good as the benefits accrue to all (they are non-excludable and non-rival).

Solutions
Compulsive taxation and provision (but not necessarily production) by the government is the typical solution in the case of market failure relating to many public goods.

Common-access resources (common-pool resources)

The 'tragedy of the commons' was a term introduced by Garrett Hardin (1968). The idea was simple. Assume a pasture open to all ('the commons') with the adjacent land owned by a number of herdsmen, as in the following illustration.

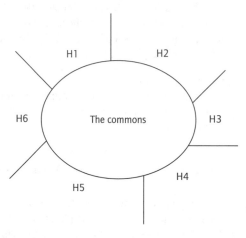

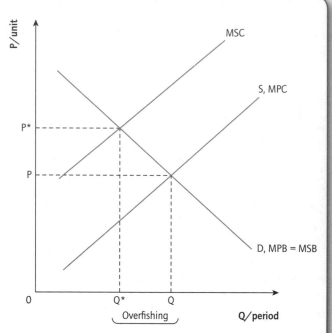

Figure 1.4.9 Overfishing

Each herdsman has the incentive to have more and more of his animals graze on the commons because he enjoys the full benefits of this but the costs are shared by all. As a result, there will be overgrazing and the commons will be destroyed.

Common-access resources (also known as common-pool resources) share two characteristics.

- It is difficult to exclude individuals from deriving benefits from the good or the resource.

- There is rivalry in the consumption of common-access resources (one individual's consumption subtracts from the benefits available to others using the resources).

Pasture is one example of a common-access resource; others include fishing grounds, forests, irrigation systems, water, the atmosphere or a city centre. The logic of the 'tragedy of the commons' may result in overfishing, deforestation, depletion of clean water supplies, global warming, etc.

Analytically, the effect of such behaviour may be illustrated through a negative externalities diagram, as in Figure 1.4.9, which illustrates the decisions of a fishing firm.

What is important to notice in Figure 1.4.9 is that the MSC of fishing exceed the MPC, as the activity of each fishing boat depletes the stock of fish available to all other fishing boats. However, these are costs external to a fishing firm's decisions. As a result, it will tend to fish more than the socially optimal level Q*.

The depletion or degradation of common- access resources poses a threat to sustainability. Sustainable development is said to exist if it 'meets the needs of the present generation without compromising the ability of future generations to meet their own needs'.

Solutions
The logic behind Hardin's 'tragedy of the commons' approach leads to a rather pessimistic outlook. Extending property rights may prove helpful in certain situations, but the time horizon of private firms and the specifics of each situation (for example the operation of multinationals in many countries) may still prove insufficient to guarantee sustainability. A different and in certain cases promising approach is devising appropriate institutional frameworks. An appropriate institutional framework is one that will protect against overexploitation and permit sustainable governance of such resources. This is the direction the work of Elinor Ostrom (who won the 2009 Nobel Prize in Economics).

In certain cases, direct regulation by governments may prove effective, for example setting fishing quotas or permitting an activity only on a limited-licence basis. In the case of GHGs, tradable pollution permits (described earlier) are a possible solution, although their implementation carries problems, the most important being that major polluting countries are not part of the process.

Lastly, educating (especially the younger generations) on the importance of adopting environmentally conscious behaviour is considered very significant.

Monopoly power as a source of market failure

Firms with monopoly power are able to restrict output below the competitive ideal and charge a higher price leading to a welfare loss. A full analysis of monopoly is given on pages 59-62.

Possible solutions

The government should ensure that competitive conditions prevail in markets. It should ensure that:

- no mergers or acquisitions materialize that excessively increase the monopoly power of any firm

- practices that seem anti-competitive are monitored; it could tax or fine firms found guilty of such practices or even break these firms up into smaller independent pieces.

A most effective way to reduce domestic monopoly power of firms is through liberalizing international trade. Free trade automatically increases competition, leading to increased efficiency and lower prices. But, one should keep in mind that there may be very significant dynamic benefits arising from the existence of such large monopoly firms in the form of faster rates of innovation, technological change and economies of scale.

Asymmetric information

In many situations either the buyer or the seller possesses incomplete or inaccurate information When an individual on one side of a transaction has more or better information than the other, we say that there is asymmetric information in the market. In such situations society's scarce resources will not be allocated efficiently. Assymmetric information can lead to the following problems.

- Adverse selection is one problem related to limitations on information. In this situation, one party possesses more information about the good being sold than the other party. Often, buyers cannot judge the true quality of the product being sold. Consider the used car market. A proportion of the used cars on sale are 'lemons', meaning that they are defective. When prices for high-quality used cars are high, owners of these cars will join the market and want to sell their cars to buy a new one, but many buyers will shy away. As the price drops though, more of the high-quality cars will be withdrawn from the market so that the proportion of lemons rises: the quality of cars is adversely affected. At the lower price the quantity demanded may even be lower. The market becomes 'thin' and it may be so thin that it is virtually non-existent.

A similar example is the market for health insurance. Individuals seeking insurance will typically be those most likely to make claims and receive payouts, in this case those in poor health or with a past history of it. If these people make up vast numbers of a health insurance company's customers, it will be forced to raise premiums, which will make people in good health withdraw from the market. The market will become thin and possibly collapse.

- When there is a misalignment of incentives then a moral hazard problem arises. Moral hazard exists when one party in a contract has more information than the other and once the contract is signed the party with the superior information changes his or her behaviour in order to benefit, while imposing costs on the other party. Individuals who purchase insurance have less of an incentive to avoid the insured-against event. They have better information regarding their behaviour than the insurers. Their behaviour cannot be easily monitored. For example, after purchasing car insurance, a driver may start driving faster and more carelessly than before. After purchasing insurance there is a decreased incentive to exercise care.

Solutions to such problems used by companies or individuals include:

- 'signalling', through which one of the parties tries to convey information about itself that will make it seem credible (for example through issuing warranties, displaying relevant qualifications or using expensive showrooms)

- 'screening', through which individuals try to infer additional information from other observable characteristics

- building a good reputation that also conveys information to buyers and is too valuable to lose

- writing contracts with contingency clauses that aim at inducing the desired behaviour (for example insurance companies offering options for an excess or deductible).

Governments can provide more information (for example labelling and awareness campaigns), can legislate minimum standards and can regulate firms' behaviour to minimize information-related market failures.

Production and costs: the short run

HL

In general, the short run is defined as the time period during which some, but not all, adjustments can take place. In the context of production theory, the short run is defined as that period during which at least one factor of production is considered fixed. Assuming two factors of production, capital (K) and labour (L), it is typically capital that is assumed constant in the short run. This means that the total product (TP), which is another term for output (Q), can change by varying the level of labour **given** the level of capital.

In the short run the behaviour of output is determined by the law of diminishing marginal returns. The behaviour of short-run costs and the shape of short-run cost curves (discussed later) are a direct consequence of the behaviour of output and of the law of diminishing marginal (and average) returns.

The marginal product of labour (MP) is defined as the extra output produced by employing one more worker or, more generally, as the change in output induced by a change in labour (L):

$$MP_L = \frac{\Delta Q}{\Delta L}$$

So, for any unit of output Q, MP is the slope of the total product (TP) curve.

The law of diminishing marginal returns

The law of diminishing marginal returns states that as more and more units of a variable factor (labour) are added to a fixed factor (capital), there is a point beyond which total product will continue to rise, but at a diminishing rate, or equivalently, that marginal product will start to decline.

Note that the law of diminishing marginal returns is a short-run law as it assumes the existence of at least one fixed factor of production (usually capital). Technology is assumed constant and the variable factor (labour) is assumed homogeneous. So, any differences in returns (output) as more units of labour are employed are not because of differences in workers' abilities but a result of the continuously changing ration of capital to labour. That is why the law is also known as the law of variable proportions. If capital and labour were perfectly substitutable factors in the production process then the law would not hold.

An example will help you understand the logic of the law. Imagine a pizzeria equipped with ovens and other equipment, tables and chairs, etc. The premises, ovens, tables, etc. are the fixed capital that exists. With zero workers working in this pizzeria, output per period will be zero. Zero workers will produce zero pizzas. Now, if one worker is employed, then some level of output (some number of pizzas) will be produced per period, say x units. The worker will have to do everything: take orders, prepare the pizzas, serve the food and take the money. If two workers are employed then it should be realized that if

the second worker simply 'copies' the first worker then double the units (2x) will be produced. But since there is so much capital available to work with compared to labour there is a lot of room for labour **specialization** to take place. The two workers may agree that one will be in charge of the whole kitchen and the other of all the serving and of taking customers' payments. Output will as a result more than double.

Focusing on Figure 1.5.1 (a) output will be initially increasing at an **increasing rate** up until some unit of labour, say L1. You should notice that the tangent on the TP curve at point b is steeper than at point a. Since we have realized that marginal product is the slope of total product and this slope is increasing up until L1, it follows that the MP curve in diagram 1.5.1(b) is rising up until L1.

At this point though, adding workers will still help **increase** total product (the TP curve in diagram 1.5.1(a) continues to rise) but now it will **rise at a slower rate** (it becomes flatter and flatter). Each extra worker contributes to the production of

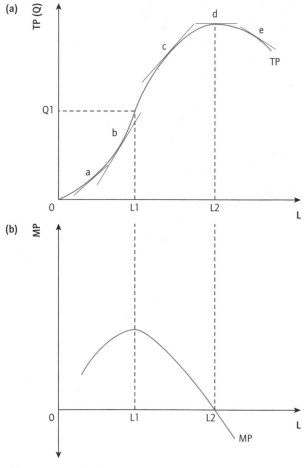

Figure 1.5.1 Total product, marginal product and the law of diminishing marginal returns

pizzas but **not as much** as the previous one. The benefits of more and more specialization are slowly exhausted. The **TP curve still rises** but now at a **decreasing rate. Marginal product,** which is the slope of the TP curve, is therefore **positive but decreasing** (dropping) **between L1 and L2.** Note that the slope of the total product curve is flatter at point c than at point b and that at worker L2 (point d) its slope is zero (it is parallel to the horizontal axis) so marginal product is zero in Figure 1.5.1 (b).

After L2 workers are employed, labour is too much for the amount of capital available (the size and equipment of the pizzeria) so total product will start declining. There are so many workers that they get in each other's way. The contribution of each extra worker (the worker's marginal product) is **negative** after L2 workers are employed. Marginal product is negative after worker L2: the marginal returns are now negative.

This shows that the law of diminishing marginal returns holds between L1 units of labour and L2 units of labour: after worker L1 total product continues to rise but at a decreasing rate; in other words, marginal product is decreasing. No firm will ever employ more than L2 workers as there would be too much labour compared to capital. Similarly, no firm will ever employ fewer than L1 workers as there would be too much capital compared to labour. Distance L1L2 is known as the economic region of production.

TIP Refer to Figure 1.5.1 (a) and (b). Draw the TP curve in three 'steps': initially with a rising positive slope (from zero to L1), then with a decreasing positive slope (from L1 to L2) then with a negative slope (past L2). At each 'switch', drop a line to the horizontal (labour) axes of both diagrams. You will have determined points L1 and L2 in the bottom diagram. Here, sketch the MP curve, remembering that it is the slope of the TP curve. It rises up to L1 and right above L1 it starts to decrease. At L2 MP is zero so the curve crosses the horizontal axis.

(HL Math and Math Methods students: draw the MP as if you were asked to sketch the first derivative of the TP function above it.)

Diminishing average returns

One can also express the law of diminishing returns in terms of the average product of labour: as more and more units of labour are added to a fixed amount of capital there is a point beyond which average product of labour decreases. In Figure 1.5.2 this occurs after worker L'.

The average product (of labour) is defined as output per unit of labour (per worker):

$$AP_L = \frac{Q}{L}$$

The average product of labour is also referred to as the productivity of labour.

Focusing on Figure 1.5.2, the average product of labour at any point on the total product curve is equal to the slope of a straight line (the 'ray') drawn from the origin to that point

on the total product curve. For example, the average product of labour at L' is equal to output (which is equal to line segment L'H) divided by the number of workers employed (line segment OL'). This ratio is the slope of the 'ray' (OH). It follows that to determine the behaviour of average product one needs to examine the behaviour of the slope of the 'ray' from the origin to successive points on the total product curve. The slope of this ray increases up to L' and then decreases. It is steepest at L' so AP has a maximum at that level of workers. Note that average product can never cross the horizontal axis and become negative as neither Q nor L can ever be negative.

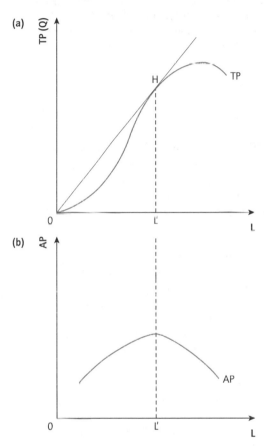

Figure 1.5.2 Total product, average product and diminishing average returns

The relationship between marginal and average product

In general, the following holds.

- If marginal is greater than average then average will rise.
- If marginal is less than average then average will drop.
- If marginal is equal to average then average will be at a maximum.

To understand the relationship, think of a student taking a series of tests in an economics course. If in the sixth test (the marginal test) the student gains a higher grade than his or her average grade to that point (in other words, if M > A) then the student's average will rise. If the student receives a lower grade than his or her average grade to that point (in other words, if M < A) then the student's average grade will fall. And if the student receives in the sixth test exactly the same grade as his or her average to that point, the student's average will not change.

Focusing on Figure 1.5.3, first draw the inverse U-shaped average product (AP) curve and then the marginal product (MP) curve, making sure that on its way down, the MP curve cuts the AP curve at its maximum point.

To the left of L', MP is greater than AP so AP should be rising. Indeed it is. To the right of L', MP is less than AP so AP should be decreasing and indeed it is. Since before L' AP is increasing and right after L' AP is decreasing, it follows that at L' AP must be at a maximum.

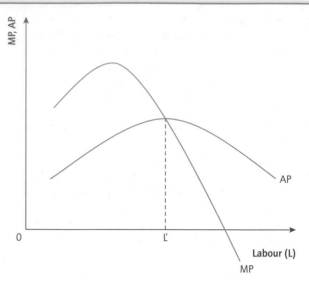

Figure 1.5.3 Marginal and average product curves in one diagram

HL

The meaning of the term 'economic costs'

To understand the meaning of the term it is important to remember that resources are scarce in any economy so whenever a resource is used in the production of a good it is automatically not available to produce other goods. In other words, it is sacrificed. From an economist's point of view, the term 'economic costs' refers to the value of all resources that are sacrificed during the production process. It implies that economic costs include not only what are defined as the **explicit** costs of a firm (the explicit payments it makes for the use of factors, also known as 'out-of-pocket' costs) but also **implicit** costs. This terms refers to the value of resources the firm owns and therefore it does not have to pay for but, from the economist's point of view, these represent sacrificed scarce resources.

Implicit costs also include the minimum reward that the scarce factor of entrepreneurship requires to remain in that line of business. This minimum reward is known as normal profits and is an element of economic costs. The idea is that to secure entrepreneurship in a business activity, some minimum reward (payment) is necessary for the risk that is undertaken. This minimum is equal to what could be earned by the entrepreneur in the next best alternative available with the same risk. If this minimum reward does not materialize, then the firm will close down and the financial capital tied up in it will be freed and moved into the next best alternative project that commands the same level of risk. If it is difficult to accept that this minimum required to attract and secure the factor of entrepreneurship is an element of economic costs, remember that for a firm to be able to use the scarce factor of labour, wages have to be paid which, of course, are an element of cost. For example, if an entrepreneur is contemplating whether to start up business A by financially investing € 1.0 million and the entrepreneur knows that he or she could be earning €80,000 a year in the next best alternative business with the same risks, business B, then the minimum return the entrepreneur requires to keep the €1.0 million invested in business A would be €80,000 per year, otherwise he or she would pull the financial capital out and instead invest it in business B. The amount of €80,000 is a production cost for business A as without this return the entrepreneur would pull out his or her scarce funds and the firm would not exist.

Economic costs include:	explicit costs	production costs for which explicit payments are made, for example wages
	implicit costs	production costs for factors owned by the firm plus the minimum payment required to secure entrepreneurship (which is known as normal profits)

Short-run costs

As mentioned earlier, the short run is a period of time during which at least one factor of production is fixed. As a result, firms in the short run face both **fixed** and **variable costs**.

Fixed costs are costs that do not vary when the level of production varies and they are unavoidable. They exist and have to be paid even if output is zero. Examples typically include rent, interest on loans, insurance costs, fixed contract costs, etc. Figure 1.5.4 (a) illustrates fixed costs as a line parallel to the quantity axis. Figure 1.5.4 (b) below it illustrates average fixed costs. Since average fixed costs are defined as fixed costs divided by output, it follows that the average fixed costs continuously decrease as output rises but they never become zero. Note that the areas beneath the average fixed costs (AFC) curve are all equal to the fixed cost the firm faces.

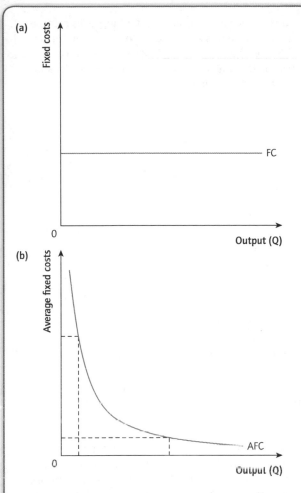

(a)

(b)

Figure 1.5.4 Fixed and average fixed costs

Variable costs include costs that vary with the level of output, for example raw materials, components and labour. **Average variable costs** (AVC) are defined as variable costs over the level of output. The **average total cost** (ATC) of producing some level of output is total costs over the level of output and it is the sum of the average variable and the average fixed costs of producing that level of output: ATC = AFC + AVC

Marginal cost (MC) is defined as the additional cost of producing an extra unit of output. This means it is the change in costs (total or variable) resulting from a change in the level of output:

$$MC = \frac{\Delta TC}{\Delta Q} = \frac{\Delta VC}{\Delta Q}$$

It is the slope of the total cost (or the slope of the variable cost) curve at each level of output.

The shape of variable and marginal costs in the short run

The shape of cost curves in the short run is a reflection of the law of diminishing marginal and average returns. Output (TP or Q) in the short run initially rises at an increasing rate up until that unit of labour at which diminishing marginal returns set in. So, as more is produced, variable costs rise but initially they rise at a decreasing rate. Producing more and more output

is initially 'easy' since with double the units of labour, the firm can produce more than double the output. If it wished to produce just double the output it would need less than double the labour: variable costs rise but they do not double.

Variable costs (VC) in Figure 1.5.5 (a) will rise at a decreasing rate up until that unit of output Q1 at which diminishing marginal returns set in production. Beyond that level of output Q1 variable costs will continue rising but at an increasing rate.

Remember that marginal costs are nothing but the slope of the VC curve: since initially variable costs rise at a **decreasing rate** and after output Q1 they increase at an **increasing rate** it follows that MC initially decrease and then at Q1 they start to increase, leading to a shape like the 'Nike-swoosh'.

The following derivation clearly illustrates the direct relationship between production and cost theory and so between marginal product and marginal costs. Remember that if labour is the only variable factor then wage costs ($\overline{w} \times L$ are the variable costs:

$$MC = \frac{\Delta VC}{\Delta Q} = \frac{(\overline{w} \times L)}{\Delta Q} = \frac{\overline{w}(\Delta L)}{\Delta Q} = \overline{w} \times \frac{\Delta L}{\Delta Q}$$

$$= \overline{w} \times \frac{1}{\left(\frac{\Delta Q}{\Delta L}\right)} = \overline{w} \times \frac{1}{MP} = \frac{\overline{w}}{MP}$$

So, MC will decrease when MP rises and MC will rise when MP decreases (i.e. when diminishing marginal returns start in production)

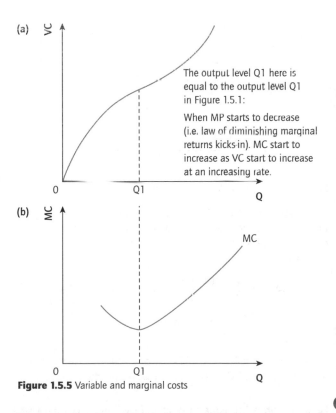

(a)

The output level Q1 here is equal to the output level Q1 in Figure 1.5.1:

When MP starts to decrease (i.e. law of diminishing marginal returns kicks in). MC start to increase as VC start to increase at an increasing rate.

(b)

Figure 1.5.5 Variable and marginal costs

The shape of variable and average variable costs in the short run

Average variable costs are the ratio of variable costs over the level of output. In Figure 1.5.6 (a) if output is Q' units then variable costs are equal to line segment Q'H. Average variable costs are therefore equal to the ratio $\frac{Q'H}{0Q'}$ which is the slope of the 'ray' OH. So, to determine the behaviour of the AVC curve one needs to check the behaviour of the slope of the 'rays' from the origin to various successive points on the VC curve. These slopes initially decrease up to output Q' and then increase, giving rise to a U-shaped AVC curve.

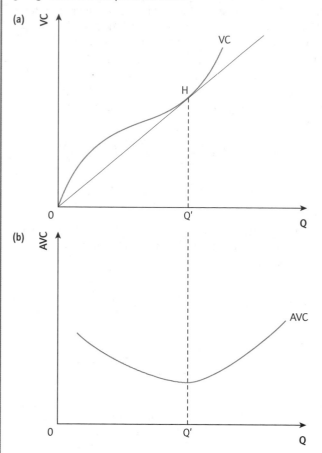

Figure 1.5.6 Variable and average variable costs

The shape of the AVC curve is the mirror image of the average product (AP) curve. The following derivation also illustrates the direct relationship between production and cost theory and in this case between AP and AVC:

$$AVC = \frac{VC}{Q} = \frac{(\overline{w} \times L)}{Q} = \overline{w} \times \frac{L}{Q} = \overline{w} \times \frac{1}{\left(\frac{Q}{L}\right)}$$

$$= \overline{w} \times \frac{1}{AP} = \frac{\overline{w}}{AP}$$

So, AVC will decrease when AP rises and AVC will rise when AP decreases (that is, when diminishing average returns occur in production).

Note that since ATC equals the sum of AVC and AFC it must be drawn above the AVC curve. The vertical distance between ATC and AVC is AFC as ATC − AVC = AFC. The ATC curve will also be U-shaped but the vertical distance between ATC and AVC

will become smaller and smaller as output increases because AFC continuously decreases and tends to zero, as shown in Figure 1.5.7. As the level of output increases the vertical distances between the two cost curves becomes smaller and smaller: (hf) < (de) < (ab).

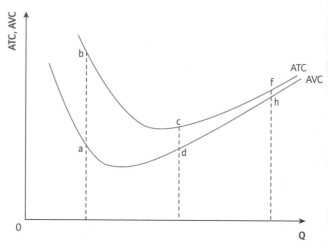

Figure 1.5.7 The ATC and AVC curves

Total costs, variable cost and fixed costs in one diagram

Now that the shape of the VC curve has been explained it is possible to include in one diagram the total cost (TC) curve, the VC curve and the fixed cost (FC) curve. In Figure 1.5.8 the TC curve is shaped just like the VC curve except it has been shifted up by the amount of the fixed costs. So, the vertical distance between the TC curve and the VC curve is the same at all levels of output. Line segment ab = fh = kj = uv and they are all equal to the fixed costs 0c.

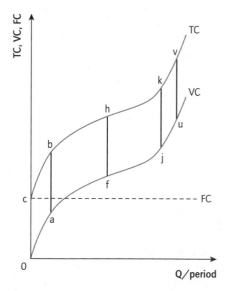

Figure 1.5.8 Total, variable and fixed costs

How to draw MC and AC curves in the same diagram

The rules that have to be followed are exactly the same as those explained in Figure 1.5.3. Both ATC and AVC curves are U-shaped and marginal cost (MC) is like the 'Nike-swoosh' shape.

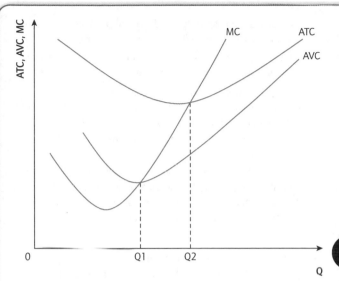

Figure 1.5.9 Marginal and average costs in the same diagram

It follows that if average is falling then marginal must be less than average, while if average is rising then marginal must be

greater than average. Lastly, on its way up MC must cut through average at its minimum point.

- If M < A then A will drop.
- If M > A then A will rise.
- If M = A then A will be at a minimum.

In Figure 1.5.9, AVC decreases for all units of output up to unit Q1. MC must lie below it. For output to the right of unit Q1 since AVC is rising, MC must lie above it. Focusing on ATC, it should be clear that for output to the left of unit Q2, MC should lie below ATC as ATC is decreasing. For output to the right of Q2, MC should lie above ATC as ATC is rising.

> **TIP**
> If you want to draw an ATC and an AVC curve on the same diagram first draw the ATC curve. Note the minimum of your ATC curve. Then draw the AVC curve **below** it, making sure that its minimum **is to the left** of the ATC minimum and also that they get **closer and closer** (but do not touch) as you move to the right.

Production and costs: the long run

The long run is defined as that time period during which all adjustments are possible. Within the theory of production it is the period during which all factors are considered variable (or, equivalently, no fixed factors exist). The firm can therefore change its scale of production. It can grow or it can shrink in size.

In the long run there are three possible effects on output from an increase in the level of use of all factors.

- **Increasing returns to scale**: the percentage increase in output is greater than the percentage increase in all inputs. For example, doubling all factors of production more than doubles the level of output Q. In other words, an increase in all inputs by 1% will lead to a greater than 1% increase in output.

- **Constant returns to scale**: the percentage increase in output is equal to the percentage increase in all inputs. For example, doubling all factors of production doubles the level of output Q. In other words, an increase in all inputs by 1% will lead to a 1% increase in output.

- **Decreasing returns to scale**: the percentage increase in output is less than the percentage increase in all inputs. For example, doubling all factors of production less than doubles the level of output Q. In other words, an increase in all inputs by 1% leads to a smaller than 1% increase in output.

Whether production in the long run is characterized by increasing, constant or decreasing returns to scale determines the behaviour of long-run average costs. More specifically, the following applies.

- If production is characterized by increasing returns to scale then average (unit) costs are decreasing as output is increasing faster than costs. The firm is benefiting from economies of scale (EOS).

- If production is characterized by constant returns to scale then average (unit) costs are constant, as output is increasing as fast as costs.

- If production is characterized by decreasing returns to scale then average (unit) costs are increasing, as costs are increasing faster than output. The firm is experiencing diseconomies of scale.

In Figure 1.5.10 a typical long-run average cost (LAC) curve is illustrated. The LAC curve shows the minimum average cost for which level of output Q can be produced in the long run; that is, when the firm can change its size and choose the optimal scale.

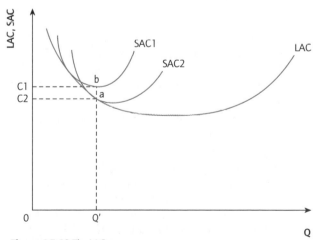

Figure 1.5.10 The LAC curve
Economies of scale (EOS) and diseconomies of scale (DOS)

Figure 1.5.10 illustrates EOS and DOS corresponding to increasing and decreasing returns to scale respectively. Initially, the LAC curve slopes downward. Average costs decrease as the size of a firm and output increases. The downward section of a LAC curve illustrates EOS. Long-run average costs are constant in the horizontal section of the LAC curve where the firm is characterized by constant returns to scale. Lastly, if the firm's size increases more then after some point, the LAC curve slopes upward. Average costs increase as the scale of a firm and output increases. The upward sloping section of a LAC curve illustrates DOS.

Note at each level of output (Q) corresponds the firm's specific size (and so a specific short-run average cost curve: SAC) with which the firm can achieve the lowest possible average costs. For example, Q' units of output can be produced both by a small firm with a short-run average costs curve SAC1 and a firm that is larger and has a short-run average costs curve SAC2. The lowest unit cost with which this firm can produce Q' units is C2 (equal to line segment Q'a) and this is achieved if the firm's size increases. Point 'a' belongs on the firm's LAC curve.

TIP Draw the U-shaped LAC curve rather shallow, making sure that on its decreasing region the SAC curves are tangent to it on the left of their lowest points while on its rising section the SAC curves are tangent to it on the right of their minima. Also note that the smallest size with which minimum average costs can be achieved in the long run is the firm's minimum optimal (or minimum efficient) scale.

EOS

These are defined as cost savings due to increased scale of production. They can be distinguished into internal EOS and external EOS. Internal EOS are cost savings due to actions of the firm itself. External EOS are cost savings originating from developments outside the firm, for example because the industry in which it operates grows.

Sources of EOS

Internal EOS can result from technical, marketing, management, financial or risk-related reasons. Specifically, these can be as follows.

- Technical EOS may arise:
  - because a firm that is large in size may be able to adopt technologies of production simply not available for smaller firms, for example capital equipment (such as an assembly line) is often indivisible and therefore unavailable for small firms
  - because larger firms offer more possibilities for labour specialization
  - as a result of the 'container principle' (or the 'law of dimensions'): cost savings may arise because volumes rise faster than surfaces. For example, a storage tank that can store double the volume of something costs less than double to manufacture than a smaller tank. This principle is related to blast furnaces, pipes, trucks and of course shipping transportation.
- Marketing EOS may arise:
  - because, on the input side, a larger firm buys inputs in bulk and so may secure better prices from suppliers (bulk buying)

  - because, on the output side, distribution costs on a per unit basis are usually lower for larger firms.
- Financial EOS may arise because a large firm can often borrow from banks at lower interest rates.
- Management EOS may arise because larger firms can employ specialists in each department, for example a large supermarket will hire financial experts to manage its cash flow on a daily basis and a large department store will hire specialist buyers.
- Risk-related EOS may arise because a larger firm is often more diversified, selling not one but many products, in not one but in many markets (or even in many countries). Risks, and the associated costs, are therefore better spread and minimized.

External EOS

Sometimes, as an industry grows, unit costs of the firms comprising it may decrease. Typically this is a result of similar firms locating together in one area (referred to also as agglomeration economies). Why?

Here are some reasons.

- A specialized labour force may develop and technical schools, catering to firms' needs, may also be established in the area.
- Complementary firms may also be established.
- Better transportation and telecommunications networks may develop.
- Marketing of by-products may be possible.

DOS

These are defined as increases in average costs due to increased scale of production. Firms may become so big that unit production costs start to rise. DOS can originate within a firm (internal DOS) or outside the firm (external DOS).

Internal DOS

After a point, size may become a problem. When firms grow beyond a certain size then unit costs may start increasing. Possible reasons for this are as follows.

- Management problems of coordination, control and communication associated with huge size may develop.
- Motivation may decrease.
- Interdependencies within a huge firm may lead to problems if there are any hold ups in any particular part of the firm.

External DOS

- After a point, congestion costs in an area may develop.
- As an industry grows, factor prices (for example for materials or specialized labour) may also start increasing as a result of the higher factor demand.

Revenues

Total revenues (TR) are defined as the product of the price per unit times the number of units sold, or:

$$TR = P \times Q$$

The behaviour of total revenues as a firm sells more units of output depends upon whether the firm can sell more units at the same price or whether in order for the market to absorb more units it must lower the price.

Case 1: The firm can sell more per period at the same price
If the firm is extremely small in size compared with the market and it sells a good that is identical to the one sold by all the other firms in the market then it will be able to sell more units without lowering the market price. In this case it will be as if it is facing a perfectly elastic (horizontal) demand for its product, as illustrated in Figure 1.5.11.

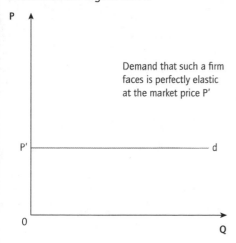

Figure 1.5.11 Demand of a firm being able to sell more units at the same price P′

Assuming that the price at which it can sell its output is P′, then its total revenues will be:

$$TR = P' \times Q$$

For example, if the price at which it can sell its output is $5.00 per unit then:

$$TR = 5Q$$

Figure 1.5.12 illustrates the total revenue function for such a firm. It is a straight line that starts from the origin because if it sells zero units it will earn zero revenues.

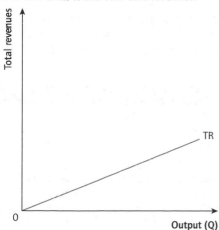

Figure 1.5.12 Total revenues when the firm can sell more units at the same price

Average revenue (AR) from the sale of Q units is defined as the revenue per unit of output sold, or:

$$AR(Q) = \frac{TR(Q)}{Q} = \frac{P \times Q}{Q} = P$$

It should be clear that AR is always equal to the price at which the output is sold. Since the demand curve shows at which price each quantity can be sold it follows that the AR curve is always the demand curve that the firm faces, as illustrated in Figure 1.5.13.

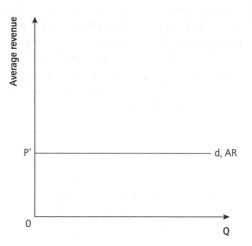

Figure 1.5.13 AR curve when a firm can sell more units at the same price

Figures 1.5.13 and 1.5.11 are identical: the demand curve that a firm faces is always identical to the firm's AR curve.

Marginal revenue (MR) from the sale of Q units is defined as the extra revenue earned from an extra unit of output sold or, the change in revenues given a change in output. So:

$$MR = \frac{\Delta TR}{\Delta Q}$$

There are two ways to understand what the MR curve will look like. One way is to realize that if a firm can sell extra units at the same price (say, P′) then:

- the MR from selling an extra unit will be of course equal to the price P′
- the MR curve will be a straight line at the price P′, identical to the demand curve it faces and its AR curve, as in Figure 1.5.14.

The other way is to realize that MR is nothing but the slope of the TR curve in Figure 1.5.12. The slope of TR is a positive and constant so MR will be a positive number and constant.

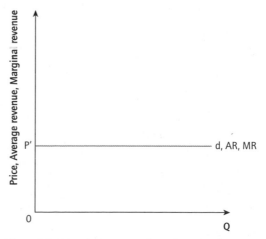

Figure 1.5.14 Marginal revenue when a firm can sell more units at the same price

Note that since AR in Figure 1.5.14 is constant it follows from the logic of marginal and average magnitudes explained earlier that MR must equal AR and must therefore also be constant.

Case 2: The firm must lower the price to sell more
If the firm is large in size compared with the market or if it sells a good that is not considered identical to those sold by other firms then it faces a negatively sloped demand curve.

Since AR is always equal to the price at which the good is sold (as shown earlier) the demand curve faced by the firm is also its AR curve, as illustrated in Figure 1.5.15:

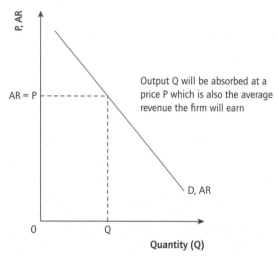

Output Q will be absorbed at a price P which is also the average revenue the firm will earn

Figure 1.5.15 AR curve when a firm must lower price to sell more

As explained earlier, what happens to total revenues in this case, when the firm lowers price, depends on the price elasticity of demand (PED). As price drops if demand is price elastic then total revenues increase while if demand is price inelastic then total revenues decrease. Total revenues, being the product of price times quantity, are zero when either quantity or price is zero. They are at a maximum where PED is equal to 1, which is at the midpoint of a straight line demand curve, as illustrated in Figure 1.5.16.

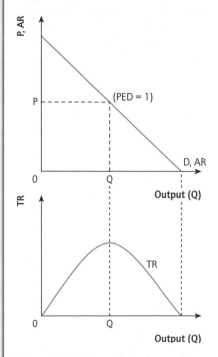

Figure 1.5.16 TR curve when a firm must lower price to sell more

Determining the shape of the MR curve is more difficult. It is important to remember that MR is the slope of TR and that since AR continuously decreases, it must be that MR is less (below on a diagram) than AR. So MR must cross the horizontal axis at Q (see Figure 1.5.17).

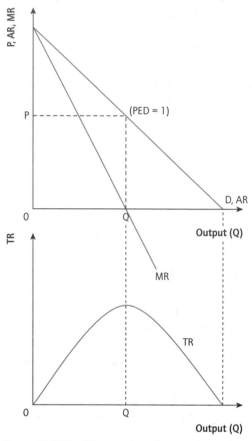

Figure 1.5.17 The MR curve when a firm must lower price to sell more

It can be shown that the MR curve when the firm faces a negatively sloped straight line demand curve will be also a straight line, will have the same vertical intercept and also double the slope.

	AR curve	MR curve	TR curve
If horizontal demand curve	Identical to the demand curve faced	Identical to the demand curve faced	Positively sloped straight line through the origin
If negatively sloped demand curve	Identical to the demand curve faced	Straight line with double the slope and same vertical intercept	Bell-shaped (parabola) with maximum below the midpoint of the demand curve where PED = 1

The meaning of the term 'economic profits' (π)

Economic profits are defined as the difference between total revenues (TR) and total economic costs (TC) of production.

$$\pi(Q) = TR(Q) - TC(Q)$$

The key to understanding economic profits is to remember the meaning of economic costs. Economic costs include not only explicit costs but also implicit costs. Remember that implicit costs refer to the cost of using resources owned by a firm for which it makes no explicit payment as well as the minimum reward that the factor of entrepreneurship requires to remain in that line of business, known as normal profits.

Since economic costs include the minimum profit required to remain in business, it follows that if total revenues are equal to total (economic) costs and the firm is making zero economic profits it is not that the firm is making no money! It is making a profit — the minimum it requires: normal profits.

This means that if a firm is making zero economic profits it will have no reason to shut down and exit the market as it is making as much as it would have been making in its next best alternative.

If now it happens that total revenues exceed total (economic) costs then the firm is earning more than the minimum (normal profits) required: it is making supernormal (or, sometimes, abnormal) profits. These are profits over and above normal. Entrepreneurs are making in this market more than they could

have made in the next best alternative available with the same risks. Other entrepreneurs will want to join this market and they will if there is nothing to deter their entry.

Lastly, if total revenues are less than total (economic) costs then the firm is not making the minimum it requires to remain in business. It may be making profits but these are less than the entrepreneur could earn in the next best alternative (less than normal profits) so, in the long run when no fixed factors tie the firm up, it will certainly exit and try to enter the next best alternative line of business.

The role of economic profits in a market economy

Economic profits are the reward to entrepreneurship. They differ from wages in that profits are not contracted, as wages are, but are a residual and so they may even be negative (losses). Supernormal profits attract resources into an industry whereas losses free up resources, allowing their use in other industries. Relative price changes coupled with supernormal profits and losses drive resource allocation in a market economy. Striving to achieve profits results in less waste and therefore in greater (technical) efficiency. Supernormal profits provide the incentive and funding for firms to finance expansion (investment). Supernormal profits can also be used to finance R&D programmes and so may lead to product and process innovations.

Remember: $\pi = (TR - TC)$ **and total costs include normal profits** **defined as the minimum required for the firm to remain in the present line of business.** **If the firm does not earn normal profits, this will lead to the firm exiting the market.**		
If $\pi = 0$	If $\pi > 0$	If $\pi < 0$
The firm is making just normal profits, enough money to keep it from exiting the market because it is making as much as it would make in the next best alternative line of business.	The firm is making supernormal profits — more than the minimum it requires — but other firms will be attracted and, if possible, will enter the market.	The firm is making losses, so even if it is making some money it is not enough to keep it operating, as in the next best alternative line of business it could make a profit.

Goals of firms

Profit maximization

The working assumption in economics is that firms aim at maximizing economic profits (that is, maximizing the difference between total revenues and total costs).

The condition for profit maximization
It can be shown that if a firm wishes to maximize profits it must choose an output level Q at which:

$$MR = MC$$
and the MC curve is rising

Many students erroneously think that this condition means that profits are zero, forgetting that the term **marginal** refers to one more unit, to the extra unit. To realize why profits are maximum when MR = MC one must consider the alternatives. There are two alternatives. MR could be either greater or less than MC.

Case 1: MR > MC
Assume for the sake of the argument that at the chosen level of output Q, MR > MC. Reading this carefully means that the

extra revenue collected from selling one more unit of output exceeds the extra cost of producing that extra unit. If that is the case, then whatever the level of profits made at Q units of output, the firm will be able to increase these profits by producing that extra unit. But if profits can be increased, they are not at a maximum. It follows that if MR > MC then profits **cannot** be at a maximum as they can be increased. Note that even if the firm was making losses at the chosen level of output Q, it would be able to decrease these losses by producing the extra unit, so the chosen Q could not have been the right (the best or optimum) choice of output.

Case 2: MR < MC
If the firm had chosen an output rate Q at which MR < MC, then, by producing one unit **less** it would not collect the associated revenues but it would not incur the greater associated cost. It follows that, whatever the level of profits, it would **increase** these (or decrease losses) by producing one less unit.

It follows from the logic of this analysis that profits **cannot** be at a maximum if MR > MC or if MC > MR.

A firm should neither increase nor decrease its output rate if MR = MC as at that level of output profits are maximized (or losses are minimized).

Profits can be increased (or losses decreased) if:	MR > MC	MR < MC
	How? By increasing output Q	How? By decreasing output Q
Profits can not be increased (or losses decreased); in other words, profits are maximized (or losses minimized) if:	MR = MC and the MC curve is rising	

Why should the MC curve be rising?

To understand why at the chosen level of output Q at which MR are equal to MC it must **also** be that the MC curve is rising, consider the alternative (that MC were declining) and assume that the firm decided to produce one more unit of output. Profits would further increase as the extra revenue would exceed the extra cost incurred. It follows that at the chosen output Q not only must MR equal MC but also the MC curve must be rising.

Other goals

Goals other than profit maximization include the following.

Revenue maximization

It may be that a firm aims at maximizing revenues. Revenues are defined as the product or the price per unit times the number of units sold. Referring to Figure 1.5.17 it should be clear that the condition that needs to be satisfied for a firm to maximize revenues is to choose that level of output Q for which MR are zero. If MR are a positive number at some level of output then by selling one more unit the firm could increase revenues so they were not at a maximum. This means that the firm should sell all units for which MR are positive up until that unit for which MR are zero.

Growth maximization

Firms may also wish to maximize the volume of output sold subject to non-negative profits. By maximizing growth the firm may be able to lower unit costs, achieving EOS. A larger firm is in better position to diversify into different markets as well as into different products. The consequence of such diversification is an overall lowering of associated risks. The condition to maximize the volume of output without incurring losses is that at the chosen level of output Q the average revenue earned should equal the average costs incurred.

Satisficing

The term satisficing was introduced by Herbert Simon (from 'satisfy and suffice'). It describes when, because of conflicting objectives of the various stakeholders within a firm as well as informational limitations, it does not aim at maximizing profits or revenues but only strives to achieve at least some pre-defined minimum level of profits or revenues.

Corporate social responsibility

Firms may depart from a strict free-market, profit-maximizing mode of operation and pursue objectives that are more closely aligned to the interests of the wider community in which they operate, both the local and global communities. Ethical ways of doing business are followed and there is a sense of obligation to satisfy long-term goals that include goals involving positive impact on the lives of the workforce and their families as well as of society at large.

Market structures

HL

It turns out that resource allocation and efficiency considerations are greatly affected by market structure. The structure of a market (whether there are many, few or one firm) is important as it determines the conduct of firms (for example whether they have the power to set prices) and, consequently, their performance (that is, whether efficiency is achieved in resource allocation).

Traditionally, markets are split into four types, namely:

- perfect competition
- monopoly
- monopolistic competition
- oligopoly.

Market structures are distinguished on the basis of the number of firms in the market (whether there are many, few or one firm), the type of product (homogeneous or differentiated) and whether entry barriers do or do not exist.

Perfect competition

Characteristics

- In perfect competition there will be very many small firms in the market.

- These firms will produce a homogeneous product, meaning that consumers consider it **identical** across sellers. There are few examples of such products. They are mostly found in the primary sector (farm products and metals are examples).

- No entry (or exit) barriers will exist. An entry barrier is anything that may deter entry into a market.

In addition, we assume:

- perfect information available to all market participants
- perfect mobility of factors of production.

Is the perfectly competitive model realistic?

Very few markets in the real world share the characteristics of perfect competition. Why? First, EOS are very common, especially in the manufacturing sector. Very often large firms can produce at a lower unit cost than smaller firms can. Firms therefore have an incentive to grow either internally (through investment in physical capital) or through mergers and acquisitions. This explains why large firms are typically found in most industries.

Firms also have the incentive to differentiate their product, for example by improving quality or changing its characteristics, in order to acquire some degree of monopoly power. Monopoly power is defined as the ability to raise price (P) above marginal cost (MC). The Lerner index of monopoly power is given by the ratio $(P - MC)/P$. A firm that manages to produce and sell even a slightly differentiated product will face a negatively sloped demand curve for its product, so it will be able to increase price without losing all customers.

Firms also try to create entry barriers so that they can maintain any supernormal profits in the long run. In addition, exit barriers in the form of 'sunk costs' also are common. Sunk costs are costs that a firm can not recover when it exits an industry.

Information in the real world is not perfect. There are cases where information is asymmetric, as explained earlier.

Lastly, perfect mobility seldom characterizes factors of production. Labour, for example, often suffers from occupational and geographical immobility.

Why is it still useful to study perfect competition?
Despite its limitations perfect competition is useful. It is simple and it is capable of successfully predicting change. Most importantly, its efficiency properties are considered desirable, so it serves as a model against which real world markets can be compared and perhaps, if necessary, 'corrected'.

Short-run equilibrium in perfect competition: a case of supernormal profits
Assume a perfectly competitive market, as illustrated in Figure 1.5.18 (b). Market forces, in other words market demand and market supply, determine the market price at P. Each firm in a perfectly competitive market is a 'price taker', meaning that the market-determined price P is a given for each firm. Since there are so many other firms offering an identical product to perfectly informed consumers, one firm cannot increase the price above the market-determined level as no one would purchase even a single unit from it. It also has no incentive to lower the

price below the market determined level as it is, by assumption, so small compared with the market that it can sell all it wants at the going market price. Imagine a sandy beach representing a market with each grain of sand being a firm. Even if one doubles its size and becomes as big as two grains of sand it would make no difference to the beach (the market). This implies that a perfectly competitive firm can sell more output per period at the same price. So, it is as if it is facing a perfectly elastic demand for its product at the going market price P.

As a result of this, the firm's average revenue (AR) and marginal revenue (MR) are both equal to the price P so that the AR curve, the MR curve and the demand the firm faces for its product coincide (Case 1 in the analysis of AR presented earlier).

This perfectly competitive firm only has to decide how much output to offer in the market per period given the prevailing market P. If we assume that the firm is a profit maximizer, we know the answer. It will choose that level of output q for which:

$$MR = MC \text{ and the MC curve is rising.}$$

The MC curve in Figure 1.5.18 (a) intersects the MR curve at point H which is right above output q*. It follows that the firm will choose to sell q* units per period at the market price P per unit. The cost per unit (the average cost) when producing q* units is given by the AC curve. Going up from q* toward the AC curve we find point F and from there we turn left and find that the AC of producing q* units is C. Total revenues collected are equal to the number of units sold times the price per unit or q* times P. This is the area of rectangle (0q*HP).

Turning to the cost side, bear in mind that total costs are equal to the number of units produced times how much it costs on the average to produce each, or q* times q*F. This is the area of rectangle (0q*FC). Economic profits are defined as the difference between total revenues collected and total costs of production, so geometrically on Figure 1.5.18 (a) they are equal to shaded area (CFHP).

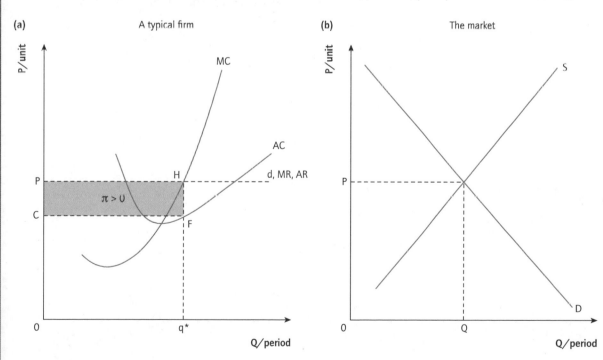

(a) A typical firm

(b) The market

Figure 1.5.18 Perfect competition
Short-run analysis: a case of supernormal profits

Economic profits for the typical firm in this case are positive. The typical firm in this market is making supernormal profits. This means that it is making more than the minimum required to compensate for the resources employed and the risk taken (remember this minimum required has been defined as normal profits).

> **TIP** A typical mistake students make is when they 'shade' the profit area. Make sure you correctly identify on your diagram the AC associated with the chosen level of output. Also, line FC on Figure 1.5.18 (a) cannot be tangent to your U-shaped AC curve in the short run as MC is shaped like the 'Nike swoosh'.

Short-run equilibrium in perfect competition: a case of losses

It is not necessary for the typical perfectly competitive firm to be making supernormal or normal profits in the short run. It could be making losses. Figure 1.5.19 illustrates this case.

In Figure 1.5.19 (b) market demand and market supply are such that the equilibrium price is determined at P. The firm in Figure 1.5.19 (a) takes the market determined price P which is equal to its MR (and AR) and selects its optimal level of output at the intersection of MR and MC at q*. AC are equal to q*F while AR (price) is only q*H. This firm is making economic losses equal to shaded area (FHCP).

Long-run equilibrium in perfect competition

Resources are attracted into an industry in which firms earn supernormal profits as this implies that these firms earn more than they would in the next best alternative. On the other hand, economic losses will induce exit of firms from the industry as the resources they employ could earn more in their next best alternative. It follows that if economic profits in an industry are zero neither entry nor exit will be observed, as firms in such an industry make just as much money as they would in

their next best alternative. Firms in perfect competition will neither enter nor exit if each firm achieves its assumed profit-maximizing goal by producing at that level of output at which MR = MC (and the MC curve is rising) and if the typical firm is making only normal profits (that is, zero economic profits). In this situation, there is no reason for new firms to enter the market or existing firms to exit. This requires that at the chosen output AR = AC.

In Figure 1.5.20, the firm will choose q* units to produce as at that level of output it achieves its goal and has no reason to change anything. In addition, at q* AC and AR are equal to q*F so the typical profit-maximizing firm is making normal profits (that is, zero economic profits). No new firms will enter and no existing firms have an incentive to exit. Nothing will change unless demand or cost (technology) conditions change in this market.

How is long-run equilibrium achieved?

Assume, as illustrated in Figure 1.5.20, a perfectly competitive market in which the typical firm is making supernormal profits. As explained, this will induce entry of new firms into the industry. As new firms enter, market supply increases, shifting the market supply curve to the right and pushing the market price lower. This process (the entry of firms) will stop when there is no incentive for more firms to enter; that is, when economic profits are driven to zero. Figure 1.5.20 illustrates this situation. The market price in Figure 1.5.20 (a) has been driven to P. The typical firm in Figure 1.5.20 (a) produces q* units. At this level of output total revenues and total costs are equal to area (0q*FP).

In the case of short-run losses, illustrated in Figure 1.5.19, loss-making firms will exit, decreasing and shifting to the left the market supply curve and pushing market price and AR higher. The process (the exit of firms) stops when AR become equal to AC, in other words when the typical firm is making normal profits (zero economic profits); that is, as much as it

(a)   A typical firm

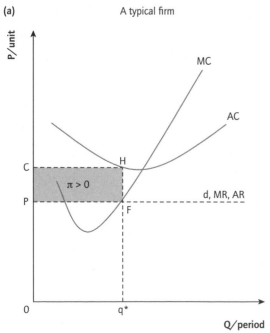

(b)   The market

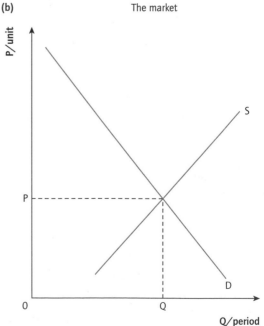

Figure 1.5.19 Perfect competition
Short-run analysis: a case of losses

(a) A typical firm

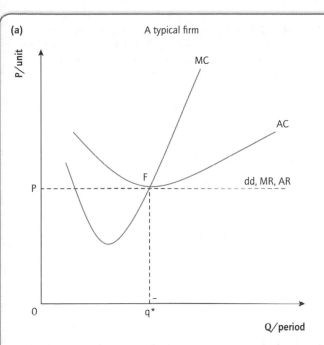

(b) The market

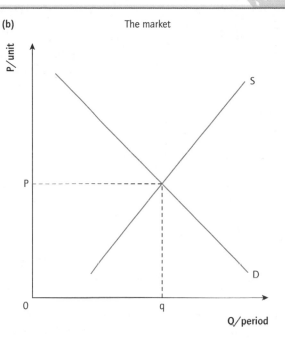

Figure 1.5.20 Perfect competition
Long run equilibrium

would earn in the next best alternative. There is no reason for more firms to exit, as illustrated in Figure 1.5.20.

The long-run equilibrium condition in perfect competition
Long-run equilibrium requires that at the chosen output rate q the typical firm is maximizing profits **and** that these economic profits are zero (normal profits) so no entry or exit is induced:

$$MR = MC \text{ (and the MC curve is rising)}$$

$$\pi(q) = zero.$$

Remember that price is always equal to AR and that in this perfectly competitive case (where the firm can sell as much as it wants at the going market price) it is also equal to MR. Also, since at the chosen output MC and AC are equal, it must be that AC is at a minimum. So, the long-run equilibrium condition in perfectly competitive markets can be written as:

$$q^*: (P = AR) = MR = MC = AC$$

Role of profits and losses in resource allocation
Note here the role of profits and losses in allocating and re-allocating scarce resources in a market economy. Profits attract scarce resources as new firms enter the industry (assuming no entry barriers) while losses force firms to exit,

TIP To illustrate long-run equilibrium in perfect competition, start by drawing a U-shaped AC curve for the typical firm and then draw, **using always a ruler**, a horizontal tangent at its minimum. This line will be the demand (and MR and AR curves) this firm faces and so determines the price. Make sure the MC curve is drawn in such a way that it cuts the AC curve at its minimum. At the intersection of the MR and the MC curves drop a line to determine the equilibrium output of the firm. When you then draw the market diagram make sure the market demand and supply curves intersect at the price you determined on the first side diagram. You could start the other way around by first determining the market equilibrium price and extending it all the way to the diagram of a typical firm.

freeing up scarce resources. Bankruptcy performs a most important role in a market economy as it makes scarce resources available again for use in other, more productive areas. Of course, whether freed-up resources may or may not be channelled into more productive uses also depends upon their mobility. In addition, the affected parties (workers and owners of capital) may face significant adjustment costs.

Shutting down in perfect competition
Assume a loss-making firm. Should it shut down immediately? The answer depends on whether it is operating in the long run or in the short run.

Long run
In the long run a loss-making firm will shut down and exit the market. In the long run all possible adjustments have been made and the firm has no fixed factors, therefore it faces no fixed (and so unavoidable) costs.

Short run
Should a loss-making firm shut down in the short run? In the short run some factors of production are considered fixed. This implies that the firm faces fixed costs. Fixed costs are unavoidable costs in the sense that the firm must pay them even if it exits the market and produces zero units of output.

The key to whether a loss-making firm should shut down in the short run is that if it does this it will still face and have to pay its fixed costs, for example monthly payments for an outstanding bank loan. Whether this firm should shut down in the short run or not depends on whether the losses incurred when the firm is operating exceed or are lower than the fixed costs incurred if it shuts down and exits. If these unavoidable fixed costs are higher than the losses faced by producing, then it should remain in business as it will be losing less. On the other hand, if these unavoidable fixed costs are lower than the losses incurred by operating then it should shut down and exit.

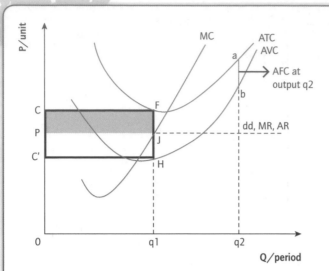

Figure 1.5.21 Shut-down rule for a perfectly competitive firm short-run analysis

Figure 1.5.21 illustrates a perfectly competitive firm operating in the short run. As a result, both the ATC and the AVC curves are present. The market price is determined at P which this firm must take and determine the optimal, profit-maximizing level of output. MR and MC are equal exactly above output level q1.

This firm is making losses. AR (price) is equal to line segment q1J while ATC are equal to line segment q1F so per unit losses are equal to distance JF. Multiplying this distance by PJ (which is equal to output 0q1) gives the loss area (JFCP), the shaded rectangle.

We need to determine now the size of the (unavoidable) fixed costs. Given that ATC = AVC + AFC so that AFC = ATC − AVC it follows that the vertical distance at each output level between the ATC and the AVC curves is equal to AFC. For example, at output level q2 the corresponding AFC are distance ab, the difference between ATC (q2a) and AVC (q2b).

We can compare fixed costs and the losses incurred at output q1 by calculating the fixed cost area using AFC at the chosen output level q1. Multiplying output C′H (=0q1) by FH (the AFC at q1) is area (HFCC′), the firm's fixed costs, the black outline rectangle.

In this case illustrated here, the loss-making firm should not shut down in the short run as the losses (JFCP) incurred by operating are less than the fixed costs (HFCC′) it would still face if it shut down.

In the short run the decision to shut down or not boils down to whether, by producing, the firm is making sufficient revenues to cover its operating (that is, variable costs). If its revenues more than cover its variable costs then it should not shut down as it will also be able to pay part of its fixed costs, whereas by shutting down it would be burdened by the full amount of its fixed costs.

Short-run shut-down rule

A loss-making firm in the short run should shut down if total revenues are less than (total) variable costs or, equivalently (dividing by Q both sides), if average revenue (price) is less than average variable cost (AVC).

So, at any price below the minimum AVC a loss-making perfectly competitive firm should shut down. This case is illustrated in Figure 1.5.22. The market determined price is assumed to be P.

Average and marginal revenue (AR and MR) are therefore also equal to P. Given the MC curve illustrated, the profit-maximizing firm will choose to produce and sell q′ units per period.

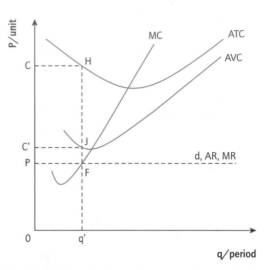

Figure 1.5.22 A loss-making perfectly competitive firm shutting down in the short run

It will be making a loss as ATC are greater than AR equal to area (FHCP). If it shuts down it will face the unavoidable fixed costs found by multiplying the profit-maximizing level of output q′ times the corresponding average fixed cost HJ. Fixed costs faced if it shuts down are equal to area (JHCC′). These are less than the losses incurred by producing. This firm's revenues (0q′FP) are insufficient to cover its variable (operating) costs (0q′JC′). AR earned − P (or q′F) − is less than the AVC incurred q′J. It will therefore choose to shut down.

Shut-down rule		
Long run	If TR < TC or if AR (= P) < ATC that is, if π < 0	Shut down and exit
Short run	if π < 0 and TR < VC or, equivalently, if AR (= P) < AVC	Shut down and exit
	if π < 0 but TR > VC or, equivalently, if AR (=P) ≤ AVC	Do not shut down: wait until no fixed costs are incurred

> **TIP** This is a tricky diagram to draw and needs some practice. Start by drawing the U-shaped ATC and AVC curves ensuring that their vertical distance (the average fixed costs) becomes smaller and smaller as output increases. Make sure the MC curve (the 'Nike-swoosh' curve) cuts through their minima on its way up. If you want to illustrate the case of a loss-making perfectly competitive firm in the short run which will not shut down, choose a price between the minima of ATC and AVC and denote the line d, AR and MR. Otherwise (if you want to show a firm which will shut down immediately and exit) choose a price below the minimum of the AVC curve you drew. Remember that the vertical distance between ATC and AVC is the AFC corresponding to the chosen profit-maximizing output so if you multiply it by this output you get the unavoidable fixed costs incurred.

Break-even price

The break-even price is defined as that price at which a firm is earning normal (that is, zero economic) profits. Given a U-shaped ATC curve, the break-even price for a perfectly competitive firm facing a perfectly elastic (horizontal) demand is the price that is equal to the firm's minimum ATC.

In the short run, the break-even price for a perfectly competitive firm lies above (that is, is greater) than the shut-down price (which is at the minimum of the AVC curve) as AVC lies below ATC for all levels of output.

In the long run, the break-even price for a perfectly competitive firm is equal to the shut-down price as both are equal to the minimum of the AC curve. (Remember that in the long run there are no fixed costs so there is no reason to distinguish between ATC and AC.)

Note, that there is another widely acceptable notion of the break-even point. It refers to the level of output for which the firm makes normal (that is, zero economic) profits. By setting TR equal to TC and solving for Q you can find the break-even level of **output** (that is, the output for which normal profits are earned).

So, for a perfectly competitive firm:

In the short run:	
break-even price is	P = min ATC
shut-down price is	P = min AVC
In the long run:	
break-even price **and** shut-down price are	P = min ATC

Figure 1.5.23 illustrates the shut-down price as well as the break-even price in the short run for a perfectly competitive firm.

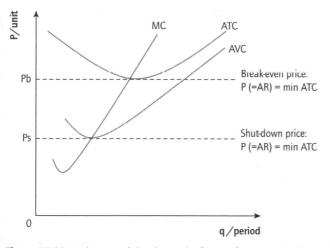

Figure 1.5.23 Break-even and shut-down price for a perfect competitor in the short run

The break-even price is at Pb as at any other price the perfectly competitive firm would be making either supernormal profits or losses. The short-run shut-down price is at Ps as that price is equal to the minimum AVC.

Note that if the firm is not a perfectly competitive firm and it faces a negatively sloped demand then it does not make sense to consider the minimum of the ATC curve as the break-even price, because a negatively sloped demand (and AR) curve can only be tangent at the falling portion of a U-shaped ATC curve.

The supply curve of the perfectly competitive firm

In the short run the supply curve of a perfectly competitive firm is that portion of its MC curve that lies above the minimum of its AVC. In Figure 1.5.24, the supply curve is the thick black segment of the MC curve. Why?

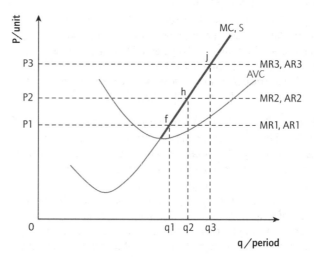

Figure 1.5.24 Short-run supply of a perfectly competitive firm

Remember that a supply curve shows how many units a firm will be willing to offer per period at each price, ceteris paribus. Referring to Figure 1.5.24, if the market price was at P1 then the profit-maximizing perfectly competitive firm would offer q1 units per period as its MR curve intersects the MC curve at point f. Similarly, if the market price was at P2 then the profit maximizing perfectly competitive firm would offer q2 units per period as its new MR curve intersects the MC curve at point h. Lastly, if the market price was at P3 then the profit-maximizing perfectly competitive firm would offer q3 units per period as its new MR curve intersects the MC curve at point j.

Points f, h and j therefore show how many units this firm will offer at different prices. It follows that the MC curve is the firm's supply curve. However, in the short run it will only be that segment of the MC curve above the minimum AVC, as at any lower price we have established that the firm will not offer any units but will choose to shut down. By the same token, in the long run, the supply curve will be that segment of the MC curve that lies above the ATC curve as the firm will not offer any units and will shut down if price is less than ATC.

Efficiency issues and perfect competition

Examining the outcome of perfectly competitive markets shows that they achieve both allocative and productive efficiency.

As discussed earlier, allocative efficiency exists if just the right amount of a good is produced from society's point of view. Assuming no externalities exist, allocative efficiency is achieved if all units of a good that are valued more by consumers than they cost to produce are indeed produced, up until that unit for which price is equal to marginal cost. Technical (or productive) efficiency exists if production takes place with minimal resource waste (that is, with minimum average costs).

Allocative efficiency in perfect competition

In Figure 1.5.25 (b) all units that are worth more to consumers than it costs to produce them are produced. Unit Q1 is worth to consumers Q1a (dollars or euro, for example); that is, as much as consumers would have been willing at the most to pay for it, while the marginal cost of producing it is Q1b (remember that the supply curve is the MC curve). So unit Q1 should be produced and in a perfectly competitive market it will be produced. In fact, all units worth producing from society's point of view are indeed produced. For the last unit Q* produced in a perfectly competitive market, P = MC.

Figure 1.5.25 (b) shows how social welfare, which has been defined as the sum of consumer and producer surplus, is maximized. Consumer surplus is equal to area (FP*E) and producer surplus is area (HEP*). Their sum, area (HEF) is at maximum since allocative efficiency is achieved. If any other quantity was produced, social welfare would be less.

Technical (or productive) efficiency in perfect competition

In the long run, firms in perfectly competitive markets are also technically efficient as they are forced to produce with minimum average costs. In Figure 1.5.25 (a) long-run equilibrium output q* is produced by the typical firm with minimum average costs (AC) equal to distance q*z. Minimal waste of scarce resources is achieved. In the long run, a firm incurring AC higher than q*z would be forced to exit the industry as it would be making losses. It follows that perfectly competitive markets not only lead to the optimal product mix but also scarce resources are not wasted. This explains why the perfectly competitive market is often considered the measuring rod against which other market structures are compared.

Evaluation of perfectly competitive markets

Even though, in general, allocative and technical efficiencies are desirable properties, there are a number of caveats to keep in mind.

- There is no guarantee that the goods produced will be distributed to the members of society in the fairest proportions. There may be considerable inequality of income in a society. So even if the right mix of goods and services is produced some may not enjoy any of them.

- Since market demand is defined as the willingness but also the ability to buy a good at each price, and ability reflects the level of income, it may very well be the case that market demand ignores very poor households. (These will not have enough dollars or euro, for example, to express their willingness to consume even basic goods). So, to take one example, the market may lead to a very limited amount of low-quality bread being produced because most resources are employed in the production of higher-quality whole wheat bread. There is no guarantee, therefore, that perfect competition leads to a **truly** socially optimum combination of goods produced.

- Perfectly competitive firms do not have an incentive to innovate. It is not only that they may not be able to afford spending on R&D but they also know that their innovation (a new product or a better process) would be copied by the other firms. Such investment would be a waste of money.

- Perfectly competitive industries produce undifferentiated products. This lack of variety might be seen as a disadvantage to the consumer.

- Price in competitive markets changes given **any** change in demand or cost (supply) conditions. These fluctuations increase uncertainty and may deter long-term investment in an industry. In contrast, the price stability often found in oligopolistic markets may seem desirable when planning investment.

- The perfectly competitive model is not compatible with increasing returns to scale; that, is with EOS. If EOS were present then this would mean that there would be a cost advantage in larger size so the industry would end up with few large firms. The absence of EOS in perfect competition may imply that, after all, price is higher than it would have been if there were few large firms involved.

(a)

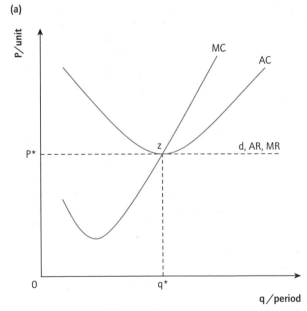

(b)

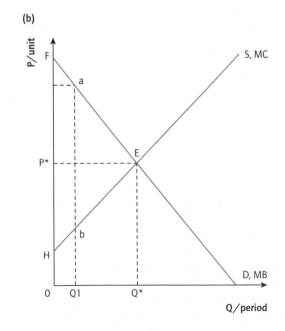

Figure 1.5.25 Efficiency in perfect competition

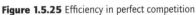

Monopoly

Characteristics

- Monopoly occurs when one firm produces a good without close substitutes; the industry coincides with the firm (a looser definition considers a firm a monopoly if it dominates the market)
- Monopolies have a unique product (as there is by definition only one firm in the market).
- There are barriers to entry.

The concept of monopoly is relative since it crucially depends on how narrowly or broadly the product and the market are defined. Note also the importance of the geographical factor, for example location in relation to transportation costs.

Here are some interesting points about monopoly firms.

- A monopoly firm can choose either the level of output or the price but not both, since the firm is still constrained by a negatively sloped demand curve.
- A monopoly firm does not necessarily make huge profits. It may even make losses; remember that profits are a function of the relative position of the demand curve (the AR curve) and the AC curve.
- A monopoly firm (and, more generally, any firm facing a negatively sloped demand curve) does not have a supply curve: the MC curve is not a supply curve for such firms; each output rate corresponds to more than one possible price as an infinite number of MR curves may go through any point on the MC curve. Remember that if we are using a supply curve in a diagram we are implicitly assuming a perfectly competitive market.
- It can be shown that if the demand curve (the AR curve) is linear, the MR curve is also linear, has the same vertical intercept and **double** the slope. (HL mathematics students: express a linear demand as $P = a - bQ$. TR are equal to $P \times Q$ or, substituting TR $= (a - bQ)Q = aQ - bQ^2$. MR is $\frac{\Delta TR}{\Delta Q}$ or, for small changes in Q the first derivative of the total revenue function, $\frac{dTR}{dQ} = a - 2Q$. The MR curve is linear, has the same vertical intercept with the linear demand curve and double its slope.)
- A monopoly firm can set the price (it is a price setter and not a price taker); the degree of monopoly power is given by the difference between the price charged and MC expressed as a proportion of price.
- A profit-maximizing monopoly firm will never choose a rate of output Q that corresponds to the price inelastic segment of the demand curve it faces. It will always locate below the elastic segment. This is because for profit maximization MR must equal MC but since MC is necessarily a positive number it follows that MR must also be a positive number at the profit maximizing output. MR is positive (it lies above the Q axis) only for that set of output rates that correspond to the elastic region of the demand curve.
- The profit-maximizing output level is necessarily **less** than the revenue-maximizing level of output (where MR = 0)

and so the corresponding price charged is higher. In other words, revenue maximization leads to more units being produced at a lower price.

Equilibrium (in the short run and the long run) of a monopoly firm

A monopoly, being the only firm in the market, faces the negatively sloped market demand curve. If it is a profit-maximizing firm it will choose that rate of output at which MR = MC and MC is rising. In Figure 1.5.26 this is the case at output Q*.

Having determined the profit-maximizing output will help us determine the price at which this quantity will be absorbed by consumers. This information is given by the demand curve. It will set the price at P*. It cannot set it any higher because at any price above P* fewer than the profit-maximizing level of output Q* will be sold.

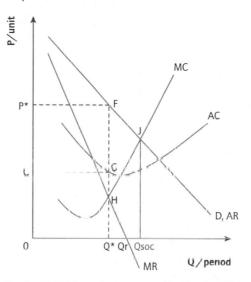

Figure 1.5.26 Monopoly: short-run and long-run equilibrium

In Figure 1.5.26, at Q* units of output per period, profits are equal to area (GFP*C). The difference between the average revenue Q*F and the average cost Q*G is the profit per unit which, if multiplied by the number of units CG (equal to Q*) gives us the profit area (GFP*C).

This firm is making supernormal profits but since we can assume that entry barriers exist, no new firms will enter the industry. If demand conditions, cost conditions and the entry barriers persist then this equilibrium (P*, Q*) will not change, so it is also a long-run equilibrium condition.

Note that if the monopolist aims at maximizing revenues instead of profits then it will choose that level of output at which MR = 0, which is at Qr where the MR curve crosses the horizontal axis.

Efficiency considerations and monopoly

Allocative efficiency is not achieved under monopoly. Monopoly is a case of market failure (as outlined earlier). Why?

At the level of output Q* chosen by the monopoly firms, price exceeds MC. Society would value more units to be produced. In Figure 1.5.26, society would like to enjoy all units up until unit Qsoc, which is valued as much as it would cost society to produce (distance JQsoc). Units Q*Qsoc are not produced, so society does not enjoy welfare equal to area (HJF). Social (or community) surplus is not maximized. Area (HJF) is the resulting welfare loss referred to as the 'deadweight loss'. It represents net value lost by society. This is a case where market forces lead to inefficient allocation of scarce resources. It is a market failure.

Productive inefficiency also results under monopoly. Why? Because the monopoly firm is not forced to produce with minimum average costs. At the chosen level of output Q* average costs are equal to line distance Q*G, which are greater than minimum.

Lastly, Harvey Leibenstein coined the term 'X-inefficiency' for a different type of inefficiency that some very protected monopoly positions may lead to. X-inefficiency refers to the **internal slackness** that characterizes some monopolies. This is the case when, on a diagram, the AC curve is not as low as it could have been given the available technology.

Is there a case in favour of monopoly and more generally, in favour of large firms with monopoly power?

The answer is yes. Assume a perfectly competitive industry with a market supply at S (also the MC curve) and market demand at D, as in Figure 1.5.27. Equilibrium price will be at Pc and equilibrium quantity at Qc. We have shown that this outcome is efficient. Assume now that somehow this perfectly competitive industry is monopolized, for example one firm buys out all perfectly competitive firms, but that the production technology remains unchanged. The MC curve for the monopoly firm remains at MC. The profit-maximizing monopoly firm will now equate its MC with its MR and choose Q* units charging a price P*. We have established that this outcome is inefficient. The monopoly firm restricts output and raises price. Welfare is reduced.

However, this result rests on the rather unlikely assumption that the larger in size monopoly firm employs the same technology that the small perfectly competitive firms employ. It is very

probable that the monopoly firm will enjoy EOS. Its cost curves may be lower than those the smaller competitive firms face, as illustrated in Figure 1.5.28. The technology available to the competitive firms lead to a set of short-run cost curves such as SACc and MCc. On the other hand, the technology available to the larger firms may, as a result of increasing returns to scale and EOS, lead to a different set of cost curves, such as SACm and MCm, located below those the competitive firms face.

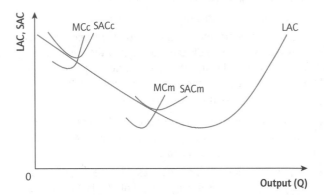

Figure 1.5.28 The lower cost curves enjoyed by the large firm as a result of EOS

If that is the case (and returning to Figure 1.5.27) then the monopoly will have a new MC curve that could be as low as MC'. MC' reflects the idea of EOS and is MCm in Figure 1.5.28. If this is the case then the monopoly may end up producing even more (Q**) than the perfectly competitive industry at an even lower price P**.

Perhaps, even more importantly, a large firm with monopoly power may lead to a faster rate of technological advancement. There are two reasons for such a development. First, such firms are in a position to keep their supernormal profits because of the existence of barriers so they are in a position to finance R&D projects which lead to innovations, defined as new products or new processes. In addition, assuming the monopoly firm is not entrenched, meaning that it is not protected by insurmountable barriers created by the state such as licenses, then in order for it to maintain its position and profits it will be forced to innovate.

In addition, the supernormal profits such firms enjoy act as bait that lures other firms to innovate in an attempt to displace the monopoly firm. Think of the cell phone market with Nokia, Apple with its iPhone and Google with Android. Perfectly competitive firms would not have the incentive to innovate because free entry would eliminate the possibility of a profitable return. These ideas are often referred to as 'dynamic efficiency' and are associated with the Austrian economist Joseph A. Schumpeter.

Barriers to entry

Barriers are defined as anything that deters entry into an industry or that prevents exit from an industry. A barrier increases the unit cost of a potential entrant above the level enjoyed by the incumbent firm.

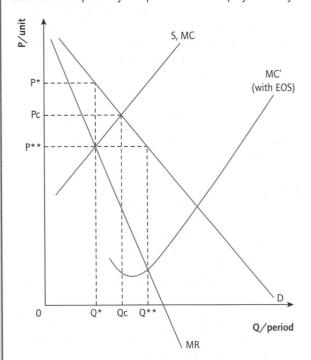

Figure 1.5.27 Monopoly compared to a perfectly competition market

Types of entry barriers
Barriers can be classified into natural, state-created and firm-created barriers, as described below.

Natural barriers: the case of a natural monopoly
Often, production technology is such that very significant EOS are present. As a result, given market size, only few or even only one firm can profitably co-exist. When only one firm can profitably exist in a market it is the case of natural monopoly. Figure 1.5.29 illustrates the point. In this diagram significant EOS are present as the LAC curve slopes downward throughout the length of the demand curve that defines the relevant market. Assume that initially there is only one firm in this market and that the profit-maximizing output is at Q while the price at which these Q units will be absorbed is P. This firm is profitable and it enjoys profits equal to ab per unit. If now this market is equally shared by two firms, each producing and selling (Q/2) units, then the total amount entering the market will still be Q units and the price will remain at P. Each firm now is making a loss equal to hf per unit. It is much too expensive to produce (Q/2) units, as the diagram illustrates.

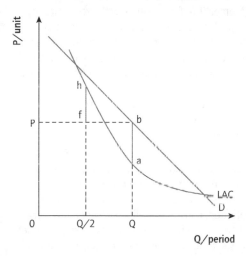

Figure 1.5.29 Natural barriers: the case of a natural monopoly

Note that exclusive ownership of some vital input which could also lead to a monopoly position is also considered a natural barrier.

State-created barriers
Examples are patents, licences and tariffs.

- Patents are granted by governments and are rights to produce exclusively for a fixed period of time. Patents aim at protecting the incentive to spend on R&D.

- Licences are exclusive permits that one or few firms have. For example, television and radio broadcasting firms require a licence.

- Tariffs limit competition from foreign firms and create monopoly power.

Firm-created barriers
Firms have every incentive to try to erect barriers in order to enjoy monopoly power and long-run supernormal profits. Advertising, and brand name and image creation is one way of erecting barriers. The stronger the brand name in a market the more difficult it is for a newcomer to enter. Also, firms

desperately try to differentiate their product. If successful, this lowers the PED of their product and permits the firm to raise price. By differentiating its product and by producing many different varieties the firm makes entry more difficult. Kellogg's cereal products are a good example.

Lastly, incumbent firms may deliberately maintain excess productive capacity. Potential entrants know that the incumbent firm can easily increase output, depressing price to unprofitable levels. A typical example of this can be found in cement firms where, in addition, transportation costs are high.

Monopolistic competition
Characteristics
- Very many small firms exist in the market (each firm has a very small share of the market).

- The firms produce differentiated products. Differentiation can be based on quality, durability, packaging, design or product service and can be real or imaginary.

- No entry barriers exist.

It is the second characteristic that gives such firms a very small degree of monopoly power. Since the product is not homogeneous, each firm faces a negatively sloped demand for the product it sells. If it increases price it will not lose all of its customers. It will lose only some of its customers so the demand curve for its product (and remember the products in monopolistic competition are differentiated) is downward sloping. Typical examples of monopolistically competitive industries include hairdressers, restaurants and DVD rental stores. Note that often, especially in manufacturing, the existence of many brands for consumers does not necessarily imply monopolistically competitive markets. For example, in the detergent industry there may be very many brands to choose from but behind these brands there are only two or three firms.

Short-run and long-run equilibrium in monopolistic competition
The illustration of short-run equilibrium in monopolistic competition is identical to the monopoly diagram (Figure 1.5.26). A monopolistically competitive firm may enjoy supernormal profits in the short run. Supernormal profits will induce entry. Entry is possible in this market structure as no barriers are assumed to exist. If hair salons in a market are enjoying supernormal profits, other such firms will be attracted. Sooner or later there will be other hair salons opening up and luring away customers from the existing firms.

As entry takes place, the demand that the typical incumbent firm faces will be affected. Note that such firms do not have a supply curve. Only perfectly competitive firms have a supply curve. Demand that each monopolistically competitive firm faces for its product will 'shrink and tilt'. Its demand will 'shrink' (meaning that it will decrease and shift to the left) because more firms in the market imply a smaller market share for each firm. At each price the quantity demanded from each firm decreases. Demand will 'tilt' (meaning that it becomes flatter) because if new firms enter the market, consumers will have an even greater selection of slightly differentiated products to choose from, so the demand each firm faces will become more price elastic. Remember that price elasticity increases when consumers face more and closer substitutes.

Entry will continue until there is no longer an incentive for it to take place. This will be the case when supernormal profits are competed away and the typical monopolistically competitive firm is making only normal profits (that is, zero economic profits). If, on the other hand, the typical firm was making losses then exit would follow, increasing demand (shifting it to the right and making it more price inelastic) until there is no reason for more firms to exit. This will be when the typical firm is earning just as much profit as it would earn in its next best alternative (that is, when it is earning normal profits).

Long-run equilibrium will be achieved when the typical firm in such a market is maximizing profits and these profits are zero (normal profits).

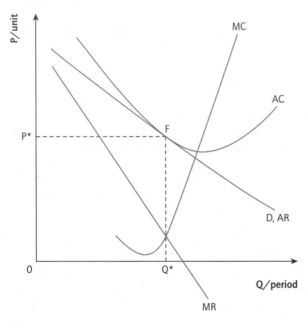

Figure 1.5.30 Monopolistic competition: long-run equilibrium

Figure 1.5.30 illustrates long-run equilibrium in monopolistic competition as at the chosen level of output Q* the firm not only equates MR and MC, so maximizing profits, but also these economic profits are zero (normal profits) as AR and AC are tangent and so equal (to Q*F) right above them. Since the typical firm is maximizing profits it is achieving its goal, so it has no reason to change its output. Since these profits are

normal there is no incentive for new firms to enter or for incumbent firms to exit. This defines long-run equilibrium.

> **TIP** Figure 1.5.30 is very tricky to draw. Either start by drawing a wide U-shaped AC curve, followed by a relatively flat demand tangent to it and its corresponding MR; determine the profit-maximizing output Q right below the point of tangency of AC with AR; lastly carefully draw the MC curve, making sure that not only does it intersect MR right above the chosen output Q but that it also cuts AC at its minimum. Alternatively, first draw a relatively flat demand curve and its corresponding MR; continue with a relatively flat MC curve and, lastly, the AC curve that is both tangent to the demand curve above the MR = MC intersection and has also a minimum on the MC curve.

Evaluation of monopolistic competition

In this market structure neither allocative nor technical (or productive) efficiency are achieved. Price exceeds marginal costs for the last unit of output each firm produces in equilibrium. Production does not take place with minimal average costs so that monopolistically competitive firms operate with excess capacity. Each firm ends up with a scale of operation that forces it to produce less output than the one that corresponds to minimum average costs. Restaurants typically have empty tables and one does not have to wait long in a queue to rent a DVD or to buy fuel. Free entry and product differentiation are responsible for this result. In addition, since these firms cannot maintain profits in the long run they are not in a position to finance R&D projects and, being small in size, they do not enjoy EOS.

On the other hand, as a result of product differentiation and non-price competition, consumers enjoy a greater variety of products, increasing the probability that they will find a closer match to their preferences. Given free entry and extensive product differentiation, consumers will have very many, very close substitutes to choose from. Price cannot be much higher than marginal costs, which is another way of saying that the monopoly power each firm enjoys is minimal. As a result, output will not be too far below the socially optimal level. Firms are forced to advertise and to resort to other methods of non-price competition, though. The higher than minimum unit costs in such markets are often interpreted as the cost of variety.

HL Oligopoly

Characteristics

- Few firms operate in the market.
- They produce homogeneous products (such as oil, steel or cement) or differentiated products (which include almost any industrial products, for example cars, detergents, appliances, air craft and banking or insurance products.
- Significant entry barriers exist.

To determine the extent of concentration in a market a concentration ratio (CR) is used which measures the proportion of total sales accounted by the largest firms in a market (or an industry). Typically, more than one CR is calculated and presented. For example, researchers provide 4-firm, 8-firm and 20-firm CRs (or 3-firm, 5-firm and 10-firm CRs) to provide a more

complete picture of the market share enjoyed by the largest firms in the market. For example, the 5-firm CR (5CR) is given by:

$$5CR = \sum_{i=1}^{5} S_i$$

where S_i is the market share of the ith firm in the market (that is, the proportion of market sales it enjoys). The market share of a firm is the proportion of the total market sales it enjoys. A 4CR or 5CR above 80% implies a highly concentrated market where a tight oligopoly (or a monopoly) is present. CRs provide no information about the size distribution of firms, so a 5CR that is 100% could be a market with five large firms of equal size each with a 20% market share, or a market where one firm has 96% of the market and four firms have the remaining 4%.

Optional material

A widely used measure of concentration in a market is the Hirschman-Herfindahl index (HHI) which is found by squaring the market share of each firm in a market and summing the resulting numbers, or:

$$HHI = \sum_{i=1}^{n} S_i^2 v$$

where S_i is defined as above. This index takes into account the distribution of the firms as it gives larger firms a bigger weight. It approaches zero as the number of firms of relatively equal size increases and in the case of a monopoly it becomes 10,000. Typically, markets with an HHI in excess of 1,800 are considered concentrated and if a merger between two firms significantly increases this HHI then it may be blocked by the competition watchdog.

Game theory and interdependence

The fact that few firms exist in an oligopolistic structure is responsible for its distinguishing characteristic, namely interdependence. Interdependence in a market exists if the outcome of any action of one firm depends on the reaction of the rival firms.

A branch of mathematics known as game theory is widely used to analyse oligopolistic set-ups. We will examine the simplest form of a game, known as the 'prisoners' dilemma'. Through it we will see the interdependence that exists in such markets and why oligopolistic firms face the fundamental dilemma of whether to collude or to compete.

Assume an oligopolistic market with only two firms, Gray S.A. and White S.A. This market is also known as a duopoly. Each firm has two policy options, to maintain the price charged or to decrease it. The outcome to either action depends on the reaction of the rival firm. The matrix below provides the pay-offs for each action given the possible reaction of the rival firm.

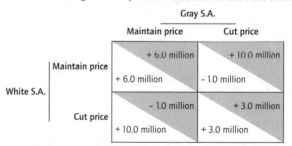

Interdependence is evident since the outcome of whichever policy Gray chooses depends on how White will react, and vice versa. For example, focusing on Gray and reading vertically, if it decides to maintain price it could earn either 6.0 million of supernormal profits or incur losses equal to 1.0 million depending on whether White also maintains its price or decides to cut price. If Gray decides to cut price it could earn 10.0 million of supernormal profits (if White maintains price) or just 3.0 million (if White also cuts price). Symmetrically, this is true for White.

To determine the dominant strategy, each firm realizes that no matter what the rival chooses, it is better off cutting price. For example, Gray realizes that if White maintains price it is better that Gray cuts price (Gray earns 10.0 million instead of only the 6.0 million it would earn it also maintained price) whereas if White cuts price Grey too should cut price as it would then earn 3.0

million whereas if it maintained price it would lose 1.0 million. In other words, no matter what White does, Gray is better off if it cuts price: cutting price is the best strategy. Symmetrically, it is the best strategy for firm White. Cutting price is therefore the dominant strategy in this game. The firms will each make only 3.0 million, which is less than the 6.0 million each would make if they were able to cooperate and maintain price.

To compete or to collude?

This dilemma characterizes all oligopolistic set-ups. Through competition these firms may increase their own market share and their profits at the expense of rivals but at the risk of a price war which could prove catastrophic. By colluding they decrease uncertainty and maximize joint profits as if they were a monopoly, but at the risk of getting caught and facing the consequences.

Collusion

Collusion exists in a market if firms agree to fix price and to engage in other anti-competitive behaviour. Agreements can be either formal or informal. If the agreement is formal we have the case of a cartel. Cartels are generally illegal. In most countries firms can not sign legally enforceable contracts. Firms that have made formal agreements try to make sure that their agreements remain secret. The Organization of the Petroleum Exporting Countries (OPEC) is a case of a formal agreement between oil-exporting countries in which deliberations and decisions are publicized, as it operates above national laws.

If the agreement is informal then we have the case of tacit collusion. If there is a dominant firm in the market and a few smaller competitors (often referred to as a competitive fringe) then the dominant firm may act as a price leader. It will set price at such a level to maximize its profits and the remaining firms will accept it. This describes what is known as the 'dominant firm price leadership' model. The price leader does not have to be the dominant firm. It could be the firm that has in the past successfully predicted changes in the market or the position of the leader may rotate from firm to firm.

To illustrate the outcome of collusive behaviour where firms behave as a monopoly firm, we can use a monopoly diagram, such as Figure 1.5.31. The joint profit-maximizing output is Q' and the price the cartel will set is P', leading to joint profits equal to area (hfP'C). Somehow, output quotas and profit shares for each member must be determined.

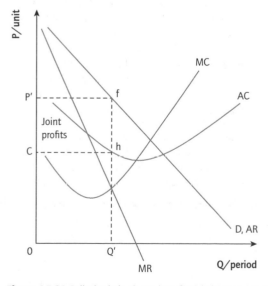

Figure 1.5.31 Collusive behaviour where firms behave as a monopoly firm

How likely is it for a collusive agreement to collapse?

Collusive structures are unstable because of the inherent incentive to cheat. Each member would prefer others to abide by the output restricting agreement (the quota) while it doesn't. The logic of this incentive is clear: if all firms except one maintain their output quota then the price of the good will remain high. To the extent that price is higher than the MC of the defector, it has the incentive to cheat and raise output above its quota. Since all members have the same incentive, such collusive agreements often collapse.

Collusive agreements are more likely to collapse:

- the greater the number of member firms (as monitoring each other's behaviour becomes more difficult)
- the smaller the proportion of total industry output members of the agreement control (as it becomes more difficult to control market price)
- if the good is differentiated and many varieties exist (as any agreement will be more difficult to reach and to enforce)
- if production costs differ (as this will make agreeing on quotas more difficult)
- if market demand is shrinking (as each member will scramble to survive).

Non–collusive oligopoly

The term refers to the case where oligopolistic firms have no agreement concerning their behaviour and tactics. Still, repeated interaction leads oligopolistic firms to avoid changing output even if cost conditions change. The kinked demand curve model illustrates this point. It was introduced by P. Sweezy in 1939 and it aimed at explaining the observed price stickiness in oligopolistic markets even when cost conditions changed. It is typically considered a model of non-collusive oligopoly.

The kinked demand curve model

Assume a duopoly. Figure 1.5.32 illustrates that currently firm A is selling Q* units at a price P*. The behavioural assumption in the kinked demand curve model is simple: the competing firm will not follow a price increase initiated by firm A but will follow a price cut. There is therefore an asymmetry in the expected response. As a result of this asymmetry in the response of its competitor, the demand that firm A faces is more price elastic for prices above the current price than for prices below the current price. Quantity demanded will fall by proportionately more if firm A increases price (since its competitor does not follow) than it will rise if firm A decreases price and its competitor follows. In the first case, firm A's product will be more expensive, while in the second case both firms' products will be cheaper. A kink will form at the current price in the demand curve that firm A faces.

In Figure 1.5.32 the kink is at point h corresponding to the initial price P* and the initial quantity Q*. Segment fh of the demand curve is relatively more price elastic than segment hg as a consequence of the asymmetry in the reaction of the

rival. Note that demand below the kink does not have to be price inelastic but only less price elastic than it is above it, as the existence of a positive segment for MR illustrates above.

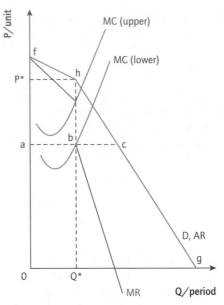

Figure 1.5.32 The kinked demand model

The kink in the demand curve is responsible for the **discontinuity** in the MR curve which has to be double the slope **of each section** of the kinked demand. Given that profit maximization is the working assumption and that profit maximization requires that MR is equal to MC, it follows that the MC curve must have intersected the MR curve right above the chosen output Q*. However, this could be the case either with $MC_{(upper)}$ or with $MC_{(lower)}$ and, by inference, with any MC within the discontinuous range of MR.

So, if MC decrease below $MC_{(upper)}$, the firm will neither change output nor price charged. Price is sticky at P* in a non-collusive oligopoly even if cost conditions change. The model is useful as it illustrates the observed price stickiness in real-world oligopolies, but it fails to explain how the original price P* is formed.

Non-price competition

Oligopolistic firms avoid competing through price cuts. Such a strategy could lead to a competitive downward spiral in prices (a price war) which could leave all firms worse off.

Non-price competition can take several forms, such as:

- heavy advertising and brand-name creation, for example for Pepsi Cola and Coca Cola
- gifts and coupons, for example in newspapers and magazines
- continuous product differentiation, for example with cars, cell phones, DVD players, television sets and television stations
- excessive product proliferation to cover all imaginable market niches, for example with ice cream or breakfast cereal

- extended guarantees (typically in electric appliances, computer hardware devices, etc.)
- after-sale service, for example the customer plans of car manufacturers
- volume discounts (often in products such as shampoo and conditioners).

If a price war occurs in the real world it is usually a case where some participants (typically with a so-called deep pocket) are looking forward to the shake-off effect of financially weaker firms being forced to fold and exit the market or be acquired.

> **TIP** The kinked demand is another tricky diagram to draw correctly. Start by first choosing the kink somewhere in the upper left corner of the graph space; then draw demand, making sure that the relatively price inelastic segment is not too steep. Next draw the MR section corresponding to the relatively elastic segment of the demand curve, maintaining the rule of doubling the slope. The MR which corresponds to the lower right segment hg of the demand curve should start at such a point b (see Figure 1.5.32) that ab = bc and also maintain the rule of doubling the slope.

Market structure	Characteristics are:	Outcomes are:
Perfect competition	• very many small firms • homogeneous product • no barriers to entry	• allocative efficiency as for the last unit produced, $P = MC$ • technical efficiency as in the long run production takes place with minimum average costs
Monopolistic competition	• very many small firms • differentiated product • no barriers to entry	• neither allocative nor technical efficiency • excess capacity • variety
Oligopoly	• few interdependent firms, leading to high market concentration • homogeneous or differentiated product • high entry barriers	• neither allocative nor technical efficiency • but, perhaps, dynamic efficiency (R&D and faster innovation; EOS)
Monopoly	• single firm • unique product • high entry barriers	• neither allocative nor technical efficiency • but, perhaps, dynamic efficiency (R&D and faster innovation; EOS)

Price discrimination

Price discrimination is a pricing policy that certain firms adopt to increase their profits further. Formally, price discrimination exists when a firm sells the same product at two or more different prices in two or more markets provided that the price differences do not reflect differences in the cost of production or provision. Examples include airline tickets; train and bus fares; theatre and cinema ticket prices; telephone services; and lawyers', private doctors' and consultants' fees. In international trade, dumping is also considered a form of international price discrimination as it involves selling abroad at a lower price than in the protected domestic market.

Conditions allowing a firm to price discriminate
Not all firms can practise price discrimination. The following conditions must hold for effective price discrimination to be possible.

- The firm must enjoy some degree of monopoly power. It must face a negatively sloped demand curve. Therefore, a perfectly competitive firm cannot practise price discrimination.
- No resale of the good (referred to as seepage) from the cheaper to the pricier market should be possible. The two markets must somehow be separable otherwise arbitrage

(buying low and selling high) will guarantee that eventually one price will dominate in both markets.

- Price elasticities of demand between markets must differ. Some consumers must be prepared to pay more either because fewer substitutes are available to them or because they enjoy a higher level of income.

Third-degree price discrimination
There are three types (or degrees) of price discrimination. The first degree is only of theoretical interest as it assumes that the firm can sell each extra unit at the highest price the consumer is willing and able to pay, and so extracts and appropriates the entire consumer surplus. Block price discrimination, also known as second-degree price discrimination, is when successive blocks of units of output are sold at a lower prices. For example, a parking lot may sell the first hour of parking at $10.00, the second and third hours at $5.00 each and extra hours at $2.00.

The commonest type of price discrimination is third degree, where the firm segments a market across some characteristic that on the one hand takes advantage of differing price elasticities and on the other hand does not allow resale of the good from the cheaper to the more expensive market. For example, airlines price tickets bought a few days in advance much higher than if they were purchased a month or so in advance of a flight. Since the consumer's name is on the ticket, resale is not possible. By pricing tickets for the same flight in this way the company tries to take advantage of the fact that if people decide to travel and book a flight only a few days in advance, either they have very important business to conduct and face few if any alternatives or they are very wealthy and the ticket expense is a small proportion of their income. On the other hand, if people book a ticket a month in advance then they are most probably travelling for pleasure, so they have many alternatives to choose from. Demand for this specific flight is quite price elastic.

Figure 1.5.33 may look a bit complicated but is actually a very straightforward and convenient illustration of third-degree price discrimination. The two markets, A and B, are drawn side by side. On the right-hand side the demand for market A is drawn as relatively price inelastic. This is the group of individuals with the fewer substitutes available and/or the higher incomes who are considering buying a ticket a few days in advance of a flight. On the left-hand side (quantities are of course not negative to the left of the origin) the demand for market B is drawn as relatively price elastic (flatter). This is the group of individuals with more available substitutes and/or lower incomes who are considering buying a ticket a month in advance of a flight. To avoid the difficulty of drawing accurately the mirror image of an MC curve shaped like the 'Nike swoosh', it is assumed that the extra cost of an extra ticket for the airline is constant and equal to 0h, and we draw the MC curve horizontal to the Q axis. Profit maximization requires that in each market MR is equal to MC so that:

$$MR(A) = MC \text{ and } MR(B) = MC \text{ or } MR(a) = MR(B) = MC$$

This is the case at Q(A) in market A and Q(B) in market B so that the firm will charge P(A) in market A and P(B) in market B.

As expected, the firm will charge the higher of the two prices in the market with the relatively more price-inelastic demand.

 TIP When drawing the two demand curves make sure their slopes differ substantially so that the resulting prices differ significantly.

Consumers and price discrimination
In general, a price-discriminating firm extracts and appropriates part of the consumer surplus. Producers are better off and the only risk they may face is the possibility of bad publicity in some cases. Viewed differently, if they were not better off with price discrimination they would not have adopted it.

Consumers, on the other hand, are generally worse off as part of their surplus is transferred to producers. There may be situations, though, where at least certain groups of consumers do benefit. One could be the group that pays the lower price, if this is set below the single price that the firm would have charged without price discrimination.

Such a pricing policy may allow a firm to sell a greater volume of output and so grow in size. For example, firms often sell at a higher price in their domestic protected market and at a much lower price in world markets. If such a firm grows and enjoys, as a result, EOS which permit it to decrease all prices charged, then even consumers in its domestic market will benefit.

Lastly, there are cases where selling a good would be unprofitable at any single price but the firm may become profitable by price discriminating and, through this, allowing consumers to enjoy the product.

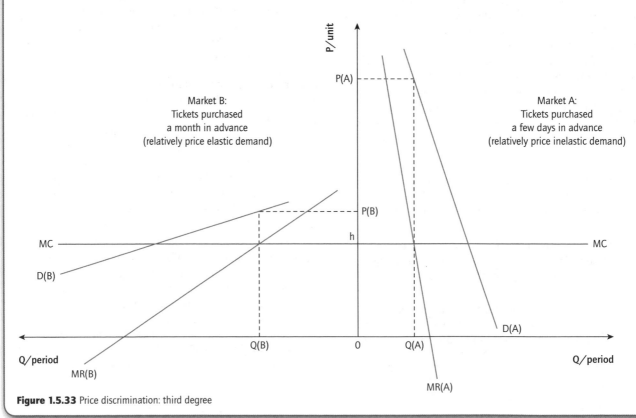

Figure 1.5.33 Price discrimination: third degree

Microeconomics: Questions

Practice part (a) long essay questions (HLP1 and SLP1)
Command terms: typically AO1/AO2 but possibly also AO4 (*not* AO3)

1. Explain what externalities are and how they may arise.

2. Explain using diagram(s) the welfare loss arising from the production or consumption of a good responsible for the generation of negative externalities.

3. Distinguish between marginal private and social costs as well as between marginal private and social benefits.

4. Explain what price, income and cross elasticities of demand measure.

5. Explain why governments provide subsidies, and describe examples of subsidies.

6. Explain why the price elasticity of demand for many primary commodities is relatively low while the price elasticity of demand for manufactured products is relatively high.

7. Analyse the concept of market failure as a failure of markets to achieve allocative efficiency.

8. Distinguish using examples between private and public goods.

9. Explain using an appropriate diagram the possible consequences of rent controls on the market for rental housing in a city of your choice.

10. Explain why a government may choose to establish a minimum wage.

11. Explain why a government may choose to support the price of an agricultural product.

12. Outline reasons for which a government may choose to use food price controls.

13. Explain why the price elasticity of supply for primary commodities is relatively low while for manufactured products it is relatively high.

14. Distinguish between movements along the demand curve and shifts of the demand curve, drawing appropriate diagrams and providing examples related to the owner-occupied housing market of your country.

15. Distinguish between movements along the supply curve and shifts of the supply curve, drawing appropriate diagrams and providing examples related to a market for an agricultural product of your choice.

16. Distinguish between specific and ad valorem taxes using appropriate diagrams and examples.

17. Explain, using the terms social surplus, marginal benefit and marginal cost, the meaning of the term allocative efficiency.

18. Analyse, using an appropriate diagram, the role that relative price changes play in the allocation of scarce resources in a free market economy.

19. Using an appropriate diagram and examples, explain why market forces may prove insufficient to address environmental concerns.

20. Explain, using examples and an appropriate diagram, why demerit goods are considered a market failure.

21. Explain, using appropriate examples and a diagram, why governments may choose to impose price ceilings.

22. Explain why governments impose price floors and describe examples of price floors.

23. Distinguish between merit goods, demerit goods and public goods.

24. Explain using examples why common access resources may be overused and depleted.

25. Explain why the over-exploitation of land for agriculture in less developed countries may pose a threat to sustainability.

26. Explain, using examples, why the global nature of the problems threatening sustainability and the lack of ownership of common access resources limit the effectiveness of individual government responses and thus require international cooperation.

27. Explain, using an appropriate diagram, why the use of fossil fuels in production processes threatens sustainability.

28. Describe the terms sustainability and common access resources using appropriate examples for the latter.

29. Explain, with reference to the free rider problem, how the lack of public goods indicates market failure.

30. Explain the role of price elasticity of demand and cross-elasticity of demand for businesses making decisions.

31. Explain why negative externalities are an example of market failure.

Higher level only

HL

1. Describe the term "tacit collusion" including reference to price leadership by a dominant firm.

2. Explain why oligopolistic firms face the dilemma to compete or to collude.

3. Using examples and an appropriate diagram, explain the meaning of the term 'natural monopoly'.

4. Explain the conditions that need to be satisfied for a firm to successfully adopt price discrimination.

5. Explain, using diagrams, under what conditions and in which market structures positive economic profits are unlikely to persist in the long run.

6. Explain why the opportunity cost of entrepreneurship, an element of normal profits, is part of the economic costs of a firm.

7. Distinguish between the three types of returns to scale.

8. Describe four factors giving rise to economies of scale.

9. Explain why interdependence is responsible for the dilemma faced by oligopolistic firms as to whether to compete or to collude.

10. Explain, using appropriate diagram(s), how a perfectly competitive market will move from a short-run equilibrium position to long-run equilibrium.

11. Outline the ways in which monopoly power might arise.

12. Explain how a monopoly producer is in a position to earn positive economic profits in the long-run.

13. Explain how a concentration ratio may be used to identify an oligopoly.

14. Explain, using diagrams, why both price elasticity of demand and price elasticity of supply are necessary to consider in order to determine the incidence of an indirect tax on consumers and producers.

15. Explain how firms operating in different market structures compete.

16. Distinguish, using diagrams, the short run and long run equilibrium positions for a perfectly competitive firm.

17. Distinguish, using examples, between monopolistic competition and oligopoly as market structures.

18. Analyse the differences between a collusive oligopoly and a non-collusive oligopoly.

19. Using appropriate diagrams, distinguish between the short run shut-down price and the break-even price for a perfectly competitive firm.

20. Distinguish between the characteristics of perfect competition and monopolistic competition.

21. Describe how a firm operating in an oligopolistic market might attempt to increase its market share.

22. Explain the role of barriers to entry in permitting a firm to earn economic profits.

23. Explain, using examples, why market failure may occur when one party in an economic transaction possesses more information than the other party.

24. Explain, using diagrams, why the profit maximizing choices of a monopoly firm lead to allocative inefficiency and productive (technical) inefficiency.

25. Distinguish between short-run average total cost curves and long-run average cost curves using appropriate diagrams.

26. Describe three goals other than profit maximization that firms may pursue.

Practice part (b) long essay questions (HLP1 and SLP1)
Command terms: typically AO3 but possibly AO1 and AO2 or even AO4

1. Discuss whether governments should always intervene in markets where significant externalities arise.

2. Evaluate the use of two market based policies to correct the market failure arising from negative externalities of production.

3. Evaluate, using appropriate diagrams wherever possible, government responses to correct the market failure arising in the case of merit goods.

4. Discuss, using diagrams wherever appropriate, the significance of price elasticity of demand for both firms and the government.

5. Explain, with the help of diagrams, (i) how the market for beer will be affected by a tax on hard liquor such as whisky and vodka, (ii) how the market for oranges will be affected if farmers can sell lemons at a higher price, (iii) how the demand for red wine will be affected if its price decreases.

6. Discuss the consequences of providing a subsidy on the stakeholders in a market.

7. Examine the implications for a business of changes in the prices goods that are related to the one it offers.

8. Evaluate a policy response adopted by a government on a market failure of your choice. Use examples and, if possible, appropriate diagrams.

9. Examine the implications of direct provision of public goods by governments.

10. To what extent do tenants (i.e. households who rent an apartment) benefit from rent controls?

11. Discuss the possible market outcomes of adopting a minimum wage policy.

12. Discuss the consequences of imposing a price floor on the stakeholders in a market for such a product.

13. Discuss the consequences of imposing food price controls on the stakeholders of such markets.

14. Discuss, using appropriate diagram(s), the consequences on the stakeholders involved of providing a subsidy to the producers of an agricultural product.

15. Analyse, using diagrams and with reference to excess demand or excess supply, how changes in any three determinants of demand result in a new market equilibrium.

16. Analyse, using diagrams and with reference to excess demand or excess supply, how changes in any three determinants of supply result in a new market equilibrium.

17. Discuss the impact of imposing an indirect tax on market outcomes.

18. Discuss the consequences of imposing an indirect tax on the stakeholders in a market.

19. Explain, using appropriate diagrams and examples, why social (community) surplus is not maximized if either more or less than the allocatively efficient output level is produced.

20. Discuss why national policies may not prove sufficient to address environmental issues and thus why an effective response to global environmental problems requires international cooperation.

21. Discuss the economic arguments relevant to a policy decision to impose substantially higher levels of taxation on the sale of alcohol, explaining reasons for which it may not induce significantly lower levels of consumption.

22. Examine the possible consequences of a decision to impose a price ceiling on basic foodstuff.

23. Discuss the consequences of imposing a price ceiling on the stakeholders in a market, including consumers, producers and the government.

24. Examine the position that consumers are necessarily worse-off in a monopoly market.

25. Contrast the use of a market-based policy versus government regulation in markets for goods such as cigarettes and alcohol.

26. Discuss legislation and funding for clean technologies as possible solutions to the threats to sustainability.

27. Evaluate, using diagrams, two possible government responses to threats to sustainability.

28. Compare and contrast carbon taxes and 'cap and trade' schemes as possible solutions to threats to sustainability.

29. Evaluate carbon taxes and 'cap and trade' schemes as possible solutions to threats to sustainability.

30. To what extent can the imposition of carbon taxes encourage sustainability.

31. Discuss the implications of direct provision of public goods by governments.

32. Examine the view that governments can best reduce smoking (or, alcohol consumption) by substantially increasing taxes on cigarettes.

33. Discuss three policies that governments might implement to reduce negative externalities associated with the environment.

Higher level only

HL

1. Evaluate the desirability of markets in which firms enjoy considerable market power.

2. Explain (i) using an appropriate diagram why price rigidity is typical in oligopolistic markets, as well as (ii) why non-price competition is usually employed by such firms.

3. Using an appropriate diagram, compare and contrast the equilibrium positions of a profit maximizing monopoly firm and a revenue maximizing monopoly firm.

4. Draw a diagram to illustrate 3rd degree price discrimination in airlines, explaining when the prices charged in the two markets you chose will differ more.

5. Explain, using appropriate diagram(s), why, despite the absence of supernormal profits in a monopolistically competitive market, firms achieve neither allocative efficiency, nor productive efficiency.

6. Explain using an example why firms will choose to operate in the long run despite earning zero economic profits.

7. Carefully define the long-run average total cost curve of firms and explain, using a diagram, the reason for its typical shape.

8. Using appropriate diagrams, compare and contrast the law of diminishing marginal returns with the decreasing returns to scale.

9. Explain, using a diagram, the shape of the perfectly competitive firm's average revenue and marginal revenue curves and why, in the long run, a perfectly competitive firm will make only normal profits

10. Explain, using a diagram, why perfectly competitive firms will be productively efficient in the long run, though not necessarily in the short run.

11. Should governments always intervene to control monopoly power?

12. Contrast formal/open and tacit collusion in oligopolistic markets.

13. Discuss the view that the greater the number of firms in a market the better off society is.

14. Contrast the short run with the long run equilibrium positions of a firm in a perfectly competitive market.

15. Compare and contrast the characteristics of monopolistically competitive markets with perfectly competitive markets.

16. Explain why price rigidity and non-price competition are typically encountered in oligopolistic markets. Use a diagram and examples to illustrate your answer.

17. Using appropriate diagrams, compare and contrast the efficiency outcomes in monopolistic competition and in perfect competition.

18. Using appropriate diagrams, compare and contrast the short-run and long run equilibrium of a profit maximizing monopolistically competitive firm.

19. To what extent do producers and not consumers benefit in oligopolistic markets?

20. Examine the view that monopoly is an undesirable market structure.

21. Discuss two possible government responses to problems arising from asymmetric information.

22. Discuss two possible government responses to the abuse of monopoly power.

23. To what extent is greater economic efficiency achieved in perfect competition compared to monopoly?

24. Explain why cartels are likely to collapse as well as the conditions that make such a development more likely.

2.1 Macroeconomic goals

Macroeconomics examines issues relating to an economy as a whole, such as unemployment, inflation, growth and the balance of payments. This means that the focus of macroeconomics is on aggregate economic variables. Whereas microeconomics may be interested in explaining why the price of corn is rising, macroeconomics investigates why the average price level may be rising. In microeconomics, the focus may be on how many workers a firm will employ but macroeconomics examines the total level of employment and unemployment in a country. In other words, in macroeconomics we zoom out of individual markets and firms and look at what is going on in the country.

Generally, governments and policy makers aim at achieving the following.

- Satisfactory and sustainable real (meaning non-inflationary) growth: total output and income of the country or economy should increase at an annual rate that is considered acceptable. We have to use caution when evaluating an economy's performance with respect to growth rates, as 'satisfactory growth' means different things to different economies at different times. In general, for advanced economies, satisfactory growth is taken to mean between 3% and 5%. Anything less than 3% is typically characterized as weak growth and anything exceeding 5% is potentially inflationary. For developing economies the range is between 5% and 10% for the same reasons. In addition, this increase in total output should be sustainable (that is, it should not come at a heavy environmental cost). The central idea of trade-offs in economics should already be apparent. Faster growth may not only prove inflationary but also unsustainable in terms of the accompanying environmental degradation.

- Price stability (which implies low inflation and no deflation): for reasons that will become clear later, prices on the average (of goods and services but also of assets) should not increase through time too fast. When prices on the average increase from one year to the next we say that there is inflation. But prices on the average should not decrease either as the costs and risks of falling prices (deflation) are also unacceptable. Price stability is usually considered to have been achieved if the inflation rate is between 1.5% to 3% annually as the measurement of inflation carries the risk of overestimating the true rate and near zero rates of inflation may actually be hiding the initial stages of deflation.

- High levels of employment (low unemployment): ensuring that whoever is searching for a job is able to find one is historically considered one of the most important objectives of governments. Given that resources are scarce, it becomes clear what a terrible waste unemployment implies.

Unemployment is also responsible for high human and social costs, over and above the associated economic costs it entails. It is clear that aiming for zero unemployment is unrealistic in a dynamic economy, one that is constantly changing. But what is considered as an acceptable rate of unemployment differs from country to country and from period to period. As a very rough rule, keep a 5% benchmark rate in mind, remembering though that such a rate may be considered unacceptably high for certain countries and unrealistically low for others.

- Long-run equilibrium in the balance of payments: the balance of payments relates to the transactions of a country with the rest of the world (exports, imports as well as investments to and from other countries) and by long-run equilibrium it is meant that the foreign sector should not impose a constraint on the country's ability to achieve the three domestic policy objectives explained above. This goal is difficult to understand even on an intuitive basis at this point but the basic idea is that a country should be in a position to pay for its imports by maintaining a sufficiently competitive export basis.

- Equitable (meaning fair) distribution of income: it may be clear that equitable does not mean equal but its precise meaning is elusive and subject to interpretation. If the distribution of income is not considered by the people themselves as fair then the process is not sustainable. On the other hand, if the fruits of economic growth are enjoyed by more than a few people, then there are benefits that may even help to accelerate the process.

		To achieve:
Macroeconomic goals	1	Satisfactory and sustainable real growth
	2	Low levels of unemployment
	3	Price stability
	4	Long-run equilibrium in the balance of payments
	5	An equitable distribution of income

The level of overall economic activity

The circular flow of income model

The circular flow model is a simplified representation of how the basic decision-making units of an economy (households, firms, the government and, in an 'open' economy, the foreign sector) interact. It describes the flows between these units. These flows can be real (flows of factors of production, flows of goods and services) or monetary (flows of expenditures on goods and services, flows of incomes generated in the production process).

At the most basic level, where only households and firms exist, it is understood that households own all factors of production which they offer to firms. Firms use these factors of production to produce goods and services which they offer back to households. These flows are real flows and are illustrated below in Figure 2.1.1.

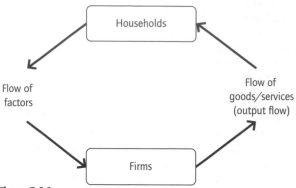

Figure 2.1.1

In exchange for the use of these factors of production firms offer payments to households in the form of wages, rents, interest and profits, the sum of which is defined as income. So, in the opposite direction of the real flow of factors there is a monetary flow of factor payments, or of income. This is referred to as the income flow. Equivalently, in the opposite direction of the real flow of goods and services from firms to households there is a monetary flow of expenditures from households to firms for the goods and services enjoyed.

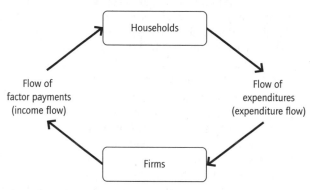

Figure 2.1.2

The flows described above must be equal. All the income generated in the production process is spent on the output produced, so the income flow is equal to the expenditure flow which is equal to the output flow.

If a time dimension is added then the issue becomes slightly more complicated, but still manageable. If there is a 'next period' then part of the income generated may be saved (a 'withdrawal' or leakage from this circular flow system) while not only households spend on domestic output but also firms spend on capital goods (that is, investment spending occurs).

This latter expenditure is an 'injection' to the circular flow system. Where this injection come from? The answer is that banks or financial intermediaries attract savings and then lend firms the funds they need to finance their investments.

It follows that the flow in this system will neither increase nor decrease if injections are equal to withdrawals. In this simplified version of an economy, without government and without a foreign sector, the equilibrium condition for national income (Y) becomes:

$$I = S$$

If a government is added then injections into the circular flow will also include government expenditures (G) on domestically produced output. Domestic output in this model can be bought by households and firms as well as the government. On the other hand, part of the income generated in this economy may not be spent as it leaks out of the circular flow of income in the form of taxes (T).

The equilibrium condition becomes:

$$I + G = S + T$$

Lastly, if we make this model more realistic and add a foreign sector then we have one more source of expenditures on domestic output, namely the expenditures foreigners make on it. Now, not only do domestic households, firms and the government spend on domestic output but also foreigners. These expenditures foreigners make on domestic output constitute the export revenues (X) of the economy and they are an injection to its circular flow system. On the other hand, part of the income generated in this economy may now be spent on foreign output. This spending represents our imports (M) and is a leakage (a withdrawal) to the circular flow.

The equilibrium condition becomes:

$$X + I + G = M + S + T$$

A simplified representation of the circular flow is also illustrated in Figure 2.1.3.

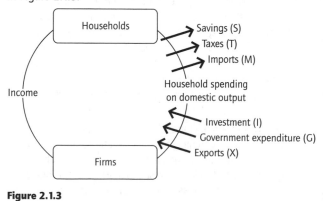

Figure 2.1.3

Measures of economic activity

Gross domestic product (GDP) and gross national income (GNI)

GDP is perhaps the single most important macroeconomic variable and it is defined as the value of all final goods and services produced within an economy over a certain period of time, usually a year or a quarter (by factors of production residing in the country). Remember the following points.

Only final goods and services are included. Intermediate goods (goods used in the production of other goods) are not included. Alternatively, instead of trying to work out which goods are final, include the 'value-added' contributed by each firm in the country, where the value added is defined as the difference between the total revenues collected by each firm and the cost of raw materials, services and components the firm purchased to produce the good or service. If all produced goods and services were included, double-counting would result and therefore overestimation of the true value of output.

Measurement of the GDP of an economy does not include transactions involving used goods, financial transactions or transfer payments as these do not represent contributions to current production of goods and services.

GDP

The output, expenditure and income approaches
There are three conceptually equivalent ways of arriving at the GDP figure for a country. These are:

- the output method, where we add all domestically produced final goods and services
- the expenditure method, where we add all expenditures made on domestically produced final goods and services
- the income method, where we add all incomes generated in the domestic production process.

Conceptually, the three methods are equivalent, and with some minor adjustments the figures arrived at through each method are equal. The value of all output produced does not become thin air but ends up in 'pockets' in the form of wages, profits, interest or rent (that is, as income to the factors of production involved). This income is then spent on output.

Each method is useful because of the breakdown it permits. The output method, for example, will give us the share of total output accounted for by each of the three sectors of an economy as well as the output of different industries:

output method: primary sector + secondary sector + tertiary sector, or

industry 1 + industry 2 + industry 3 + ... + industry n

The expenditure method permits us to monitor the level of investment spending through time or the proportion of government expenditures in total economic activity:

expenditure method: spending by households + spending by firms + spending by the government + net spending by foreigners, or

consumption + investment + government expenditures + net exports

The income method provides information about the proportion of total income earned by labour in contrast to owners of capital:

income method: wages + profits + interest + rents

Nominal GDP versus real GDP
Note that even though we are truly interested in an output measure, we are forced to add values (prices times quantities) which makes our GDP measure dependent not only on output changes (in which we are interested) but also on price changes (which typically do not interest us).

Comparison of GDP figures in successive years therefore becomes a problem since, assuming that an increase in GDP is recorded, we cannot know whether the bigger figure is due to

an increase in output of goods and services produced or whether it is due to an increase in prices (an increase in the general or average price level; that is, due to inflation). In other words, we cannot know to what extent the increase in the nominal (or money) GDP figure recorded is 'real' and to what extent it is 'inflationary'. For example, if GDP measured at current prices increased from one year to the next by 5.5%, it cannot be known what proportion of this increase is due to an output increase and what proportion is due to inflation. It could be, for example, that output increased by, say, 4% (that is, real GDP increased by 4%) and that the remaining 1.5% was due to price level increases (that is, to inflation), or it could be that output increased only by 0.5% and prices by 5.0%.

So, nominal GDP (money GDP or GDP at current prices) is a measure of output of a certain period valued at the prices prevailing in that same period.

Real GDP (or GDP at constant prices) is a measure of output of a certain year (say, year 't') valued at the prices prevailing at some reference period (known as the base period or base year). So, the output of each good in year 't' is multiplied by its price that prevailed in the base year chosen.

Real GDP is therefore a measure of output after having isolated (or adjusted for) the effect of inflation. Real GDP figures reflect the volume of production, not the value.

Define the GDP deflator as the ratio of nominal GDP to real GDP of a year times 100.

$$\text{GDP deflator} = \frac{\text{nominal GDP}}{\text{real GDP}} \times 100$$

By manipulating the above we arrive at:

$$\text{real GDP} = \frac{\text{nominal GDP}}{\text{GDP deflator}} \times 100$$

The GDP deflator is a comprehensive price index which measures the average level of prices of all goods and services included in the GDP of a country.

GNI

A variation of the measure of output given by GDP is given by GNI. GDP focuses on what is produced within the boundaries of an economy independently of the nationality of the factors of production involved. In contrast, GNI focuses on the nationality of the factors of production involved and the incomes they earn independently of their geographic location. The major difference between the two is a result of the operation of multinational corporations. Let's take two countries, Greece and France. Assume that in Greece the French bank BNP operates, while in France the Greek yogurt and ice cream manufacturer DELTA operates. Focusing on Greece:

$$\text{GNI} = \text{GDP} + \text{DELTA} - \text{BNP or, more generally,}$$

GNI = GDP + (factor income earned abroad − factor income paid abroad)

where 'factor income earned abroad' refers to the profits of the Greek firm in France and 'factor income paid abroad' refers to the profits the French bank earns in Greece. Of course, factor income includes not just profits but also wages, interest and rent.

Per capita figures
By dividing GDP or GNI by the population of a country we arrive at per capita GDP and per capita GNI respectively.

Per capita figures scale the variable for country size, making comparisons between countries meaningful.

Problems in GDP measurement

GDP measurement is fraught with problems. Official GDP figures in many countries understate the true level of economic activity because of the existence of a large parallel ('black' or shadow) economy. Individuals in many countries under-report their incomes to avoid taxation. A heavy tax burden, especially high marginal (top) tax rates may be responsible for this tax-evading behaviour. Some productive activity may also be illegal per se (involvement with drugs, prostitution, etc.). Furthermore, 'do it yourself' activities are not included. If I repair my car instead of taking it to the mechanic, the value of the service I produce will not show up in official statistics. This becomes an important issue in the case of many developing countries because subsistence farming (defined as farming to feed one's family) is not included in GDP measurements and this leads to underestimation of per capita income levels. Lastly, data collection in many countries is poor and unreliable.

Comparisons over time and across countries using national income statistics

For meaningful comparisons over time it is important that the effect of changing price levels is isolated. Real GDP or GNI must be used. In addition, if we are not just interested in the size of an economy then it is advisable to use per capita figures. Conversion of national income figures to a common currency, usually the US dollar, should also be made using purchasing power parity (PPP) dollars and not market exchange rates. PPP dollars incorporate cost of living differences, making cross-country comparisons of these variables more meaningful.

Living standards and GDP/GNI statistics

Per capita GDP or GNI statistics are often used to make inferences about the living standards of a country. Despite being a useful summary measure of material welfare of the population of a country, this method suffers from major deficiencies and should be employed with extra care. The following is a list of the associated problems.

■ This method fails to incorporate income distribution considerations. Per capita income is a simple average that provides no information on whether income is equitably or very unequally distributed.

■ It fails to value the environmental degradation often associated with increased production. Green GDP is an attempt to correct this problem as it factors in the detrimental effect of production on the environment. Green GDP is estimated by subtracting from GDP the cost of natural resource and environmental depletion.

■ It fails to include non-marketed subsistence production which may be relatively significant in some low-income countries. Non-marketed subsistence production refers to food and other goods and services produced by a family for its own consumption. More generally, it fails to include the size of parallel ('black' or shadow) economies in developing (and developed) countries.

■ It fails to reveal the composition of output. Two economies with equal per capita income levels may differ with respect to living standards because of different output mix. A country that devotes a large proportion of its GDP to, say,

defence, sacrifices resources in this area that could otherwise have been used in the production of pro-development goods.

■ It fails to include the value of leisure, a most important 'good' an individual may enjoy. It makes a big difference to workers if their average working week is over 50 hours and they can seldom take time off, or if the working week is only 35 hours.

■ It fails to incorporate the value of the stream of services flowing from the accumulated social and other capital of an economy. Living standards at any point in time are affected not just by current income but also by the stock of accumulated wealth. For example, the existence of a high-quality and free public school system implies that households with children may devote more of their income to other goods and services.

The trade (or business) cycle

The trade or business cycle is defined as the short-term fluctuations of real GDP around its long-term trend. Periods of expansion (booms) are followed by periods of contraction (recession or busts). The downturn's major characteristic is increasing levels of unemployment. If, on the other hand, expansion is too rapid it may give rise to inflationary pressures. Ideally, steady, sustainable, non-inflationary long-term growth is desirable.

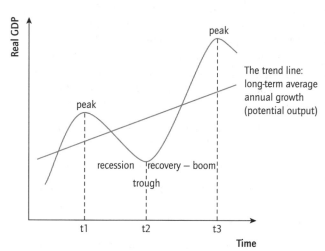

Figure 2.1.4 The trade (or business) cycle

The economy depicted in Figure 2.1.4 is a growing economy. Growth exists when total output, measured by real GDP, increases through time. It follows that this economy is growing between time period t2 and t3 but also over the long term as the trend line is upward sloping. The trend line is equal to the average annual long-term growth of the economy and is considered to reflect the potential output of the economy. When the economy is at its potential output we say that there is full employment. Full employment does not mean that everyone who is looking for a job has one. In a dynamic economy, one that continuously transforms, this is not possible. Instead, full employment incorporates what economists refer to as natural unemployment. Natural unemployment is usually defined as the unemployment that exists when the labour market is in equilibrium and includes people in between jobs, people who lack the necessary skills and are training or re-training, people who are relocating, etc.

In figure 2.1.4, between time t1 and t2 the economy is in recession. Real GDP is decreasing (technically, for at least two consecutive quarters), so the economy is registering negative growth rates. At t1 it was at a peak (as well as at t3). At t2 it is at a trough and it is about to enter recovery.

Note that if the growth rate is decreasing (from, say, 2.1% to 0.8%) real GDP continues to increase but at a slower and slower rate. Various expressions are used to describe this phase, for example 'the economy is losing steam', 'it is peaking out' or it is 'approaching recession'. An economy about to enter recession is, in Figure 2.1.4, somewhere right before a peak.

If actual output is greater than potential output then unemployment must be lower than the natural rate.

If actual output falls short of potential output then unemployment is greater than the natural rate.

When actual output is not equal to potential output an output gap is present.

TIP Make sure that after you finish drawing the trade cycle there is only **one** level of real GDP corresponding to **each** time period t. A common error is to draw it in such a way that at each point t on the horizontal axis there are more than one corresponding levels of real GDP.

A time line of macroeconomics

- The distinction between macroeconomics and microeconomics did not always exist. In fact, it is relatively new and started to be widely recognized only after the Second World War as a result of the publication in 1936 of the *General Theory of Employment, Interest and Money* by John Maynard Keynes, who transformed the theoretical landscape of economics.

- The time line below serves as a very broad guide to the evolution of ideas in macroeconomics and policy making.

Time line

```
----|--------------------|----------|------|--------------------------|--------------------|--------------------|------------------------------------>
1870      1929         1936                      1970      1980    1990      1997              2007
|--------------------------|----|----------------------------------|--------------------|
```

Pre-1929: The Classical School of thought; 'Laissez faire, laissez passer'. Market forces guarantee that an economy will rest at, or close, full employment. There is no need for the government to intervene. (Non-activists)

Keynes' 'General Theory' is published in 1936. There is no guarantee that a market economy will rest at 'full employment' so there is an active role for the government. Through fiscal policy the government can stabilize the economy and achieve full employment. **Keynesian interventionist** ideas reign after the Second World War until the mid 1970s. (Activists)

In the 1970s, **monetarism** emerges at the **University of Chicago** with Nobel prize laureate **Milton Friedman** being the most widely known advocate of monetarist ideas. Monetarists slowly deconstructed the Keynesian edifice, initially doubting the effectiveness of fiscal policy and later suggesting that even monetary policy should be avoided. Markets 'rule'.

In the 1980s the **rational expectations school (new classical)** approach emerges through the work of **Lucas, Sargent** and others; the **supply side** is emphasized. The role of the government is further questioned and reliance on market forces is further emphasized.

The **East Asian crisis**, 1997–1998, cast doubts on extreme pro-market policies and on the **'Washington Consensus'**. Many speak of the necessity to **manage** globalization. Inequalities within and between countries are rising.

The **financial and economic crisis that began in 2007** brings back Keynesian interventionist policies. The state of macroeconomics is questioned. 'Saltwater' and 'freshwater' economists openly debate issues.

Aggregate demand

Aggregate demand (AD) is a term that refers to total spending on domestic goods and services per period of time. More precisely, AD is defined as the planned level of spending on domestic output at different average price levels per period of time.

Spending on output can originate either from the private sector (which includes households and firms) or from the public sector (the government). Private sector spending includes consumption expenditures (C) that households make and investment expenditures (I) that firms make. The public sector expenditures are usually termed government expenditures (G) in which both current and capital public spending are included.

Spending on domestic output can also originate from abroad as foreigners buy domestic goods and services. These are the exports (X) of an economy. Since though part of the spending that households, firms and the government makes is on foreign goods, we must subtract imports (M) to arrive at AD. So, AD is given by the relationship:

$$AD = C + I + G + (X - M)$$

$$AD = C + I + G + NX, \text{ where } NX = (X - M)$$

When plotted against the average price level, AD is negatively sloped illustrating, as in Figure 2.2.1, that at a higher average price level, planned spending on domestic output decreases.

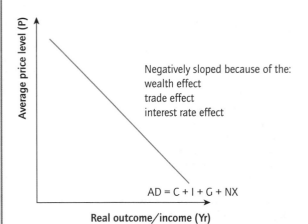

Figure 2.2.1 The AD curve

The AD curve is downward sloping but not for the same reasons that the demand for a single good is downward sloping as on the vertical axis we have the average price of all goods and not of a single good.

AD is negatively sloped because of the wealth effect, the interest rate effect and the trade effect. Here are specific details.

- The wealth effect: if the average price level increases the real value of the money that people have in their pockets or in bank accounts, as well as the real value of other financial assets such as bonds, decreases. If people feel poorer they tend to spend less.

- The interest rate effect: if the average price level increases then more money will be needed to effectuate a given level of transactions. If the supply of money is fixed but the demand for money increases then interest rates will increase, which decreases both consumption and investment expenditures as people and firms borrow to purchase durables and capital goods respectively.

- The trade effect: if the average price level increases then exports become less competitive abroad while imports seem more attractive at home so net exports, a component of AD, decrease.

As in all diagrams, the function will not shift when a variable on either of the axes changes. So, if there is a change in the average price level there will be no shift in the AD curve but only a movement along it. Changes in national income cannot initiate a shift in the curve either. AD will shift only if a non-income factor induces a change in any of its components.

Components of AD

Consumption expenditures

Consumption expenditures (C) are defined as spending by households on durables, non-durables and services per period of time. Consumption expenditures depend on the level of interest rates (IR), on the degree of consumer confidence (CC), on the level of household wealth (W), on personal income taxes (PIT), on household indebtedness (HD) etc.

$$C = f (IR, CC, W, PIT, HD, ...)$$

The above simply states that consumption expenditures are a function of (that is, depend on) the variables listed inside the parentheses.

More specific details are as follows.

- Interest rates (IR): the interest rate can be simply defined as the price paid per period for borrowing money on a percentage basis. If interest rates, for example, increase, then consumption expenditures are expected to decrease, shifting AD to the left for three reasons. First, borrowing to finance the purchase of consumer durables such as cars, appliances and furniture will become more expensive so households will tend to cut down on such purchases. Note that the housing market will also be negatively affected as it will become more expensive to finance the purchase or construction of a house, but technically this expenditure is classified under investment. Second, higher interest rates make saving more attractive (saving is defined as income not spent). If people tend to save more then it automatically implies that they will tend to spend less. Lastly, the single largest expenditure of a typical household is the purchase of its house. Households borrow from banks to finance this purchase through specialized very long-term loans known as mortgages. The interest rate charged on such loans is often adjustable, meaning that if market interest rates increase, mortgage rates will also increase and so will the monthly payments. People who bought houses in the past with a mortgage and still owe money will therefore have less money available every month to spend on goods and services, as they will need to pay a higher monthly mortgage payment to the bank. If, for example, a family must pay the bank $550.00 per month instead of $500.00 then in a year it will have $600.00 less available to spend on goods and services.

■ Consumer confidence (CC): households feeling secure and confident about their future will tend to spend more. A stable and growing economy with low inflation and unemployment will boost consumer confidence and favourably affect household spending, shifting AD to the right. On the other hand, uncertainty over future job prospects and insecurity about one's future income adversely affect present consumption. Spending on durable goods, such as cars and appliances, as well as on housing, are greatly affected by consumer moods.

■ Wealth (W): the total value of a household's assets may affect the level of its spending. If, for example, wealth increases, then consumption will be positively affected. A stock market boom or rising property values tend to increase spending and lower savings. AD will tend to increase and shift to the right.

■ Personal income taxes (PIT): If, for example, the government increases PIT then disposable income (Y_d), defined as income (Y) less such taxes (T) plus transfer payments (Tr) will decrease $(Y_d = Y − T + Tr)$. Lower disposable income as a result of higher PIT will tend to decrease consumption expenditures and so decrease AD, shifting it to the left.

■ The level of household indebtedness (HD): if private (household) debt (from taking out loans and/or from paying credit card charges) has accumulated, household spending will to decline as households will need to pay more and more to service their debt. This will put a damper on consumption expenditures and so tend to decrease AD, shifting it to the left.

Investment expenditures

Investment expenditures (I) are defined as spending by firms on capital goods per period of time. Investment increases the stock of capital of an economy. Investment is important both because of its short-run influence on AD and because in the long run it affects aggregate supply (AS) and so the rate of (actual and potential) growth of an economy. Investment spending is the most volatile component of AD. Investment expenditures depend on the level of interest rates (IR), on the degree of business confidence (BC), on technology (T), on business taxes (BT), on corporate indebtedness (CD), etc.

$$I = f (IR, BC, T, BT, CD, ...)$$

The above simply states that investment expenditures are a function of (that is, they depend on) the variables listed inside the parentheses.

Again, more specific details follow.

■ Interest rates (IR): if interest rates increase, then investment expenditures by businesses are expected to decrease, shifting AD to the left. Borrowing to finance the purchase of capital goods such as machines, tools, equipment and factories will become more expensive so firms will find that fewer possible investment projects are now profitable. Even if a firm uses its own funds to finance an investment project, the opportunity cost of using these funds instead of keeping them tied in banks or as bonds increases.

■ Business confidence (BC): the greater the degree of business confidence in an economy, the more willing firms will be to invest and expand. Economic and political stability are necessary for a positive business climate to evolve and so for investments to take place. Keynes considered the behaviour of entrepreneurs with respect to private investment decisions similar to that of a herd ('imitation') and, in his opinion, the observed instability of investments was due to these 'animal spirits'. Expectations can be greatly changed by many unpredictable factors, leading to swings in the prevailing business climate and so to changes in the level of investment spending.

■ Technology (T): industries and sectors where technology advances at a rapid rate will register higher rates of investment spending. Firms in such industries will be forced to undertake such spending in order to remain ahead or keep up with rivals.

■ Business taxes (BT): changes in business taxes affect the expected profitability of an investment project. An increase in business taxes will mean that fewer investment projects pass the profitability test and this will tend to dampen investment and, consequently, decrease AD.

■ Corporate indebtedness (CD): companies that are highly indebted will be very hesitant to take on more debt in order to make more investments.

In addition to the above factors, the following are also thought to affect investment spending in an economy and so AD.

■ Public policy toward investment: governments often attempt to influence investment by offering tax incentives to firms, subsidies, preferential loan terms, protection from foreign competition, etc. Note that the size itself of the public sector in an economy may influence the growth of private investment. Also remember that institutions affect private investments. A large bureaucracy (or 'red tape') and complicated regulations will burden the operation of firms in a country and negatively affect the rate of investment. Investment levels are, ceteris paribus, higher in countries with low levels of bureaucracy and with transparent economic and business environments. Lastly, corruption adversely affects investment, especially foreign direct investment (investment by multinational corporations in foreign countries).

■ The overall macroeconomic environment: a 'sound' macroeconomic environment where policy makers ensure low inflation, low budget deficits, a sustainable public debt and flexible labour markets usually leads to higher rates of investment spending. A sound macroeconomic environment leads to higher confidence level for businesses.

■ Income and its growth: rising income leads to rising consumption, which may induce more investments as firms may be forced to increase their capacity to meet the increased demand for goods and services.

Government spending

Government spending (G) is in many economies a large part of total spending on goods and services. Government spending is distinguished into **current** spending on goods and services, **capital** (public investment) spending which refers to spending on roads, ports, telecommunications, schools and other infrastructure and also on **transfer payments** which basically refer to pensions and unemployment benefits. Note that transfer payments are not included in national income since they do not represent rewards to current productive effort. Governments spend to ensure that adequate amounts of public and merit goods and services are consumed, such as national defence, educational services and health-care services. They spend to regulate markets in their attempt to guarantee product safety, environmental standards, competitive conditions, etc. They may also spend to redistribute income so that a socially acceptable minimum is guaranteed. Such spending includes funding state pensions, unemployment benefits, subsidies, disability benefits, for example. Lastly, governments spend to affect AD. An increase or decrease in government expenditures will cause AD to increase or decrease, shifting to the right or to the left. This is part of what is known as fiscal policy. We may therefore conclude that economic and political priorities affect the level of government spending.

Net exports

Net exports (NX or X−M) are defined as the difference between spending by foreigners on domestic output minus domestic spending on foreign output or, more simply, as the difference between export revenues and import expenditures per period of time. Net exports depend on foreign income (Y_f), the exchange rate (ER), the level of trade protection or of commercial policy (CP) etc.

$$NX = f(Yf, ER, CP, ..)$$

The above simply states that net exports are a function of (that is, depend on) the variables listed inside the parentheses.

A more specific explanation follows.

- Foreign income (Y_f): if, for example, income enjoyed by foreign trading partners increases, their level of consumption will increase. Part of their increased spending will be on imports. But their imports are our exports. It follows that the exports of an economy will tend to increase if the income of its trading partners increases and vice versa.

- Exchange rate (ER): the exchange rate of a currency is its price expressed in terms of a foreign currency. If, for example, the exchange rate decreases (depreciates or devalues) then exports become cheaper and so more competitive abroad while imports become pricier and less attractive domestically. As a result, net exports are expected to increase, shifting AD to the right.

- Trade protection or changes in commercial policy (CP): trade protection or commercial policy refers to any policy that governments may implement to discriminate against foreign suppliers. If, for example, trading partners lift trade barriers (for example if they decrease tariffs, which are taxes on imports; or eliminate quotas, which are quantitative restrictions on imports) then exports will increase and so will AD.

So, if any of these factors change in the described direction, AD will tend to increase and shift to the right. Remember though that there is no *a priori* guarantee that the expected change will be significant or that it will even materialize, as each component of AD is affected by many variables. So, if, for example, interest rates decrease, we expect that consumption expenditures will be positively affected but we cannot be certain that this will indeed happen, as perhaps the decrease in interest rates is too small or households happen to be very pessimistic or highly indebted. This is why we qualify our conclusion stating that 'consumption will tend to increase'.

TIP Draw the AD either as a straight line or slightly curved. It is easiest, though, to draw it with a ruler. Make sure you label the axes properly. The vertical is not 'price' but the 'average price level' as it shows AD and not demand for one good or a service. The horizontal is often denoted as 'Q'. This should be avoided as again it may lead to confusion. 'GDP' should also be avoided as GDP refers to the actual output produced and not to planned output. 'Real output/income' and 'Yr' are often considered an appropriate choice. Remember that output and income are conceptually identical terms.

Consumption expenditures will tend to increase if:	interest rates decrease
	consumer confidence increases
	wealth increases
	personal income taxes decrease
	household indebtedness decreases
Investment expenditures will tend to increase if:	interest rates decrease
	business confidence increases
	technology rapidly advances
	business taxes decrease
	corporate indebtedness decreases
Government expenditures will tend to increase if:	economic priorities change and dictate this
	political priorities change and dictate this
Net exports will tend to increase if:	foreign income levels increase
	the exchange rate decreases
	the level of trade protection faced decreases

Aggregate supply

Aggregate supply (AS) is defined as the planned level of output that domestic firms are willing to offer at different average price levels per period of time. The shape of the AS curve is rather controversial in macroeconomics as it reflects the different assumptions used by different schools of thought. We will initially discuss what is known as the short-run aggregate supply (SRAS) curve. The monetarist or new classical model will follow and, lastly, we will present the Keynesian model.

SRAS

The short run is defined in economics as the time period during which not all adjustments have taken place. Within the framework of an AS analysis this is taken to refer to fixed money wages: money (or nominal) wages are assumed fixed over the short run and unable to adjust to changes in the average price level. Why? Two explanations may be offered. The first rests on labour contracts which fix wages for relatively long periods of time. The second explanation rests on the idea that workers are slow to adjust their expectations of inflation (of a rising average price level) and only after some time do they realize that rising prices have affected their purchasing power.

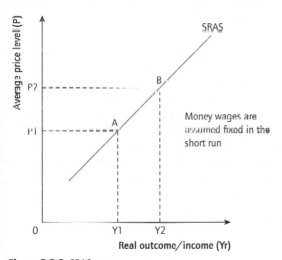

Figure 2.2.2 SRAS curve

Figure 2.2.2 illustrates a typical SRAS curve. It is upward sloping because if the average price level rises from P1 to P2 while money wages remain fixed, then firms enjoy greater profitability which induces them to offer more output. Remember that the real wage is the ratio of the money wage divided by the average price level so if the latter is rising while the former is constant then the real wage is decreasing. There is a movement along the SRAS curve from point A to point B reflecting the direct (positive) relationship that exists in the short run between the price level and real output.

SRAS will shift to the left or to the right if resource prices and, more specifically, nominal wages change, as well as if business taxes or subsidies change. In general, across the board changes in production costs will tend to shift the SRAS curve of an economy. For example, assume that money wages increase. The SRAS curve will shift to the left as production costs for firms will have increased. Or, assume that business taxes decrease in

an economy. This is equivalent to a decrease in production costs which will tend to shift the SRAS to the right. Now consider the effect of an increase in the price of oil. Since oil is the predominant form of energy, it will increase production costs, shifting the SRAS curve to the left.

Lastly, in a principally agricultural economy, temporary supply shocks (such as generally poor weather, a destructive hurricane or floods) will have adverse effects, decreasing SRAS and shifting the curve to the left.

Alternative views of AS
The monetarist or new classical AS
According to the monetarist or new classical school of thought, an economy will in the long run – when all adjustments are possible and more specifically money wages have adjusted to changes in the average price level – produce whatever its resources and technology allow it to produce. In the long run, output will be at its potential or natural level, which is considered the full employment level of output for the economy. This level of output in the long run is independent of the average level of prices because money wages are assumed to adjust fully so that the real wage is constant.

Figure 2.2.3 illustrates a monetarist or new classical long-run aggregate supply (LRAS) curve. It is drawn vertical to show that increases in the average price level will not induce any increase in real output in the long run. Why? Because in the long run, money wages will have adjusted and matched the increase in prices so firms' profitability will not have changed.

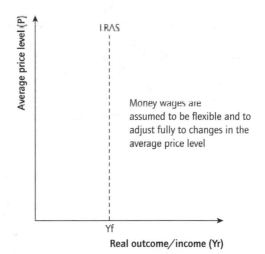

Figure 2.2.3 The monetarist or new classical LRAS curve

It is drawn vertical at the level of potential output, Yf, to show that in the long run when all adjustments have been made an economy will produce whatever its resources and technology normally allow it to produce. At this level of potential output there is full employment, but that should not be taken to mean that there is no unemployment in the economy. At the full employment level of output there is some unemployment, which is referred to as natural (or 'normal') unemployment and, as mentioned earlier, is the unemployment that exists when the labour market is in equilibrium.

The Keynesian version of AS

The Keynesian version of the AS curve typically has three distinct sections, as illustrated in Figure 2.2.4.

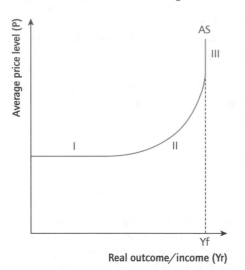

Figure 2.2.4 The Keynesian AS curve

Section I is horizontal, implying that higher levels of output can and will be produced without the average price level rising. The explanation lies with the realization that the real output levels corresponding to this region are significantly below the full employment level of real output denoted with Yf. Such an economy operates presumably in deep recession or depression-like conditions.

Section III is vertical at the full employment level of output Yf. This full employment level of output is typically considered within the Keynesian framework of analysis as a 'wall', implying that there is no unemployment in the economy. Real output cannot increase beyond Yf. If one wishes to include the idea of natural (or 'normal') unemployment within this framework then the level of Yf must be chosen slightly to the left of the vertical

section. Within such a set-up, at full employment there is some unemployment, the natural or normal rate of unemployment; and output can increase beyond that level, implying that unemployment may fall below that level. It is perhaps advisable to keep the two models separate as their origins and implications differ.

Section II illustrates an upward sloping AS curve. It depends on the realization that an economy consists of many different sectors and industries that employ differing types of resources which do not reach full employment conditions together. Some industries may reach full employment earlier than others. This situation is referred to as 'bottlenecks' in production: spare capacity may coexist with full employment. Real output may continue to rise but, as a result of the full employment conditions in some industries, wages and more generally production costs may also be rising and so will prices.

Shifting AS over the long run

If the LRAS increases and shifts to the right it implies that the full employment level of real output has increased. In Figure 2.2.5 the effect of an increase in AS over the long run is illustrated. On the left-hand side the monetarist or new classical version is depicted with the LRAS shifting to LRAS'. On the right-hand side the Keynesian version is shown with AS shifting over the long term to AS'.

Note that, strictly speaking, it is a mistake to refer to 'long-run Keynesian aggregate supply' as Keynes was not interested in the long run in his analysis of the workings of an economy. We show on the right-hand side of Figure 2.2.5 an increase in AS over the long run within the Keynesian framework.

Whichever approach one chooses to adopt, the reasons behind the shift are the same. They include increases in the amount or the quality of the factors of production available in the economy and in how efficiently these are employed, as well as technological and institutional improvements.

Monetarist or new classical and Keynesian versions

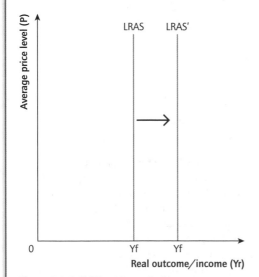 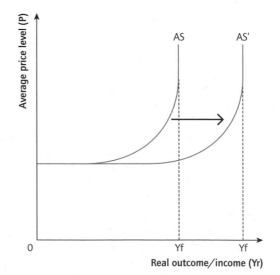

Figure 2.2.5 Shifting AS over the long run

Equilibrium

Short-run equilibrium

Macroeconomic equilibrium in the short run exists at that level of real output at which AD is equal to SRAS, as illustrated in Figure 2.2.6.

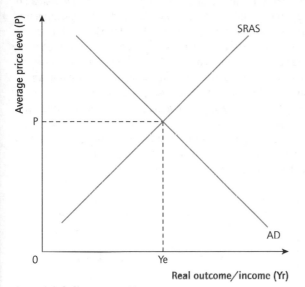

Figure 2.2.6 Short-run equilibrium

The equilibrium level of real output Ye is determined at the intersection of AD with SRAS. The average price level of the economy is also determined at level P. It should be clear that any shift in AD will induce a change in the equilibrium average price and output levels in the same direction as the change in AD. For example, if AD increases, say, as a result of lower interest rates, then it will shift to the right, leading in the short run to higher real output as well as to a higher average price level. Shifts in the SRAS will induce changes in the average price level and of equilibrium output that are in the opposite direction. For example, if oil prices increase then SRAS will decrease, shifting to the left and inducing a higher average price level accompanied by lower equilibrium real output.

Equilibrium in the monetarist or new classical model

Within the monetarist or new classical model, equilibrium in the long run will necessarily be at the economy's potential or full employment level of output, while any deviation from the potential level of output can only exist in the short run as a result of the prevailing fixed money wages. It follows that such deviations of short-run equilibrium from the potential level of output will be temporary and the economy will always return in the long run to the full employment level of output as a result of money wages fully adjusting. Figure 2.2.7 illustrates this.

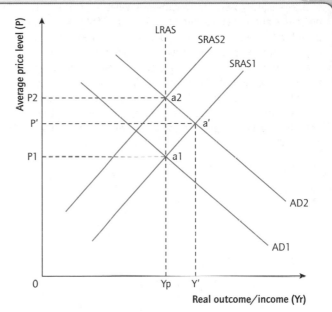

Figure 2.2.7 Returning to full employment following an increase in AD

Assume an economy initially in long-run equilibrium determined at the intersection of AD1 and SRAS1 on the LRAS curve (point a1). Real output is at its potential (full employment) level Yp and the average level of prices is at P1. Assume now that, for whatever reason, AD increases and the curve shifts to the right to AD2. The average price level will increase to P' and this will induce firms to increase real output to Y' as money wages in the short run are fixed, so profitability is higher. Short-run equilibrium is at point a' at the intersection of AD2 with SRAS1. Real output is above its potential (full employment) level. The economy is characterized by an **inflationary gap** equal to the difference between the potential level of output and the greater equilibrium level of output YpY'.

In the long run though, money wages within this model are assumed to adjust fully and match the increase in prices. If money wages increase to re-establish the original real wage rate in the labour market, then SRAS will decrease and the curve will shift to SRAS2. Remember that an increase in money wages is a factor that shifts the SRAS curve to the left. The real wage is back to its original level so firms will be forced to cut back output and produce at Yp, the potential (full employment) level of output. Long-run equilibrium is re-established with real output at its original full employment level but with the average price level higher at P2. The flexibility of money wages in the long run guarantee that the economy returns to its 'normal' rate of real output.

The symmetric adjustment process unfolds with a decrease in AD. More specifically, Figure 2.2.8 illustrates an economy initially in long-run equilibrium determined at the intersection of AD1 and SRAS1 on the LRAS curve (point a1). Real output is ▸▸

at its potential (full employment) level Yp and the average level of prices is at P1. Assume now that, for whatever reason, AD decreases and the curve shifts to the left to AD2. The average price level will decrease to P' and this will induce firms to decrease real output to Y' as money wages in the short run are fixed, so profitability is lower. Short-run equilibrium is at point a' at the intersection of AD2 with SRAS1. Real output is below its potential (full employment) level. The economy is characterized by a **deflationary gap** equal to the difference between the potential level of output and the lower equilibrium level of output Y'Yp.

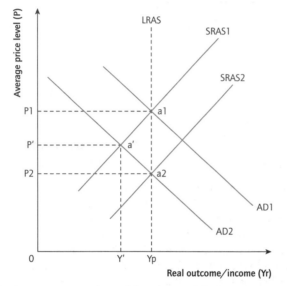

Figure 2.2.8 Returning to full employment following a decrease in AD

In the long run though, money wages within the monetarist or new classical model are assumed to be fully flexible. This means that they are assumed to adjust and match the decrease in prices. If money wages decrease to re-establish the original lower real wage rate in the labour market, then SRAS will increase and the curve will shift to SRAS2. Remember that an decrease in money wages is a factor that shifts the SRAS curve to the right. The real wage is back to its original level, so firms will be induced to increase output and produce at Yp, the potential (full employment) level of output. Long-run equilibrium is re-established with real output at its original full employment level, but with the average price level lower at P2. The downward flexibility of money wages assumed by the monetarist or new classical school guarantees that in the long run the economy will return to its normal rate of real output. The market economy in this model is capable of returning to its potential rate of real output with flexible money wages doing the trick.

> **An inflationary gap exists when actual equilibrium output is greater than potential (full employment) output.**

> **A deflationary gap (also referred to as a recessionary gap) exists when equilibrium output is below the potential (full employment) level of output.**

Equilibrium in the Keynesian model

The major difference between the monetarist or new classical model described above and the Keynesian model is that the latter is not equipped with an automatic adjustment mechanism. Within the Keynesian framework an economy may find itself stuck at an equilibrium level of real output with less than full employment. No endogenous forces exist that will restore full employment. More specifically, money wages are assumed 'sticky downwards' (the 'ratchet' effect: money wages may increase but they do not easily adjust downwards). It follows that within the Keynesian world, AD is the driving force behind economic activity. Instead of believing in 'supply creating its own demand' (Say's law from the classical school of thought, which included the intellectual fathers of monetarism and the new classical school), Keynes turned things inside out, postulating that it is 'effective' demand (which we call AD) that determines the equilibrium level of real output in an economy. If, for whatever reason, AD proves insufficient to establish full employment then a market economy will suffer a system-wide failure as it will be unable on its own (that is, without the help of the government) to restore full employment conditions. Figure 2.2.9 illustrates equilibrium in a Keynesian model of national income determination.

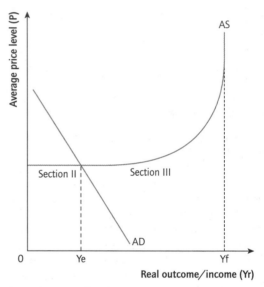

Figure 2.2.9 Equilibrium in a Keynesian macroeconomic model

Assume that AD is at an extremely low level (as on Figure 2.2.9) perhaps because of extremely low consumer and business confidence and a general wave of pessimism in the country. Equilibrium real output will be determined at the intersection of AD with the Keynesian AS curve at the level of output Ye. In this model, and as a result of the assumed downward stickiness of money wages (perhaps as a result of labour unions), equilibrium below full employment may persist for an unacceptable period of time, forcing the government to intervene and attempt to increase AD by increasing its own spending levels, as will be explained later. Note that if AD increases it is not necessary for the economy within this Keynesian framework of analysis to experience rising price levels (that is, inflationary pressures) at least until it reaches section II of the AS curve.

Again, when equilibrium output is less than full employment output a deflationary (or recessionary) gap exists, equal to YeYf. An inflationary gap is more cumbersome to illustrate within a Keynesian diagram as Keynesian analysis was originally not interested in investigating inflationary conditions. In any case, if AD increases within the vertical section of a Keynesian AS curve (section III) then an inflationary gap is said to be created, as illustrated in Figure 2.2.10.

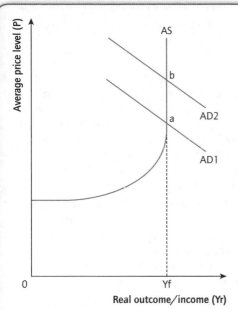

Figure 2.2.10 An inflationary gap within a Keynesian AS diagram

Assume that AD is originally at AD1, leading to an equilibrium level of real output equal to the full employment level of real output Yf. If, for some reason, AD increases and the curve shifts to AD2 then the economy will remain at its full employment level of output Yf but the average price level will rise, proving purely inflationary. Distance ab in Figure 2.2.10 is often considered to illustrate an inflationary gap within the Keynesian model.

Low unemployment

An individual is considered unemployed if he or she is actively searching for a job and cannot find one. The unemployment rate is the ratio of the number of unemployed over the size of the labour force (also referred to as the workforce or the working population) times 100. The labour force includes the employed and the unemployed:

$$\text{Unemployement rate} = \frac{\text{number of unemployed}}{\text{labour force}} \times 100$$

Measurement problems

It is difficult to get an accurate estimate of the unemployment rate. The official unemployment rate may underestimate or overestimate the true level of unemployment in a country, as follows.

It may understate the true level of unemployment because of the existence of discouraged workers and of underemployed individuals. The first category of discouraged workers includes individuals who would like to work and would happily accept a job offer but who have stopped actively searching for one because they have remained unemployed for too long and their past search effort was unsuccessful. Since they are demonstrating no effort in seeking employment they are not considered unemployed, so they are not included in the official unemployment rate. The second category, the underemployed individuals, includes people who do have a job (so are considered employed) but who are working as part-time employees fewer hours per week than desired. These are involuntary part-time workers.

The official unemployment rate may overstate the true level of unemployment as some individuals may intentionally conceal their true employment status either fearing loss of transfer payments, such as unemployment benefits, that are granted only to the unemployed or because they are employed in illegal activities such as gambling or prostitution.

In general, during recessions the number of part-time workers and of discouraged workers increases. Also, some who were falsely claiming to be unemployed in order to collect benefits may actually become unemployed. As a result, actual or true unemployment is more likely to be higher during the downturn of the business cycle than the official figure suggests. Symmetrically, during a boom actual unemployment may be lower than the reported official figure as fewer people will become discouraged or will be forced into accepting part-time positions when jobs are plentiful. In addition, more people may continue reporting as unemployed even though they have actually found a job.

Remember that the reported official unemployment rate does not reveal any information pertaining to age, gender, ethnic or regional disparities. Concerning demographic groups, unemployment among young workers and minorities is typically the highest. It is therefore important to examine disaggregated unemployment data to get a better picture of the labour market of a country.

Consequences of unemployment

Perhaps the biggest cost of unemployment is the opportunity cost of lost output. Goods and services that could have been produced are sacrificed. One way of viewing this cost is by examining the size of the distance between actual output and potential output in a business cycle diagram. This is referred to as the output gap. Another way of visualizing this cost is through a diagram showing a production possibilities curve (PPC) – also known as a production possibilities frontier (PPF) – as unemployment implies that the economy is operating inside the curve.

The government's finances are also affected by unemployment. Tax revenues collected are lower because of the lower incomes and the resulting decreased private spending. Government spending increases because of the unemployment benefits paid to the unemployed and the increased number of training and re-training programmes that need to be implemented.

For individuals who lose their jobs, the single most important cost incurred is the lost income. Living standards of the unemployed are adversely affected, especially if wages were the only source of income. Another cost for individuals is the loss of up-to-date skills. In certain professions this may be very important and the longer people remain unemployed the less employable they become as their human capital is eroded. Employers prefer to hire individuals currently employed elsewhere as not only will their skills be up to date but also the risks created by asymmetric information are avoided as the employer cannot know why the unemployed lost their jobs in the first place. Other possible private costs of unemployment include the loss of self-esteem that often results and the increased probability that the person will resort to alcohol or drug abuse.

If unemployment is high and prolonged, society may experience a higher incidence of crime and violence and other negative externalities resulting from drug and alcohol abuse. If unemployment is heavily concentrated in regions or in age groups such problems may become even more pronounced.

There may be some benefits arising from moderate unemployment. Many quote that union power weakens, so there is reduced wage inflation in the economy. If the real wage decreases then profitability and competitiveness of domestic firms increases. Increased geographical and occupational mobility is also mentioned as a possible positive side effect of unemployment as workers are forced to relocate or change occupation. These benefits must be viewed in context though, otherwise the harsh reality of unemployment may be distorted.

Types and causes of unemployment and policies to lower it

There are three main types of unemployment.

- **Seasonal unemployment** is a result of predictable variations in the demand and supply of labour. Weather patterns are responsible for construction workers being laid off in the winter and snow ski instructors in the summer. Labour supply surges in June every year as college and secondary school graduates start looking for a job. This type of unemployment is expected and there is not much a government can do about it. Unemployment statistics though are often corrected ('seasonally adjusted') so that policy makers can determine true changes in unemployment, not those due to the changing seasons.

- **Frictional unemployment** refers to people in-between jobs as it takes time to match a job seeker with an available job vacancy. This is unemployment of a short-term nature and is largely also unavoidable in an economy since people will always voluntarily switch jobs, searching for better ones or relocating. Faster and better information about the labour market will decrease but not eliminate frictional unemployment. Governments can minimize frictional unemployment by ensuring that job vacancies as well as the profiles of those available for work become known wider and faster.

- **Structural unemployment** is perhaps the most serious type of unemployment since it is of a long-term nature. It represents those remaining unemployed long after recovery is under way in an economy. An economy may be booming but structural unemployment will not decrease. It is the result of the evolving structure of an economy because of rapid technological advancement or shifting comparative advantage. The changing structure of an economy results in a 'mismatch' between the skills available among the unemployed and the skills required by the labour market. New technologies render certain professions obsolete but at the same time create new job opportunities. For example, in some cases the Internet may have decreased the demand for shop assistants but it has created new jobs for web designers and software engineers. But if the redundant shop assistant is not trained in computer science then he or she may find it difficult to get a job. Or, consider the case of an industry in a country losing its export markets to lower-cost foreign firms. If Korean shipyards become more competitive then specialized workers in other countries will lose their jobs. Lastly, the mismatch can also be geographic, with the unemployed clustered in one region of the country while job vacancies exist elsewhere.

Figure 2.3.1 is an illustration of the structural unemployment resulting in some specific industry if, for example, some of the firms are forced to shut down as a result of increased foreign competition or because of some firms switching to automated processes that render some of the workers redundant.

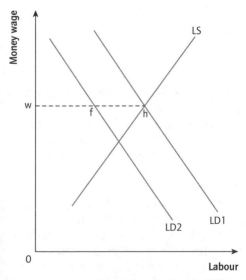

Figure 2.3.1 Structural unemployment in a specific industry as a result of a shift in comparative advantage or the introduction of new technology

Note that labour demand (LD) shows how many workers firms are willing to hire at each wage rate while labour supply (LS) shows how many workers are willing to offer their labour services at each wage rate. Initially, we assume equilibrium in this specific labour market with the wage rate determined at the intersection of LD1 with LS. If automated processes or shifting comparative advantage decrease labour demand to LD2 and money wages are sticky then distance fh may be thought of representing the resulting structurally unemployed.

Structural unemployment, though, may not be a result of mismatches but of what are known as labour market rigidities. Minimum wage laws and wages set through collective bargaining between industries and labour are examples of labour market rigidities. They both result in higher unemployment as wage rates are set above their equilibrium, market clearing level. If pension plans in one industry are not easily transferred to another industry then occupational mobility is hampered. Consider a worker losing his job in industry A but prevented from taking a job offer in industry B because he can not transfer his pension rights. He will end up unemployed. Lastly, institutional disincentives are considered as causes of structural unemployment. Laws preventing firms dismissing employees except in certain circumstances and high unemployment benefits are examples.

Eliminating structural unemployment is not possible in a dynamic economy as its structure is constantly changing but there are policies considered helpful in reducing it. Perhaps the most important of these policies are related to facilitating the training and re-training of those with non-marketable skills. Governments may directly provide training programmes or they may subsidize private provision of such programmes. They may also provide low-interest loans to individuals willing to enroll in such skill-creating courses who otherwise lack the necessary financing, as well as assistance to individuals willing to relocate to ease their adjustment costs. Governments offer incentives in the form of tax breaks or wage subsidies to firms hiring structurally and long term unemployed individuals. They also revise school curricula to prepare individuals better for the labour market.

If labour market rigidities are responsible for some of the structural unemployment in a country then the obvious solution is to render the labour market more flexible, but this is difficult. At the top of the list of policies to achieve this are those that reduce the power of labour unions. This is because labour unions are responsible for the increased power insiders (workers with jobs) hold that increase turnover costs for firms and prevent outsiders (workers looking for a job) from getting hired. The government may also try to eliminate minimum wage laws as well as collective bargaining since both create excess supply of labour in particular labour markets. Reducing non-wage labour costs, such as national insurance contributions that firms are obliged to pay, could increase demand for labour. Reducing the level of unemployment benefits and the length of time for which benefits can be collected will force some workers to accept a job offer instead of remaining unemployed and collecting benefits. Lastly, eliminating legislation relating to job security may mean that firms are more willing to hire workers as it will be less costly to fire them in a downturn.

However, the reduction in structural unemployment that some of these measures may bring about may come at a significant cost to society. Decreasing workers' protection may lead to labour and social unrest which may hamper growth instead of accelerating it. Segments of the population may become marginalized and income distribution more unequal, again with adverse effects on growth and development.

It is worth noting that the policies that should be employed to lower structural unemployment are of a microeconomic nature.

Cyclical (or Keynesian or demand-deficient) unemployment

This type of unemployment is directly related to the business cycle. Higher unemployment will necessarily accompany a recession because of the lower level of economic activity. A decrease in AD will force some businesses to shrink and others to close down.

On the left-hand side of Figure 2.3.2 the decrease in AD is shown from AD1 to AD2 which results in lower level of economic activity and lower real output Y2. The economy has entered a recession. As a result of the lower of economic activity, firms decrease their demand for labour. Some firms may shrink, others may even shut down because of the recession. On

the right-hand side of Figure 2.3.2 the economy's labour market is illustrated. Note that in Figure 2.3.2 the labour market as a whole of a country is depicted whereas Figure 2.3.1 focused on the labour market relating to a specific industry. In Figure 2.3.2, labour demand decreases from DL1 to DL2. Money wages are assumed 'sticky downward' and so remain at w. Excess supply of labour in the country results equal to distance ab, reflecting the resulting cyclical unemployment.

Unemployment due to cyclical reasons is dealt with using what are called expansionary demand-side policies. Effectively, through these policies the government will attempt to close the deflationary gap. The policies aim at increasing AD. They include interest rate cuts in the hope that households and firms will be convinced to spend more, as well as lower taxes and increased government expenditures.

TIP Even though it sounds counterintuitive, a growing economy may over the long term suffer from higher structural unemployment. This is because the different income elasticities of demand of the different industries and sectors of an economy will change its structure.

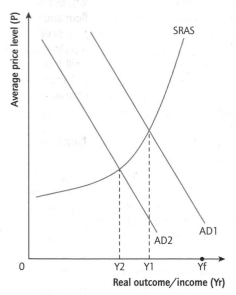

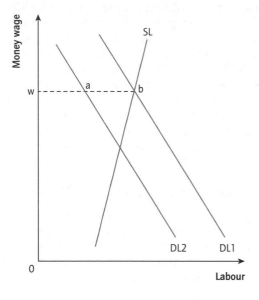

Figure 2.3.2 Illustrating cyclical unemployment

Low and stable rate of inflation

Inflation is defined as a sustained increase of the average level of prices. The inflation rate is the percentage by which the price index has risen between two periods. For example, if annual inflation in India in 2010 was at 10.9% this means that prices in India increased in 2010 compared with 2009 by 10.9%.

Deflation is defined as a sustained decrease in the average price level. It implies a negative rate of inflation. For example, in February 2010 the Japanese inflation rate was −1.2% on a year-on-year basis, meaning that on average prices in February 2010 were lower than in February 2009 by 1.2%.

Disinflation characterizes an economy experiencing a decrease in inflation. The inflation rate remains positive but it is lower than it was in the previous period. In other words, prices

continue to increase but at a slower rate. For example, inflation in India in 2004 was at 3.8% while in 2003 it was at 5.4%. Since inflation in 2004 decreased compared with 2003, this means that there was disinflation in India. Prices continued to rise in 2004 but at a slower rate than in the previous year.

Measuring inflation

The average level of prices is measured through a price index which is a weighted average of the prices that the typical consumer faces expressed as an index number. It is referred to as the consumer (or retail) price index (CPI). Statisticians determine the CPI through surveys of the basket of goods and services that the typical household buys. The average is a weighted average as goods and services are not of equal significance to the typical consumer. The weight for each good is the expenditure on it expressed as a proportion of total expenditures made. The cost of purchasing the basket is recorded and then expressed as an index number. This means that using statistical criteria some year is chosen to be the 'base' (or reference) year and all other years are expressed as a percentage of it. It follows that the price index for the base year will be equal to 100. By expressing a variable as an index number we get rid of its units of measurement which makes comparisons through time easier. If we have constructed the consumer price index for period t and the consumer price index for period (t + 1) then the inflation rate of period (t + 1) is given as the percentage change of these two price indices. Note that a negative percentage change implies deflation.

$$\text{Inflation}\,(t + 1) = \%\,\Delta(\text{CPI}) = \frac{\text{CPI}(t + 1) - \text{CPI}(t)}{\text{CPI}(t)} \times 100$$

Problems of measurement

The typical consumer is a fictitious person. This person is both young and old, lives both in a city and on a farm and is both well off and relatively poor. As a result, it is problematical to use the inflation rate figure to determine, for example, by how much a government should increase pensions, as older people consume more health care and less entertainment than a younger individual. Since the patterns of consumption across different demographic groups differ, the price differences experienced by each group will not be accurately reflected by the national or official inflation rate of the country.

There are also several other measurement problems of a more technical nature. The weights used to construct the average price level are fixed. As a result, the effect on the inflation rate of an increase in the price of a particular good is overestimated. Even though consumers will switch away from it and purchase other cheaper substitutes, its significance (its weight) in the construction of the average will be the same. In this way, the official inflation rate may overestimate true inflation. This is referred to as the substitution bias. New products are not immediately taken into account in the construction of the average price level. It took a few years for the price of mobile phone services to enter the typical basket of goods and services in many countries. This is referred to as the new product bias. Prices from new retail outlets such as online stores (for example Amazon) or mega and discount stores may not be sufficiently sampled. Since these retail outlets usually have lower prices, the official inflation rate may overestimate true inflation. This is referred to as the new retail outlet bias. Improved quality of goods and services may not be properly accounted for in the construction of the average price level. A better version of a product may be 10% more expensive but may last 50% more than the older version, rendering it effectively cheaper. Again, the official inflation rate may overestimate true inflation. This is referred to as the quality bias.

Core (or underlying) inflation

The CPI is affected significantly by changes in (fresh) food prices and energy prices. Spending on food items together with spending on gasoline and heating oil represent a significant chunk of the typical consumer's budget. Food prices, though, are affected by weather and other random factors. For example, a bad season will increase the price of most food products while a good crop will decrease it. Oil prices are affected by decisions made by the Organization of the Petroleum Exporting Countries (OPEC), political developments in countries producing and exporting oil and by speculators. Oil prices may therefore increase and decrease significantly for reasons unrelated to the fundamentals of an economy. This is why what is known as core inflation is estimated and reported. The core or underlying rate of inflation simply excludes food and energy prices from the set of prices comprising the basket of goods that the typical consumer purchases. As a result, swings in food and energy prices that are unrelated to the fundamentals of an economy are isolated, permitting a more accurate interpretation of the workings of an economy.

The producer price index

An alternative price index that has certain advantages over the CPI is the producer price index (PPI). The PPI includes the prices that producers receive for goods (services are not included) at all stages in the production process, including not just finished goods (such as price-scanning devices and tractors) but also semi-finished and intermediate goods (such as flour and steel) as well raw or crude materials (such as coal and crude oil). The main advantage of the PPI over the CPI is that it picks up and signals price changes that the typical consumer will face before those changes actually materialize. In this sense changes in the PPI are considered 'leading indicators' of future consumer inflation rates.

The GDP deflator used as a comprehensive measure of price movements

The GDP deflator (see page 69) measures price changes of all goods and services included in a country's GDP. It is in this sense broader and more useful than the CPI or the PPI for measuring the overall changes in the price level. It includes not only consumer goods and services but also investment goods and services, government goods and services as well as goods and services sold to foreigners. It does not, though, include prices of imported goods and services which do feature in the basket of goods and services that the typical consumer buys, and this is considered a disadvantage. The GDP deflator is typically used to adjust money (or nominal) GDP for price changes.

Consequences of inflation

- Inflation increases uncertainty in business, making it even more difficult for firms to judge and decide whether an investment project will or will not be profitable. This is more so the case if inflation is variable. How fast will wages and production costs rise in the future? How much will it be possible to sell the good for in one, two or three years' time? How fast will prices of substitutes and complements increase? The increased uncertainty means that firms will undertake fewer investments. Slower rates of investment spending will slow down economic growth and so, in the long run, employment rates may decrease.

- Inflation also renders exports less competitive in foreign markets. As a result, the export sector shrinks, making it more difficult to earn the necessary foreign exchange to pay for imports, which will tend to increase as foreign goods will also become more attractive. Trade imbalances will widen. Pressure on the currency to depreciate will be exerted which could further aggravate inflation as imports will become more expensive.

- Households on fixed money incomes (such as wage earners and pensioners) suffer a decline in their purchasing power. Income distribution may worsen.

- If actual inflation proves higher than expected inflation then borrowers will gain at the expense of lenders. The money they will be paying back to lenders will be worth less than expected at the time of the loan.

- Inflation also transfers purchasing power from the people to the government, acting as an additional tax if the tax brackets of a progressive income tax system do not adjust in line with inflation. Assume that someone earns 10% more income with inflation also at 10%. In real terms this individual is not better off but he or she may be moved to a higher tax bracket with a much higher marginal tax rate, so in real terms will pay proportionally more tax than before.

- Inflation, in general, may redistribute national income from the poor to the rich since the former have fewer choices to hedge against inflation and, in addition, they cannot borrow easily. The wealthy have the necessary collateral to borrow from the banking system and proceed to invest in assets (for example land or gold) the value of which is expected to rise faster than inflation. On the other hand, the real value of money deposited in a typical savings account decreases.

- The efficiency of the price mechanism is lost because inflation distorts the signalling and incentive power of relative price changes. A consumer or a firm witnessing the price of good X rising cannot be sure that it truly is becoming relatively more expensive as the person or firm cannot know whether the prices of other similar goods have increased by the same percentage or not. If they have, then the relative price of the good in question has not changed and no substitution process should kick in. With inflation (which is unbalanced, meaning that prices are not all rising at the same rate) this becomes impossible to determine, confusing decisions of consumers and of firms and leading to inefficiency in the allocation of scarce resources. In this sense, inflation is 'noise'.

- Keep in mind that mild inflation reduces the real wage costs of firms, so it may help their competitiveness. This is especially important in a world where money wages do not easily adjust downwards because of contracts and resistance of labour unions.

> **TIP** Remember that the costs of inflation may easily be re-written in an essay as the benefits of price stability.

Consequences of deflation

- The biggest risk of deflation is that the economy may enter a deflationary trap. A vicious circle may start, with deflation creating more deflation.

- Deflation induces consumers to delay purchases since they come to expect further price decreases. As a result, AD decreases even more, pushing even lower the average price level.

- Deflation decreases firms' revenues, squeezing their profit margins and forcing them to cut down on costs. Wages fall and redundancies follow. Some firms are forced to go bankrupt. AD shifts further to the left.

- The real value of outstanding debt increases. Indebted consumers become hesitant to make purchases and indebted firms hesitant to make investments. AD decreases even more and so does the average price level.

- Since the real value of outstanding debt increases, some households and some firms cannot service their loans. Banks accumulate 'bad' loans (loans that are not repaid), so the risk of a banking crisis with repercussions on the real economy increases.

- As AD falls it is not only the average price level that falls but also real output, leading to higher unemployment.

- Easy monetary policy is a policy used by a central bank to stimulate economic growth by lowering interest rates but, when there is deflation, the central bank cannot use this policy to reflate the economy as (nominal) interest rates cannot decrease below zero. Expansionary fiscal policy may also prove ineffective as households may prefer to save and postpone spending. Even 'sitting on' cash earns a real rate of return, meaning that with falling prices it will buy more in the future.

- However, exports become more competitive abroad and AD may increase as a result of a rise in net exports.

Types and causes of inflation and of deflation

Through the AD/AS diagram it should be clearly realized that any factor that persistently increases AD or leads to an adverse shift in AS may lead to an increasing price level (that is, to inflation). The former is known as demand-pull inflation and the latter as cost-push inflation, even though once an inflationary process begins it is difficult in practice to distinguish between the two.

Demand-pull inflation
In the case of demand-pull inflation the extent of the inflationary effect resulting from the increase in AD depends on how steep the AS curve is, in other words on how close to the full employment or potential level of real output the economy is operating. The closer to the potential level of real output (that is, the steeper AS is) the greater the effect on the average price level of AD increasing.

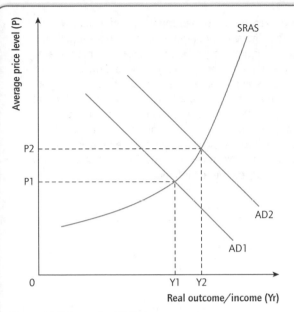

Figure 2.3.3 Demand-pull inflation

In Figure 2.3.3 demand-pull inflation is illustrated, employing a generic SRAS curve. Keep in mind that, in the long run, any increase in AD is purely inflationary as the LRAS curve is vertical at the potential level of output. Within the monetarist or new classical model any increase in real output and corresponding decrease in unemployment will be short lived since money wages will adjust. Within the vertical section of a typical Keynesian-style AS curve an increase of AD will also prove purely inflationary. In the Keynesian model an increase in AD may not prove inflationary if the economy is in a deep recession and is operating on the horizontal section of the AS curve.

Causes of demand-pull inflation

An increase in any component of AD may prove responsible for demand-pull inflation. Demand-pull inflationary pressure may originate from a rapid increase in consumption and investment expenditures caused by excessively optimistic and confident households and firms. Surging exports may also exert upward pressure on prices. Export growth may accelerate, as a result of an undervalued or depreciating currency or faster growth abroad.

Most often, governments are responsible for demand-pull inflation. Profligate government spending and poorly designed tax-cuts, especially before elections, may increase AD too fast and create inflation.

Inflationary expectations themselves are a common cause of continuing inflation. If prices are expected to continue climbing then firms and workers with pricing power will increase their prices and wages to keep ahead of the game, adding to the inflationary spiral.

Perhaps the single most important cause of inflation is excessive monetary growth. The easiest way to understand this is by quoting Milton Friedman's famous saying that inflation exists when 'too much money chases after too few goods' and so inflation is a purely monetary phenomenon. If the money supply increases faster than output then part of the resulting increased spending will manifest itself in the form of rising prices.

TIP Remember that increases in AD will affect not only the average price level but also real output. A rise in real output and in employment may accompany demand-pull inflation.

Cost-push inflation

Figure 2.3.4 illustrates cost-push inflation as the average price level is shown to increase from P1 to P2 following a shift to the left of AS (an adverse supply shock) from AS1 to AS2.

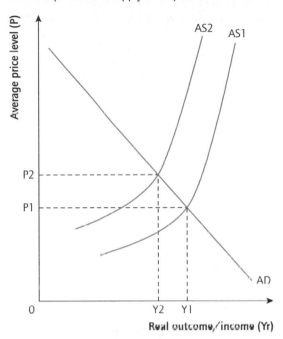

Figure 2.3.4 Cost-push inflation

Causes of cost-push inflation

Any factor that is responsible for a decrease in AS and a shift of the AS curve to the left may lead to cost-push inflation. Perhaps the most common cause of cost-push inflation is a rise in the price of oil. Oil is still the predominant form of energy for firms so a sustained and sharp increase in its price will increase production costs across the board and so increase prices. More generally, rising commodity prices can create cost-push pressure as commodities are products used as inputs in manufacturing.

Powerful labour unions may also create cost-push pressure as they may be in a position to achieve for their members money wage increases higher than any productivity gains. Effectively, this increases production costs for firms and so increases prices.

A devaluation (or a sharp depreciation) of the currency renders import prices higher. The average price level will automatically increase as the typical basket of goods and services consumed includes imported products. This may lead workers to demand higher wages, initiating a wage-price spiral. Also, if domestic firms rely for their production process on imported raw materials and intermediate products then production costs will increase, with the same effect on prices.

An increase in indirect taxation will increase production costs and so increase prices. This would be a one-off increase in the average price level so it would hardly qualify as a cause of inflation (a **sustained** increase in prices) unless it led to demands for higher wages and an inflationary spiral began. ▸▸

Lastly, a productivity slow-down may initiate cost-push inflation as production costs would increase. Such a development would typically require some unfavourable institutional change.

> **TIP** Stagnant GDP or even falling GDP will accompany cost-push inflation.

Causes of deflation
Figure 2.3.5 illustrates a case of deflation since the average price level is shown to decrease from P1 to P2 as a result of decreasing AD from AD1 to AD2.

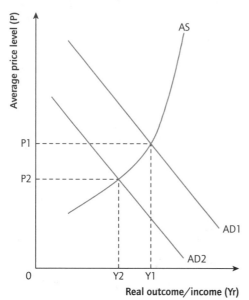

Figure 2.3.5 Deflation

Deflation can be caused by continuing decrease in AD, often the result of a significant domestic crisis, such as a banking crisis or a crisis related to government debt. Typically, interest rates have already been driven down to zero as a result of unsuccessful attempts by the central bank to increase private spending and the government has little room to spend more and boost AD.

Deflation may also result from AD rising slower than originally expected. Optimistic firms may have overinvested in new capacity, leading to a large shift to the right of AS. If AD fails to rise as fast then a decreasing average price level may result.

Policies to deal with demand-pull inflation
In the case of demand-pull inflation, policy makers must attempt to decrease (or, more correctly, slow down the increase) of AD in the economy. Spending in the economy must be restrained. It follows that the government may decrease its own expenditures (fiscal restraint). Government expenditures are a component of AD, so if they decrease then AD will also decrease. Taxation may also increase as higher direct taxes will decrease disposable income and so consumption expenditures. The policy mix of decreasing government expenditures and increasing taxation is referred to as contractionary or deflationary fiscal policy and will be evaluated later.

Policy makers could try to restrain private spending (consumption expenditures by households and investment expenditures by firms) through an increase in interest rates.

Interest rates are set by the central bank of a country and changes of interest rates (and/or of the money supply) are referred to as monetary policy. An increase in interest rates (known as tight monetary policy) makes borrowing from banks more expensive for households and businesses. It also makes saving more attractive and it leaves families with adjustable mortgage loans with less to spend every month as their monthly bank installment to pay off their mortgage will be higher. The bottom line is that private spending is expected to decrease (or to slow down). Figure 2.3.6 illustrates the effect of contractionary policies on inflation.

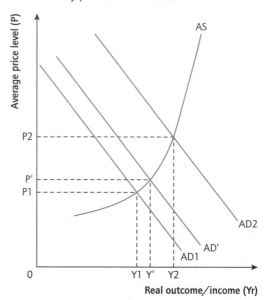

Figure 2.3.6 Dealing with demand-pull inflation

Given AD1 and AS the average price level is at P1. As a result of demand-pull inflation, AD would increase from AD1 to AD2 and the price level all the way to P2. If contractionary fiscal and/or tight monetary policies are adopted then the hope is that AD will not increase as fast all the way from AD1 to AD2 but would increase only to AD'. The price level will rise but not as much. Inflation will be lower.

Note though that whereas real output would rise to Y2 it will now, as a result of the contractionary policies employed, rise only to Y'. Output will increase but not as fast, so the cost of decreasing inflation is slower economic growth, even recession.

Policies to deal with cost-push inflation
The policy response is less obvious in the case of cost-push inflation. It may seem that policies that aim at increasing AS (supply-side policies) are in order but these policies are difficult to adopt and implement and take a long time to have any effects. For example, policy makers may try to decrease the power of labour unions or they may initiate policies that aim at making product markets more competitive. There is no doubt that appropriate supply-side policies are always helpful to contain inflation since by shifting AS to the right any increase in AD will be absorbed without the average price level rising. Non-inflationary growth will therefore be achieved.

Because of the difficulties related to policy initiatives that try to increase AS even if inflation is cost-push inflation, it is contractionary demand management policies that are employed by policy makers. The typical immediate real-world response to any inflationary pressures emerging in an economy is for policy makers to tighten monetary policy (that is, to increase interest rates, making borrowing more costly).

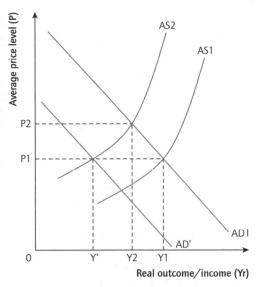

Figure 2.3.7 Dealing with cost-push inflation

Figure 2.3.7 illustrates the situation. Initially, AD and AS are such that real output is at Y1 and the average price level at P1. Assume an adverse supply shock (for example a lasting rise in oil prices) shifting AS from AS1 to AS2 and leading to a higher price level P2. Cost-push inflation is even more costly than demand-pull inflation as real output decreases from Y1 to Y2 and unemployment rises.

Policy makers respond by increasing interest rates (tight monetary policy) in an attempt to keep the average price level at P1. If the policy is successful and the increased borrowing costs lead to a decrease in spending by households and firms then AD will decrease and shift left from AD1 to AD', maintaining the price level stable at P1. Inflation will have been eliminated. Note though that the negative effect on economic activity (that is, on real output) will be more severe. This will further decrease to Y' and unemployment will increase even more. Often, this is considered a short-run cost worth suffering as the resulting price stability helps accelerate economic growth and, consequently, employment generation in the long run.

> **TIP** Increased exposure to international competition also exerts a dampening effect on inflation. Not only are domestic firms forced to become more efficient and lower their prices but also they may benefit from cheaper sources of supply.

How to deal with deflation

Deflation is a difficult problem to deal with. Japan, a major advanced economy, has suffered the consequences of deflation for many years. Deflation creates a vicious circle of decreasing prices leading to decreasing AD, leading in turn to decreasing prices that is extremely difficult to break (a deflationary trap). Monetary policy is ineffective and fiscal policy is weakened. Somehow policy makers have to convince the public that inflation should be expected. Governments have resorted to printing dated vouchers to force recipients to spend them and not save them. Deflation is often corrected through the increase in AD that results from cheaper exports.

The Phillips Curve

The original Phillips Curve

Since the early 1960s and until the mid-1970s economists relied on an empirical result that Alban W. Phillips, a New Zealand economist at the London School of Economics, made in 1958. His work, the Phillips curve, became one of the most famous relationships in macroeconomics. It showed that there was a stable trade-off between the inflation rate and the unemployment rate of an economy.

His original empirical (statistical) work examined UK data on the annual percentage change in money wages and the annual unemployment rate over a period of 96 years (from 1861 to 1957). The left-hand side of Figure 2.3.8 shows what he found: that the percentage change in money wages and the unemployment were inversely related. If unemployment was low (referred to as a 'tight' labour market) then money wages rose a lot as employers were forced to bid up wages to find employees, In contrast, if unemployment was high (a 'slack' labour market), then money wages increased by just a little, or even decreased, as firms could hire workers without having to offer more or even by offering less than last year's prevailing money wage.

Moving from wage inflation to price inflation was the next step. Since wages typically form a big proportion of production costs and since firms in the real world often set prices as a percentage of their unit costs (mark-up pricing) it seemed sensible to explore how the annual inflation and unemployment rate were related. The right-hand side of Figure 2.3.8 illustrates what was found by many empirical studies in the 1960s. Inflation and unemployment were inversely related. If unemployment decreased then inflation increased, while if inflation decreased unemployment would increase. The negatively sloped curve on the right-hand side of Figure 2.3.8 is the original Phillips curve.

If this inverse relationship was stable then governments could perhaps exploit it. The Phillips curve was considered as presenting policy makers with a 'menu of choices'. They could achieve a lower unemployment rate but at the cost of higher inflation, or they could achieve lower inflation but at the cost of higher unemployment. The issue was to determine the politically desired combination of the two variables and then through demand-side policies policy makers could achieve it.

This statistically determined relationship was compatible with the ruling Keynesian theory. Remember that the Keynesian perspective stressed the importance of AD in the determination of equilibrium income. If AD increased then real output would increase and so unemployment would decrease. But this rise in AD would also lead to inflationary pressures. So, as shown on the right-hand side of Figure 2.3.8, if policy makers were to succeed in reducing unemployment from U1 to U2 then inflation would increase from $\pi 1$ to $\pi 2$.

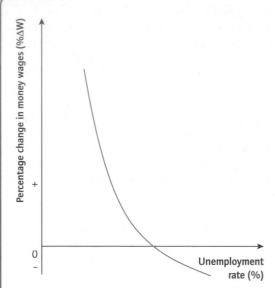

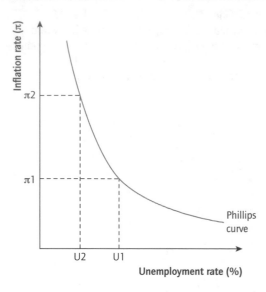

Figure 2.3.8 The original Phillips curve

The breakdown of the Phillips curve

Since the late 1960s the original Phillips curve relationship suffered both empirical and theoretical setbacks. Inflation and unemployment were both increasing in the 1970s in the USA and in other advanced economies. The term 'stagflation' was coined, implying recession together with rising inflation. The original inverse relationship had collapsed and traditional Keynesian analysis, relying on the importance of shifts in AD to explain movements in output and prices, found it hard to explain what was going on. Stagflation implied higher inflation and higher unemployment and this suggested that the Phillips curve was not stable but shifted out and to the right, as illustrated in Figure 2.3.9.

In Figure 2.3.9 the Phillips curve is shifting outwards through time. Point A2 on Phillips curve PC2 illustrates a both a higher rate of unemployment and a higher rate of inflation compared with Phillips curve PC1 and point A1.

How could this happen? One explanation was that AS had shifted left in the 1970s. The oil price shocks at this time increased production costs of firms across the board. Back then the US economy relied much more on manufacturing than it does these days. The price shocks shifted AS on the left-hand side diagram of Figure 2.3.10 from AS1 to AS2. Equilibrium has shifted from point

A1 to point A2 which is characterized by rising prices and by lower real output and higher unemployment as the same point illustrated on the right-hand side diagram of Figure 2.3.10. The adverse supply shock resulted in stagflation and analytically this is shown with a shift to the right of the Phillips curve.

But beyond this empirical refutation of the original Phillips curve there came a theoretical attack. Milton Friedman and Ed Phelps (both Nobel Laureates; 1976 and 2006 respectively) independently made a distinction between a short-run Phillips curve (SRPC) and a long-run Phillips curve (LRPC) and claimed that in the long run the Phillips curve was vertical at the equilibrium rate of unemployment (the natural rate introduced earlier which corresponds to the potential level of real output of an economy where the LRAS is vertical). Therefore, they claimed, any trade-off between inflation and unemployment could exist only in the short run. This became known as the Phelps–Friedman critique and the theory as the expectations-augmented Phillips curve.

If a government tried to lower unemployment below its natural or equilibrium rate using expansionary policies (that is, by increasing AD) it would succeed only **temporarily** and at the cost of permanently higher inflation. The short run trade-off between inflation and unemployment was only because workers suffer

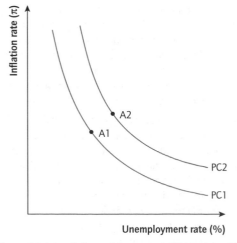

Figure 2.3.9 Stagflation and the outward shifting of the Phillips curve

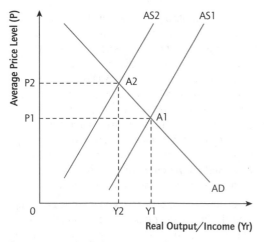

Figure 2.3.10 Stagflation as a result of adverse supply shocks

from 'money illusion': they form their expectations about inflation **adaptively** (meaning that they form their expectations about next year's inflation by looking at **past** inflation rates) so they are **slow** to realize that inflation accelerates and does not remain the same as a result of the expansionary policies pursued.

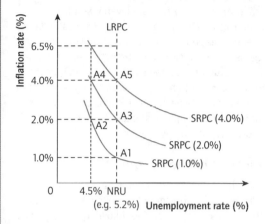

Figure 2.3.11 The LRPC
(The expectations-augmented Phillips curve or the Phelps–Friedman critique)

In Figure 2.3.11 it is assumed that the natural rate of unemployment (NRU) is at 5.2% and that the economy has been experiencing inflation equal to 1.0% for some time now so that workers again expect 1.0% inflation next year (point A1). Assume now that the government adopts expansionary policies to try to lower unemployment to 4.5% below the equilibrium (natural) level. It is essentially trying to expand output beyond its potential level. As a result of the higher AD, inflation accelerates to 2.0%. The real wage rate decreases and firms hire more workers. We are moving along the economy's SRAS curve where the average price level is higher and real output greater. Unemployment decreases to 4.5%

and the economy has moved to point A2 on the figure. Workers are slow to realize that inflation is actually higher than previously at 2.0%, so the real wage is lower. But when their expectations adjust they will demand higher money wages, increasing the real wage for firms back to its original equilibrium level. The SRAS curve of the economy will have decreased and shifted to the left. Firms will fire workers so unemployment returns to its natural rate at 5.2% (point A3) and real output to its potential level Yp.

If the government insisted on trying to decrease unemployment below its natural rate using expansionary demand-side policies it would need to 'engineer' higher and higher inflation rates so that workers would be temporarily fooled and accept job offers. In Figure 2.3.11, inflation would have to accelerate to 4.0% for unemployment to drop below the natural rate again and for the economy to move to point A4 before adjusting back to A5, while workers would expect inflation still to be at 2.0%.

The policy implication predominantly associated with the monetarist or new classical school is clear: governments should not try to lower unemployment below its natural rate using expansionary demand-side policies because it is futile. Any decrease in unemployment will be temporary and at the cost of higher inflation. Equivalently, in terms of real output, the implication is that it is futile to try to expand real output beyond its potential level by employing expansionary demand-side policies as any increase will be short lived and will in the long run prove purely inflationary. In the long run, when expectations have adjusted and there is no money illusion, there is no trade-off between inflation and unemployment. There is only one rate of unemployment and it is compatible with any rate of inflation as long as this rate of inflation does not accelerate. In the long run the Phillips curve is vertical at the NRU which is also known for this reason as the non-accelerating inflation rate of unemployment.

Economic growth

Economic growth exists if a country's real GDP increases through time. It can be illustrated in several ways. In Figure 2.3.12 economic growth is depicted by the movement towards the northeast from point A to point B (closer to the frontier within a country's production possibilities curve or PPC) as this movement illustrates an increase in the economy's actual output.

Point B reflects production of more of good X and more of good Y compared to point A (as X2 > X1 and Y2 > Y1). This increase in actual output (real GDP) represents economic growth. It can be a result of lower unemployment in the country and, more generally, better (more efficient) use of existing resources.

Lower unemployment does not imply in this set-up more labour becoming available but that, given the existing amount of labour, fewer individuals remain unemployed. If you think about it, strictly speaking, you could have a movement from point A to point B

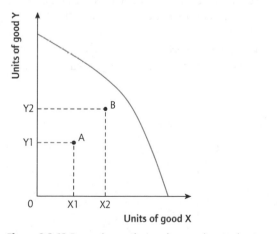

Figure 2.3.12 Economic growth as an increase in actual output

with the unemployment rate remaining the same if the number of unemployed increases at the same rate as the labour force. In this case, though, there would also be a shift of the curve outwards.

Economic growth can also be illustrated through an outwards shift of the PPC, as illustrated in Figure 2.3.13.

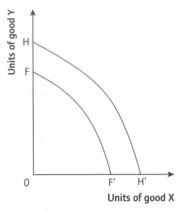

Figure 2.3.13 Economic growth as an increase in the production possibilities of a country

The production possibilities of this economy have expanded and the PPC has shifted from FF' to HH'. Remembering that each point in this space represents a specific combination of output it should be clear that this economy is now in a position to produce and enjoy combinations of good X and of good Y that were previously unattainable. If we recall the assumptions made to construct the PPC it should be clear that such a shift is possible if the quantity or quality of available resources increases or improves and/or if the available technology advances.

An alternative visualization of economic growth employs the concept of the LRAS curve with the economy's potential output increasing. It would not be technically correct, though, to consider the level of potential output as being the same with any point on a PPC: the former is not a technological but an economic concept; the latter are purely technological as they are defined solely on the basis of what the technological capabilities of an economy are with some specific set of resources and technology.

Figure 2.3.14 illustrates an economy which experiences a shift to the right of its LRAS and a corresponding increase in its level of potential output.

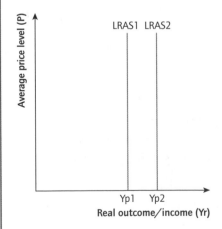

Figure 2.3.14 Economic growth as an increase in potential output and a shift to the right of the LRAS

Potential output has increased from Yp1 to Yp2, shifting the economy's LRAS curve from LRAS1 to LRAS2. The factors that could be responsible for such developments include all the factors that could shift a PPC outwards but, in addition, any factor that may decrease the natural rate of unemployment.

In the long run, economic growth is achieved when the economy experiences improved labour productivity as improved productivity means great output per unit worker. For such productivity gains to be achieved, investments in natural capital, physical capital and human capital are prerequisites. Improvements in the institutional framework should also not be overlooked. These are the same factors responsible for a shift outwards of the PPC. The single most important driving force in productivity growth is technology though.

Consequences of economic growth

Economic growth has many benefits and this may explain why it is considered the single most important macroeconomic goal, but it may also entail serious costs. The following consequences of economic growth are significant.

■ Economic growth has an effect on living standards. It allows more output to be enjoyed per person, assuming of course that the economic growth is greater than population growth. If output per person increases then increased levels of consumption of goods and services are possible. Assuming a direct relationship between welfare and consumption it follows that growth may improve living standards. Economic growth is considered a prerequisite for poverty reduction.

■ A growing economy will affect unemployment. Economic growth is typically, but not necessarily positively, correlated with employment creation. Usually, in a growing economy more jobs are created and unemployment decreases. Successful policies that accelerate growth also decrease unemployment so that a second macroeconomic objective is achieved. It is possible, though, for a country to experience 'jobless growth'. This could be the case if growth is achieved using inappropriate technologies, which in the case of developing countries means that they do not rely on labour, the relatively abundant factor of production. Also, growth may not lead to a reduction of unemployment if it is not fast enough so that the net increase in the labour force exceeds the jobs that are created.

■ A growing economy affects inflation. Economic growth can both alleviate and create inflationary pressures. If the growth in the productive capacity of the economy is not faster than the growth in demand that rising income levels create then the economy may overheat. This will mean that prices (the average level of prices) will start rising. Whether economic growth is responsible for (demand-pull) inflation depends on how fast AD rises compared to LRAS. In addition, if the growth process puts pressure on input prices (wages for labour, raw material prices, etc.) it may also initiate a cost-push inflationary spiral. The flip side of this is that if the growth process increases LRAS at least as fast as AD increases then the economy will be able to enjoy non-inflationary growth.

■ Economic growth has consequences for government finances (the 'fiscal dividend'). A growing economy implies higher incomes and more spending. Tax revenues from both direct and indirect taxation will therefore automatically increase (that is, without the government imposing any new taxes). More money flowing into the government's coffers permits financing of more government projects, not only without the government resorting to higher taxation but also without it incurring any additional borrowing costs.

- Economic growth can both improve and worsen income distribution. It can alleviate income inequality as it permits government a redistribution of income from the wealthy to the poor. Redistribution can be direct by permitting the establishment of a social welfare net such as pensions and unemployment benefits or permitting an increase in such benefits. It can also be indirect through spending on poverty alleviation programmes (to increase agricultural productivity; to improve sanitation; to improve basic infrastructure, etc.) as well as on improved health and education facilities that increase human capital and labour productivity. Unfortunately, economic growth often leads to higher income inequality. There is no guarantee that he benefits of growth will be fairly distributed. If growth is driven by only a handful of industries; if it is concentrated in certain regions; if it relies only on certain skills or if it is 'jobless' then many may be left out and income inequality in the country may widen.

- Economic growth affects trade. If the growth is export driven (that is, if it is a result of growing exports as in the case of China) then it will decrease any trade deficit or lead to a trade surplus. If, though, it is driven by domestic demand then the resulting higher income levels may be responsible for a widening trade deficit as part of the higher incomes will be spent on imports.

- There are also consequences for sustainability: the effect of economic growth on the environment may entail certain benefits but it also creates very significant costs. The possible benefits can best be understood through the so-called environmental Kuznets curve (associated with Gene Grossman) which shows that there is an inverted U-shaped relationship (that is, a 'hump-shaped' curve) between certain environmental costs (such as water pollution, air pollution and deforestation) and per capita income levels of countries. The basic idea is that as per capita incomes increase, pollution increases, but some threshold level of income exists. Beyond this threshold, not only is there significantly increased demand for a cleaner environment by the population, but there are also more resources available to expend on cleaner technologies. The issue here is that output growth not only requires the use of more natural resources but also leads to more emissions and wastes that may exceed the earth's 'carrying capacity', rendering growth unsustainable. The environmental Kuznets curve provides an optimistic view in the sense that it claims that economic growth does not 'unavoidably harm the natural habitat' but it is strongly criticized in many respects. First, it may empirically hold for local externalities (that is, for indoor household pollution which does decrease after some relatively low per capita income level) but it does not seem to hold for many dispersed externalities such as carbon emissions. Also, different pollutants behave differently across countries and across income levels. In addition, with global pollution levels still rising, wealthier countries may choose not to produce but to import pollution-intensive goods. In general, the effect of economic growth on the environment is a function of the scale of production, the composition of production (whether changing tastes lead to the production of fewer pollution-intensive goods) and the techniques of production (whether less pollution-intensive technologies are employed).

Equity in the distribution of income

The fourth macroeconomic goal is to ensure that income distribution is equitable. Equitable does not mean equal. It means fair. But fairness is an elusive concept and it means different things to different people. Unequal ownership of factors of production may be responsible for income inequality as well as a distorted institutional framework that is tilted in favour of certain social groups and grants them exclusive privileges and preferences.

Indicators of income inequality

Inequality ratios
Income inequality can be described using inequality ratios. These examine the ratio of (disposable) income of the top 10% (decile) over the bottom 10% of the population (also known as the 'interdecile P90 to P10 income ratio') or of the top 20% (quintile) over the bottom 20% (quintile). Income inequality ratios in the world of the highest to the lowest decile range can range between roughly 5 to 40: the top 10% may earn 5 to 40 times more than the bottom 10% of the population. In Denmark the figure in the mid-2000s was the lowest at 2.72.

Income inequality can also be described through the Lorenz curve and its degree can be measured through the Gini coefficient.

The Lorenz curve and the Gini coefficient
In Figure 2.3.15 population (income recipients) is plotted on the horizontal axis in **cumulative** percentages (that is, from poorest to richest households). So at, say, the 20% point, we have the poorest 20% of the population and at the 40% point, we have the poorest 40% of the population. On the vertical axis we measure the percentage of income received by each percentage of the population.

The Lorenz curve shows the proportion of national income earned by each income group. For example, the poorest 20% of people in Figure 2.3.15 receive only 5% of national income. Note that 100% of the population will of course receive 100% of national income. Also note that the diagonal is the line of equality (perfectly equal income distribution).

The further away from the diagonal, the more unequal the distribution of income is. The closer to the diagonal, the more equal the distribution of income is. If income distribution worsens in a country it means that the Lorenz curve moves further away from the diagonal.

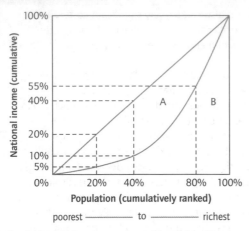

Figure 2.3.15 The Lorenz curve and the Gini coefficient

The Gini coefficient measures the degree of income inequality in a population. It is the ratio of the area between the Lorenz curve and the diagonal over the area of the half square in which the curve lies. The Gini coefficient is the ratio of the area between the Lorenz curve and the diagonal over the area of the half-square or, focusing on Figure 2.3.15, area (A) divided by area (A+B):

$$\text{Gini coefficient} = \frac{\text{area (A)}}{\text{area (A + B)}}$$

The Gini coefficient can vary from 0 (denoting perfect equality: each person gets the same income) to 1 (denoting perfect inequality: all income goes to the share of the population with the highest income).

Range of values of Gini: (0,1)

Typically, highly unequal income distributions are distributions with a Gini coefficient between 0.50 and 0.70. Some representative values of this coefficient are: Brazil 0.57, Zimbabwe 0.50, Argentina 0.49, Uganda 0.46, the USA 0.38, the UK 0.34, Australia 0.30, Austria 0.27, and Denmark and Sweden at 0.23. The Organisation for Economic Co-operation and Development (OECD) average in the mid-2000s was around 0.31.

Keep in mind that often what matters most is not the level of income distribution but the direction of change (that is, whether income distribution is becoming more or less unequal).

Poverty

Absolute poverty is defined by the minimum income necessary to satisfy basic physical needs; the 2008 World Bank international poverty line is set $1.25 (purchasing power parity – PPP) per day.

Relative poverty measures the extent to which a household's income falls below the national average.

Causes and consequences of poverty
Poverty locks individuals into a vicious poverty cycle or trap. Low income is both a cause and a consequence of poverty. As a result of their low income, these individuals' human capital is very low. They cannot afford the opportunity cost of schooling. Their savings are non-existent, so they are not in a position to invest in physical capital and (in developing countries) they are forced in their effort to survive to deplete or destroy any natural capital they may have access to. Low human, physical and natural capital implies low productivity, which in turn leads to low income, closing the cycle.

Possible benefits and costs of a more equitable income distribution

A more equitable distribution may help accelerate growth and promote human and economic development in many ways.

- The very poor will be able to afford access to crucial resources, such as education and medical care, so the amount and quality of productive resources available to a country increases. Better education and health improves labour as productivity will be higher.

- The propensity of the poor to consume is higher than that of the rich so redistribution will increase AD, especially for basic goods and services.

- Social tensions will be lower, so governments can more easily undertake important economic reforms requiring a high degree of consensus within the population. If people feel that they enjoy the fruits of economic growth then they will be willing to work harder and sacrifice more now in order for them or their children to enjoy more at a later date. They will be willing and able to save more, allowing higher rates of investment and so growth. Fewer social tensions decrease uncertainty and risks for domestic and foreign investors.

- Trust increases among the population so the cost of economic transactions decreases. More economic activity will take place so growth will accelerate.

On the other hand, consider the following.

- An excessively equal income distribution could lower economic efficiency. It could lower the incentives for people to work hard and for risk taking. In this way, growth may be undermined.

The role of taxation in promoting equity

Direct and indirect taxes

Direct taxes are taxes on income, on profits and on wealth. The characteristic of a direct tax is that its burden cannot be shifted onto another entity. Indirect taxes include taxes on goods and on expenditures and they have been discussed earlier. The burden of an indirect tax can be shifted onto a different entity.

Progressive, proportional and regressive taxation

To explain the difference between these types of taxes it is important to define the marginal tax rate (MTR) and the average tax rate (ATR).

The MTR is the percentage taken by the government on the last dollar earned, or the extra tax paid as a result of extra income earned.

The ATR is the ratio of the tax collected over income earned or, more generally, the ratio of the tax collected over the tax base. The tax base refers to whatever is taxed, for example income, spending, profits and wealth.

MTR	ATR
$MTR = \dfrac{\Delta T}{\Delta Y}$	$ATR = \dfrac{T}{Y}$

A **progressive** tax system is one in which individuals with higher incomes pay proportionately more so the ATR rises as income rises. In a progressive income tax system the MTR is greater than the ATR. (Remember that if the average increases it follows that the marginal is greater than the average.)

A **proportional** tax system is one in which all individuals pay the same proportion of their income independently of the level of their income. In a proportional tax system the ATR remains constant as income rises so the MTR is equal to the ATR. A flat rate (proportional) income tax exists in several countries, such as Latvia, Russia, and Estonia, and is being considered by many others. It presents many advantages to the progressive income tax systems that most countries have. Disincentives are lower, administrative costs are lower, the system is simple and more transparent and it is potentially even fairer, as loopholes do not exist which usually higher-income households take advantage of.

A **regressive** tax system is one in which poorer individuals pay a greater proportion of their income. In a regressive tax system the ATR decreases as income rises so the MTR is less than the ATR. Indirect taxes are proportional with respect to expenditure but regressive with respect to income. This is why indirect taxation on food and basic goods is lower than in other systems, or set at zero.

In Figure 2.3.16 the horizontal axis measures the tax base (say, income) and the vertical the amount of tax paid. A proportional tax system is illustrated by any straight line through the origin. In a progressive tax system the slope of the line is increasing while in a regressive tax system the slope of the line is decreasing.

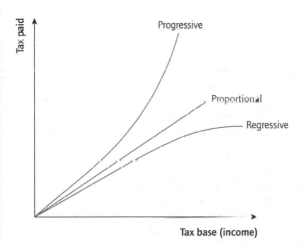

Figure 2.3.16 Progressive, proportional and regressive taxation

Measures to promote equity

Short-run solutions

Usually governments resort to a mixture of progressive income taxes coupled with a system of transfer payments. Transfer payments include pensions, unemployment benefits, disability benefits, child allowances and subsidies. By taxing households with higher incomes more heavily than those with lower incomes and spending more on transfer payments, national income may be redistributed in an attempt to satisfy the equity goal. Social health insurance and a system of public education is usually part of a package that aims at effectively increasing the income of the lower-income strata.

Long-run solutions

In the long run, the most effective route to a more equitable income distribution is by improving the quality and access to education and health-care services for the most deprived income groups. Schools, health-care centres, improved infrastructure that includes better roads, as well as sanitation and clean water supplies will all contribute to an increase in human capital. A healthier population with better education, training and skills will increase labour productivity and lead to higher incomes. The importance of a fair judicial system, better institutions in general and lower corruption should not be underestimated.

Progressive tax	Proportional tax	Regressive tax
A tax is progressive:	A tax is proportional:	A tax is regressive:
if the ATR ↑	if the ATR constant	if the ATR ↓
that is, MTR > ATR	that is, MTR = ATR	that is, MTR < ATR
which means that higher income individuals pay proportionately more,	which means that higher income individuals pay proportionately the same,	which means that higher income individuals pay proportionately less,
or, more generally, that tax paid rises faster than the tax base.	or, more generally, that tax paid rises as fast as the tax base.	or, more generally, that tax paid rises slower than the tax base.

2.4 Fiscal policy

Fiscal policy is a demand-side policy. Demand-side policies attempt to increase or decrease AD (or, more precisely, to slow down the increase of AD) in order to affect real output (growth), employment and the inflation. Later we will see that these same policies are also used to correct a trade imbalance and are referred to as expenditure-changing policies.

Fiscal policy refers to the manipulation of the level of government expenditures (G) and/or government revenues (T) in order to influence AD and, through this, economic variables such as real output and growth, employment and inflation.

The government budget

Sources of revenue and types of expenditures

Governments typically earn most revenues from direct and indirect taxation. They may earn also revenues from the sale of goods and services (for example, revenues from the sale and export of oil are a major source of government revenues for countries producing and exporting oil). The proceeds from the sale of government-owned assets, such as state-owned enterprises that are then privatized or government land, are also one-off revenues.

Spending is classified into current spending, capital expenditures and transfer payments. Current expenditures include wages and salaries of public sector employees as well as spending on consumables (day-to-day items) such as stationery. Capital expenditures refer to public investment spending. These expenditures include all spending on infrastructure, for example spending on the construction of roads, harbours, hospitals and schools. Transfer payments represent transfers of money from one group to another and as such are not included in the calculation of GDP but are part of income redistribution policies. Transfer payments include social security (welfare) expenditures, for example pensions, unemployment benefits, disability payments and scholarship grants.

The budget outcome

The relationship between the size of government expenditures and government income (tax revenues) determines whether there is a budget deficit, a budget surplus or a balanced budget. Here are specific definitions.

- A budget deficit exists if government expenditures (G) exceed government revenues or income (T).

- A budget surplus exists if government revenues or income (T) exceed government expenditures (G).

- A balanced budget exists if government expenditures (G) are equal to government revenues or income (T).

The public (national or government) debt

Assume the formation of a new country in, say, 2006. Assume that its government in 2006 had spent 150 million of its own dollar currency and had collected 120 million dollars. It incurred a budget deficit equal to 30 million dollars. Assume now that in 2007 it had spent 180 million dollars and had collected in tax and other revenues 170 million dollars. In 2007 it recorded a budget deficit equal to 10 million dollars. Its public debt is at 40 million dollars. If in 2008 it spent 210 million dollars and collected in tax and other revenues 215 million dollars, it recorded in 2008 a budget surplus of 5 million dollars. Its public debt will now stand at 35 million dollars. The public debt is defined as the 'the cumulative total of all government borrowings less repayments' or the sum of all money owed by a government at a point in time. Budget deficits or surpluses and the public debt are therefore not the same but they are linked, as the public debt grows when the government runs a budget deficit and shrinks when it runs a budget surplus.

> **TIP** The public (national or government) debt should not be confused with a country's external debt. The external debt refers to what a country (public and private sector) owes to foreigners and is denominated in foreign exchange.

If:	then:	and:
G > T	a budget deficit is recorded	the national debt grows
T > G	a budget surplus is recorded	the national debt shrinks
G = T	the budget is balanced	the national debt is unchanged

Expansionary and contractionary fiscal policy

Expansionary (or reflationary) fiscal policy

Keynes introduced the idea that the (equilibrium) level of output was demand-driven. The level of AD (effective demand) determines the level of overall economic activity. There was no guarantee, according to this school of thought, that equilibrium output and full employment output will coincide. There could very well be a deflationary (or recessionary) gap. AD could be insufficient if, for whatever reason, the private sector (households and firms) decided to hold back on their spending. A recession could result. So, through this, Keynes introduced the idea of expansionary fiscal policy.

Expansionary (or, reflationary) fiscal policy aims at increasing AD in order to increase national income (real output) and employment and so close a deflationary gap.

It requires an increase in government spending (G) and/or a decrease in taxation (T). Since government spending is a component of AD, a rise in G will directly increase AD, shifting it to the right. In other words, if private spending (C + I) is not sufficient to generate full employment, then the government should increase its spending (G) by borrowing from the private sector (deficit spending: G >T). A decrease in taxation (T) will indirectly also increase AD as it will increase disposable income that people have (defined as income minus direct taxes) and will induce more spending. If through an increase in government expenditures and/or a decrease in taxes, AD increases (that is, shifts to the right) then a deflationary (or recessionary) gap can be closed, as Figure 2.4.1 illustrates.

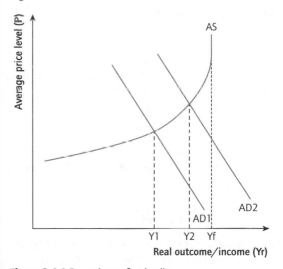

Figure 2.4.1 Expansionary fiscal policy

Assume an economy in equilibrium at real output level Y1. Given that the full employment (or potential) level of output is at Yf, there is a deflationary (or recessionary) gap equal to distance Y1Yf. Let's say the government decides to employ expansionary fiscal policy in an attempt to close this gap. The increase in government expenditures (G) and the decrease in taxes (T) will increase AD (as explained above), in this case, say, from AD1 to AD2. The new equilibrium level of real output is at Y2, which is closer to the full employment level Yf. It should be realized though that the opportunity cost of such a policy is the risk of accelerating

inflation. In Figure 2.4.2 this risk is shown to depend crucially on the shape of the AS curve and, more precisely, on how close or far from full employment the economy is operating.

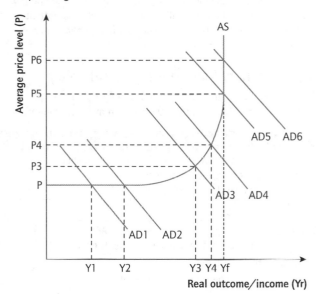

Figure 2.4.2 The shape of AS and the effects of expansionary fiscal policy

Assuming that the economy was in equilibrium at Y1, the increase in AD from AD1 to AD2 leads to an increase in real output without the average price level being adversely affected. If, though, the deflationary gap was smaller and the economy was in equilibrium at Y3, then the increase in AD from AD3 to AD4 would lead not only to an increase in real output but also to some increase in prices (that is, it would be responsible for some inflation). If the economy is at full employment and government expenditures increase and/or taxes decrease, the resulting increase in AD will prove only inflationary.

If we employ a monetarist or new classical AD and AS framework then the effects are similar, as shown in Figure 2.4.3.

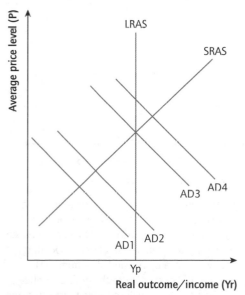

Figure 2.4.3 Expansionary fiscal policy in a monetarist or new classical framework

If there is a deflationary gap then expansionary fiscal policy will increase AD from AD1 to AD2. The result is higher real output but also inflationary pressures. If, though, the economy is at its potential output and AD increases as a result of reflationary fiscal policy from AD3 to AD4, then no lasting increase in real output will result. Any increase in real output will be temporary. In the long run, real output will return at its potential rate at the cost of higher inflation. Expansionary fiscal policy will not have succeeded in increasing real output.

Contractionary (deflationary) fiscal policy

On the other hand, an overheating economy, defined as an economy where AD is rapidly increasing, creating inflationary pressures, requires contractionary fiscal policy. The government must decrease government expenditures and increase taxes so that AD decreases.

The decrease in government expenditures (G) will directly decrease AD (or slow down its increase) while an increase in direct taxes will decrease disposable incomes, lowering consumption (C) and so AD.

In a diagram, AD will shift left, alleviating inflationary pressures (shown as a decrease in the average price level) but also risking a contraction of the economy (that is, a lower level of output and a higher rate of unemployment). The risk of contraction depends on the shape of the AS curve facing the economy.

	Expansionary fiscal policy	Contractionary fiscal policy
Goal	To reflate a failing economy increasing real output and decreasing unemployment (to help close a deflationary gap)	To cool off an overheating economy (to help close an inflationary gap)
How?	G↑ and/or T↓	G↓ and/or T↑
Why is AD affected?	An increase in G directly increases AD; a decrease in T will increase Yd and so C and AD	A decrease in G directly decreases AD; an increase in T will decrease Yd and so C and AD
Possible costs	Higher inflation; wider trade deficit; crowding out	Slow down in growth or even a recession; increased unemployment
Note:	The shape of the AS curve is crucial in evaluating the impact on an economy	

HL The multiplier effect

Expansionary fiscal policy according to the Keynesian school is very powerful tool to lift an economy out of a recession, as a result of the operation of the multiplier effect.

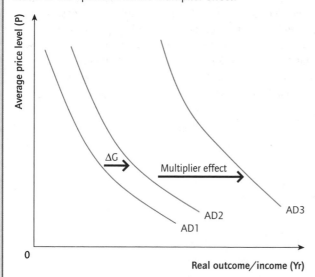

Figure 2.4.4 The Keynesian multiplier effect

Assume that a government wishing to close a deflationary gap employs expansionary fiscal policy and decides to increase its expenditures by some amount, say, ΔG (the difference between the new level of spending and the original level of spending). AD will automatically increase by ΔG and shift from AD1 to AD2, as in Figure 2.4.4. But according to the multiplier effect, the process will not end there. AD will continue to increase and shift to the right all the way to AD3.

The multiplier effect states that an increase in government expenditures will lead to a greater change in income:

$$\Delta Y = k\Delta G$$

where ΔY is the resulting change in national income, ΔG is the change in government spending and k is the multiplier.

It can be shown that the multiplier k is equal to:

$$k = \frac{1}{(1 - MPC)}$$

where MPC is the marginal propensity to consume defined as the extra spending induced by extra income:

$$MPC = \frac{\Delta C}{\Delta Y}$$

Since whatever is not spent on domestic output is either spent on imports, or saved or paid as taxes to the government, k is also equal to:

$$k = \frac{1}{(MPM + MPS + MRT)}$$

MPM is the marginal propensity to import, MPS is the marginal propensity to save and MRT is the marginal rate of tax. They are defined respectively as the extra spending on imports, the extra savings and the extra taxes paid from extra income earned and they represent the withdrawals (leakages) in our circular flow of income model.

The logic of the Keynesian multiplier

Why will national income increase by more than the increase in government expenditures? The explanation rests on two ideas. First of all, one person's spending is automatically someone else's income. In addition, as the circular flow diagram (see Figure 2.1.3 on page 68) clearly illustrates, economic activity takes place in successive rounds. An example will help clarify the point. Assume that the government decides to increase expenditures by £10 million and hires unemployed workers to dig holes and bury bottles, and other unemployed workers to dig them up. National income has directly increased by £10 million the income that these workers earned for the 'service' they produced. Spending by the government is income for the workers. But, economic activity will not stop there. There is a 2nd and a 3rd and an nth round that follow. Why? Because these workers will spend **part** of this extra income on domestic goods and services that others produce and the process will continue.

Let the MPC be constant and equal to b; for example, b could be equal to 0.8 which means that out of every extra pound earned in income, 0.80 of it will be spent on domestic goods and services. The increase in government expenditures by £10 million pounds will lead to an eventual increase in national income equal to £50 million if the MPC is equal to 0.8 as k, the multiplier, is equal to $\frac{1}{(1 - 0.8)} = \frac{1}{0.2} = 5$ and so the resulting change in income ΔY is equal to $5 \times £10$ million $=$ £50 million.

Since only £8 million out of the £10 million was spent on domestic goods it follows £2 million was not spent on domestic output. This income must have been spent on foreign goods (imports) or paid in taxes or simply saved.

Import expenditures, tax payments and savings are all withdrawals in the circular flow model. It follows that $(1 - MPC)$ is the marginal propensity to withdraw (MPW) as shown above. The multiplier effect is therefore greater, the greater the proportion of any increase in income that is spent on domestic output; or the smaller the proportion of any increase in income that is saved, spent on imports or taxed by the government

TIP The multiplier can be generalized for all injections, namely not just for G but also for I (investments) and X (exports). According to the Keynesian multiplier, an increase in any injection will lead to a greater increase in national income.

Note that one mechanism through which trade cycles are transmitted internationally is the export multiplier. A recession in the US economy will lead to lower US imports and so lower European and, say, Japanese exports. Depending on the size of this decrease, as well as on the openness of these economies, economic activity in Europe and Japan will be adversely affected (their AD will shrink) and this effect will be magnified through the export multiplier, which is the change in national income resulting from a change in export revenues.

Also, note that the effect is not instantaneous as there is a time lag between receipt of income and subsequent spending.

Optional material

Algebraically the following holds:

(1) $\Delta Y = \Delta G + b\Delta G + b^2\Delta G + b^3\Delta G + b^4\Delta G + ...$ →

(2) $\Delta Y = (1 + b + b^2 + b^3 + b^4 + ...)\Delta G$ →

(3) $\Delta Y = \left(\frac{1}{1 - b}\right) \Delta G$ →

(4) $\Delta Y = k \Delta G$,

where k is the multiplier

Since b is the marginal propensity to consume (MPC) domestic goods and services the multiplier k can be rewritten as:

$$k = \frac{1}{(1 - MPC)}$$

In (1) the change in income ΔY is equal to the initial change in government spending (ΔG) which workers earned and is the direct, first-round effect and the first term in the equation. The second term ($b\Delta G$) is the proportion b of this income that was spent on other domestic goods by these workers and which is income to others in the economy. For example, if I earned from the government £100 pounds for fixing a window in a government building and my MPC is 0.8 then I will spend £80 pounds, say on luxury cakes that the baker Roxanne across the street baked. Now, income has increased by 180 and represents the service (window fixing) and the good (cakes) produced up to this point. If Roxanne in turn spends 0.8 of her extra income on say, cheddar cheese that Bob produces, then his income will have increased by £64 pounds (this the third term, $b^2\Delta G$) representing the extra cheddar produced. Up to this point, national income has increased by 100 + 80 + 64 or, generalizing, by $\Delta G + b\Delta G + b^2\Delta G$. Bob will then spend a portion b of his extra income $b^2\Delta G$ or, $b^3\Delta G$ on some other goods, and so on.

In (2) the term ΔG is factored out and it should be realized that inside the parentheses we have the sum of infinite terms of a geometric progression which converges (as $0 < b < 1$) to $\frac{1}{(1 - b)}$.

The crowding out effect

Crowding-out is a monetarist criticism of Keynesian-inspired expansionary fiscal policy. If the government increases government spending then, as a result of the multiplier effect, AD will increase by more than the original increase in government expenditures. Fiscal policy therefore seems, according to the Keynesian school of thought, like a very powerful tool to reflate an economy in a recession.

Not so, claim the monetarists. The increased government spending and resulting greater budget deficit needs to be somehow financed. For example, if a government decides to spend $787 billion more without resorting to increased taxation, then it must borrow. If the government borrows by selling bonds to the non-bank private sector, then interest rates may rise as there is going to be greater demand for loanable funds in the loanable funds market. In Figure 2.4.5 the market where funds are borrowed and lent is illustrated. Initially, demand for loanable funds (by businesses and others planning to spend more than they have available) and supply of loanable funds (by parties that wish to spend less than they have available) is such that interest rates are at r1.

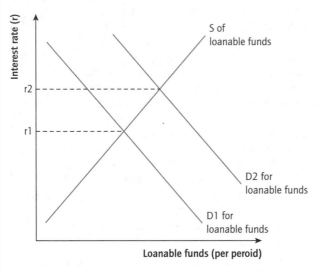

Figure 2.4.5 The loanable funds market and the effect of government borrowing on interest rates

If the government enters this market and also asks to borrow, then demand for loanable funds may increase to D2. Interest rates are shown to increase from r1 to r2. Private sector investment spending is therefore expected to decrease as long as it is inversely related to interest rates. Consumption expenditures may also decrease. Figure 2.4.6 shows that since AD includes not only G but also C and I it may not increase to AD2 after all but only (if, at all) to AD3.

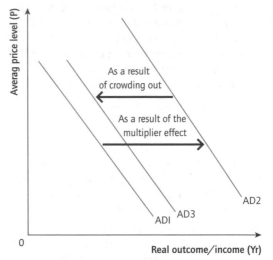

Figure 2.4.6 The crowding-out effect

In this way, expansionary fiscal policy is shown to be not as powerful as Keynesians thought.

> **TIP** The effects of crowding out also depend on the type of government expenditures financed. If capital (investment) expenditures are financed then, given that infrastructure investments may create substantial positive externalities to private firms, economic growth may even accelerate. This is an especially valid argument for developing countries where improved infrastructure is much needed and is considered complementary to market forces. Also, if the budget is financed by foreigners then domestic interest rates may not increase (but other problems may result: for example, the external debt, which has to be paid off in foreign exchange, will increase).

Automatic fiscal stabilizers

Tax revenues as well as some government expenditures change automatically as the level of national income changes without the government having to initiate any legislative changes. More specifically, a progressive income tax system and the existence of social insurance in the form of unemployment benefits will exert a stabilizing effect on the economy, making the business cycle smoother. With these systems in place, recessions will be slightly milder while an overheating economy will somewhat cool off, alleviating inflationary pressures.

How do automatic fiscal stabilizers work?

For example, assume an economy entering recession. As the economy contracts and real output/income (Y) decreases, tax revenues collected by the government will automatically fall proportionately by more so disposable incomes will not decrease as fast. At the same time, as a result of people losing their jobs, unemployment benefits will automatically kick in, providing the unemployed with at least some disposable income to spend. The effect of what has just been described is to mitigate the downturn of the economy: automatic stabilizers will not allow disposable income to decrease as fast in a recession, slowing down the decrease in consumption and AD. Figure 2.4.7 illustrates the point.

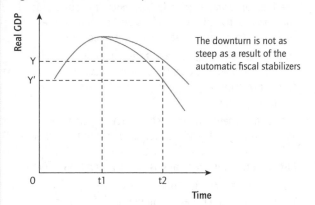

The downturn is not as steep as a result of the automatic fiscal stabilizers

Figure 2.4.7 How automatic stabilizers mitigate an economic downturn

The economy enters recession at time t1. Real GDP begins to decrease. At time t2, as a result of the automatic stabilizing effect of unemployment benefits and progressive taxes, real output falls only to Y whereas it would have decreased to Y' without their existence. The downturn is milder.

Assume now an economy starting to overheat as AD is growing faster than AS. An inflationary gap is emerging. Real output is growing above potential output. Here, progressive taxes will do their trick as they increase faster than income, slowing down the increase in disposable incomes and so the spending power of households and firms. AD will not be increasing as fast as it would have had taxes not been progressive. The existence of a progressive tax system cools off the economy, relieving it to an extent from the build-up of inflationary pressures. The upturn of the business cycle is milder, as Figure 2.4.8 illustrates.

At time t1 the economy starts to recover. At time t2 real output has grown above the (thick black) trend line that reflects potential output. An inflationary gap emerges. Real output would have grown to Y' without the automatic stabilizing effect of progressive taxation. The stabilizing effect allows output to grow only to level Y, in this way decreasing the size of the inflationary gap the economy experiences. The upturn is milder.

Figure 2.4.8 can also illustrate why automatic stabilizers can retard recovery. As, right after time t1, the economy begins to recover, growth would have been faster and potential output could have been attained earlier were it not for the decrease in government outlays (payments for unemployment benefits will decrease as the unemployed find jobs) and the proportionately faster increase in tax revenues. This problem is known as fiscal drag.

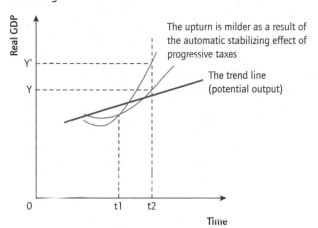

The upturn is milder as a result of the automatic stabilizing effect of progressive taxes

The trend line (potential output)

Figure 2.4.8 How automatic stabilizers cool-off an overheating economy

Impact of fiscal policy on potential output and LRAS

Not all government expenditures are the same. A distinction introduced earlier was between current spending, capital spending and transfer payments. An increase in current spending and transfer payments is unlikely to have an impact on potential output but that does not hold true for public investment (capital) spending. Let's take the example of government expenditures on infrastructure, which can be defined as physical capital that creates significant positive externalities in lowering the overall cost of economic activity and so potentially having a high social rate of return. This type of expenditure can increase an economy's potential output and shift its vertical LRAS to the right. The construction of an improved road system, of a necessary bridge or harbour, or of a better system of telecommunications has the potential to expand the productive capacity of an economy. Of course, we should keep in mind though that a 'bridge to nowhere' is just a waste of scarce resources.

Expenditures on schools and health care can increase and improve the stock of human capital an economy has available. More and better primary schools, secondary schools and colleges as well as more and better health-care centres are

crucial in increasing labour productivity. An increase in labour productivity translates to faster long run growth and so a higher level of potential output.

It can be argued that a decrease in tax rates may unleash more work and investments as incentives could be positively affected. To the extent that lower taxes provide the incentive for more work and investments, potential output can also increase. On the other hand, tax revenues have to be sufficient and equitably shared so that the financing of necessary government expenditures does not require more and more borrowing which may prove unsustainable.

Lastly, prudent fiscal management may indirectly affect potential output and long-run growth. The term is elusive but it is generally considered to mean that budget deficits are not excessive and that the national debt does not grow at unsustainable rates. As explained earlier, high-budget deficits, especially if they are not incurred in a deep recession, can lead to increased interest rates and the crowding out of private sector investment and consumption. An unsustainable national debt, as a result of profligate government spending and an ineffective tax system, may lead to default with huge costs on the real economy.

Evaluating fiscal policy

Possible strengths of expansionary fiscal policy

- Fiscal policy is direct: any increase in government spending will automatically increase national income by at least as much, if not more, as it is a component of AD.

- A decrease in taxes to reflate an economy as part of an expansionary stimulus plan may also have beneficial supply-side effects as lower taxes may improve the incentives to work and to invest.

- In an economy in deep recession (or depression) interest rates may be at or close to zero, so monetary policy is totally ineffective; in such a case policy makers have only fiscal policy to turn to.

- If the institutional framework of the economy is equipped with unemployment benefits and a progressive income tax system then policy makers have the benefits of 'built-in stabilizers'.

- If the increased government expenditures of a stimulus package include spending on infrastructure (for example roads, bridges, harbours or telecommunications; that is, physical capital typically financed by governments that create very significant positive externalities decreasing transaction costs across the board), along with health and education then a positive supply-side effect will also result.

- If the increased government expenditures of a stimulus package include spending on the development of green technologies then an additional long-run benefit will be the improvement of the environment, allowing sustainable growth.

> **HL**
> - If the government expenditure multiplier is greater than one then it is also a very powerful tool to help a lagging economy recover. The Chief Economist of President Obama's Council of Economic Advisors, Christina Romer, estimates the US government expenditure multiplier at 1.6. In general, the size of fiscal multipliers depends on specific characteristics of each economy with more open economies (those, for example, with few restrictions on trade) having larger multipliers than less open economies.

Possible weaknesses of fiscal policy

- There are significant time lags associated with fiscal policy that may even end up destabilizing instead of stabilizing an economy. Specifically, we can break down the overall lag from the moment an economic problem is encountered to the moment the policy switch has an impact into:
  - the detection lag (it takes time to collect and evaluate data in order to detect a problem)

  - the administrative lag (it takes time for the government to decide, for example, exactly how much it needs to spend and on exactly what projects, as well as to have the package approved by the parliament or congress)

  - the execution or impact lag (it takes time for whatever policy response was chosen to have effects on the economy, especially since the cumulative impact of the multiplier is long).

- Large deficit spending may increase national debt to unsustainable levels and may force significant tax increases in the future (so, in a sense, the cost of such a policy is shifted on to future generations) or may even lead to default.

- There is also the chance that if an expansionary fiscal effect continues for longer than required then inflationary pressures may arise.

- Expansionary fiscal policy and deficit spending may end up crowding out private investment and therefore be less effective. The resulting budget deficit must somehow be financed. Government borrowing from financial markets may drive interest rates up and, as a result, private investment will decrease (and so will consumption expenditures). If this decrease in private spending matches the increased government spending, the crowding out is said to be complete and fiscal policy is totally ineffective.

- Fiscal policy suffers from an 'expansionary bias' because politicians are often irresponsible and prefer to spend more and tax less rather than spending less and taxing more because the former maximizes their short term re-election chances.

- Expansionary fiscal policy may also lead to a widening trade deficit. A higher level of income will lead to more imports absorbed. If the average price level increases then exports will shrink as they become less competitive and imports will rise as they become relatively more attractive than domestic goods.

- Contractionary fiscal policy to fight inflationary pressures is often difficult to employ. Societies usually do not welcome decreases in spending related to social welfare or in education and health or even in defence programmes. Increasing taxation beyond a point will adversely affect incentives in the economy.

- An increase in government expenditures as part of an expansionary fiscal policy cannot be easily reversed if policy makers realize that it leads to overheating: for example, it is not easy to stop the construction of a bridge.

> **HL**
> - The government expenditure multiplier may even be less than one as some economists claim.

2.5 Money and monetary policy

Money

Money is defined as anything generally acceptable as a means of payment. If nothing serves this function, then we have a barter economy, where goods are exchanged for goods. Barter requires double coincidence of wants and implies extremely high transaction costs for individuals who will therefore prefer to avoid specialization in order to minimize dependency on exchange. Introducing money permits specialization to take place, expanding dramatically the production possibilities in both a static and dynamic sense.

Functions of money

- Money is a medium of exchange: it is acceptable as a means of payment in market transactions.

- It is a unit of account: it serves as a yardstick, with which values can be measured, expressed and compared.

- It is a store of value: people may hold their wealth through time in the form of money ('money at rest').

- Money provides a standard of deferred payments: it allows inter-temporal contracts; it serves as a link between the past, present and future.

The banking system

The modern banking system is known as a 'two-tier' system since it comprises commercial banks and a central bank.

The role of a central bank

The role of central banks has evolved a lot over time and their importance has changed. A central bank is considered as the banker to the government and the banker of commercial banks.

- It is the sole note-issuing authority in a country. Remember, though, that the supply of notes is a small percentage of the money supply which includes at the least demand deposits (also known as sight deposits, chequing accounts or current accounts).

- It issues and redeems government bonds.

- It manages the government's banking account.

- It carries out monetary policy by influencing interest rates and banks' lending practices. For many economists, the single most important duty of a central bank is to ensure price stability through monetary policy.

- It has responsibility for exchange rate policy.

- It is the 'lender of last resort'; it stands ready to provide any required liquidity to the banking system in case of an emergency (a 'credit crunch').

- It regulates and supervises commercial banks to ensure that bank lending is prudent and that banks are sufficiently liquid to meet their obligations to depositors.

Commercial banks

These are profit-maximizing firms specializing in bringing borrowers and lenders together. They belong to the larger class of so-called financial intermediaries. These profit-oriented firms accept people's money and lend to those wishing to invest.

They pay interest to savers and are paid interest from borrowers. Their profitability to a large extent depends on the difference (the 'spread') between the two interest rates. Interest is what is earned when lending money and what it costs to borrow money and typically is expressed on an annual basis and as a percentage. There are very many interest rates depending on who borrows or lends, how much is borrowed or lent, the level of risk involved, etc. The central bank, as will be explained later, can influence market interest rates.

It is important to understand that lending by commercial banks is performed by the stroke of a pen. Nowadays, it's actually more like a computer click of a mouse. The bank issues a loan to a business by opening up a account allowing cheques to be written for the business (that is, a current account). Note though that for every $1.00 cash deposited by a customer in a bank, credit can be extended by a multiple which is greater, the smaller the 'cash drainage' (the use of cash) in the economy. This is known as a fractional reserve system: commercial banks need only to keep as reserves (in their vaults or in their deposits at the central bank) a fraction of the total value of loans (credit) they have issued. This is because at any point in time only some customers will require to be paid in cash (by cashing their cheques); most transactions (in terms of value) involve the transfer of cheques, the computer crediting of one account and the debiting of another.

Demand for money: the concept

The term 'demand for money' seems strange as most people would claim that the demand is infinite. But the term makes sense once you realize that holding money will not earn you interest while holding bonds will. The term 'money demand' refers to the case where an agent (an individual or a firm) has a choice to hold bonds (an interest-bearing asset) and money (a non-interest bearing asset; that is, cash and an account on which cheques can be drawn). It becomes clear that there is no reason to hold money and sacrifice interest unless there is a desire to purchase goods or services. According to Keynes there are three motives for holding money (he termed this 'liquidity preference', meaning demand to be liquid, to hold cash).

- The transactions motive: you need money (liquidity) to buy goods and services. The transactions demand for money is a positive function of national income as at higher levels of income, more transactions will take place.

- The precautionary motive: you need to hold money to meet unexpected expenses. The precautionary demand for money is also a positive function of income.

- The speculative motive: the speculative demand is inversely related to the interest rate since the opportunity cost of holding cash rises as interest rates rise and people will prefer to hold bonds instead.

Figure 2.5.1 illustrates the demand for money. As the interest rate increases, demand for holding money instead of bonds decreases as the opportunity cost of holding cash rises. If the level of income increases from Y1 to Y2 then the demand to hold money at each level of interest rates will increase, shifting the demand for money to the right.

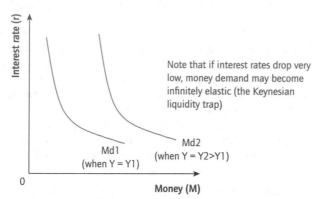

Note that if interest rates drop very low, money demand may become infinitely elastic (the Keynesian liquidity trap)

Figure 2.5.1 Demand for money (liquidity preference)

Money supply

Money supply is considered at this level to be 'exogenous', meaning that it is not affected by the level of AD and interest rates but that it is fixed at some level by the central bank. The money supply includes cash (coins and notes) as well as current account deposits (also known as sight account deposits). The definition may be expanded to include more assets. Figure 2.5.2 illustrates the typical shape of the money supply provided by the central bank.

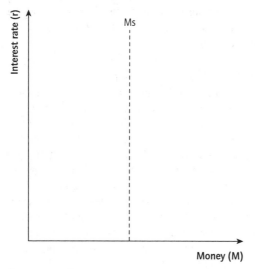

Figure 2.5.2 The money supply (exogenous and fixed by the central bank)

The central bank can affect the size of the money supply as follows.

- It can change the required reserve ratio. Commercial banks need to keep only a fraction of the money deposited in their vaults and can lend out the rest. They need to do that to ensure that they are sufficiently liquid to meet their obligations to depositors. If the central bank increases the required reserve ratio then they will be able to lend out less so the money supply will decrease, shifting the curve in Figure 2.5.2 to the left.

- The central bank can change the discount rate. There are very many interest rates in an economy. One such rate is the

discount rate which is the interest rate at which commercial banks can borrow if they need to from the central bank. If the central bank wants to decrease the money supply and shift the curve to the left then it could increase this discount rate, making it more costly for commercial banks to get hold of extra cash to lend out to their customers.

- The central bank can conduct open market operations. If it decides to buy orange juice on the open market costing 100 million euros then its vaults will fill up with orange juice and the 'market' will have an extra 100 million fresh euros. The money supply will have increased and shifted to the right. If the central bank decides to sell some of the orange juice for 80 million euros then the market will have more orange juice but 80 million less euros, (that is, the money supply will have decreased). The central bank does not buy and sell orange juice because, first, this would significantly disrupt the price of a basic good that many of us buy and also the good would be costly to store. Instead it buys and sells (outstanding) bonds in the open market. If it buys bonds it can increase the money supply and if it sells bonds it can decrease it.

Interest rate determination by the central bank

The interaction of the supply and the demand for money will determine, as in any market, the interest rate which influences all other market interest rates. Figure 2.5.3 illustrates the point.

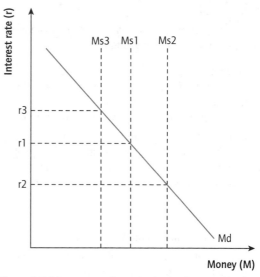

Figure 2.5.3 Interest rate determination by the central bank

Given a money demand Md and money supply at Ms1 the market interest rate will be determined at r1. If the central bank wishes for some reason to lower interest rates it can increase the money supply to Ms2. It can do this by decreasing the required reserve ratio, lowering its discount rate or conducting open market purchases of (outstanding) bonds. The interest rate in the money market will decrease to r2. On the other hand, if for some reason the central bank wishes to increase interest rates it can decrease the money supply to Ms3. This can be done by increasing the required reserve ratio, raising its discount rate or conducting open market sales of (outstanding) bonds. The interest rate in the money market will increase to r3.

Monetary policy

Monetary policy is, together with fiscal policy, a demand-side policy. It aims to affect economic variables such as real output and growth, employment and inflation. If the goal is to increase AD then the central bank will adopt easy or loose (expansionary) monetary policy, increasing the money supply and, through this, lowering interest rates. This would typically be the policy choice for an economy in recession or about to enter one (that is, when a deflationary or recessionary gap is present). If the goal is to decrease AD (or to slow down its increase) then the central bank will adopt tight or contractionary monetary policy, decreasing the money supply and, through this, increasing interest rates. This would typically be the policy choice for an overheating economy (that is, when an inflationary gap is present).

Easy or loose monetary policy

If an economy is about to enter recession or if it already is suffering negative growth rates and a deflationary gap then the central bank may decrease interest rates (r) (or, equivalently, decrease the money supply) in an attempt to increase AD and so output and employment. How does it work? How are lower interest rates expected to reflate a failing economy? It is hoped that AD will increase because consumption expenditures, investment expenditures and net exports will tend to rise.

Consumption expenditures of households may increase as borrowing to finance the purchase of durables (for example cars or household appliances) becomes cheaper so households may spend more on these goods. Also, monthly payments on adjustable mortgage loans will decrease so households will have more available to spend in general. Lastly, the lower rate of return will make saving a less attractive option so households will tend to spend more.

Investment spending by firms may also increase as borrowing costs to finance purchases of capital goods (for example machines, tools and other equipment) and expansions (such as new factories) are lower. Also, lower interest rates imply that the opportunity cost to firms of using their own past retained profits to finance investments is also lower.

Lastly, as a result of lower interest rates, the exchange rate will tend to depreciate (see the section on exchange rates later) so exports will become more competitive abroad and imports less attractive domestically, increasing net exports and so AD.

Tight monetary policy

Assume an overheating economy in which inflation is becoming a problem and an inflationary gap is forming. The central bank may increase interest rates (or, equivalently, increase the money supply) in an attempt to decrease AD. AD is expected to decrease as higher interest rates will work in the opposite direction to the one described when an easy or loose monetary policy is adopted. With tight monetary policy, borrowing costs will increase for both households and firms, monthly loan repayments for many types of loans will increase and saving will become more attractive. Spending by households and firms is therefore expected to slow down or even decrease. The exchange rate will also tend to appreciate, rendering exports pricier and therefore less competitive abroad and imports more attractive domestically, decreasing net exports.

Note that the term 'quantitative easing' refers to purchases by the central bank of long-term bonds so that the money supply increases.

Evaluation of monetary policy

Central banking is both an art and a science: the timing of an interest rate change, the statements issued by the central banker and the size of the interest rate change are all crucial for the success of any policy change. There are very many factors that determine the extent to which a policy response will or will not be successful. In general, monetary policy is extensively used throughout the world to regulate the strength of total spending on domestic goods and services.

- It is considered rather flexible as the central bank can alter interest rates often.
- Interest rates can be altered gradually or incrementally (by 0.25% at a time).
- The central bank can also easily reverse any decision if it becomes clear that a policy reversal is in order.

On the other hand, it is also characterized by several problems.

- Most importantly, spending of both households and firms does not only depend on interest rates. Consumption and investment expenditures depend on a host of other factors. The degree of consumer and business confidence is extremely important in determining the response of household and business spending to a change in interest rates. The degree of household and firm indebtedness is also of paramount importance. For example, let's say the central bank lowers interest rates in an attempt to prevent a recession. If businesses are pessimistic and/or if households are already burdened by heavy debts there is no guarantee that they will be convinced to borrow and spend more, and the policy may fail.
- Also, if the borrowing rate is already too low (close to zero) then it can not be lowered any further as negative interest rates do not make any sense (see Figure 2.5.1 and consider the liquidity trap case where money demand becomes flat, that is, infinitely elastic).
- Just like fiscal policy, monetary policy is characterized by potentially destabilizing time lags. These time lags may be shorter than those characterizing fiscal policy but they are still variable in length, creating uncertainty as to the success of any policy change.
- Under a fixed exchange rate system monetary policy is ineffective. Interest rate changes have to be used only to ensure that the exchange rate remains fixed at the chosen level. This will become clear in a later section.
- Today, financial markets are largely global so most firms and even households can and do borrow from anywhere in the world. These developments weaken the effectiveness of any domestic monetary policy choice.

	Easy or loose monetary policy	Tight monetary policy
Goal	To increase AD of an economy that is in or about to enter recession (to close a deflationary gap)	To decrease AD of an economy suffering from inflationary pressures (to close an inflationary gap)
How?	By r ↓ (or, by ↑ Ms through open market purchases of bonds, lower required reserves or a decrease in the discount rate)	By r ↓ (or, by ↑ Ms through open market sales of bonds, higher required reserves or an increase in the discount rate)
Why is AD affected?	By lowering interest rates the central bank hopes that C and I and NX will ↑ and so AD will ↑	By increasing interest rates the central bank hopes that C and I and NX will ↓ and so AD will ↓
But	other variables also affect the decision to spend; financial markets are global; there is a lower interest rate limit beyond which it is ineffective (the liquidity trap); it is ineffective under a fixed exchange rate regime, etc.	
On the other hand	monetary policy is flexible, gradual and easily reversible; in addition, if the central bank is independent, monetary policy is less yielding to political pressure and manipulation	

Supply-side policies

Supply-side policies are policies that aim at increasing the production side of an economy and so aggregate supply, shifting the LRAS curve to the right.

Supply-side policies attempt to enhance the institutional framework of an economy, increase the quantity and improve the quality of factors of production, as well as improve incentives. They may be distinguished into interventionist and pro-market policies. In the former, the government takes on an active role, whereas in the latter the role of the government is supposed to be minimized in order to unleash the powers of the free market.

Interventionist supply-side policies

- Investments in human capital, including investments in education and health care, are one example. Investments in primary and secondary education yield the highest social rate of return, the resulting external benefits are the highest and investment ensures that all children have access to education. Investments in better health-care services made available to the general population also help increase the stock of human capital of an economy. An increase in human capital leads to increased labour productivity, so to an increase in the productive capacity and the potential output of an economy. The LRAS will shift to the right.

- Investments in infrastructure will also boost the supply side. 'Build yourself a road to get rich' is not an exaggeration as a better transportation system creates massive positive externalities. Infrastructure refers to physical capital that government typically but not necessarily finances which decreases the costs of economic activity and creates sizable external benefits. Roads, railways, harbours, airports and telecommunications all serve to lower production costs of all economic agents in a country.

- Investments in technology are another example. In their attempt to increase AS, governments fund R&D projects. Provision of basic R&D is responsible for significant positive externalities that a private firm would not be able to capture. Markets alone would lead to fewer R&D projects being undertaken, which implies a slower rate of technological progress. Labour productivity does not only depend on the level of human capital (education and training) but also on the quality and the level of technology embodied in the physical capital that employees work with. It follows that a faster rate of technological advancement will increase labour productivity and so the LRAS of an economy.

Note that all of the above public investments imply an increase in government expenditures and as such will also have a short-run effect on AD, increasing it and shifting it to the right before the LRAS is positively affected and also shifts to the right.

- Improving the institutional framework is a supply-side policy. The institutional framework of an economy includes the laws, the regulations, the customs and traditions within which economic activity takes place. They define the 'rules of the game'. Improving the institutional framework of an economy implies improving the capacity of the economy to produce. Unfortunately, there is no unique set of laws, rules and regulations that can be transplanted to any economy and prove optimal. Movements that reduce bureaucracy, increase transparency and accountability, simplify processes and procedures, and reduce corruption are, in general, considered to be steps in the right direction.

- Industrial policies are championed by policy makers who consider government intervention and guidance necessary for the productive capacity of an economy to increase. This group considers market forces inadequate to guide financial capital and investments to their most productive uses and so believe that government is necessary to do the job and 'pick winners' (that is, industries and firms to support as they are thought to have the most potential for growth). Subsidized low interest loans, tax breaks and tax allowances and protection from foreign competition are some of the measures employed. Some successful as well as unsuccessful developing countries have adopted such measures. Many, if not all, advanced economies have also employed such policies in varying degrees.

Pro-market supply-side policies

The measures included in this group are measures that the 'supply-siders' espouse. Supply-siders are a group of economists who are known for their often extreme pro-market ideas and biases. Their basic principle is less government and more free and unfettered markets. Their ideas include the following.

- Policies related to the labour market including polices that try to make it more flexible. Some examples are policies aimed at:

  – lowering or even abolishing the minimum wage

– decreasing the power of labour unions

– reducing non-wage labour costs to employers (such as national insurance contributions) so that labour becomes cheaper to firms and more labour is hired

– making hiring and firing of workers easier so that managers do not hesitate to hire more labour when demand rises

– making pension plans transferable across occupations (so that labour mobility increases)

– reducing unemployment benefits to make job acceptance faster for firms searching for labour.

■ Their policies related to product markets include ones that aim to increase the extent of competition and decrease the degree of any monopoly power in markets so that the economy reaps the resulting benefits from increased efficiency and lower prices. Deregulation and privatization as well as trade liberalization are typical candidates. Deregulation refers to the decrease in regulations related to conducting business in a certain market. In many countries there are many laws that prevent competition from working. For example, in Greece only pharmacists have the right to open up a pharmacy and they may not open a new pharmacy less than a 100 metres from an existing one. Dismantling such regulations is considered to increase competition and, through this, improve efficiency and lower prices. Privatization refers to the transfer of state-owned assets (most often this refers to state-owned firms) to the private sector. The idea is that the private sector, as a result of the profit motive, will cut costs and improve efficiency and this will lead to lower prices. Trade liberalization refers to the decrease or elimination of trade barriers and is considered the fastest way to decrease any domestic monopoly power.

■ Supply-siders' incentive-related policies decrease tax rates to improve the incentive to work, save and invest. A decreased marginal tax rate will increase the opportunity cost of leisure so individuals will supposedly have a greater incentive to work. The increase in labour supply will exert a positive effect on LRAS. A lower capital gains tax or business profit tax aims at increasing the incentive to invest.

Evaluation of supply-side policies

Overall, the benefits expected from implementing supply-side policies are a result of:

■ increased levels of competition and the expected enhanced efficiency

■ fewer distortions to the price mechanism

■ fewer built-in disincentives

■ increased flexibility in labour markets.

There is no question that in many economies product markets are severely distorted as a result of years of government intervention and that an institutional overhaul can create real long-term benefits for society. In many economies labour markets may also be distorted, with privileged groups of workers reaping rents that increase inefficiencies, create unemployment and decrease overall competitiveness. Reform can improve social welfare in the long term.

On the other hand, pro-market supply-side policies can be criticized on the following grounds.

■ Benefits usually take a long time to materialize. Pro-market supply-side policies are effective in the long run but incapable of dealing with short-run problems.

■ Tax cuts may induce more leisure and less labour and investment, proving more of a gift to the better-off segments of the population and further skewing an inequitable income distribution.

■ Privatization often has led, at least in the short run, to increased unemployment and it may lead to monopoly pricing and related inefficiencies.

■ Deregulation may prove unsuccessful in raising competition and lowering prices. The deregulation of the banking sector in the USA is considered by many prominent economists the cause of the 2008–09 financial and economic crises.

■ The smaller safety net that results from lower and stricter unemployment benefits and other welfare-related cuts, as well as the squeeze of real wages (especially for the unskilled), may lead to increased income inequality as segments of the population may get marginalized. This may create significant economic and social costs in the future.

Optional material

Schools of economic thought: a very brief outline of ideas

Classical school

- Given that scarcity is the fundamental economic problem, an economy will always fully utilize its scarce resources. An economy will therefore produce whatever its scarce resources and its technology allow it to produce.

- 'Supply creates its own demand' is known as Say's Law (Say was a French economist). Say's Law means that production creates income and this income will necessarily be used to purchase whatever was produced.

- Overproduction was ruled out in this school of thought, as overproduction implies excess supply which in competitive markets leads to lower prices and so to the market clearing (reaching equilibrium).

- Prolonged unemployment was also ruled out as it implies excess supply in labour markets. Excess supply leads to lower wages, forcing the labour market to clear (that is, for demand for labour to equal supply of labour).

- Flexibility of prices and wages guarantees that the product and labour markets would clear (that demand would equal supply).

- The economy will tend to operate at or near the full employment equilibrium. Any deviation from this would be temporary.

- It follows that there would be no need for the government to intervene. This is known as 'laissez-faire, laissez-passer'.

Keynesian school

- Demand for output creates the supply of output. It is 'effective' demand that determines equilibrium output and income. An economy's total output depends on the level of effective demand, later referred to as aggregate demand (AD).

- There is no guarantee that an economy will find itself (will be in equilibrium) at the full employment level of output. Equilibrium may occur below full employment (a deflationary or recessionary gap may exist).

- If the private sector (which includes households and firms) for whatever reason – perhaps just psychological – is unable to express sufficient demand for goods and services in an economy to lead to full employment of resources, then the government can act. It can raise its own spending on goods and services (as well as lower taxation) to increase the level of total demand to that level that all resources are fully employed. This is known as expansionary (or reflationary) fiscal policy.

- The inherent instability of a market (a capitalist) economy leads to the observed short-run fluctuations of output around its long-run trend. This instability is a result of consumption and investment being unstable, as well as the existence of the multiplier effect and the interaction of the multiplier and the accelerator.

- Instability (the business or trade cycle) requires government intervention. Counter–cyclical demand-side stabilization policies need to be introduced. These include fiscal and monetary policies.

- Fiscal policy is considered most effective in times of deep recessions.

Monetarist or new classical school

Two major developments in the 1970s were responsible for the change in direction in economics: the great inflation of the 1970s and the deconstruction of the Keynesian interventionist approach by Milton Friedman and the Chicago School (or, more generally, by the monetarists). Friedman's pro-market ideas began to dominate economic theory and with Margaret Thatcher in 1979 in the UK and Ronald Reagan in 1980 in the USA they also started to dominate policy making.

In 1973, the first oil crisis erupted, leading to the quadrupling of the price of a barrel of oil in one day. The effect was 'stagflation', the coexistence of rising unemployment and rising inflation. This was a blow to Keynesian economics as the two were thought as being inversely related through the Phillips curve.

- Monetarists are considered the intellectual heirs of the classical school of thought.

- Friedman and the monetarist school tried to show that a market economy is inherently stable, so there is no need for an active role for the government. Consumption expenditures were not thought to depend on the current level of income and the role of expectations on the business investment spending decision was diminished. Private spending was more stable.

- Monetarists first pointed out the possibility of 'crowding-out', in this way weakening deficit spending as a tool to reflate a flagging economy.

- Inflation for Friedman was a 'purely monetary phenomenon' with 'too much money chasing after too few goods'. Monetary policy was even considered potentially destabilizing and this school of thought preferred to rely on pro-market supply-side policies.

- The monetarists discredited the Phillips curve inflation–unemployment trade-off, trying to show that in the long run the Phillips curve is vertical at the natural rate of unemployment, a term that Friedman himself coined.

- Extreme monetarists considered that anything the government can do the market can do better. Government failure was even more likely than market failure.

- Several ideas related to monetarism are the basic ingredient of what is known as the 'Washington Consensus' which pushed stabilization, liberalization and structural adjustment onto developing nations, often with very debatable results.

- New classical economists (Bob Lucas, Thomas Sargent, Neil Wallace, Ed Prescott, et al.) tried to build macroeconomic theory on the basis of neoclassical microeconomic theory. They considered agents aiming at maximizing utility and possessing rational expectations so that no systematic errors were made. Their analysis concluded that only unanticipated policy changes could temporarily affect real economic variables (policy ineffectiveness). Real business cycle theorists regard changes in productivity as the driving force of business cycles.

2 Macroeconomics: Questions

Practice part (a) long essay questions (HLP1 and SLP1)
Command terms: typically AO1/AO2 but possibly also AO4 (*not* AO3)

1. Describe the circular flow model of an open economy and explain the meaning of the terms 'income flow' and 'expenditure flow'.

2. Explain how the size of the income flow within the circular flow model depends on the relative size of the withdrawals (or, leakages) and the injections.

3. Outline the difference between GDP and GNI as well as between nominal and real values of these measures of economic activity.

4. Explain why the income approach, the output approach and the expenditure approach in measuring national income are equivalent.

5. Explain the meaning and significance of the term 'green GDP'.

6. Using an appropriate diagram, distinguish between the phases of the business (or, trade) cycle and explain the meaning of the term 'long term growth trend', identifying it on your diagram.

7. What is the difference between the demand for a product and aggregate demand? Explain two reasons for which aggregate demand is negatively sloped.

8. Define any three of the four components of aggregate demand and explain, for each of these three components chosen, one factor that may increase it and thus lead to a rightward shift in the AD curve.

9. Define the term 'consumption expenditures' and explain three factors that may increase their level in an economy and thus increase aggregate demand.

10. Define the term 'investment expenditures' and explain three factors that may increase their level in an economy and thus increase aggregate demand.

11. Define the term 'government expenditures' and explain the three types that these expenditures are typically classified into as well as factors that may increase their level in an economy and thus increase aggregate demand.

12. Define the term 'net exports' and explain three factors that may increase their level in an economy and thus increase aggregate demand.

13. Explain why the short run aggregate supply within the Monetarist/New Classical framework is upward sloping and suggest two reasons it may shift to the left.

14. Explain the distinction between the short run aggregate supply and the long run aggregate supply within the Monetarist/New Classical framework.

15. Explain each of the three discreet sections of a typical Keynesian aggregate supply curve.

16. Explain factors that may shift the Monetarist/New Classical long run aggregate supply curve right. Are these *exactly* the same factors that are responsible for shifting the production possibilities curve (or, frontier) of an economy outwards?

17. Distinguish between the reasons the Keynesian aggregate supply curve is upward sloping (section II) and the reasons the Monetarist short run aggregate supply is upward sloping.

18. Explain the impact of an increase in aggregate demand within the Monetarist/New Classical and the Keynesian analytical framework.

19. Using appropriate diagram(s), explain the mechanism that guarantees, within the Monetarist/New Classical framework, how any gap (inflationary or deflationary) will automatically close.

20. Explain the role of aggregate demand within the Keynesian framework of analysis and contrast it with its long run role in the Monetarist/New Classical framework.

21. Compare and contrast the significance of shifts of the aggregate demand within the Keynesian and the Monetarist/New Classical framework.

22. Explain what prevents real output returning to its full employment (or, potential) level following a decrease (or, an increase) in aggregate demand within the Keynesian framework.

23. Explain why a deflationary gap requires government intervention within the Keynesian perspective but does not within the Monetarist/New Classical perspective.

24. Explain how the unemployment rate is calculated as well as the difficulties in measuring unemployment.

25. Describe using examples the types of unemployment distinguishing between the causes of each type.

26. Explain using diagram(s) the cause of cyclical unemployment.

27. Explain using diagram(s) the cause of structural unemployment.

28. Distinguish between inflation, disinflation and deflation.

29. Explain how inflation and deflation are measured.

30. Explain the problems of measuring inflation.

31. Explain why **core** inflation is important to monitor.

32. Explain what a **producer price index** measures and why it is useful to measure it.

33. Explain the causes of both demand pull and cost push inflation.

34. **(HL only)** Explain the view that the short run Phillips curve may shift outwards.

35. Explain the meaning of the term 'natural rate of unemployment' and its relationship to the Monetarist/New Classical idea of potential output.

36. Define economic growth and, using appropriate diagrams, describe various ways it may be achieved.

37. Explain the significance (or, role) of different types of investment (in natural, physical and human capital) for economic growth and illustrate using an appropriate diagram.

38. Explain the role of productivity gains in the process of economic growth.

39. Does equity and equality in the distribution of income mean the same thing? Explain.

40. Explain why markets may lead to increased income inequality.

41. Explain two ways the distribution of income may be described.

42. Explain how inequality in the distribution of income is typically measured.

43. Distinguish between absolute and relative poverty.

44. Explain possible causes of poverty.

45. Explain possible consequences of poverty.

46. Using examples, distinguish between direct and indirect taxation and explain the role of each type in distributing national income (or, ... of direct taxation in redistributing income).

47. Distinguish between progressive, proportional and regressive taxes, providing examples of each and illustrating with an appropriate diagram (last point not in syllabus).

48. Explain, using examples, how government expenditures and transfer payments may be used to redistribute income.

49. Distinguish, using examples, the sources of government revenue and the types of expenditures a government makes and comment on the possible budget outcome.

50. Explain using a numerical example the relationship between budget deficits/surpluses that a government runs and the public debt of a country.

51. Explain using appropriate diagram(s) how expansionary fiscal policy can influence macroeconomic aggregates such as inflation, employment and output, with special emphasis on the shape of aggregate supply (note that this could easily be also a part (b) long essay question as it is quite demanding).

52. Explain using appropriate diagram(s) how contractionary fiscal policy can influence macroeconomic aggregates such as inflation, employment and output (note that this could easily be also a part (b) long essay question as it is quite demanding).

53. Explain how automatic stabilizers may help to stabilize overall economic activity. Use a diagram to illustrate your analysis.

54. Explain both the direct and indirect channels through which fiscal policy may impact on long term growth.

55. Outline the typical role and responsibilities of a Central Bank.

56. Explain how the level of interest rates in an economy is determined, describing how the Central Bank can affect the money supply.

57. Explain using appropriate diagram(s) how easy monetary policy can influence macroeconomic aggregates such as inflation, employment and output, with special emphasis on the shape of aggregate supply (note that this could easily be also a part (b) long essay question as it is quite demanding).

58. Explain using appropriate diagram(s) how tight monetary policy can influence macroeconomic aggregates such as inflation, employment and output (note that this could easily be also a part (b) long essay question as it is quite demanding).

59. Describe the channels through which looser (easier) (∕ tighter) monetary policy can help close a deflationary (∕ inflationary) gap.

60. Explain what is meant by the expression 'inflation targeting' when referring to the mandate of a Central Bank.

61. 'Supply side policies may be of an interventionist nature or may be market oriented'. Outline the meaning of this statement, explaining through an appropriate diagram their aim.

62. Define the term 'infrastructure' and explain the impact of a decision to improve a country's infrastructure both in the short term and in the long term.

63. Define the term 'human capital' and explain why many countries make significant investments to increase its stock.

64. What do we mean by the expression 'industrial policies'? List three examples that may be considered part of an industrial policy initiative and explain their impact on aggregate demand and long run aggregate supply.

65. Outline any two interventionist supply side policies explaining both their short term impact on aggregate demand and their potential impact on long run impact on aggregate supply.

66. Explain how two different types of market-based supply-side policies are expected to affect the long run aggregate supply of an economy.

67. Analyze how labour market reforms may affect the supply-side of an economy.

68. Analyze how policies to encourage competition may affect the supply-side of an economy.

69. Analyze how incentive-related policies may affect the supply-side of an economy.

Practice part (b) long essay questions (HLP1 and SLP1)
Command terms: typically AO3 but possibly AO1 and AO2 or even AO4

1. To what extent can national income statistics be useful in deriving conclusions concerning changes in living standards of a country through time or comparisons of living standards between countries at a point in time?

2. Examine the impact of an increase (and, separately, a decrease) in aggregate demand on short run and long run equilibrium within the Monetarist/New Classical.

3. Examine the impact of an increase (and, separately, a decrease) in aggregate demand within the Keynesian analytical framework.

4. Examine why an increase in aggregate demand may have different implications concerning inflationary pressures within the Keynesian and the Monetarist/New Classical frameworks of analysis.

5. **(HL only)** Explain, using an appropriate diagram, the meaning and significance of the Keynesian multiplier outlining the factors that may increase its size.

6. Discuss economic consequences of unemployment.

7. Discuss personal and social consequences of unemployment.

8. Evaluate policies to deal with different types of unemployment.

9. Discuss possible consequences of inflation.

10. Discuss possible consequences of deflation.

11. Evaluate policies to deal with different types of inflation.

12. **(HL only)** To what extent (or, discuss whether) a trade-off exists between inflation and unemployment using appropriate diagram(s).

13. Discuss the consequences of economic growth on living standards, unemployment, inflation, income distribution, the balance of payments and sustainability.

14. Evaluate possible government policies employed to redistribute income with special reference to how efficiency issues are affected.

15. Evaluate the effectiveness of expansionary fiscal policy, taking into consideration the Keynesian – Monetarist/New Classical viewpoints as well as short run versus long run considerations.

16. Evaluate the effectiveness of contractionary fiscal policy, taking into consideration the Keynesian – Monetarist/New Classical viewpoints as well as short run versus long run considerations.

17. Evaluate the effectiveness of easy monetary policy, taking into consideration the Keynesian – Monetarist/New Classical viewpoints as well as short run versus long run considerations.

18. Evaluate the effectiveness of tight monetary policy, taking into consideration the Keynesian – Monetarist/New Classical viewpoints as well as short run versus long run considerations.

19. Discuss the strengths and weaknesses of market-based supply-side policies.

20. Discuss the strengths and weaknesses of interventionist supply-side policies.

The benefits of free trade

- It permits specialization of scarce resources which leads to higher levels of output and so higher levels of consumption. Through trade countries can consume combinations of goods outside their production possibilities curve (PPC).

- Free trade decreases the power of domestic monopolies by exposing them to international competitive forces. The increased level of competition increases efficiency and forces domestic firms to lower prices.

- It may allow domestic firms to achieve economies of scale (EOS) by increasing the size of the markets they sell or export their products. This is especially significant for small countries with small domestic markets.

- It allows firms to import capital goods (machinery, equipment, tools and intermediate products) that meet much more closely their exact specifications and this further increases their productivity and profitability.

- It enables transfer and diffusion of technology and ideas across borders.

- It stimulates growth by increasing productive resources, by accelerating technological change and by spurring competition, as well as through the multiplier effect resulting from the increased export revenues.

- The resulting growth in real incomes allows higher savings, increasing the availability of domestic funds for investment.

- It presents consumers with a greater variety of goods to choose from.

Free trade: summary of key points

Free trade	allows specialization of resources increasing output
	increases competition, lowering domestic monopoly power
	leads to greater efficiency
	leads to lower prices which benefit buyers and keep the cost of living lower
	may induce domestic firms to grow and achieve EOS
	allows domestic firms to import exactly what they need
	enables technology and ideas to spread faster
	stimulates faster growth
	allows higher savings that may be used to finance investments
	presents consumers with more options

Figure 3.1.1 may be used to illustrate the welfare gains from free trade. The market for good X is shown and initially no trade is assumed. This could be the result of prohibitive trade barriers that permit no imports from abroad (known as the 'autarky case').

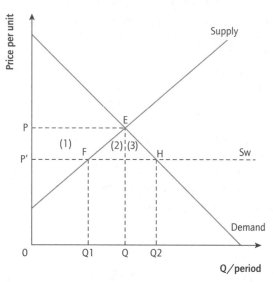

Figure 3.1.1 Benefits of free trade

The equilibrium market price will be determined at P and the equilibrium quantity at Q. Now assume trade barriers are eliminated and trade becomes free. If the world price of the good is at P' then the world price would prevail in the domestic market.

HL Note that since Figure 3.1.1 is a demand and supply diagram we are implicitly considering a perfectly competitive market where the good is homogeneous; so one price will prevail, the lower world price P'; we are also considering a 'small country' case which means that the country is so small that the world price of the good is not affected by how much the small country demands.

At the lower world price P' domestic firms will produce less (Q_1 units instead of Q) and consumers will consume more (Q_2 units instead of Q). As a result, consumer surplus increases by area (1, 2, 3) whereas producer surplus decreases by area (1). Area (EFH) or area (2, 3) therefore represents the net welfare gain resulting from free trade. The additional consumer surplus is greater than the lost producer surplus. Consumers can, in principle, fully pay (compensate) producers and still be better off.

Absolute and comparative advantage

The question that arises is in which goods should each country specialize? According to Adam Smith, mutually beneficial trade is based on the principle of absolute advantage. A country may be more efficient in the production of some commodities and less efficient in the production of others relative to another nation. Each country should specialize in the production of the good in which it has an absolute advantage.

A country has an absolute advantage in the production of a good if it can produce more of it with the same resources or, equivalently, if it can produce a unit of it with fewer resources than another country. In absolute advantage the absolute resource cost of producing a good is relevant.

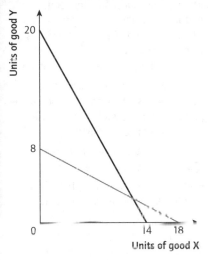

Figure 3.1.2 Absolute advantage

On a diagram, the country with the PPC further out on an axis has the absolute advantage in the production of the good measured on that axis. In Figure 3.1.2 Country Grey has an absolute advantage in the production of good X (it can produce 10 units with the same resources while Country Black can produce only 14 units). Country Black has an absolute advantage in the production of good Y (20 units instead of 8). Country Grey should therefore specialize in and export good X and import good Y, and vice versa for Country Black.

If a country happens to be absolutely more efficient in the production of both goods then, according to the principle of absolute advantage, there is no reason for it to specialize and engage in trade. This would be the case in a diagram where the PPCs do not intersect.

In 1817, David Ricardo showed that absolute advantage is not necessary for mutually beneficial specialization and trade to take place. Even if a country is absolutely at a disadvantage in the production of every good compared with another country (that is, its PPC is inside the other country's PPC) there is still room for mutually beneficial trade.

According to Ricardo only comparative advantage is necessary. Each country should specialize and export those goods that it can produce at relatively lower cost. Relative costs are what matter and not absolute costs.

A country has a comparative advantage in the production of a good if it can produce it at a lower opportunity cost (that is, by sacrificing fewer units of another good compared to another country).

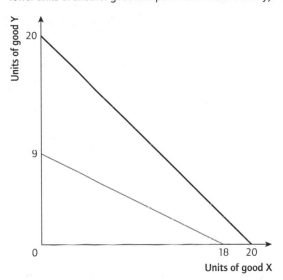

Figure 3.1.3 Comparative advantage

In Figure 3.1.3, Country Grey can produce 18 units of good X or 9 units of good Y at the most, whereas Country Black can produce 20 units of good X or 20 units of good Y. Country Black has an absolute advantage in the production of both goods as it can produce more of both.

Since their PPCs are not parallel, their opportunity cost ratios differ. This means there is room for specialization and mutually beneficial exchange.

Country Grey has a comparative advantage in the production of good X and Country Black has a comparative advantage in the production of good Y. Grey should specialize and export good X while Black should specialize and export good Y.

How do we know that Country Grey has a comparative advantage in the production of good X?

First, we can see this as Country Grey's PPC is flatter. On a figure with two linear PPCs, the country with the flatter PPC has the comparative advantage in the production of the good on the horizontal axis, while the other country has the comparative advantage in the production of the other good.

We can also calculate the opportunity cost of producing good X by each country.

For Country Grey: If it produces 18 units of good X it cannot produce (that is, it must sacrifice) 9 units of good Y, so (dividing both sides by 18) in producing 1 unit of X it must sacrifice $\frac{9}{18}$ or $\frac{1}{2}$ units of good Y.

For Country Black: If it produces 20 units of X it cannot produce (that is, it must sacrifice) 20 units of Y, so (dividing both sides by 20) in producing 1 unit of X it sacrifices 1 unit of Y.

More generally, the opportunity cost of producing the good on the horizontal axis is the slope of the PPC:

Opportunity cost of producing the good on the horizontal $= \frac{\Delta Y}{\Delta X}$

Note that if the PPCs are parallel, as in Figure 3.1.4, then there is no room for specialization and mutually beneficial trade because the opportunity cost ratios are equal.

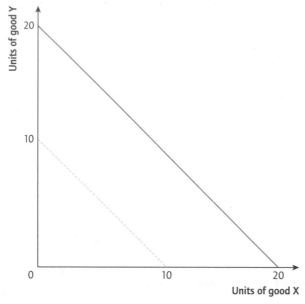

Figure 3.1.4 No room for mutually beneficial specialization and trade

Sources of comparative advantage

The ultimate determinants of a country's comparative advantage include differences in factor endowments and differences in technology. Differences in the quantity and quality of factors of production available include differences in the stock of natural capital and its productivity, differences in the stock of human capital and its productivity and differences in the stock of physical capital and its productivity. Differences in technology are manifested indirectly as technology is embodied in the physical capital available (it is 'inside' the machines available) and affects the productivity of human capital.

In addition, comparative advantage and trade flows can be affected by movements in the exchange rate (the price of a currency expressed in terms of another). For example, if the exchange rate rises (appreciates) then exports become less competitive. Changes in the relative inflation rates also affect competitiveness. For example, if average inflation in country X is 8% while in country B it is 4%, the goods and services produced by country X will become relatively more expensive over time. This worsens their competitiveness and causes a loss in comparative advantage. Export subsidies can also be used to create an artificial comparative advantage for a country's products – US cotton producers, recipients of massive state subsidies, provide a good example. Lastly, non-price factors can lead to the creation or the loss of comparative advantage and competitiveness (such as product design, reliability, quality of after-sales support). Export sales of German capital goods, for example, are not easily affected by an appreciating euro as their reputation is excellent in foreign markets.

Assumptions on which the principle of comparative advantage rests

These assumptions are:

- constant (average and marginal) costs of production reflected in the linear PPCs we draw
- perfect factor mobility within each country (but, immobility between countries)

- no transport costs
- perfect competition in all markets
- free trade (no trade barriers).

Criticisms of the principle of comparative advantage

The above assumptions do not accurately reflect real world conditions. These assumptions are the basis for the criticisms of the comparative advantage model and its predictions. The criticisms are as follows.

Costs of production need not be constant. They may be decreasing, in which case the gains from specialization may even be greater. Increasing returns to scale in production and the resulting EOS are very often the case in the real world.

Labour and the other factors of production suffer from both occupational and geographical immobility. It may not be costless or even possible for a country to specialize. Real adjustment costs, such as unemployment for certain regions or groups, will result when a country responds to a shift in its comparative advantage.

Transportation costs do exist in the real world and, depending on the ratio of weight to value, will decrease the scope of foreign trade opportunities. Note though that transport costs have dramatically decreased since the advent of the container in shipping.

Perfect competition is not common at all. Large firms with monopoly power and EOS dominate world trade.

Trade barriers are also a reality which prevents world trade flows from reflecting comparative advantage conditions among nations.

For these and other reasons the actual pattern of trade flows does not fully reflect comparative advantage. Still, comparative advantage is a most useful concept in understanding and explaining much of what is going on in the world of trade.

Limitations of the theory of competitive advantage: summary

Limitations of the theory of comparative advantage are that	increasing returns to scale and so EOS exist
	labour suffers from occupational and geographical immobility so it may be costly to specialize
	transportation costs exist, limiting the scope for trade
	perfectly competitive conditions are rarely approximated
	trade barriers exist, limiting the scope for trade

Comparative advantage is a dynamic concept

Comparative advantage is a dynamic concept as it can and does change over time. Governments can and historically have promoted policies that help to create a comparative advantage in specific industries. A government could invest in education, increasing the stock of human capital and raising labour productivity and lowering average costs in specific industries. It could create favourable investment conditions for private firms by ensuring price stability (low inflation), long-run equilibrium in the exchange rate and, more generally, a conducive business environment. It could also import technology by attracting foreign direct investment (FDI) in high-tech sectors.

An example of a country that did not rely on a static interpretation of comparative advantage but instead created a comparative advantage in several other areas is Korea. If it had relied on its original comparative advantage, it would have still been an exporter of rice.

The World Trade Organization

The World Trade Organization (WTO) was set up in 1995 and has 153 member countries, replacing another international organization known as the General Agreement on Tariffs and Trade (GATT). GATT was formed in 1948 when 23 countries signed an agreement to reduce tariffs.

The WTO is an international institution aiming at promoting free trade by persuading countries to abolish import tariffs and other barriers. It has become closely associated with globalization. It ensures that trade rules are adhered to, it settles trade disputes between countries and it organizes trade negotiations. WTO decisions are final and every member must abide by its rulings. So, when the USA and Brazil are in dispute over frozen orange juice, it is the WTO which acts as judge and jury. The WTO empowers its members to enforce its decisions by imposing trade sanctions against countries that have broken the rules.

The WTO is criticized on several grounds. It is accused that it is controlled by the rich nations, especially the USA, and that it does not sufficiently consider the needs and problems of the developing world. For example, agricultural products from developing countries do not have free access to the US market but the USA insists that the poor open up their markets to US goods and, especially, services. It is claimed that the WTO is too powerful, trying to force nations to change policies, laws and regulations by declaring them in violation of its rules. It is charged that does not consider the possible adverse effects of trade liberalization on workers, on the environment and health or on child labour. Lastly, some consider that it lacks transparency in its decision making on trade disputes as it is closed to the media and the public.

On the other hand, even if the benefits of freer trade have not been shared equally, many believe that the trade liberalization efforts of the WTO have improved living standards across the globe.

The WTO: summary of key points

The WTO	was set up in 1995 as a successor of the GATT (1948).
	has 153 member countries.
	promotes trade liberalization.
	sets trade rules and ensures that they are followed.
	is the arbitrator of trade-related disputes.
Criticisms of the WTO include that it is	biased in favour of US and European Union interests.
	inconsiderate to the needs of developing countries.
	paying insufficient attention to increasingly important issues such as child labour, health, the environment and workers' rights.

Restrictions on free trade: trade protection

Does trade protection make sense?

If the benefits from free trade are so many and, as shown earlier in Figure 3.1.1, net welfare increases with free trade, why do so many countries restrict trade and employ various degrees of trade protection? Why is 'managed' trade so common?

The simple answer is that not all parties involved gain from free trade. There are groups that are worse-off. Free trade creates winners and losers.

In Figure 3.1.1 the increase in the consumer surplus exceeds the decrease in the producer surplus. The winnings of the winners are greater than the losses of the losers. The problem in the real world is that there is no guarantee that the losers will be compensated.

In addition, the winnings from free trade are spread over a very large number of people (consumers) each getting a very small addition to his or her income while the resulting losses are spread over a much smaller number of individuals (producers) each suffering a significant cut in their income. It follows that losers have a big incentive to put up a fight against free trade.

To ensure that the adjustment costs for the losers are small, governments often judge that some level of trade protection is necessary.

Non-economic arguments in favour of trade protection

■ Governments often erect trade barriers to ensure that a country is self-sufficient in the production of crucial goods in the case of a war; in other words, for strategic reasons. The weapons and aerospace industries as well as the food industry are often classified as being of such strategic importance. The validity of this argument is doubtful, at least for countries belonging in wide strategic and/or political alliances.

■ Trade barriers are also employed to restrict imports of drugs and other harmful substances or to put pressure on and weaken politically unfriendly countries (embargoes).

■ Some countries resort to trade protection to preserve a way of life or cultural identity as part of a broader social strategy. For example, the television stations in many countries face restrictions on the hours of programmes broadcast in foreign languages.

■ Trade barriers also exist to ensure that certain minimum safety and health standards are met. The goal is purportedly to protect the public but often such standards are a pretence through which domestic producers are protected.

Economic arguments in favour of trade protection

■ A very common argument in favour of restricting trade is to protect domestic jobs. Many claim that free trade decreases employment as cheaper and better-quality foreign products flood the domestic market, forcing domestic firms to shut down. Foreign cheap labour is often blamed for increasing rates of unemployment.

These claims must be carefully evaluated. First, higher domestic wages do not necessarily imply higher labour costs as labour productivity is important. If domestic wages are higher because of higher labour productivity then labour costs may be lower than abroad, so there is no reason to fear imports. If, though, the higher domestic wages are not a reflection of higher labour productivity then the domestic industry has a comparative disadvantage. Theory then suggests that labour and other resources should be channelled to other, more efficient uses. Workers and owners of capital, and perhaps whole regions, will have to face real adjustment costs and of course will resist these changes. They will try to blame foreigners for their plight and will demand protection. Instead of protection though, which will reduce the incentive to restructure and adjust, other policies could be adopted to smoothen the transition, especially for displaced workers. Note that in the case of poorer developing countries shifting resources from one use to another may be almost impossible without some government assistance which itself could be too costly to implement. In such a case, trade liberalization should proceed gradually. Also, if employment in a whole region relies on the distressed industry with few or no employment alternatives for the population, then the liberalization process must be gradual.

- Another common argument in favour of protection is to improve a trade deficit. A trade deficit exists if the value of imports of goods and services (the import bill) is greater than export revenues. The idea is that trade protection will render imports more expensive and therefore less attractive. Spending on imports will therefore decrease, shrinking and correcting the trade imbalance.

  There are several potential problems with this argument. First, it invites retaliation from trading partners as any improvement in the trade balance comes at their expense. Second, restricting foreign products into the country lowers foreign incomes and, consequently, foreign consumers' ability to buy our exports. Third, and most importantly, such a policy does not treat the root cause of a widening trade deficit problem. The ballooning trade deficit may be the result of domestic products being uncompetitive: domestic goods and services are unable to penetrate foreign markets (so that exports decrease) and they are not the choice of domestic households which find it cheaper to buy imports instead (so that imports rise). High inflation, structural rigidities and uncompetitive domestic markets, as well as issues of poor quality, reliability, delivery, design or marketing may be the real reasons behind a growing trade imbalance. In these cases trade protection will not prove helpful but may possibly prove detrimental as it will delay the adoption of appropriate adjustment policies.

- Governments may decide to erect import barriers to assist the growth of certain industries in their initial stages of development. Once these industries acquire the necessary know-how and achieve EOS they will be able to meet international competition. At this point protection should be removed. This is the well-known 'infant industry' argument.

  This argument also needs to be carefully evaluated. It is indeed theoretically sensible and the policy has been used by all developed economies in the past, including the USA,

as well as by all Asian export achievers, in varying degrees. But it also suffers from potential major drawbacks. How does a government pick a 'winner'? It may be difficult to determine which industry qualifies for such treatment. If a mistake is made, will it be possible for the government to reverse its course and withdraw its support? Removing the protection could be fiercely resisted by the industry stakeholders. If trade protection is not lifted then we have the case of the 'perpetual infant'. There is an inherent risk of making the industry over-reliant on state support, sluggish and inefficient.

- If dumping is suspected (which is selling abroad at a price below average costs or lower than the domestic price) then even the WTO allows a country to impose tariffs (taxes on imports which in this case are referred to as anti-dumping duties) on the exporting industry. An investigation follows and if dumping is proved then trade protection is permitted to ensure a 'level playing field'.

  Dumping is not easy to prove, though. The question arising relates to firms' average costs. It could be that the foreign firm is much more efficient, so it has much lower unit costs of production. Or it could be that the foreign firm is illegally being subsidized by its government, creating an artificial cost advantage. In the former case there is no case of dumping whereas in the latter there is. As anti-dumping duties are automatically imposed when dumping is suspected until the issue is investigated and a verdict is reached, many industries 'cry' dumping to gain time in order to restructure and, they hope, become more efficient.

- Another argument is the strategic trade policy argument. According to this, in a framework of international oligopolies (where few large firms dominate world markets) a government can tilt the balance and the profits away from foreign competitors and towards domestic firms by using trade policies. The government's assistance can be in the form of subsidies, grants, loans at below market interest rates and tariffs. The classic example is the aircraft manufacturing industry, with Boeing and Airbus monopolizing the world market and where each side accuses the other of massive government assistance. In other cases (typically in high-tech industries), where there are 'first mover advantages' (implying that firms that are first to succeed will dominate the world industry), the assistance could take the form of setting industry standards in favour of domestic firms.

  The problem with strategic trade policy is that it carries the risk of destabilizing trade disputes and retaliation as it is a 'beggar thy neighbour' policy. If one country succeeds then another country necessarily fails. There is also the risk of protecting the wrong industries.

- Tariffs (taxes on imports) provide a government with revenues. Tax systems in certain developing countries are ineffective, making it difficult for their governments to collect sufficient revenue to finance pro-development activities. Since points of entry into a country are few, taxing imports to collect revenue may be a last resort that cannot be given up. If this is the case then trade liberalization must be gradual to ensure that the provision of basic government services is not interrupted.

Arguments in favour of trade protection: summary

Economic arguments in favour of trade protection are that	it will protect jobs from foreign competition.
	it can correct a trade deficit.
	it will protect against possible dumping.
	it can enhance government revenues.
Other arguments in favour are	the 'infant industry' argument.
	the strategic trade policy argument.

Arguments against trade protection

- Trade protection breeds inefficiency as domestic firms are exposed to less competition and are faced with captive domestic markets.

- Less competition implies greater domestic monopoly power.

- Greater monopoly power for domestic firms implies higher prices, distortion of the signalling power of the price mechanism and misallocation of scarce resources.

- Higher prices for imported and domestically produced consumer goods imply a decrease in consumer surplus and lower purchasing power for households and so constrained ability to express demand for all other goods and services in the economy. This could have negative effects on output and employment levels.

- Higher prices for domestic firms importing intermediate products (products used in their own production process) imply higher production costs and so a decrease in aggregate supply and cost-push inflationary pressures. If these domestic firms happen to be export-oriented their competitiveness in international markets will be eroded, hurting their sales and adversely affecting overall employment levels in the economy. Trade protection usually destroys more jobs than it preserves or creates.

- Trade protection may induce retaliation ('tit for tat'). If the trade frictions escalate then a trade war may result, in the long term, in hurting all parties involved.

- Domestic firms will not be exposed to the technological advancements embodied in imported capital goods.

- Only special interest groups benefit from trade protection, with society at large worse off in the long run. Owners and workers of protected industries and their stakeholders are better off at the expense of all others.

- Trade protection is responsible for 'directly unproductive profit-seeking (DUP)' activities, a term introduced by Bhagwati (1989), which includes activities such as rent and revenue seeking and tariff and quota evasion that take place in response to an existing trade barrier and lead to the use and waste of real resources.

- Consumers and firms are faced with limited options to choose from. The reduction in choice is a cost as buyers (consumers as well as firms) have to settle for their second or third choice. Utility decreases for households while competitiveness decreases for firms.

Arguments against trade protection: summary

	it breeds inefficiency.
	it limits competition and increases monopoly power.
	it is responsible for misallocation of scarce resources.
Arguments against trade protection are that	it leads to higher prices for consumers.
	it increases the production costs of firms importing intermediate goods.
	it increases the possibility of retaliation.
	it limits awareness of firms to technological progress embodied in imported capital goods.
	it is responsible for DUPs.
	it limits options to consumers and firms.

Types of trade protection

Trade protection can take various forms. The most common forms are: tariffs, quotas, voluntary export restraints, subsidies and regulatory barriers (product standards), as well as a host of other measures such as antidumping duties, exchange controls, non-automatic import authorization (import licenses) etc. Remember that non-tariff barriers include those barriers that do not directly affect the price of the good.

Tariffs

A tariff is defined as a tax imposed on imports aimed at restricting their flow into the country and at protecting domestic producers. It has been the most common form of protection. It may be specific or ad valorem. A tariff will tend to raise the domestic price and domestic production while lowering the amounts consumed and imported. These effects are illustrated in Figure 3.1.5.

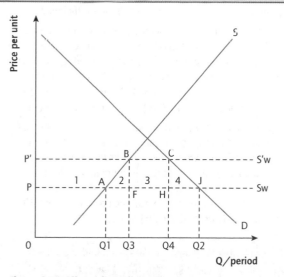

Figure 3.1.5 Effects of a tariff ('small country' case)

Assume the market for a particular good and let the world price be at P. At the price P, domestic firms will offer Q1 units per period while domestic consumption will be Q2 units per period. Imports will make up the difference (that is, Q1Q2 units per period).

Let a tariff equal to t dollars or euros be now imposed. The tariff will raise the domestic price to P'. The tariff t is equal to P' dollars or euros per unit. Note that the tariff will not affect the world price as it is assumed that the country is 'small'. This means that the world price P is not affected if the country, as a result of the tariff, demands less. The country is small in the sense that its production and consumption decisions are insignificant, so they do not affect the world price.

Given the new price P' established in the domestic market, domestic production will rise to Q3 units per period while domestic consumption drops to Q4 units per period. The volume of imports shrinks to Q3Q4 units per period.

The higher price implies that the consumer surplus decreases by area (P'PJC) or area (1, 2, 3, 4) while the producer surplus increases by area (PABP') or area (1).

Area (FHCB) (area (3)) is the tariff revenue collected. This is the case because tariff revenues are the product of the tariff per unit times that number of units imported. The tariff per unit is line segment P'P (equal to segment BF) and the volume of imports is Q3Q4 (or segment FH).

Examining the changes in social welfare that result from the imposition of the tariff we realize that:

Δ(producer surplus) = plus area (1)

Δ(consumer surplus) = minus area (1 + 2 + 3 + 4)

Area (3) represents the tariff revenues collected, so it cannot be considered a welfare loss as this money can be spent on schools and health care centres, for example.

So: Δ(social welfare) = minus area (2 + 4)

A tariff leads to a net welfare loss equal to areas (2) and (4).

Area (2) represents the resulting production inefficiency while area (4) represents the resulting consumption inefficiency.

Area (2) reflects production inefficiency because the cost of domestically producing units Q1Q3 (which is equal to area Q1Q3BA, the sum of all the marginal costs of producing these units) is greater than what it would have cost the country to import these units at the world price OP (which is equal to area (Q1Q3FA), the product of units Q1Q3 times the world price).

Area (4) reflects consumption inefficiency. Units Q4Q2 are now not consumed by domestic consumers as a result of the tariff even though these units are valued by consumers more than what it would cost them to import. These units are worth area (Q4CJQ2) to consumers, which is the sum of how much consumers would be willing to pay for each of these units. They would have cost only area (Q4Q2JH) to import.

> **TIP** Remember that despite the welfare loss a tariff may make sense. It is a source of government revenue that may be impossible to replace. Also, the adjustment costs for the displaced workers may in some cases be prohibitively high.

Tariffs: summary of effects

Tariffs	increase the domestic price of the protected good.
	increase domestic production of the good.
	decrease consumption of the good.
	decrease consumer surplus by area (1 + 2 + 3 + 4) in a typical tariff diagram.
	increase producer surplus by area (1) in a typical tariff diagram.
	create tariff revenues equal to area (3) in a typical tariff diagram (but the effect on total government tax revenues collected is ambiguous).
	lead to production inefficiency equal to area (2) in a typical tariff diagram.
	lead to consumption inefficiency equal to area (4) in a typical tariff diagram.
	are responsible for a welfare loss equal to area (2 + 4) in a typical tariff diagram.

Quotas

A quota is defined as a quantitative restriction on the volume of imports. Figure 3.1.6 illustrates the effect of a quota.

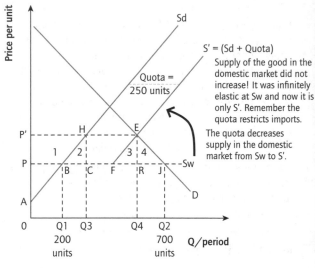

Figure 3.1.6 Effects of a quota

Let the world price for some good be at P. At price P, domestic firms are willing to offer Q1 units per period (say, 200 thousand tons of frozen orange juice per period) while domestic consumption will be Q2 units (say, 700 thousand tons). The volume of imports will be Q1Q2 units or, in this example, 500 thousand tons of frozen orange juice).

Let the government now impose a quota of 250 thousand tons of frozen orange juice in an attempt to protect domestic producers. No more than 250 thousand tons of imported frozen orange juice may enter the domestic market.

Prior to the quota, domestic consumers faced an infinitely elastic supply of frozen orange juice Sw as they were offered whatever amount they wished at the world price. We are again assuming a small country so that the world price remains unaffected no matter how much the small country decides to buy.

After the imposition of the quota, at the unchanged world price P, as well as at any other price above it, supply of frozen orange juice in the domestic market will be constrained to whatever amount domestic producers of frozen orange juice are willing to offer plus the 250 thousand tons of frozen orange juice that can now only be imported.

It follows that the new effective supply of frozen orange juice is at S', which is parallel to the right of the domestic supply curve Sd by the amount of the quota, in this case by 250 thousand tons (more precisely, the new supply is the line ABFS'). At each price above P, the amount of frozen orange juice available to domestic consumers will equal to whatever quantity domestic producers are willing to offer plus the 250 thousand tons quota of frozen orange juice.

At price P, the total quantity supplied will equal Q1 units of domestic frozen orange juice plus the 250 thousand tons of the quota equal to distance BF. At that price P though, quantity demanded is greater and equal to Q2 units. Excess demand equal to distance FJ units per period will result. Since we are implicitly assuming perfectly competitive markets, the domestic market price for frozen orange juice will rise until it reaches P'.

Price P' is the new equilibrium price in the domestic market because at that price the total amount supplied to the market by both domestic and foreign producers is equal to the quantity domestically demanded by consumers. More specifically, at P' domestic producers offer Q3 tons (or distance P9H), consumers buy Q4 tons (or distance P9E) and the difference of Q3Q4 tons (or distance HE) is made up of the imported frozen orange juice which is equal to the 250 thousand tons quota.

A quota therefore increases the domestic price of the protected good as well as domestic production while it reduces domestic consumption and, of course, the volume (quantity) of imports.

Examining the changes in social welfare that result from the imposition of the quota we realize that:

Δ(producer surplus) = plus area (1)

Δ(consumer surplus) = minus area (1 + 2 + 3 + 4)

Δ(social welfare) = minus area (2 + 3 + 4)

Area (3) is known as 'quota rents' and represents money typically earned by the foreign exporting firms which can now export the product at a higher price. Area (3) may also end up in the hands of foreign governments. It is even possible that the money that area (3) represents ends up in the hands (the coffers) of the domestic government if, for example, it auctions off the quota licenses.

Area (2) again represents the resulting production inefficiency while area (4) represents the resulting consumption inefficiency, as explained in the case of a tariff.

The effects of a quota are the same as those of an 'equivalent' tariff with one exception: the tariff revenues area (3) now represents quota rents which are usually collected by foreigners and represent an additional welfare loss.

The existence of quota rents helps explain why quotas are often imposed instead of tariffs even though the associated welfare loss is bigger. Foreigners are 'happier' as they usually pocket these rents. If the foreign exporting firms pocket the quota rent, then their export revenues (and equivalently, the

import bill from the point of view of the importing country) are bigger than if an equivalent tariff was imposed and may even be greater than what they would have been under free trade. With free trade their export revenues were equal to area (Q1Q2JB) whereas with a quota appropriated by the foreign exporter they are area (Q3 Q4EH), which could be greater. This possibility minimizes the probability of retaliation.

TIP The quota diagram is one of the most difficult to draw and is a source of many avoidable mistakes. An easy way to do the job is to draw a free trade diagram, determine the amount of imports under free trade (Q1Q2 in Figure 3.1.5) and find the midpoint of this segment (conveniently assuming that the quota is set at half the free trade level of imports). Do not label this new point! Very lightly trace with your pencil (so that you can erase it later) a line up to Sw to determine the point from which you draw a parallel to the domestic supply curve Sd (in Figure 3.1.5 the point you determine on Sw is point F). This is the new effective supply curve S'. Lastly, from the intersection of S' and your demand curve D (point E in Figure 3.1.5) determine the new equilibrium price P'.

Quotas: summary of effects

Quotas	increase the domestic price of the protected good.
	increase domestic production of the good.
	decrease consumption of the good.
	decrease consumer surplus by area (1 + 2 + 3 + 4) in a typical quota diagram.
	increase producer surplus by area (1) in a typical quota diagram.
	create 'quota rents' equal to area (3) which are typically pocketed by foreign firms (but the domestic government may also collect these).
	lead to production inefficiency equal to area (2) in a typical quota diagram.
	lead to consumption inefficiency equal to area (4) in a typical quota diagram.
	are responsible for a welfare loss equal to area (2 + 3 + 4) in a typical quota diagram (assuming that the quota rents are collected by foreigners).

Voluntary export restraints (VERs)

Setting up VERs is a form of trade protection that is a slightly different version of imposing quotas. VERs are agreements between an exporting and an importing country limiting the maximum amount of exports in a given period. The domestic (importing) government asks the foreign government to restrict the exports of the good; the term 'voluntary' is misleading since the request is really a demand and it is made clear that unless the foreign government 'voluntarily' complies, more restrictive protectionist barriers will be imposed. The effects are similar to that of a quota so area (3) may still end up in the pockets of foreigners, making it less costly than if a tariff was imposed.

Subsidies

Subsidies lower production costs of firms and therefore artificially increase their competitiveness. As a result, subsidies will decrease imports and may even lead to exports. The US cotton industry is the recipient of huge government subsidies and ranks number one in world cotton exports. The effects of a subsidy are illustrated in Figure 3.1.7.

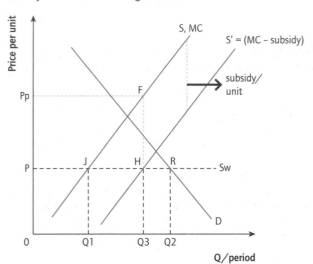

Figure 3.1.7 The effect of a subsidy to domestic producers on imports

Initially, assume free trade with the world price of the product at P. The domestic industry will be willing to produce and offer Q1 units per period whereas consumption (quantity demanded) will be at Q2 units per period leading to Q1Q2 units of imports.

If a subsidy is granted to the domestic firms then their production (marginal) costs will decrease by the amount of the subsidy. Supply will increase, shifting vertically downward by the amount of the subsidy to S′.

The world price P is not affected (assuming again a 'small country' case) but now at the world price P, domestic firms are willing to offer more. Domestic production at P is now, as a result of the subsidy, at Q3 units per period. Consequently, the volume of imports will shrink from Q1Q2 to Q3Q2 units.

Domestic firms will earn P per unit plus the per unit subsidy which is the vertical distance HF between the two supply curves (that is, their new average revenue is Pp).

Total revenues for the domestic industry have increased from area (0Q1JP) to area (0Q3FPP). Consumers enjoy the same

amount at the same price but the government and so, eventually, taxpayers are burdened by the cost of the subsidy which is equal to area (PHFPP).

Subsidies: summary of effects

Subsidies	do not affect the domestic price of the protected good.
	do not affect consumption of the good.
	increase domestic production of the good.
	do not affect consumer welfare.
	make domestic producers better-off.
	lead to wasteful domestic production and resource misallocation.
	lead to increased government spending burdening taxpayers.
	can create trade frictions.

Administrative or regulatory barriers

Perhaps this is the most common form of protection. Regulatory barriers include product standards (to meet certain domestic requirements), sanitary standards (to protect the domestic consumers), pollution standards, etc.

Often these standards are set to protect domestic producers rather than domestic consumers by making it more difficult (and costly) for foreign firms to comply.

Perhaps the most famous example of an administrative barrier is the one related to the city of Poitiers in France. In 1981, the French government ordered that all Japanese video imports were to be inspected and pass customs there. Poitiers is located inland, is far from ports and was staffed with only a few officers ordered to inspect fully each and every truck. The delays were huge and the volume of imports entering France per period was effectively reduced. Following complaints this absurd requirement was withdrawn.

Anti-dumping duties

Domestic firms may file a complaint that foreign firms are dumping their goods in the domestic market. Dumping is said to exist if a firm sells abroad at a price below unit (average) costs or below its domestic price. A duty (a tax) is automatically imposed that raises the foreign firms' price and the issue is investigated and resolved by the WTO.

Very often, firms file such claims only to buy time to restructure and, they hope, become more efficient.

Why have cries for trade protection been increasing?

A growing number of developing countries (especially China) have achieved rapid, export-led growth. Export success by these countries means deep import penetration in Europe and the USA. Protectionist response is expected from those groups most affected.

Large trade imbalances between large trading nations (the most prominent example being that between the USA and China) have strained relationships between these countries and have led to various protectionist measures. The USA, for

example, has accused the Chinese of achieving export penetration as a result of keeping their currency (the yuan or renminbi) undervalued.

Exchange rate instability has added risk and uncertainty to trade and since it can lead to sudden shifts in comparative advantages it may lead to calls for protection for domestic industry. Many claim that the choice is between managed trade or managed exchange rates.

Of course, rising unemployment has always been a reason for demanding increased trade protection. Recessions and unemployment always put political pressure on governments to limit 'job threatening' imports.

The exchange rate of a currency is defined as the price (or the value) of a currency expressed in terms of another currency.

For example, on 7 April 2011, 1.00 EUR = 1.38 USD. One needed 1.38 US dollars to purchase 1 euro. This automatically means that one needed 0.73 euro to buy 1 US dollar as 0.73 is the inverse of 1.38.

Foreign exchange markets

A foreign exchange market is a market in which currencies are exchanged for other currencies. An example is the market where euros and dollars are traded. This is a 24-hour, 365-days-a-year world market that is a good approximation of a perfectly competitive market, as follows.

- The 'good' is homogeneous as it makes no difference whether a dollar is bought in Frankfurt or in Singapore or in London.

- There are very many buyers and sellers of currencies (all major world banks participate, non-financial corporations as well as financial corporations such as pension funds, insurance companies, hedge funds, etc.) No single player is large enough to influence the market price of a currency.

- No entry barrier into the market exists as any new bank or corporate financial or non-financial major can enter and participate.

A distinctive characteristic of this market is that all buyers are at the same time also sellers, and vice versa. Also, if the price of currency A expressed in terms of currency B is e then the price of currency B expressed in terms of currency A is $\left(\frac{1}{e}\right)$.

Floating, fixed and managed exchange rate systems

A currency is traded in a floating (or flexible) exchange rate system if market forces alone without any government or central bank intervention determine its value. The dollar, the euro and the British pound all float against each other.

A fixed exchange rate system refers to the case where the exchange rate is set and maintained at some level by the government (or the central bank) of a country.

A managed exchange rate system is one where there is no announced level or band but either the exchange rate is allowed to float within some implicit upper and lower bound or authorities intervene whenever they consider the direction or the speed of adjustment of the currency undesirable.

Appreciation and depreciation
These terms refer to changes in the price (the value) of a currency in a floating (or flexible) exchange rate system. More specifically, a currency appreciates if its price increases within a floating exchange rate system. A currency depreciates if its price decreases within a floating exchange rate system. It should be clear that if currency A depreciates in terms of

currency B it follows that currency B appreciated in terms of currency A, as the one exchange rate is the inverse of the other.

In a floating exchange rate system exchange rate changes are continuous and even if the trend is upward, there is a lot of short-term volatility.

Revaluation and devaluation
The terms refer to official changes in the price of a currency in a fixed exchange rate system. More specifically, a currency devalues if its official price decreases within a fixed exchange rate system. A currency revalues if its official price increases within a fixed exchange rate system.

Who demands (and supplies) a currency in the foreign exchange market and why?
Consider for example the demand for the British currency: pounds sterling. Who will demand pounds in the foreign exchange market and for what reason?

- Demand for pounds sterling arises from the demand for UK exports of goods and services. For example, Koreans purchasing British engines or measuring instruments will need to pay in pounds sterling so the Korean currency, the won, will have to be exchanged for pounds sterling at some point in the foreign exchange market. The equivalent will happen when an American spends her holiday in London.

- Demand for pounds sterling also arises when foreigners want to make deposits in this currency or to purchase UK bonds or shares of UK firms. Demand for the British currency also arises when multinational corporations want to establish a presence in the UK. These are all investment (capital) flows (portfolio investments and foreign direct investment; FDI, respectively) into the UK.

- Lastly, speculators may buy British currency not to buy a good, a service or some asset but instead hoping to sell it at a higher price at a later date and so make a profit.

Remember that the demand for a currency is at the same time the supply of another currency. In the market for British currency the supply of pounds sterling will originate from holders of that currency who offer it in the market, wishing to buy another currency in order to:
- purchase foreign goods and services (that is, UK imports)
- make investments (portfolio and FDI) abroad (that is, investment or capital outflows from the UK)
- buy foreign currencies as part of pure speculative activities.

It should be added that central banks may also buy or sell a currency as part of their exchange rate policy.

Demand and supply of currency: summary

The demand and the supply of a currency in the foreign exchange market reflects international trade flows as well as cross-border investment and speculative flows		
	Demand for the currency reflects	Supply of the currency reflects
More specifically:	the value of its exports of goods and services	the value of its imports of goods and services
	as well as the inflow of investments into the country.	as well as the inflow of investments into the country.

In Figure 3.2.1 the market for British pounds sterling (GBP) is illustrated against the US dollar (USD).

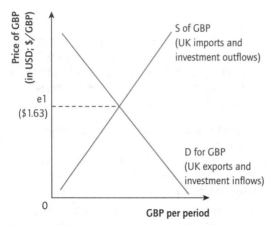

Figure 3.2.1 What the demand and the supply of a currency reflect

In Figure 3.2.1 the vertical axis is the price of the pound sterling and we choose to express it in US dollars. So, it is US dollars per one pound sterling or $/£. Since the vertical axis is the price of the pound sterling it follows that the horizontal axis will be quantity of pounds sterling traded per period or more simply pounds sterling (£) per period. In general, and to avoid a common mistake, remember that whatever is below on the ratio of the vertical axis is the label on the horizontal axis.

The demand for pounds sterling reflects the value of UK exports as well as inflows of capital from abroad to buy US assets. The supply of pounds sterling reflects the value of UK imports as well as outflows of capital from the UK to buy foreign (US in this case) assets. Remember that we also have speculators on both sides and perhaps central banks.

The interaction of the daily or hourly demand and supply of a currency determines the exchange rate in a flexible exchange rate system.

Exchange rate adjustments in a flexible exchange rate system

To simplify the analysis let's assume that there are no cross-border investments so that only exports and imports of goods and services (trade flows) create a need to exchange currencies. In a US–EU17 framework, Americans demand euros to buy EU17 goods and services and Europeans supply euros to buy dollars (and so US goods and services). (EU17 refers to the members of the eurozone. See page 131 for more on this.)

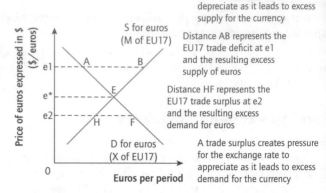

Figure 3.2.2

At the exchange rate e1 the supply of euros is equal to distance e1B and reflects the value of imports into the EU17 while the demand for euros is distance e1A and reflects the value of EU17 exports to the US. Import expenditures exceed export revenues at e1 so the EU17 has a trade deficit and in the foreign exchange market an excess supply of euros exists equal to distance AB. This excess supply creates pressure for the euro to depreciate.

This depreciation has two effects: EU17 exports become cheaper and more competitive abroad while imports become pricier and therefore less attractive within the EU17. Eventually, the value of EU17 exports will increase and the expenditures on imports will shrink, tending to balance out trade flows. This will happen when the exchange rate reaches e*. At e*, demand for euros is equal to supply of euros per period and trade balance is restored. Remember we are assuming there are no cross-border investment flows or central bank intervention.

At the exchange rate e2 the supply of euros is equal to distance e2H and reflects the value of imports into the EU17 while the demand for euros is equal to distance e2F and reflects the value of EU17 exports to the USA. Export revenues exceed import expenditures at e2 so the EU17 has a trade surplus and in the foreign exchange market an excess demand for euros exists equal to distance HF. The excess demand creates pressure for the euro to appreciate.

This appreciation has two effects: EU17 exports become more expensive and therefore less competitive abroad, while imports become cheaper and more attractive domestically. Eventually the value of EU17 exports will decrease and the expenditures on imports will increase, tending to balance out trade flows. This will happen when the exchange rate reaches e*. At e*, demand for euros is equal to supply of euros per period and trade is balance is restored.

It follows that a trade deficit (more generally, a current account deficit) creates pressure for the exchange rate to depreciate whereas trade surplus (more generally, a current account surplus) creates pressure for the exchange rate to appreciate.

In the real world though there are a number of issues that complicate matters. First, exchange rates are very much affected by cross-border investments (the buying and selling of bonds and stocks and speculation) and not only by trade flows. For example, any change in interest rates or in investors' expectations may prevent the adjustment process described above.

Second, whether a depreciating currency will increase the value of exports (that is, export revenues) depends on the price elasticity of exports. The lower-priced exports will definitely increase the volume (quantity) of exports per period but whether their value (revenues) actually increases or not depends on their PED.

Causes of changes in the exchange rate

The demand and the supply of a currency in the foreign exchange market reflect trade flows and investment flows between countries. Trade flows refer to exports and imports of goods and services. This means that the first factor that may change the exchange rate of a currency is a change in exports or in imports.

Changes in trade flows

■ **One example is a change in the foreign demand for a country's exports.** Assume that a country is experiencing growing demand for its exports. To simplify the analysis let's further assume that demand for its imports remains constant. Growing exports implies that demand for the currency by foreigners will be increasing, shifting to the right. At the original exchange rate a trade (current account) surplus will be created as well as excess demand for the currency. Excess demand for the currency will create pressure for the currency to appreciate. Note that a decrease in the foreign demand for a country's exports will exert downward pressure on its currency.

■ **Another example is a change in the domestic demand for imports.** Assume that domestic demand for imports increases, with demand for exports remaining constant. Supply of the currency will increase as there will be growing need to buy with it foreign exchange. The supply for the currency will be shifting to the right. At the original exchange rate a trade (current account) deficit will form as well as excess supply for the currency. Excess supply for the currency will create pressure for the currency to depreciate. Note that a decrease in domestic demand for a country's imports will exert upward pressure on its currency.

Figure 3.2.3 illustrates the first point focusing on the Australian dollar (AUD) and assuming that Australia experiences increased demand for its exports.

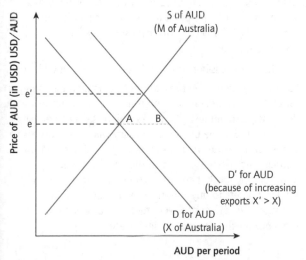

Figure 3.2.3 Growing demand for a country's exports and its effect on the currency

Initially, assume that demand and supply for the Australian dollar are equal so that the exchange rate against the US dollar is at point e on the vertical axis. Australia's trade in good and services is balanced (we are assuming there are no investment flows). If there is growing demand for Australian exports then demand for AUD will shift to D' reflecting the growth in export demand (X'>X). At the original exchange rate e there is a trade (current account) surplus equal to distance AB and excess demand for Australian dollars in the market. This means there is pressure on the Australian dollar to appreciate all the way to e'.

In Figure 3.2.4 we assume increased demand in Australia for imported goods and services.

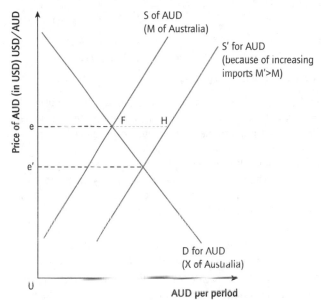

Figure 3.2.4 The effect of increased domestic demand for imports on a currency

The increased demand for foreign goods and services (imports) in Australia will increase supply for the Australian dollar to S'. At the original exchange rate, e, a trade (current account) deficit will appear as well as excess supply of Australian dollars in the foreign exchange market (equal to distance FH) which will exert pressure on the Australian dollar to depreciate to e'.

Since changes in the foreign demand for a country's exports and changes in the domestic demand for imports affect the exchange rate, it follows that any factor that affects a country's trade flows will in turn affect its exchange rate.

■ **Factors that may affect trade flows include changes in relative growth rates.** A higher growth rate implies that incomes in the country are rising faster. Since rising incomes imply rising consumption expenditures, and household consumption includes spending on not only domestic but also foreign goods and services, it follows that in a growing economy demand for imports will rise. If incomes are rising then more imports will be absorbed.

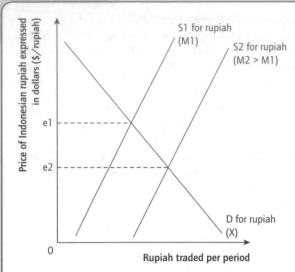

Figure 3.2.5 Effect of a growing economy on the exchange rate

In Figure 3.2.5 the price of the Indonesian rupiah is initially assumed at e1. If Indonesian growth accelerates then Indonesians' incomes are rising so their consumption expenditures will rise. This means that they will also buy more foreign products. Indonesians will have to supply more of their currency, the rupiah, in the foreign exchange market to buy the necessary dollars they need to buy more imports. Supply of the rupiah will shift to the right to S2 as imports are now greater (M2 > M1).

As a result, the rupiah will tend to depreciate to e2. This is a very interesting result that is seemingly counterintuitive. A growing economy may witness a depreciating currency.

- **Factors that may affect trade flows include changes in relative inflation rates.** If inflation in a country accelerates it means that prices in that country are rising on the average faster than previously. As a result, its products will be less competitive abroad while imported goods and services will seem more attractive domestically.

  Foreign demand for its exports will decrease and so will the demand for its currency in foreign exchange markets. In addition, domestic demand for foreign products (imported goods and services) will increase, increasing the supply of its currency in foreign exchange markets (as more foreign exchange will be needed to pay for these imports).

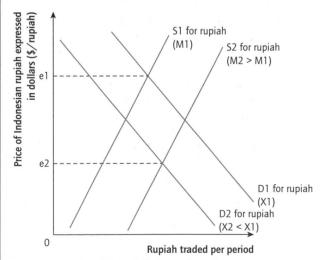

Figure 3.2.6 Effect of higher inflation on the exchange rate

Figure 3.2.6 illustrates the effect of higher inflation in Indonesia on its currency, the rupiah. Initially, the rupiah against the dollar is at e1.

The higher inflation in Indonesia will have an adverse effect on its exports as they will become less competitive abroad and therefore decrease, decreasing the demand for the rupiah from D1 to D2.

At the same time inflation will mean that Indonesians find foreign products more attractive. Imports will tend to increase, leading to more rupiahs being supplied in the foreign exchange market, shifting the supply of rupiahs from S1 to S2. The rupiah will tend to depreciate to e2.

Inflation in an economy will tend to depreciate a currency.

Changes in cross-border investment (capital) flows

The exchange rate is also affected by cross-border investment and speculative flows. For Americans to buy EU17 bonds or to set up a new firm in the EU17 first they need to get their hands on euros. If, on the other hand, EU17 bonds do not seem as attractive anymore then holders of EU17 bonds will want to get rid of them to switch to, say, British bonds. They will sell euros to buy pounds sterling, so the supply of euros will increase.

Investment flows include portfolio investments (the buying and selling of bonds and stocks and of other financial assets) and FDI, which refers to investors establishing a presence in a foreign country either by setting up a new firm or by acquiring controlling share of an existing domestic firm.

Much of these capital flows are short term and speculative in nature. Currency speculation is also included in this section. These transactions are included in the financial account of the balance of payments of a country.

Bear in mind that not all countries have fully liberalized their financial account. This means that foreign investment may be constrained. Many economies limit the types of foreign investment flows they permit as some of these investments may prove very destabilizing. Short-term speculative capital may suddenly be withdrawn, leading to a sudden sharp depreciation and, consequently, to adverse real effects on the economy. There is a lot of discussion on the desirability of such private capital inflows (referred to also as hot monies or footloose funds, for obvious reasons) especially for developing countries.

Factors affecting cross-border capital flows are explained below.

- **Factors that may affect investment flows include changes in relative interest rates.** If interest rates in a country decrease, then domestic bonds as well as savings deposits denominated in the domestic currency will be less attractive to foreign investors. As a result, not only will demand for that currency decrease but also there will be an increase in the supply for that country's currency as investors will sell their assets to buy currencies and bonds of other countries. The effect of lower interest rates will be a tendency for the currency to depreciate.

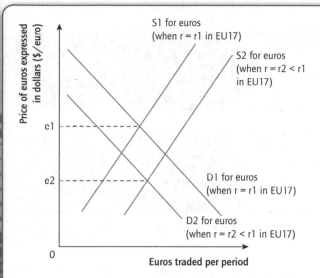

Figure 3.2.7 Effect of a decrease in interest rates on a country's currency

In Figure 3.2.7 we assume that the dollar price of the euro is initially at e1. Let's say the European Central Bank decreases interest rates. Now the rate of return on European bonds as well as on deposits in euros is lower, so these assets are less attractive to investors. Demand for the euro will decrease from D1 to D2, reflecting the lower demand for European bonds and euro deposits. Also, some holders of such assets will decide to sell them, increasing the supply of euros from S1 to S2 as they switch to more attractive bonds issued by other countries. The euro will tend to depreciate from e1 to e2.

A note of caution here: if interest rates rise there will be a tendency for the exchange rate to appreciate **assuming** that foreign investors do not expect the currency to depreciate. For example, if interest rates in country A rise then investors will not all flock into that country if they expect its currency to depreciate. So interest rates do matter, but so does the expectation about the future path of the exchange rate itself.

- **Factors that may affect investment flows include expectations about future growth.** A growing economy will tend to absorb more and more imports, putting pressure on the exchange rate to depreciate, as illustrated in Figure 3.2.8. At the same time, though, there will be other forces in the foreign exchange market that will tend to appreciate the currency.

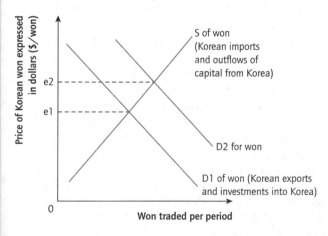

If the future prospects of this growing economy are good (if, in other words investors expect it to continue growing in the future) then they will want to buy stocks and/or establish a business presence themselves in the country so that they can receive the expected profits. Demand for the country's currency will tend to increase, pushing the exchange rate upward. Remember that a growing economy implies growing and profitable firms and plentiful business opportunities which foreigners will also want to take advantage of.

In Figure 3.2.8 the Korean currency, the won, is illustrated. Initially, the equilibrium exchange rate is assumed at e1. If data projections point out strong and continuing growth for the Korean economy, then growing interest will be expressed in Korean company stocks as well as FDI into Korea.

These increased portfolio investments and FDI into Korea imply an increase in the demand for Korean won in the foreign exchange markets. Demand for won will increase from D1 to D2, so the won will tend to appreciate from e1 to e2.

- **Factors that may affect investment flows include expectations concerning the future path of the exchange rate.** Often a currency is demanded in foreign exchange markets not to buy foreign goods or services or to buy foreign bonds, stocks or companies but just to sell it at a later date, perhaps even in a matter of hours, at a higher price, making a profit out of the price difference.

Market participants who act in this way are known as currency speculators. Their demand for the currency is purely speculative. Obviously, the driving force behind their demand is the expected future path of the exchange rate itself.

In the simplest scenario if they expect the exchange rate to appreciate they buy the currency now, hoping to sell it later at a higher price, making a profit. If others believe and do the same thing then the demand for the currency will increase.

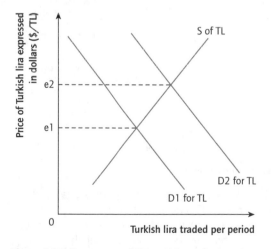

Figure 3.2.9 Currency speculation and the exchange rate

In Figure 3.2.9 currency speculation increases the demand for the Turkish Lira from D1 to D2, leading it to appreciate from e1 to e2. In this way, expectations can often be self-fulfilling.

Exchange rate appreciation and depreciation: summary

If foreign demand for a country's exports increases and/or domestic demand for imports decreases, creating or widening a trade (current account) surplus, then	**the exchange rate will tend to appreciate.**
If domestic interest rates increase (or, foreign interest rates decrease) then	
If it is expected that the country will continue to grow then	
If speculators expect the exchange rate to appreciate then	

On the other hand, the following applies.

If domestic demand for imports increases and/or foreign demand for its exports decreases, creating or widening a trade (current account) deficit, then	**the exchange rate will tend to depreciate.**
If domestic inflation increases then	
If domestic interest rates decrease (or foreign interest rates increase) then	
If speculators expect the exchange rate to depreciate then	

Government intervention

Fixed exchange rate systems

How does a fixed exchange rate system work?

A fixed exchange rate system is defined as a system in which the exchange rate is set by the government at some desired level (usually against a major currency, say, the US dollar) and is then maintained at that level through intervention in the foreign exchange market by the central bank. How is the exchange rate maintained at the set level? What can and should the government or the central bank do to maintain the rate at the desired level if, for example, there are pressures for it to devalue?

How do they work?

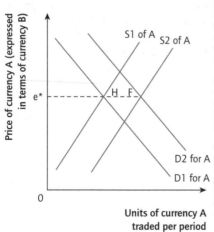

Currency A pegged against the dollar at e*

S of A rises to S2 because inflation makes imports seem more attractive, creating an excess supply that will push A below e*, unless:

central bank of A starts buying HF units of A per period artificially increasing demand for it to D2

or instead the central bank could increase interest rates inducing greater demand for A by investors (i.e. inducing capital inflows).

Figure 3.2.10 Fixed exchange rates

In Figure 3.2.10 it is assumed that currency A is pegged against, say, the US dollar at e*. If demand and supply forces are at D1 and S1 the exchange rate will be at e* so there is no reason for the authorities to intervene. Assume now that supply for currency A increases to S2, perhaps as a result of accelerating domestic inflation which induces residents to switch to more attractive imports. As more of the currency will be supplied in the foreign exchange market (supply of A, say, shifts to S2) there will be excess supply for the currency equal to FH per period at e*, putting pressure on the currency to devalue.

Remember that in a fixed exchange rate system we use the terms devaluation and revaluation.

The exchange rate will be maintained at the desired level e* only if authorities somehow manage to increase demand for the currency to D2. How could they do this? One obvious option is for the central bank of country A to enter the foreign exchange market and start buying FH units of its currency per period using its foreign exchange reserves, for example pounds sterling or euros. What this really means is that the central bank is increasing demand for currency A from D1 to D2.

To defend the currency, the central bank can also increase interest rates. This would be the next line of defence as foreign exchange reserves are limited and the central bank cannot go on selling, for example, euros forever to buy its own currency: there will come a point when it has no more euros left to sell. The higher interest rates in country A will attract financial capital from abroad as domestic bonds and deposits in currency A will earn a higher rate of return, so will be more attractive. Foreigners will buy currency A in the foreign exchange market in order to buy country A's bonds or make deposits in currency A. Higher interest rates impose a real cost on the economy, though, as growth in country A will slow down and unemployment will increase.

The government may also resort to official borrowing of foreign exchange in an attempt to maintain the currency at e*. This borrowing to defend the currency cannot continue for long, though, as repayment will impose significant future costs on an economy. Alternatively, the government may try to limit pressure on the currency to devalue by restricting imports into the country and in this way restricting the supply of its currency in the foreign exchange market.

Lastly, it can also restrict access to foreign exchange, reducing the supply of its currency in the foreign exchange market. Exchange controls may lead to a parallel ('black' or shadow) market.

On the other hand, if there are forces pushing up the currency's value the central bank will sell its currency, buying US dollars in the foreign exchange market, or it may lower domestic interest rates. Note that both options increase the money supply, so may lead to accelerating inflationary pressures in country A.

Fixed exchange rate system: summary

In a fixed exchange rate system	
If there are pressures for the currency to devalue	then the central bank must start buying it using foreign exchange reserves (but these are limited).
	or the central bank must increase interest rates to attract foreign capital inflows (but high interest rates choke off economic activity).
	or the country must resort to official borrowing of foreign exchange (but borrowing imposes future costs).
	or the government may restrict imports and access to foreign exchange (but inefficiencies and 'black' markets will emerge).

The following applies in relation to revaluation.

In a fixed exchange rate system	
If there are pressures for the currency to revalue	then the central bank must start selling it to buy dollars (foreign exchange). or the central bank must decrease interest rates to create an outflow of foreign capital. (but both options increase the risk of inflation).

Managed exchange rate systems

Managed float

In a managed exchange rate system the government tries to decrease exchange rate movements without keeping exchange rates rigidly fixed. The central bank periodically intervenes if authorities consider the exchange rate moving in a direction or a speed that is considered undesirable. Usually there is an implicit targeted band within which exchange rate movements are considered acceptable, but it is not announced.

Intervention involves buying and selling the currency in foreign exchange markets or of manipulating interest rates to induce the desired capital flows, as described earlier when discussing fixed exchange rates.

Maintaining disequilibrium exchange rates

Keeping the currency overvalued

Sometimes countries try to keep the exchange rate of their currency overvalued. This means that they try to maintain it at a level above the free market equilibrium level. Why would policy makers decide on something like this and what are some of the consequences?

Many developing countries have in the past tried to keep their currency overvalued as part of an import substitution strategy which will be explained in more detail later. The basic idea is that they were trying to shift out of agriculture and into manufacturing by substituting domestic production for imports. They erected trade barriers to protect their 'infant industries' and at the same time kept their exchange rate overvalued. This sounds absurd because when the exchange rate increases then imports become cheaper. But the goal was to lower the price of imported machines and other inputs (that is, the price of capital goods and raw materials that would decrease the production costs of the new industries). The trade barriers would be used to keep out of the country any goods that could be considered substitutes in the eyes of domestic buyers, allowing the growth of the domestic infant industries.

This may make sense but at the same time the overvaluation of the currency acted as a tax on exports because exports became more expensive abroad. In the case of traditional primary export commodities (for example coffee) for which the price was determined in commodity markets and was quoted in US dollars, farmers earned fewer units of domestic currency for each US dollar of their exports as a result of the overvaluation. The bottom line was that an overvalued exchange rate hurts the export sector.

On the other hand, keeping the currency overvalued may be part of a policy to combat inflationary pressures. Export demand, which is part of aggregate demand (AD), will decrease, cooling off the economy. In addition, cheaper imports also help. First, the cost of living of the population is lower (as the typical consumer's basket of goods includes imports). Also, it forces domestic import-competing industries to cut costs, increasing their efficiency and keeping their own prices low. Lastly, production costs of domestic firms using imported inputs remain low. With inflation contained, the country can keep interest rates low, which spurs investment and growth. These are some of the benefits the US economy has enjoyed as a result of the US dollar being overvalued in relation to the Chinese yuan (as the Chinese have been accused of keeping their currency undervalued). US export demand may have been hurt but there have been also some very significant side-benefits that cannot be overlooked.

Keeping the currency undervalued

Sometimes countries try to keep the exchange rate of their currency undervalued. This means that they try to maintain it at a level below the free market equilibrium level. Why would policy makers decide on something like this and what are some of the consequences?

An undervalued currency automatically implies cheaper exports. This is the biggest advantage of such a policy. The foreign price of a country's goods and services is pushed lower. Exports gain a competitive advantage. The increased export penetration and resulting export revenues increase AD and, through the export multiplier, accelerate growth. Undervalued currencies have significantly contributed to the spectacular export–led growth that several developing countries have achieved.

Such a benefit does have its costs. First, the export success from keeping the currency undervalued creates trade frictions with trading partners. One country's export success means that import-competing industries of the trading partner will suffer and the distress caused will increase the cries for retaliation and trade protection. Another risk of such a policy is that it may result in inflationary pressures. To keep the currency undervalued in the face of growing export demand requires massive selling of a currency in the foreign exchange market. To keep the yuan undervalued, China must sell yuan buying US dollars. The resulting increase in the money supply may prove inflationary and in the long term undermine the export success and growth of the country.

Comparing and contrasting flexible and fixed exchange rates

In general, the advantages of one system can be considered disadvantages of the other.

Advantages of flexible exchange rates

- Policy makers are free to use monetary policy. For example, they can use easy monetary policy to boost the economy as not only is the currency allowed to depreciate but depreciation may lead to an increase in net exports, a component of AD.

- A trade (more generally, a current account) deficit or surplus may be automatically corrected. A trade deficit implies that more of the currency is supplied than demanded in the foreign exchange market. The excess supply will depreciate the currency and, assuming proper elasticities, the value of exports will rise and import expenditures will drop. There is therefore less need for the government to adopt costly contractionary demand-side policies which slow down growth and increase unemployment if there is a widening trade deficit.

- Exchange rate adjustments through time are usually smooth and continuous, so currency crises are avoided.

- On the one hand, there is less speculation as there is no exchange rate target that may be perceived by speculators as fundamentally undervalued or overvalued and therefore eventually impossible to defend. But, if the fundamentals of an economy (for example inflationary pressures) point to a weakening currency, speculators may start selling the currency en masse, leading to a unnecessarily sharper decrease in its value.

- There is less need for the central bank to carry large foreign exchange reserves as there is no need for it constantly to intervene to maintain the exchange rate at a fixed parity.

Advantages of floating exchange rates: summary

Advantages of floating exchange rates are that	policy makers can use monetary policy to achieve domestic goals.
	trade imbalances are in principle automatically corrected.
	exchange rate adjustments are smooth and continuous.
	typically, less speculation exists.
	there is less need for the central bank to keep foreign exchange reserves.

Disadvantages of flexible exchange rates

- Since in a floating system the exchange rate bobs up and down, often in an very unpredictable manner with any world economic or political development capable of affecting it, there is a lot of uncertainty in the foreign exchange market. Exporters and importers as well as investors face significant exchange rate risks against which they can only partially hedge. As a result, both the volume of international trade in goods and services and the volume of cross-border portfolio investments are negatively affected. Smaller firms especially, with fewer resources available to protect themselves against such risks, will drop out of the market.

- Governments lack the 'policy discipline' that a fixed exchange rate system imposes. A country may therefore be more prone to inflation. For example, easy monetary policy to accelerate growth could be more easily adopted by a government even if it means that the resulting growth will be inflationary.

Disadvantages of flexible exchange rates: summary

Disadvantages of flexible exchange rates are that	increased uncertainty hurts trade and cross-border investment flows.
	a government may be more prone to adopt inflationary policies for short-term gains.

Advantages of fixed exchange rates

- Less uncertainty and exchange rate risk means that firms engaged in international trade can easier predict their export revenues or import bill. Portfolio investors avoid exchange rate risk which could lower their return from any investment. A fixed exchange rate regime may even lead to more FDI as the value of repatriated profits depend on exchange rate movements. This will mean that the volume of exports and imports is higher and more cross-border investments will result.

- Since inflation is not compatible with a fixed exchange rate system, governments cannot easily pursue expansionary fiscal policy that may prove inflationary: fixed exchange rates impose fiscal discipline on governments. In addition, firms are forced to be efficient and keep their costs and prices down to maintain whatever competitive advantage they have.

- Fixing the exchange rate has often been a policy choice for governments determined to curb inflation in high-inflation economies.

Advantages of fixed exchange rates: summary

Advantages of fixed exchange rates are that	there is less uncertainty and exchange rate risk increases the volume of trade and cross border investments.
	policy discipline on governments as inflationary growth is not an option.
	they provide a policy option to curb high inflation.

Disadvantages of fixed exchange rates

- The government is deprived of monetary policy as a tool to affect domestic economic activity. Monetary policy may be used only to ensure that the exchange rate remains fixed.

- The government is also deprived of exchange rate policy to deal with domestic objectives.

- Even the use of reflationary fiscal policy is constrained as budget deficits need to be somehow financed and a financing a large budget may lead to either a faster growth in the money supply or higher interest rates.

- Devaluation or revaluation can prove disruptive as they imply an abrupt realignment of the currency.

- To avoid the need to resort to devaluation a trade deficit must be corrected by adopting contractionary fiscal policy to lower national income and import absorption. But this means slower growth or even inducing a recession with unemployment increasing.

- Central banks must maintain large foreign exchange reserves to be able to intervene in the foreign exchange market and maintain the parity. This involves a high opportunity cost as reserves earn either no or low interest.

Disadvantages of fixed exchange rates: summary

Disadvantages of fixed exchange rates are	the government cannot use monetary policy to achieve domestic goals.
	the government is deprived of an exchange rate policy.
	the use of expansionary fiscal policy is restrained as financing a deficit may affect the money supply or interest rates.
	exchange rate adjustments are abrupt and potentially disruptive.
	trade deficits are not automatically corrected requiring use of painful contractionary fiscal policy.
	the central bank may maintain large foreign exchange reserves.

Purchasing power parity (PPP)

Economists often use the concept of PPP to help predict long-run movements in the foreign exchange value of a currency. PPP is a measure of the equilibrium value of a currency, defined as the exchange rate towards which the currency will move over time. The PPP rate is the rate that will equate the cost of purchasing the same basket of goods in two countries.

If a currency's market exchange rate is presently below its PPP value, PPP advocates will argue that the currency is undervalued and will therefore tend to appreciate in the future. For example, consider a basket of goods and services purchased by the typical consumer in two countries. Assume that it can be bought in Europe (EU17) with €100.00 whereas one needs $160.00 to buy it in the USA and that the market exchange rate is €1.00 = $1.47. One may argue that the dollar is overvalued and will tend to depreciate (or, equivalently, that the euro is undervalued and will tend to appreciate). An American could go to the foreign exchange market and purchase €100.00 with only $147.00 and buy the same basket of goods and services in Europe for which he or she would need $160.00 to buy in the USA. The theory therefore suggests that in such a case US imports of goods and services will rise. But, as more US dollars will be offered in the foreign exchange market to buy the necessary euros, the US dollar will be pushed down (and the pushed euro up) until the US dollar falls (the euro rises) to €1.00 = $1.60.

PPP theory may be helpful to forecast the long-run value of a currency but its usefulness to predict short-run variations is very strongly doubted. Not only will it take a long time for the equilibrium value as defined to be reached but, in addition, there are many other economic forces that may keep the value away from equilibrium.

Overall, empirical support for PPP is mixed, as exchange rates do not necessarily move towards their long-run equilibrium value. Why? The basket of goods and services consumed by the typical consumer in each country differs substantially and also includes non-traded goods (such as haircuts or real estate). If given the market exchange rate, real estate is cheaper in the 'other' country we cannot import land, buildings and housing from it. Trade barriers and transport costs also decrease the scope of trade but, most importantly, exchange rates are highly influenced by capital flows.

PPPs are still used as conversion factors. PPPs should be used instead of market exchange rates as conversion factors (to a single currency, usually the US dollar) of GNI and per capita GNI figures, in order to incorporate cost of living differences that will make cross-country comparisons of these variables more meaningful. Care should be taken that the PPP value used in the conversion accurately reflects recent and true cost of living differences.

The balance of payments is defined as a record of all transactions of a country with the rest of the world over a period of time, usually a year.

Transactions which lead to an inflow of currency enter the account with a plus sign and are known as credit items whereas those that lead to an outflow of currency enter with a minus sign and are called debit items.

The balance of payments is divided into three major components, the current account, the capital account and the financial account. The sum of these by construction equals zero. The balance of payments balances.

For the same reason a household's monthly budget must balance: Assume Zoi earned $2,000 and spent $2,300 in January. This is not possible unless she drew on her savings and/or borrowed a total of $300. If these $300 dollars are added to her income then, since all her expenditures were necessarily somehow financed, her budget for January was balanced. If more currency flowed out of a country to pay for imports and investments than flowed in from exports and investments then this difference must have been somehow financed. Foreign exchange reserves decreased and/or official borrowing took place in sufficient amounts to balance her external account.

The current account

The current account includes the following three accounts.

- **The goods and services account** which includes exports and imports of goods (physical merchandise) and exports and imports of services. The difference between export revenues and import expenditures is the balance of trade in goods and the balance of trade in services respectively. Tradable services include transport, construction, postal and courier services, insurance and pension services, financial services, communication services, computer services, personal and business travel, etc.

- **The primary income account** which includes the differences between primary income received from abroad and payable abroad. Primary income includes profits, interest and dividends (PIDs) from portfolio and direct investments, compensation of employees (wages and salaries) and the returns from renting natural resources (for example from granting fishing, grazing, mining, and forestry rights). Note that this difference ('net income from abroad') is what distinguishes GDP from GNI in macroeconomics.

- **The secondary income (or current transfers) account** which includes unilateral current transfers with nothing received in return, for example workers' remittances, donations, transfers related to international cooperation between governments (such as receipts and payments to EU institutions), food aid and emergency aid after natural disasters.

The sum of net exports of goods and services, net income and net current transfers over a period is defined as the current account balance. If this is positive we say that there is a current account surplus. If it is negative we say that there is a current account deficit. If we focus only on the exports and imports of goods and services we can say that if export revenues

from the sale of goods and services is greater or smaller than import expenditures on goods and services over a period then we have a current account surplus or deficit respectively.

The capital account

The capital account includes the following.

- It includes capital transfers receivable and payable, such as the provision of resources for capital purposes by one party without anything of economic value being supplied as a direct return to that party. Debt forgiveness is also included in capital transfers.

- It also includes the acquisition and disposal of non-produced, non-financial assets such as sales and purchases of intangible assets (patents, copyrights, trademarks, franchises and leases, etc.).

Typically, the capital account is small and of minor importance.

The financial account

The financial account includes investments and assets, as follows.

- **FDI** exists when a resident in one country acquires control or a significant degree of influence on the management of a firm in another economy. It mostly refers to multinational corporations.

- **Portfolio and other investments** refer to the acquisition and sale of stocks and bonds as well as changes in loans and deposits. When a resident of Egypt buys stocks of Turkish companies or buys Turkish bonds then an outflow of money is recorded in the Egyptian financial account and an equal inflow of money in the Turkish one. Note that the next year, when the Egyptian resident receives dividends and interest payments from the investments, the inflow of money will be recorded in the Egyptian current account as a receipt of income and the equal outflow of money in the Turkish current account as a payment of income.

- **Reserve assets (official reserves)** include assets that the central bank holds to finance balance of payments needs and to intervene in the foreign exchange market in order to affect the exchange rate.

The current account is equal to the sum of the capital and financial accounts. It is the inclusion of changes in reserve assets (that is, in official reserves that force the balance of payments always to balance). It would be impossible over a specific period of time (say, a year) for more currency to flow out of a country than had flowed in the same period unless somehow this deficit was financed: either by drawing on foreign exchange reserves and/or by official borrowing. Since we add the financing of a deficit as a decrease in foreign exchange reserves assets (and/or as official borrowing) in the financial account, the balance of payments account will necessarily balance. Conversely, if over a period more currency had flown into a country than flown out of a country then official reserves would increase and/or official lending would take place for the overall balance of payments to balance.

Unfortunately there are always errors and/or omissions. Not only is estimation of credits and debits into and out of a country imprecise but there are always unrecorded illegal cross-border activities, for example involving drugs or weapons. As a result, the balance of payments account does not balance despite the inclusion of the official financing (reserves) item. To balance the accounts artificially the balancing item is included with the same magnitude but the opposite sign of the error item. If the balancing item is large then this is an indication of poor data collection and statistical services and/or of illegal sales or purchases.

Is a current account deficit a problem?

As explained earlier, a rising current account deficit will exert pressure on the exchange rate to depreciate (in a floating exchange rate system) or devalue (in a fixed system). Why? Because rising foreign import demand means that residents are offering in the foreign exchange market more of their currency while decreasing export revenues means that foreigners are demanding less of the currency in the market. If supply of a currency increases and/or demand for it decreases the currency will tend to decrease in value.

Beyond this effect on the exchange rate the question remains whether a current account deficit is or is not a problem. The answer is 'it depends'. First of all, it depends on the size of the deficit. To determine the importance of a current account balance (deficit or surplus) we always express it as a proportion of GDP so that the size of the economy is 'scaled out'. Typically a current account deficit is considered a potential problem if it is widening and exceeds between 5% and 6% of the country's GDP.

It also depends on the reasons for which it exists. More specifically it depends on whether it is temporary or persistent (also referred to as fundamental).

Temporary deficits are short term being either of a transitory nature (for example because of a crop failure) or of a reversible nature (for example as a result of a booming economy). In the latter case, a short-term current account deficit implies an improvement in living standards as the nation is consuming more than it is producing. A strong and growing economy typically records trade deficits as a result of the increased import absorption (assuming of course that growth was not export led in the first place, as in the case of, say, China). Also, a developing economy in the process of establishing certain industries may initially be forced to rely on imported capital goods, leading to trade deficits.

On the other hand, fundamental or persistent imbalances are chronic. They tend to last for a long time and they are the result of structural problems of the economy. These are indeed serious as they reflect a 'sick' economy. To understand the issue, consider an economy with chronic inflation, uncompetitive product markets and rigid labour markets. Export competitiveness will be eroded and export revenues will shrink while spending on imports will increase as many domestic households will turn to better and cheaper imports. A ballooning current account deficit will result.

HL

Implications of a persistent current account deficit

A current account deficit must be somehow financed and it is this financing that may create future problems in the economy. The bottom line is that the economy is not earning enough foreign exchange from its exports and income earnings from abroad to finance its imports. Running down foreign exchange reserves may only continue for short periods of time because these reserves are limited. The remaining options are few. A surplus is required in the combined capital and financial accounts and it may result either from the sale of domestic assets (such as businesses, stocks or property) to foreigners or from borrowing from abroad.

Selling assets requires willing buyers. Buyers are willing to buy domestic assets if the future prospects of the economy look good and/or if the selling price is exceptionally low. If the future growth prospects of the economy look good then the sale of assets does not have to signal a problem. For example, foreigners will buy shares or acquire companies because they expect growth in sales and therefore high dividends and high profits. But since we are discussing here a persistent current account deficit problem, any sale of assets must be a result of very low sale prices. The assets sold to foreigners can be both sizeable and of significance (for example sale of significant natural resources, sale of banks or of large industries) so such a development carries the threat of loss of economic sovereignty.

On the other hand, borrowing involves future repayment of the capital plus interest. This implies that in the future part of national income must be diverted away from domestic uses towards the repayment of past borrowing. This income could have been used to finance increased consumption expenditures, increased investment expenditures or increased government spending on, say, social capital formation. In addition, since repayment of such borrowing must be made in foreign exchange it means that future foreign exchange earnings from exports will need to be diverted away from the purchase of imports of consumer and capital goods. If the economy is not growing fast enough to finance these obligations then these developments will jeopardize any future growth prospects of the economy. Living standards of the population will decrease. Also, if the lending is of a short-term nature (from hot money inflows) then there is the risk of a sudden exodus of this capital with the resulting sell-out sharply depreciating the currency.

More importantly, a mounting foreign debt creates snowballing effects on an economy. Foreigners will be willing to lend only at higher and higher interest rates to compensate for the additional risk they face. Higher interest rates imply surging interest costs though, worsening the foreign debt problem. As the risk of the country defaulting increases, its credit rating by international credit rating agencies such as Moody's could be downgraded. This tightens the squeeze on the country as such a development will further increase interest rates.

It should be clear that an unsustainable current account deficit cannot and will not last forever. Some adjustment process eventually will restore balance. But adjustment may be abrupt and very unpleasant. Correcting a current account deficit may require expenditure-reducing or expenditure-switching policies and/or supply-side policies.

Methods to correct a persistent current account deficit

Expenditure-reducing policies

These include policies that decrease the level of AD. The goal is to reduce the level of national income and so decrease spending on imports.

Policies that decrease the level of AD include contractionary fiscal policy and tight monetary policy. Since the decrease in AD will also decrease inflation, the export sector may benefit from increased competitiveness. All in all, shrinking imports and perhaps rising exports will help narrow the current account deficit.

Note though that such an adjustment policy comes at a high cost. Growth will surely slow down or even turn negative. Incomes and output will decrease. Firms will contract or shut down and unemployment will surge.

Expenditure-switching policies

These are policies aiming at switching spending away from imported goods and services towards domestically produced goods and services. To induce such a switch, imports have to become more expensive and therefore less attractive.

A devaluation (or a rapid depreciation) of the exchange rate is one such policy choice. If the price of a currency decreases then foreign goods and services (imports) become more expensive in domestic currency. In addition, exports will become cheaper abroad and may rise in value. Both effects will tend to correct the foreign deficit.

A potential risk of a rapid depreciation or devaluation of the currency is that inflation may accelerate. Why? First, a rise in export demand will tend to increase AD, shifting it to the right. The rapid depreciation will also increase import prices and increase the cost of living. If this development initiates a rise in wages then a wage-price inflationary spiral may follow. In addition, domestic production processes that require the use of imported raw materials and/or intermediate products will experience an increase in their production costs so cost-push inflation may follow.

Alternatively, policy makers could instead resort to trade protection which will render imports more expensive. Tariffs and quotas, for example, increase the price of imports and lower import spending. Domestic households and firms will substitute domestic products for imports, decreasing the country's import bill.

Such protectionist policies create trade frictions and invite retaliation from affected exporting nations. In addition, they run against WTO membership rules. If they are implemented then inefficiency increases as resources are misallocated. The country suffers the costs of trade protection.

Note that certain expenditure-reducing policies may also end up switching expenditures. For example, a tight monetary policy will decrease national income and so decrease imports, induce capital inflows which could help finance the current account deficit but also decrease inflation, leading to increased international competitiveness. On the other hand, it may lead to an appreciation of the currency, hurting exporting industries.

Supply-side policies

Solutions of a more long-run nature include certain supply-side policies aiming at increasing the competitiveness of the economy and especially of the export sector. Remember that a persistent current account deficit may be a result of uncompetitive product markets characterized by a high degree of monopoly power and of rigid labour markets with high labour costs and low labour productivity. Supply-side policies can prove useful to restore the competitiveness of an ailing economy and cure a fundamental disequilibrium in the current account.

On the other hand, supply-side policies have their drawbacks, which have been discussed earlier (see page 108).

Policies to correct a persistent current account deficit: summary

Expenditure-reducing policies	include policies that decrease AD, for example contractionary fiscal and monetary policies.
Expenditure-switching policies	include devaluation, as well as increased trade protection that renders imports more expensive.
Supply-side policies	include decreasing domestic monopoly power, increasing labour market flexibility and improving incentives.

Is a current account surplus a problem?

Remember a current account surplus exists if the sum of net exports of goods and services plus net income and net current transfers is positive. It is acceptable, even though not strictly speaking correct, to say that it exists when export revenues from the sale of goods and services over a period of time exceeds the import bill.

In general, one may argue that if the surplus is small or transitory it is not considered an issue. Also, if it is part of a growth and development strategy known as export-oriented growth its benefits may exceed its costs but, still, a persistent current account surplus does involve risks for an economy which should be addressed.

First, a persistent surplus implies that the economy is consuming inside its production possibilities. From a static point of view this implies that living standards are lower than they need be but from a dynamic point of view this argument may be turned on its head. Foreign markets can and have proved an engine of long-run growth and development for many countries. The most prominent recent examples include Japan, the four East Asian Tigers (Hong Kong, Taiwan, Singapore and South Korea), Malaysia, Thailand, Vietnam and, of course, China and India.

More importantly, large bilateral trade surpluses carry the risk of retaliatory protectionist measures by the deficit country. To the extent that the surplus country relies on foreign demand for its

growth this may pose a serious risk. The deficit country may suddenly adopt highly protectionist policies, blocking out imports which could grind growth of the exporting surplus country to a halt.

It is also argued that if the current account surplus is the result of trade barriers erected in key markets of the economy then the surplus country is not fully exploiting its comparative advantage and is inefficiently employing its scarce resources. On the other hand, given that comparative advantage is not a static but a dynamic concept that countries can, and should try to change, this argument is significantly weakened. The trade protection policies employed may help the country develop competitive industries.

Perhaps the most serious problem associated with a persistent and widening current account surplus is that it puts pressure on the exchange rate to appreciate. This is even more serious if the trade surplus is mostly due to one export, for example oil or natural gas. The appreciation means that all other exports become less and less competitive in foreign markets and as result suffer (this is referred to as the Dutch disease). On the other hand, the appreciation puts pressure on firms to cut down on waste and become more efficient.

Lastly, if the current account surplus is the result of the country keeping its currency undervalued then, as explained earlier, the country runs the risk of inflation.

The Marshall-Lerner condition and the J-curve effect

Devaluation implies that the foreign price of exports decreases and the domestic price of imports increases. This of course assumes that the domestic price of exports does not change nor does the foreign price of imports. So if, for example, Germany exports BMW cars to the USA and imports Abercrombie and Fitch shirts from the USA, we are assuming that the euro price of BMW cars does not change nor does the US dollar price of an Abercrombie and Fitch shirt.

With exports more competitive abroad and imports less attractive domestically, we expect that export revenues will increase and import expenditures will decrease. So if a country has a current account deficit this will improve. Such a development rests though on the size of the PED for exports and the PED of imports. Why? Because the behaviour of revenues and expenditures when price changes depends on PED.

The Marshall-Lerner condition states that for devaluation or a sharp depreciation of a currency to improve, a current account deficit the sum of the PED for imports and the PED for exports must be (absolutely) greater than 1.

The Marshall-Lerner condition: summary

Marshall-Lerner condition:

devaluation (sharp depreciation) will improve a trade deficit

if: PED (X) + PED (M) > 1

The proof needs some elementary calculus but this may serve to illuminate the condition.

If we express the German trade balance in US dollars, then a sharp depreciation of the euro will make US Abercrombie and Fitch shirts pricier in euros even though their US dollar price is constant. Let PED(M) = 0 so that exactly the same quantity of Abercrombie and Fitch shirts is bought in Germany. With their US dollar price the same **and** the quantity demanded and imported the same, import expenditures expressed in US dollars will necessarily remain the same.

Germany's trade balance will improve if export revenues (expressed in US dollars) increase. Since the depreciation of the euro made the US dollar price of BMW cars in New York lower, Germany's export revenues in US dollars will increase if the quantity of cars demanded by Americans increase by proportionately more, so that PED(X) > 1.

The sum of the two elasticities would therefore exceed 1. It follows that if the Marshall-Lerner condition is satisfied then the German trade balance, following a sharp depreciation of the euro, will improve.

Why are PED for exports and PED for imports low in the short run?

Firms and especially households may not even be aware of the new prices. A sharp depreciation of the euro will mean that European cars are now cheaper in the USA. Will the average US household immediately realize that European cars are cheaper? Not really. Access to new information is never instantaneous.

But even if it becomes widely known that European cars are now cheaper in the USA, the typical American may need some time to switch away from buying American cars if all his or her life the person has bought Fords – buying habits also need time to be overcome.

Most importantly, it is commercial contracts between exporting and importing firms that slow down the response to a currency change. Importers of foreign cars may have signed long-term contracts with foreign firms that are difficult to terminate or change. It takes time to change business contracts.

The J-curve effect

Since PED of exports and PED of imports are low in the short run the Marshall-Lerner condition will not be immediately satisfied. It will take some time before the sum of the two elasticities exceed unity. So, in a figure with time on the horizontal axis and the trade balance (X-M) on the vertical, the path through time of the trade balance following devaluation traces a J-shaped curve. This is known as the J-curve effect.

In Figure 3.3.1 assume an economy with a trade deficit equal to $250 million deciding to devalue its currency (or let it sharply depreciate). Initially, the deficit becomes larger and

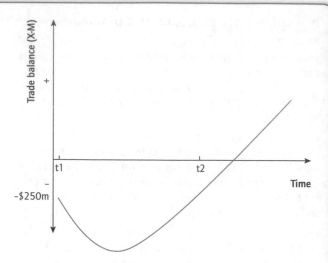

Figure 3.3.1: The J-curve effect

larger because the Marshall-Lerner condition is not satisfied: PED for exports and PED for imports are very low and do not exceed unity.

Only after time t2 in Figure 3.3.1 is the condition satisfied and the trade deficit shrinks below the $250 million mark.

Note that an inverted J-curve results after a revaluation (appreciation), where the surplus initially becomes bigger and only later it starts to shrink.

Preferential trade agreements

Globalization implies greater interconnectedness of countries in the world. This greater interconnectedness is also expressed in the area of international trade. Economies are becoming more open, meaning that the size of exports and imports as a proportion of GDP is increasing. The volume and value of annual trade flows has been rising in the past decades as a result of trade liberalization.

Trade liberalization, defined as a process of reducing or even eliminating trade barriers, may be achieved through preferential trade agreements (on a bilateral or more generally, regional basis) or multilaterally through the WTO. The WTO has been discussed earlier – see page 110.

Preferential trade agreements are the weakest form of economic integration where tariff reductions are only offered to some product categories from certain countries. The term, though, may also refer to all forms of regional trading blocs.

Regional trading blocs or agreements

The regional approach to trade liberalization refers to agreements among governments of two (bilateral) or more countries to liberalize trade. They do this by reducing or eliminating tariffs and other trade barriers and perhaps coordinating other trade-related activities while keeping protectionist barriers with outsiders. There are four types of regional trading arrangements: free trade areas, customs unions, common markets and economic (and monetary) unions.

- Two or more countries can form a **free trade area** if tariffs and non-tariff barriers between members are abolished or agreed to be phased out, but each member country maintains its own tariffs on imports from non-member countries so that no common trade policy exists towards non-members. NAFTA (the USA, Mexico and Canada) are EFTA (Iceland, Norway, Liechtenstein and Switzerland) and the best known examples.

- A **customs union** is a free trade area where members additionally establish a common tariff and agree to other trade policies with non-member countries. Examples include:
    - MERCOSUR, set up in 1991, in which Argentina, Brazil, Paraguay and Uruguay are full members

    - the 1996 agreement between the EU and Turkey
    - the East African Customs Union between Ethiopia, Sudan, Kenya, Tanzania, Uganda and Zambia.

- If, in addition, unrestricted factor flows are agreed then the member countries have formed a **common market.** Free flow of labour and capital means that individuals have the right to work in any of the member countries without any special permits and that cross-border investment is liberalized. A common market can be summarized as an agreement for the free flow of goods, services, people and capital.

- Lastly, an **economic union** is formed when members of a common market make additional provisions for the harmonization of certain macroeconomic and regulatory policies. If they also adopt a common currency they have formed a monetary union. The European Union and the eurozone are the only such examples.

Dismantling of trade-related barriers within a trading block will increase competition between the firms of member countries, which is considered a positive outcome, but at the same time certain inefficiencies may arise as a result of tariffs being lowered or eliminated only between members. Remember that preferential trading agreements are discriminatory while WTO multilateral agreements are non-discriminatory.

Regional trading blocs: summary

A free trade area is formed if	members eliminate or agree to phase out trade barriers between them but each member country maintains its own external tariff to nonmembers.
A customs union is formed if	free trade area members agree to adopt a common external tariff.
A common market is formed if	members of a customs union additionally agree to permit the free flow of factors of production.
An economic union is formed if	members of a common market additionally harmonize certain macroeconomic and regulatory policies.
A monetary union is formed if	members of an economic union agree to adopt a common currency and establish a common central bank.

HL

Evaluation of trading blocs

The big question is whether preferential trade agreements are a 'stumbling block' or a 'building block' to multilateral trade liberalization through the WTO. Since almost all WTO members are also members of at least one preferential trade agreement but, at the same time, non-members of most agreements, the significance of evaluating the role of trading blocs becomes apparent.

The static analysis of trading blocs rests on the work of Jacob Viner in 1950, who introduced the terms 'trade creation' and 'trade diversion'.

Trade creation refers to an increase in imports that displace less-efficient domestic production. The elimination of the internal trade barriers will lead members to import from one another goods and services that were previously produced domestically. This increases efficiency since production shifts away from a higher-cost domestic producer to a lower-cost foreign producer, leading to fewer scarce resources being wasted.

Trade diversion arises when imports shift from an efficient non-member to a less-efficient member due to the preferences the latter enjoys. The remaining external tariff only for non-members may render some member artificially cheaper in the production of a good. Another member will then switch importing from the truly efficient and lowest-cost non-member to the artificially cheaper member. This is inefficient since it implies production against what comparative advantage would dictate, but it is still possible that the effect is to improve welfare, as both consumers and producers within the importing country face prices closer to the true world price levels. It follows that by examining trade creation and trade diversion it is not simple to determine whether the preferential agreement enhances or decreases welfare. The relative size of trade creation and trade diversion will vary from case to case and determine whether the agreement enhances or diminishes static efficiency. Whether a particular trading bloc promotes global welfare is an empirical question.

In addition to the above static analysis, the expected dynamic effects should be weighed in. On the plus side, a trading bloc expands the size of the market so faster and higher investment rates will follow, allowing firms to grow in size so EOS may result. This has been an argument used for developing countries. By forming a trading bloc they could accelerate the process of industrialization. Protection from developed economies would be retained and members would enjoy a bigger market, faster investment and EOS. Seamless borders also enable faster technology transfer. Lastly, the bargaining power of members increases, so they can exercise greater economic leverage than if they acted individually.

Are there any potential long-run disadvantages of such trading blocs?

Firms could grow to such sizes that they suffer from diseconomies of scale (DOS). This is rather unlikely though. What is more likely is that trading blocs may form by self-interested member producers hoping to benefit from any resulting trade diversion effects.

Most importantly, the role of the WTO is undermined. Multilateral agreements which are superior to any regional trading agreement may become more and more difficult to achieve. There is a risk that the world may end up split into major blocs, each a potential 'fortress' to the others.

An additional risk arises from a large economy (for example the USA, China or the European Union) signing a sequence of preferential agreements with smaller individual countries which allows it to use its huge bargaining power more effectively than engaging in simultaneous bargaining (through the WTO).

There were 474 regional agreements in July 2010 according to the WTO. This proliferation of preferential trade agreements has also resulted in a 'spaghetti bowl' of tariffs that complicates trade as it increases business and administration costs of adhering to rules.

Monetary union

If members of an economic union adopt a single currency and transfer the responsibility of monetary policy to a common central bank then they have also established a monetary union. In 1999 a subset of countries of the European Union adopted a common currency, the euro. The eurozone in 2011 has 17 member countries.

Advantages are mostly of a microeconomic nature and include the following.

- There are lower transaction costs as currency conversions are not necessary. Every time an individual or a business has to exchange one currency for another, a fee has to be paid to the bank. This cost is eliminated for any transactions within a monetary union.

- There is greater price transparency, which makes comparisons of prices of goods, services and resources much easier. Buyers (consumers a well as firms) are able to spot quickly the lowest price available in the market for

whatever good or service they are looking for. This increases competition, forces inefficient producers to become more efficient and prices gravitate towards the lowest offered in the union.

- Exchange rate risk and of the resulting uncertainty costs are eliminated. Flexible exchange rates are often very volatile and even if an exchange rate is pegged it may always revalue or devalue. This implies increased uncertainty for firms engaged in exports and imports of goods and services as well as for investors buying and selling stocks and bonds. They cannot be sure what the exchange rate will be at a future date and even though there are financial instruments that help them hedge against exchange rate volatility they are still costly, especially for smaller firms. A single currency encourages more trade and a greater volume of investment within member countries.

- A group of countries with a common market and a common currency will enjoy greater influence and bargaining power in world affairs.

On the other hand, here are some possible disadvantages, mostly of a macroeconomic nature, of monetary union.

- Member countries are deprived of an independent monetary policy. Since there is one currency and one central bank there is one monetary policy for all members. This 'one size fits all' approach may make things very difficult for some members if business cycles are 'asynchronous'. This is a fancy term that just means that when one economy is booming and overheating another may be losing steam and about to enter recession. Theory dictates that the former should tighten monetary policy, increasing interest rates, while the latter should loosen monetary policy, decreasing interest rates. If they are members of a monetary union, most probably the smaller country will suffer.

- Members are deprived of an independent exchange rate policy. A central bank is responsible for conducting monetary and exchange rate policy. Being a member of a single currency area deprives a country the possibility to devalue or sharply depreciate its currency to boost its exports in a recession, or to do the opposite in the face of mounting inflationary pressures. Not only is there no exchange rate to manipulate between members (when trade between members is probably the biggest), but one member alone cannot influence the external value of the common currency as there is an independent central bank.

- There is limited room for pursuing independent fiscal policy. Even though each government can manipulate its own expenditures and taxes, the available degrees of freedom are limited as fiscal irresponsibility within a monetary union can create havoc. Remember that budget deficits and public debts have to be financed somehow so that fiscal and monetary policies are not independent as they may at first seem.

- Members lose economic sovereignty. If a country is deprived of an independent monetary policy, if it cannot exercise an independent exchange rate policy and if its fiscal finances have to be aligned with other members, then it has transferred at least part of its economic sovereignty outside the country. This has been a major argument for many European Union countries against adopting the euro.

Advantages and disadvantages of monetary union: summary

Possible advantages of a monetary union include	lower transaction costs as currency conversions are unnecessary.
	greater price transparency, facilitating price comparisons.
	no exchange rate risks and associated uncertainty costs.
	greater negotiating and bargaining power in world affairs.
Possible disadvantages of a monetary union include	no independent monetary policy.
	no exchange rate policy.
	limited room for independent fiscal policy.
	loss of economic sovereignty.

3.5 Terms of trade

HL

Meaning and measurement

The terms of trade (TOT in the equations below) of a country are defined as the ratio of the average price of exports over the average price of imports, expressed as index numbers times 100.

$$TOT = \frac{\text{Average price of exports expressed as an index number}}{\text{Average price of imports expressed as an index number}} \times 100$$

The terms of trade therefore measure the volume of imports attainable by a unit of exports. They show the volume of foreign goods that can be bought by a country by exporting a given amount of domestic output. They reflect the rate at which one country's goods exchange for those of another country.

A couple of examples will illustrate the above points. On a personal everyday basis, if the price of a pizza is $12.00 and the price of a cheeseburger is $2.00 then the ratio

$$\frac{\text{Price of a pizza}}{\text{Price of a cheeseburger}} = \frac{12}{2} \times 6$$

shows that you can exchange 6 cheeseburgers for 1 pizza. You should realize immediately that even though it is a ratio of prices, it shows the rate at which quantities can be exchanged.

Now assume that we are referring to international trade and that a country exports coffee and imports a certain type of machine. Further assume that the price of a ton of coffee is $20,000 and the price of these machines is $10,000 each. The country's terms of trade are

$$TOT = \frac{20,000}{10,000} \times \frac{2}{1} = 2$$

showing that this country can import two of the machines by exporting one ton of coffee.

Changes in the terms of trade

If the terms of trade increase through time it is referred to as a favourable movement (an improvement) in the sense that now the country can attain a greater volume of imports with the same exports (or, equivalently, the same volume of imports with a smaller volume of exports). For example, if the price of a ton of coffee increases to $30,000 then the terms of trade increase to 3/1 meaning that a ton of coffee buys three of the machines in world markets and not just two.

If the terms of trade decrease over time this is referred to as an unfavourable movement (a deterioration or a worsening) in the sense that now the country can attain a smaller volume of imports with the same exports (or, equivalently, the same volume of imports with a greater volume of exports). For example, if the price of a ton of coffee decreases to $10,000 then the terms of trade decrease to 1/1 meaning that a ton of coffee now buys one of the machines in world markets and not two.

An increase in the terms of trade (a favourable movement) will occur if the average price of exports rises relatively to the price of imports, and vice versa. An decrease in the terms of trade (an unfavourable movement) will occur if the average price of exports rises relatively to the price of imports, and vice versa. By using the word 'relatively' we avoid having to mention all the possible ways that a fraction may increase or decrease in value.

TIP Volume refers to the quantity of exports or imports. Think of Qx and Qm respectively.

HL

Causes of changes in the terms of trade

One must be careful as to the cause of any change in the terms of trade as it affects the interpretation of the effects. For example, it makes a big difference whether export prices rise as a result of increased demand for a country's exports, or as a result of an appreciation of the exchange rate.

■ Take the case of changes in the world demand for a country's exports or imports. If the world demand for a country's exports increases (decreases) then, ceteris paribus, its terms of trade will increase (decrease): there will be a favourable (unfavourable) movement. If the world demand for a country's imports increases (decreases) then, ceteris paribus, its terms of trade will decrease (increase): there will be an unfavourable (favourable) movement.

Let's, consider Australia. It predominantly exports commodities (they make up 80% of goods it exports). A surge in the world demand for commodities

(raw materials) will lead to an increase in the average price of Australian exports. Australia's terms of trade will increase (assuming no change in the average price of its imports). This is a favourable movement. On the other hand, for countries importing raw materials, their terms of trade will decrease (deteriorate; experience unfavourable movement) to the extent that the average price of all imports is affected.

■ Now let's look at changes in the world supply for a country's exports or imports. A change in the world supply will affect the price of a product. For example, if technological progress or higher productivity or reduced input costs increase the supply of a good that a country exports then its price will drop and its terms of trade will decrease (worsen). Note that we are implicitly referring to a country with significant concentration of its exports in one or few products or product groups, for example agricultural products. For importers of the product or product group their terms of trade increase (improve).

Or, consider a decrease in the world supply of an export (or an import). A good example is the case of commodity agreements which aimed at restricting exports to increase their world price. Oil is in a similar category as the Organization of the Oil Producing and Exporting Countries (OPEC) is a cartel which typically, but not always, restricts oil exports of members to push the world price of oil up. The terms of trade of oil exporters increase (a favourable movement) but given oil's significance as an energy input, the terms of trade of importing countries will decrease (worsen).

- Changes in the exchange rate will result in changes in the terms of trade. If a the external value of the currency changes then the terms of trade are affected as export prices and import prices change. For example, assume an appreciation (or, in a fixed exchange rate system, a revaluation). Since exports become pricier and imports cheaper, the terms of trade are affected. They will increase (that is, a favourable movement will take place); conversely, for a depreciation (or devaluation).

- Changes in the relative rates of inflation will affect the terms of trade. If prices in an economy are increasing faster than they are abroad, then the average price of its exports will be increasing faster than the average price of its imports. Ceteris paribus, this means that the terms of trade of the country with the higher inflation are improving.

- When a large country imposes tariffs and other trade barriers this can improve its terms of trade. A large country is defined as a country that is in a position, through its decisions, to affect the world price of a product. Assume that a large country imposes a tariff on a product it imports. The domestic price of this product will rise but at the same time the resulting decreased demand for it will tend to decrease its world price. The decrease in the demand in the importing country was big enough to adversely affect world demand for the product. The large country has managed to improve its terms of trade as the average price of its imports has decreased.

Consequences of changes in the terms of trade

Consequences for the trade balance in goods and services (current account)

A change in the terms of trade will affect the trade balance of a country as it implies that export and/or import prices have changed. For example, to determine whether a trade deficit will improve or widen it is important to determine whether the cause of the change in the terms of trade has affected the average price of exports and the volume of exports in the same or opposite directions (or, symmetrically, whether the average price of imports and the volume of imports have moved in the same or opposite directions).

The discussion is similar to the discussion in microeconomics of whether an increase in the price of a good will increase or decrease the revenues of a firm. If the increased price is a result of an increase in the demand for the good, then both the price and the quantity (volume) increase, so revenues unambiguously increase. If the increased price is a result of a decrease in supply (and so a movement along the demand curve), then quantity (volume) will decrease and price elasticity will determine the answer. If demand is price elastic then the increase in price will decrease revenues whereas if it is price inelastic the increase in price will decrease revenues.

Returning to trade flows, if an improvement in the terms of trade is the result of an increase in world demand for the good then price and quantity (volume) move in the same direction, so export revenues increase. A trade deficit (ceteris paribus) will narrow (or a trade surplus will grow). If the improvement is a result of a decrease in world supply that increased export prices then quantity (volume) of exports decreases so the effect on export revenues (or the import bill) depends on PED. If it is price inelastic, as in the case of oil, then export revenues of OPEC members will increase and their trade surpluses will grow (and the import bill of oil importers will also increase, with their trade deficits widening).

A change in the terms of trade as a result of exchange rate movements affects prices and volumes (quantities) of tradables in the opposite direction, so again price elasticities are important

in determining the effect on the trade balance. For example, if the terms of trade of a country have increased because of an appreciation, then prices of exports rise. Exports become less competitive abroad and more difficult to sell. The volume of exports falls. The country will earn more foreign currency only if the volume of exports drops by proportionately less (that is, if the demand for its exports is price inelastic; similarly for imports). The Marshall-Lerner condition enters this discussion.

- If the sum of the Price elasticity of demand (PED) for exports and the PED for imports of a country exceed unity then an appreciation will decrease a trade surplus (that is, narrow it).

- On the other hand, a depreciation which lowers export prices and makes imports more expensive will decrease (worsen) the terms of trade. However, if the sum of the PED for exports and the PED for imports of a country exceed unity, then the depreciation will decrease a trade deficit (that is, narrow it).

Lastly, an import tariff imposed by a large country will, ceteris paribus, tend to improve its trade balance as both the world price of the good will decrease and the volume of its imports.

Long-term consequences

A long-term deterioration in a country's terms of trade means that the country will have to export ever-increasing volumes of goods to attain the same volume of imports. It implies that a unit of its exports commands a smaller slice of world output. The distribution of world income (output) changes against the country experiencing the worsening terms of trade.

Terms of trade and developing countries

Short-term fluctuations

Many developing countries specialize and export a narrow set of primary products, while they import mostly manufacturing sector products. Supply in the short run of primary agricultural commodities is typically very low and can be considered for analytical purposes as perfectly inelastic (that is, vertical). This is the result of the long time lags that characterize their production. Demand for most commodities is also very price inelastic as they lack close substitutes. Given that output of agricultural products is affected by random and uncontrollable factors, such as weather conditions, it follows that prices of such exports are quite volatile.

The resulting short-term fluctuations of the terms of trade of developing countries exporting a narrow range of agricultural commodities creates high uncertainty both for producers and the government. Uncertainty over export prices and, consequently, export revenues hurt planning and deter productivity, enhancing investments as farmers are afraid that they may not be in a position to pay back any bank loans they take.

Fluctuating export revenues means that foreign exchange may not always be enough to finance the purchase of necessary imports of food, capital or intermediate products.

Foreign debt payments may be impossible to make, requiring more borrowing. Growth and development become even more difficult to achieve.

Long-term deterioration

Developing countries specializing in and exporting a narrow range of agricultural commodities have over the long term suffered a deterioration of their terms of trade. World prices of such products have in general decreased over the long term because supply has in general grown faster than demand. World supply has dramatically increased, both as a result of technological advancements in agriculture and as a result of massive subsidies granted to farmers in developed countries by their governments.

On the other hand, world demand for agricultural commodities has not increased as fast. The reason for this is that income elasticity of demand (YED) for food products is low.

This long-term decline of the terms of trade of many developing countries signified a shrinking slice of world output and income for these countries to enjoy. Distribution of world income became more unequal. Development based on primary sector exports was considered a dead-end. Decreasing export earnings forced these countries to try to produce more and more which, given the competitive structure of these markets, pushed prices even lower.

Short-run instability and long-term decline in export earnings were responsible for low rates of investment, unstable employment and increased poverty, as well as environmental degradation because of more intensive cultivation of land, deforestation and soil erosion.

The long-term decline in the terms of trade of many developing countries is the principal argument in favour of industrialization and diversification. The logic behind import substitution, industrialization and export promotion as growth and development strategies rests on the long-term deterioration of the terms of trade of many developing countries.

Variations on the following may be asked in questions (b) and (c) of HL/SL Paper 2

1. Explain the gains from trade that a country may expect.

2. Explain using appropriate diagrams absolute and comparative advantage.

3. Describe the possible sources of comparative advantage for country X.

4. Describe the objectives and functions of the WTO as well as some of the criticisms it faces.

5. Explain, using an appropriate diagram, the effects on different stakeholders of a tariff imposed on good X.

6. Explain, using an appropriate diagram, the effects on different stakeholders of a quota (or, of a VER) imposed on good X.

7. Explain, using an appropriate diagram, the effects on different stakeholders of the government granting a subsidy to the domestic producers of good X.

8. Describe administrative (regulatory) barriers to trade.

9. Discuss arguments in favour of trade protection.

10. Discuss arguments against trade protection.

11. Explain, using an appropriate diagram and an example, how the value of a currency is determined in a floating (flexible) exchange rate system.

12. Describe, using an appropriate diagram, two factors that may be considered responsible for an appreciation/ depreciation (or, revaluation/devaluation) of currency X.

13. Distinguish, using real world examples, between an appreciation and a revaluation of a currency (or, between a depreciation and a devaluation of a currency).

14. Describe a fixed exchange rate system and explain the actions required to maintain currency X fixed.

15. Explain how a managed exchange rate system operates.

16. Outline (or, describe) the role of the balance of payments.

17. Distinguish between credits and debits in the balance of payments, illustrating with examples (from the extract).

18. Explain the four components of the balance of payments providing an example from each.

19. Explain the difference between a current account deficit and a current account surplus.

20. Explain (using examples from the extract) two components of the capital account.

21. Explain the three (main) components of the financial account providing an example for each.

22. Explain the meaning of the expression 'current account balance'.

23. Examine how the current and the financial accounts are interdependent.

24. Explain the pressure on the exchange rate of a currency of a sizeable current account deficit (or, surplus).

Variations on the following may be asked in part (d) of HL/SL Paper 2

1. Compare and contrast a fixed exchange rate system with a floating exchange rate system.

2. Compare and contrast the different types of trading blocs.

3. (HL only) Discuss the real-world relevance and limitations of the theory of comparative advantage.

4. Discuss the arguments in favour of trade protection.

5. Discuss the arguments against trade protection.

6. (HL only) Discuss the implications of a persistent current account deficit.

7. (HL only) Discuss the possible consequences of a rising current account surplus.

8. Discuss the possible advantages and disadvantages of a monetary union for its members.

9. Evaluate the effect of different types of trade protection.

10. Evaluate the possible economic consequences of a change in the value of a currency.

11. (HL only) Evaluate the effectiveness of the policies to correct a persistent current account deficit.

12. Examine the possible consequences of overvalued and undervalued currencies.

13. Examine how the current account and the financial account are interdependent.

14. (HL only) Examine the effects of changes in the terms of trade on a country's current account.

4.1 Economic development

Defining growth and development

Development is a multidimensional qualitative concept that refers to an improvement in living standards in an economy encompassing material consumption, education and health, as well as environmental concerns. Development involves poverty reduction, increased employment opportunities for the individual and a more equitable distribution of income.

Development focuses attention on the individual and on the three dimensions of well-being, which are:

- health: the ability to live a long and healthy life
- education: the ability to read, write and acquire knowledge
- income: command over the income needed for a decent life.

The term sustainable development focuses attention on intergenerational equity along with environmental, social and economic issues. A widely accepted definition is: 'development which meets the needs of the present without compromising the ability of future generations to meet their own needs'. A development process is typically considered unsustainable when insufficient attention is paid to the environmental consequences as well as to the resulting changes in the distribution of income. Ignoring these dimensions threatens to reverse any progress made.

Economic growth, on the other hand, is a purely quantitative concept. Growth refers to increases in the real GDP (total output) of an economy through time. Growth and development are related but at the same time very different. Growth does not necessarily imply development. A country may grow without any development objective being achieved. The United Nations Development Programme (UNDP) has described four types of growth to avoid, defined as:

- jobless, where employment opportunities for the poor do not expand
- ruthless, where income inequality widens
- futureless, where natural resources are wasted and the impact on the environment is neglected
- voiceless, where individual empowerment lags behind.

On the other hand, development typically necessitates growth. Even though some limited improvement in living standards may be achieved without any growth taking place, long-term progress on the development front requires that developing countries grow.

Sources of long-term growth

A useful way of remembering the sources of growth is to realize that output may grow if all of the following conditions apply.

- The amount of available resources increases.
- The quality of available resources increases.
- The available technology improves.
- The framework within which economic activity takes place (referred to as the institutional framework) improves.

Growth may take place as a result of the following factors.

- More or improved natural resources (land) becomes available. This usually implies either the discovery of new mineral or oil deposits or the improvement of existing land. Irrigation, fertilization and improved land management may all improve the quality of existing land and contribute to growth. An increase in the natural capital may lead to growth. Remember, though, that many poor countries rich in natural resources have grown spectacularly while several rich countries with abundant natural resources have miserably failed to grow.
- There is investment in physical capital. New factories, machinery and equipment increase the physical stock of capital. As a result, labour productivity (defined as output per worker) increases. Also, increased public investments in infrastructure such as roads, ports, communications, power supplies, water and sanitation facilitate and also lower the cost of economic activity.
- The labour force grows. A larger labour force means more manpower while a larger population increases the demand

side of domestic markets. However, a larger labour force may not be able to find productive employment. In addition, short-term growth may result from better utilization of existing idle human (and other) resources.

- Investment in human resources can exert a most powerful effect on growth as it has a direct positive effect on labour productivity. Improving health services and increasing the stock of human capital, defined as the experience, skills and education embodied in the labour force of a country, are considered the best policy choices to achieve growth and development.
- Technological progress is a very influential determinant of growth. If labour is the relatively abundant resource then labour-saving technologies where higher output levels are achieved with the same quantity of labour are considered 'inappropriate' as this leads to the UNDP's category of jobless growth. Employing the 'appropriate' technology (which relies on the relatively abundant factor) to accelerate the growth and development process is a highly complex issue, especially if environmental considerations are included.
- An institutional framework conducive to growth and development is devised. The institutional framework of a country refers to the set of rules and laws, norms and conventions within which economic activity is conducted. There is no unique set of institutions that singularly promotes growth. However, some institutions have worked better than others. Attempts to transplant a template of westernized institutions into developing countries may not prove fruitful.

Characteristics of developing economies

Developing countries in our world are many and diverse. Their initial conditions, geography, climate, history, political systems, institutions and available resources vary significantly. This means that the list of characteristics that follows does not apply to all developing countries, or to the same extent for them all. It is very dangerous to generalize as there are huge differences in these characteristics between developing countries and within each one.

Per capita real income levels

Extremely low per capita real income levels characterize many developing countries. Low per capita real income levels result in low saving and so low investments. Low investments in natural, human and physical capital lead to low productivity gains and so low incomes, creating a vicious circle of poverty that extends across generations and which may require some kind of intervention.

The degree of income inequality is generally greater in developing than in developed economies. Income distribution is often highly unequal, with the top quintile (20%) of people often receiving 10 to 50 times more than the bottom 40%.

The percentage of people in absolute poverty, defined as the specific minimum income needed to satisfy the basic physical needs to assure 'continued survival', is also high in developing countries. Interestingly enough, there is recent research showing that often an increase in income will not lead to more food purchased. There may be households at or even below poverty line who will instead choose to spend any extra income earned on a television or a cell phone (Banerjee and Duflo, 2011).

In addition, as a result of very low per capita income levels, large segments of the population suffer from ill health, malnutrition and debilitating diseases and infant mortality rates are also very high. Remember that there are significant variations both between and within developing countries.

Population growth rates and/or size

Many developing economies are still characterized by high population growth rates or, if the population growth rates are not very high, the size of their population may be very high. This may be the result of high birth rates (fertility) coupled with a reduction in death rates (mortality) because of improved health conditions. A major implication of high birth rates is that children under the age of 15 often make up almost one half of the total population. This means that the active labour force has to support almost twice as many children as it typically does in richer countries. In some developing countries a large proportion of the population is attracted to cities (urban centres) where most economic activity takes place in the informal sector (that is, where it is neither officially registered nor regulated).

Unemployment and underemployment

High unemployment is a common feature of most developing countries. Unemployment, especially in urban areas, may affect 10–20% of the labour force. On the other hand, the underemployed include those working less than they would like to as well as those who have near zero contribution to total output. In rural areas unemployment suffers from large seasonal variations. Unemployment is a much more complex problem in developing economies and the necessary policy approaches go beyond traditional demand-side or pro-market supply-side prescriptions.

Dependence on the primary sector

Agriculture in developing countries contributes around 30% of GDP compared to less than 2% in high-income countries. As per capita income levels rise the structure of demand changes, leading first to a rise in manufacturing and then to a rise in services. The share of services in high-income countries is around 70% of GDP. Of course, there are variations in the structure of output within each income group.

Dependence on exports of primary commodities

Since a significant proportion of output in low-income countries originates from the primary sector, primary commodities often also form the basis of their exports to other nations. Some countries may even depend on exporting a single non-oil primary commodity.

The Millennium Development Goals

In 2000, world leaders promised to improve living standards in the developing world by achieving eight UN Millennium Development Goals (MDGs) by 2015. These goals encompass education, health, gender and the environment and are stated as follows.

- Eradicate extreme poverty and hunger.
- Achieve universal primary education.
- Promote gender equality and empower women.
- Reduce child mortality.
- Improve maternal health.
- Combat HIV/AIDS, malaria and other diseases.
- Ensure environmental sustainability.
- Develop a global partnership for development.

Progress has been made on several issues but for very many countries and regions these goals remain out of reach. The best way to monitor up-to-date progress on each of these goals is to visit www.un.org/millenniumgoals/reports.shtml. The World Development Report also includes useful information on the MDGs. Check, for example, Table 3 (Millennium Development Goals: Eradicating poverty and improving lives) on page 382 of the 2010 report.

Bear in mind that one important drawback of these goals is that they overlook inequality and process freedoms. In addition, according to the World Bank, climate change and conflict may compromise the efforts to improve standards of living and to achieve these goals.

Indicators used to measure development

Per capita income figures

Per capita GNI or per capita GDP represent measures of per capita income. The difference between GDP and GNI is that GNI excludes incomes earned domestically by foreign factors (which are paid abroad, for example the profits of multinational corporations) but it includes incomes earned abroad by nationals of the country. Per capita income figures are computed by dividing GNI or GDP of a country by the mid-year total population of the country. Usually, per capita income figures are in so called PPP (purchasing power parity) dollars, sometimes referred to as 'international dollars', which have the same purchasing power over GDP as a US dollar in the US. The idea behind using PPP as a conversion factor, and not the market exchange rate, is that cost of living may differ substantially between countries and market exchange rates do not necessarily adjust to capture these differences.

The World Bank uses per capita GNI to determine the following income classifications: low income was defined as $975 or less in 2008; middle income was $976 to $11,905; and high income was $11,906 or more. A further division at GNI per capita – $3,855 – is made between lower-middle income and upper-middle income economies.

This classification is useful and may provide us with some information on the level of development of a country as there is a positive correlation between per capita income and social welfare. Few would question that Norway is more developed than Zimbabwe. But since growth in per capita income does not necessarily imply improved living standards, classification based on per capita income is also fraught with problems. Using per capita income may mask very significant differences between countries.

These are some issues to be aware of when using per capita income figures to determine the level of development of countries.

- Per capita income fails to incorporate income distribution considerations. Per capita income is just a simple average providing no information on whether income is equitably or very unequally distributed.

- Using per capita income figures does not take into account the value of the environmental degradation often associated with increased production. The pressure on agriculture to produce more food products is responsible for soil erosion and the burning of forests. Industrialization is also often accompanied by massive migration from rural to urban areas, leading to heavily polluted and congested cities. Emissions from industry and increased energy requirements also decrease the quality of life.

- Per capita income figures fail to include non-marketed subsistence production which may be relatively significant in some low-income countries. Non-marketed subsistence production refers to foods and other goods and services produced by a family for its own consumption. More generally, per capita income figures fail to include the size of parallel ('black' or shadow) economies in developing countries.

- Relying on per capita income also conceals useful information on the composition of output. Two economies with equal per capita income levels may differ with respect to living standards because of different output mix. A country that spends a large proportion of its GDP on, say, defence, devotes resources there that could have been used otherwise in the production of pro-development goods. The value of leisure, a very important 'good' an individual may enjoy, is not included in the calculation of GNI or GDP. As pointed out in Section 2, it makes a big difference to workers if the average working week is over 50 hours and they can seldom take a holiday, or if the working week is only 35 hours and everyone enjoys four weeks' paid leave every year.

- Lastly, per capita income does not include the value of the stream of services flowing from the accumulated social and other capital of an economy that individuals enjoy. Living standards at any point in time are not affected just by current income but also by the stock of accumulated wealth. For example, as mentioned in Section 2, the existence of a high-quality and free public school system implies that households with children may devote more of their income to goods and services not related to education.

Despite these and other shortcomings, per capita income remains the best single indicator of development available but must be employed with caution in any analysis.

Other single indicators

Single indicators of the level of development of a population include the following.

- Health-related indicators may be used, such as health expenditure per capita; life expectancy at birth (years); infant mortality (per 1,000 live births); mortality of children aged under five years (per 1,000); malnutrition prevalence, weight and/or height for age (of children under five years old); births attended by skilled health staff (% of total); maternal mortality ratio (per 100,000 live births); immunization, DPT and measles (% of children aged between 12 and 23 months); improved sanitation facilities (% of population with access); prevalence of HIV (% of population aged between 15 and 49 years); physicians (per 10,000 people); hospital beds (per 10,000 people).

- Education-related indicators may be taken into account, such as literacy rate (% of people aged 15 years and older); mean years of schooling (of people aged 25 years and older); expected years of schooling (years); expenditure per student, primary, secondary and tertiary (% of GDP, per capita); pupil–teacher ratio, primary; ratio of girls to boys in primary and secondary education (%); school enrolment, primary, secondary and tertiary (%); trained teachers in primary education (% of total teachers).

- Other indicators include newspaper circulation per 1,000 population, energy consumption per capita, percentage of GDP derived from each sector of the economy and urban population.

An excellent source of current data on health, education and other development-related indicators are the statistical tables at the end of the World Development Report published annually by the World Bank (www.data.worldbank.org).

Composite indicators

No single indicator is powerful enough to illustrate satisfactorily the complex issue of development. It is therefore preferable to rely on several indicators synthesized into a single variable.

A number of composite indices have been devised. They integrate economic, social and even political aspects of development. The most widely quoted and used composite indicator is the human development index (HDI). The HDI measures average achievements of a population in terms of health, education and access to goods and services and was devised as a simple rival to GNP concentrating only on longevity, basic education and minimal income. The HDI 'succeeded in challenging the hegemony of growth-centric thinking' (that is, it was successful in displacing per capita income as a summary measure of development).

The health dimension of the HDI is captured by life expectancy at birth. In 2010 the indicators used to measure progress in education have been revised and now include the mean years of schooling of people aged 25 and older and the expected years of schooling that a child of school entrance age could expect to receive if prevailing patterns of enrolment were to stay the same (instead of adult literacy and gross enrolment rate). Access to goods and services is measured by per capita income which in 2010 has also been revised and now refers to GNI per capita in PPP dollars, replacing GDP per capita. The reason for the change to GNI is that in a globalized world it is preferable to focus on the income of the residents of a country as this income may significantly differ from domestic production.

Major drawbacks of the HDI include:

- a reliance on national averages which conceals skewed distributions in the variables included within a population
- the absence of 'a quantitative measure of human freedom'

(UNDP, 2010).

Being an average it may conceal important differences within a country. Women and rural populations as well as the very old and the very young often suffer disproportionately but this is not illustrated through the HDI. In addition, environmental concerns are not addressed. It is possible for a country to have a high HDI and be 'unsustainable, undemocratic and unequal'.

Note that three new composite indicators were introduced by the UNDP in 2010 capturing multidimensional inequality (the inequality-adjusted HDI, known as the IHDI), gender disparities (the gender inequality index) and extreme deprivation (the multidimensional poverty index).

- The IHDI is a measure of human development that takes into consideration the extent of inequality in the country. Under perfect equality the HDI and the IHDI are equal. Inequality in the distribution of health, education and income lowers the HDI of an average person in a society below the aggregate HDI of the country (based on the UNDP Human Development Report, 2010).

- The gender inequality index attempts to reveal differences in the distribution of achievements between women and men in a country. Often women and girls are discriminated against in health, education and in the labour market, which negatively affects their freedoms.

- The multidimensional poverty index replaces the human poverty index. It complements money-based measures of poverty by considering 'multiple deprivations and their overlap'. Low level of income is but one dimension of the poverty experienced by people in many countries of the world – poverty extends to other dimensions such as poor health and nutrition, low education and skills, inadequate livelihoods, bad housing conditions, social exclusion and lack of participation. The multidimensional poverty index shows the number of people who are poor (suffering a given number of deprivations) and the number of deprivations with which poor households typically struggle.

Domestic factors

Education and health

Labour productivity is defined as output per worker, or the quantity of goods and services a worker can produce per hour of work. It critically depends on the education, skills and training of workers as well as on the type of capital they use in the production process. Growth in productivity is the key to long-term growth which in turn is a prerequisite for development.

Investments in human capital formation are necessary to achieve higher labour productivity, faster long-term growth and improved living standards. Better health and education increase labour productivity and allow individuals to have more, better and higher-paid employment opportunities. Better education and health are also responsible for numerous external benefits (both are the most important examples of merit goods). Remember too that achieving better health and education are themselves development goals.

Appropriate technology

Growth is necessary for any long-term progress in development but not all types of growth do lead to development. The technology employed determines whether any acceleration in growth will translate into human development gains or not.

In general, technologies can be distinguished into capital-intensive or labour-intensive. Capital-intensive production processes rely mostly on the use of physical capital (on machines) whereas labour-intensive production processes rely mostly on the use of labour (on workers). Remember that in many production processes there is no choice: you cannot construct a labour-intensive oil refinery.

Since in most developing countries labour is the relatively abundant factor of production, it follows that appropriate technologies are labour-intensive. A labour-intensive technology translates to increased employment and income generation for the population of the country and an exit from poverty. On the other hand, capital-intensive technologies lead to what is referred to as jobless growth, which is a type of growth that does not lead to improved living standards.

Credit and microcredit

The importance of credit and microcredit institutions lies in the simple fact that typically, if you cannot borrow, you cannot make any investment in physical, natural or human capital. It follows that a functional credit system is vital in breaking the poverty cycle explained earlier.

Credit institutions induce people to save, as they offer not only safety for whatever income people do not spend but also a rate of return. Banks allow people to borrow money that can be used to increase their human capital or to start a small business, which may enable them to break the poverty cycle. Unfortunately, a functional credit system is not enough as very often it is also the absence of well-defined property rights that prevents poor people from borrowing from commercial banks.

Microcredit, on the other hand, focuses on making available very small loans to the very poor, helping them to start a small business or expand an existing one or meet an emergency arising from disease, theft or bad weather. The pioneer of microfinance is Bangladeshi economist Muhammad Yunus who created the Grameen Bank several decades ago. Yunus won the Nobel Peace prize for his efforts in 2006. The Nobel Committee adopted the view that reducing the gap between the rich and the poor is necessary to decrease conflict in the world.

Many microfinance loans have been offered to women who have not only shown that they spend the money carefully and productively but also that they are more likely to pay the loans back. Lending money to women has helped them in their empowerment. Their participation in such programmes gives them greater bargaining power and enables them to take part in family decision making while it also increases their mobility.

Microfinance has been considered to play a significant but rather limited role in the development process of nations. Microcredit has lately come under attack: '...most borrowers do not appear to be climbing out of poverty, and a sizable minority is getting trapped in a spiral of debt, according to studies and analysts' (*New York Times*, 2011).

Women and their empowerment

Policies that aim at improving gender equity have been found to improve human development. Not only will deprived girls and women benefit from such policies but also the growth and development process will accelerate: 'Human development if not engendered, is endangered.'

There are numerous routes through which this can be accomplished. Educating girls is considered one of the most significant investments for a developing country as it results in even greater, gender-specific benefits. An educated mother will enjoy higher earning ability outside the home for each extra year of schooling. She will have fewer children so will create conditions for capital deepening (which means more capital will be available per worker), resulting in even higher long-term productivity and output gains. Her children will be healthier and she will make sure that her children are also educated, creating a virtuous circle. Educating women decreases mortality in children younger than five years old, decreasing the costs of health-care intervention.

Lastly, better and more educated women can lead to higher women's participation in the labour force as well as in politics, allowing them to influence policy.

The distribution of income

High and rising income inequality is considered a major barrier to economic development. It follows that policies aiming at reducing income inequality and making growth inclusive will encourage development. Poverty reduction depends not only on income growth but also on how income is distributed: poverty is reduced and development is achieved if there is growth accompanied by narrowing income inequality.

A more equitable distribution of income will make it easier to reach consensus among different population groups. This is a necessary condition for a government to be willing and able to undertake successfully the required institutional and economic reforms that accelerate growth. Lower income inequality decreases the prevalence of corruption in a country and corruption is considered a major obstacle to the development process as it increases the costs of doing business and it distorts efficiency. Trust between economic agents increases, also decreasing the cost and increasing the likelihood of doing business, another necessary condition for growth to accelerate. A more equitable distribution of income will decrease the number of the very poor so that more people will have access to education and health resources and so become more productive members of society. The probability of civil unrest will be lower, decreasing the risks for investors and leading to more domestic and foreign investment spending in the country. Lower income inequality may accelerate savings and result in more investment and greater demand for locally produced goods and services, which may increase income and further decrease inequality.

Trade-related barriers

Barriers to primary export-led growth

Overspecialization on a narrow range of primary exports cannot effectively lead the way to economic development. Here are some of the reasons for this.

- Demand for most primary exports is income inelastic and, as a result, markets for such products in high-income countries do not grow fast enough to help accelerate growth.

HL

- The terms of trade of countries exporting primary products will deteriorate in the long run. They will need to export a greater volume of primary exports to be able to import one unit of manufacturing goods. However, this will only lead to a further decrease in the price of these primary products as most of these markets are competitive.

- Export earnings may exhibit significant year-to-year fluctuations as prices of farm products are affected by the weather and other random factors. This may mean that domestic aggregate demand becomes unstable and investment spending is more risky.

- Primary exports may be dominated by a few multinationals and middlemen so that linkages with the rest of the economy may prove ineffective.

- Prices received for many primary products have decreased through time. For example, technology and an increase in the number of coffee-producing countries have pushed down the world price for coffee.

- Agricultural exports have to face the trade protection that advanced economies (the USA, the European Union and Japan) grant their farmers in the form of subsidies. The resulting inability to access these markets is a more general barrier developing countries face. This statement does not indiscriminately apply to all developing countries, though, as many falsely believe. It mainly applies to the so called Cairns Group of developing countries, which includes Argentina, Brazil, Chile, Colombia, Costa Rica, Indonesia, Malaysia, Philippines, South Africa, Thailand and Uruguay which are mostly middle-income countries with a strong comparative advantage in agriculture. It follows that the main beneficiaries of liberalizing trade in agriculture would be this group of countries. The least developed countries as defined by the UN (which include all countries in Sub-Saharan Africa; Afghanistan, Bangladesh, Bhutan, Cambodia, Lao, Maldives and Nepal in Asia; and Haiti in Central America) will actually be hurt by this liberalization, the main reason for this being that most of these countries are net food importers and elimination of agricultural subsidies will translate into higher food prices for them.

Trade-related strategies for growth and development

The strategy of protection: import-substitution industrialization (ISI)

In the 1950s it was thought that the problem of development was a structural problem in that developing countries relied too heavily on the primary sector and did not have a manufacturing sector. The creation of an industrial base to substitute domestically produced manufactured goods for imports became known as ISI. The goods targeted were non-durable manufactured goods (for example textiles) that were simple to produce and were for domestic consumption. Trade barriers were erected to protect the newly established domestic firms. These barriers would stay in place until the firms grew sufficiently in size and acquired the necessary know-how to lower average costs. Trade barriers were reduced when the firms were able to compete with imports and survive within the domestic markets.

Typically, the exchange rate was kept overvalued so that prices of necessary imported materials and intermediate products (machines and other manufactured inputs) used by the infant industries were artificially low.

Several problems are associated with an inward-oriented strategy. Since the domestic industry had its own 'captive' market to sell its products, it never had the incentive to become efficient. The price and cost disciplines that competition imposes on firms were totally absent. In some cases, low-quality, high-cost and high-priced goods were produced.

The overvalued exchange rate acted as a tax on traditional primary exports as farmers earned less domestic currency for each dollar of primary exports. Poverty for large segments of the population therefore increased. In some developing countries the ISI strategy created a privileged élite which became more and more powerful as the industrial sector grew. In many cases, the protective trade barriers were never eliminated. In addition, the newly established industries were often capital-intensive, employing inappropriate technologies which led to jobless growth as minimal employment opportunities were created. Remember that jobless growth is a type of growth to avoid as development does not follow.

Export promotion: outward-oriented strategies

In some East Asian countries, including those known as the four East Asian Tigers (Korea, Taiwan, Hong Kong and Singapore), the structural change that the ISI strategy represented was followed by an attempt to export the simple, non-durable, manufactured goods these countries had been producing for their domestic market. These, and later other developing countries, adopted an outward orientation.

In this process, the role of the state varied among countries but, in all of them, it played a significant, complementary role. It provided guidance and assistance to the private firms but only if they achieved specific performance standards typically associated with export targets. These firms were forced to produce low-price, high-quality goods in order to continue to enjoy any state subsidies or cheaper loans from banks.

Export promotion is not sufficient to promote development and to ensure the sustainability of the process. The state in these countries invested heavily in education, slowly creating a more productive labour force with higher skills. The state also ensured that the fruits of economic growth were enjoyed by all. This meant that these countries avoided the costs associated with rising income inequality.

The first Asian country to initiate such an approach to the growth and development problem was Japan. It was followed by the four East Asian Tigers (and other countries, such as Malaysia, Indonesia, Thailand and Vietnam, have been added to this list). China and India are the current stars of the export- or outward-oriented strategy.

Advantages of outward-oriented strategies

- Focusing initially on the production and export of simple, manufactured non-durable goods changed the structure of these economies. Employment opportunities increased for the rural migrants, as these industries were mostly labour-intensive.

- The export revenues earned alleviated problems with the balance of payments as they were used to finance the importation of necessary intermediate and capital goods. There was less danger of the economy running into foreign exchange and foreign debt problems. Rising export revenues also increase aggregate demand (AD), so they can fuel growth in output and incomes.

- Focusing on the larger export markets forced firms to grow in size and acquire economies of scale (EOS). This is especially important for small countries.

- Firms were forced to learn more about manufacturing their products more efficiently. International competition provided the stimulus. The state also invited technical assistance from abroad but it usually limited contracts so that they lasted no more than three years, forcing domestic firms to learn the necessary technology. Operating successfully in world markets enabled firms to acquire the marketing, financial, managerial and, most importantly, entrepreneurial skills. Exposure to world competition allowed a local entrepreneurial class to evolve and mature.

- Through varying degrees of state guidance these economies slowly shifted their comparative advantage and production to more sophisticated and complex manufactured products and later to knowledge-based and technology-intensive products. Their economies therefore diversified and were more insulated from industry-specific risks.

Possible disadvantages of outward-oriented growth

- Since the growth process is driven by exports, it depends on how fast the advanced economies are growing. If their incomes are rising fast then they will be absorbing more imports which are the exports of the developing countries. A deep recession in the USA or in Europe, though, will be costly as it will slow down the process, especially if domestic demand is weak and the government is not in a position to adopt expansionary fiscal policy. In response to the 2008 global crisis China was able to adopt a huge fiscal stimulus programme, but not all countries were able to do the same.

- Outward-oriented growth must successfully overcome the barriers created by trade protection in developed countries.

- Outward-oriented strategies may lead to worsening income distribution as the rural sector may be left behind. A larger share of national income will accrue to those involved in the export sector. It follows that only if there are redistributive policies in place will development ensue (using the term 'redistributive policies' in its broad sense here – that is, including spending on better health and education).

- The drive to produce cheaply for export markets may lead policy makers to ignore the costs of environmental degradation. This is very evident in China where export-driven growth is seriously damaging the natural resource base of the country and generating major environmental costs, undermining the sustainability of the country's long-term growth and development prospects.

- Achieving outward-oriented growth forces policy makers to keep the exchange rate artificially undervalued to provide an extra competitive edge to their exports, risking not only rising protectionist sentiment abroad but also inflation at home.

- Focusing on outward-oriented growth may lead policy makers to postpone the creation of a social safety net that would include state pensions and health insurance, as the growth process does not rely on the ability of the population to spend on domestic goods and services.

Preferential trading agreements

Regional integration among developing countries is often referred to as south–south integration. Originally, in the 1960s and 1970s, developing countries had attempted to create a number of preferential trading agreements as a way of reducing the cost of ISI through opening their markets to other developing countries. A bloc would increase the size of the potential market for each exporting firm and so it would lead to EOS. Any complementarities in production would also help reduce costs and allow specialization. The regional agreements since the 1990s are referred to as 'new regionalism' and are part of a broader trade liberalization scheme where export promotion is featured as the growth and development strategy of choice.

Examples of preferential trading agreements among developing countries include the Latin America Free Trade Association (LAFTA), formed in 1961; MERCOSUR, a customs union among Argentina, Brazil, Uruguay, and Paraguay formed in 1991; the Asia-Pacific Economic Cooperation (APEC), a group of 21 nations that border the Pacific Ocean, established in 1989 and promoting freer trade and cooperation among its members; the Economic Community of Central African States (ECCAS), established in 1983 and including Burundi, Cameroon, Central

African Republic , Chad, Congo, Equatorial Guinea, Gabon, Rwanda, São Tomé and Principe; and the Economic Community of West African States (ECOWAS), established in 1975, with 16 member countries.

Possible benefits of increased regional cooperation among developing countries include:

- increased trade creation as a result of the resulting expanded market
- the possibility of EOS that may lead to more exports outside the bloc
- greater political and bargaining power in negotiations with developed economies
- a decreased level of dependence on developing countries' markets.

Here are some reasons many attempts at regional cooperation among developing countries have failed or have resulted in limited success.

- The structure of production and of trade in developing countries lacks a sufficient complementary nature. The similarity of their economies has resulted in more trade diversion than trade creation.
- Many attempts have encountered significant organizational and administrative problems.
- Political rivalry both between and within countries and lack of commitment have also prevented progress.
- Transaction costs are often high due to the high share of raw materials and non-durables in these countries' mutual trade. There are high transport costs, especially since infrastructure is poor (for example, there are few roads).

The role of foreign direct investment and the multinational corporation

Foreign direct investment (FDI)

FDI is long-term investment where a firm based in one country establishes a presence in another country. It may either refer to investment in new facilities ('de novo' or 'greenfield' investment) or it may refer to acquiring controlling percentage of the shares of existing local companies. The key characteristic of FDI is that the investor has control of the acquired asset.

FDI leads to the creation of multinational corporations. A multinational corporation is a firm which has established, through FDI, production or other operations in more than one country.

Why do multinational corporations invest in developing countries?

The obvious reason for corporations to expand into other countries is that by doing so they are able to increase their sales and/or decrease their costs so that they increase their profits.

Most FDI flows into developed countries (about 70% of the total in 2009) and most of it flows out of developed countries (about 88% in 2009). Flows into developing countries have been almost steadily increasing though. Some of the most important explanations for the expansion of a multinational corporation into developing countries are listed below.

- The multinational corporation is involved in extraction of natural resources such as oil, copper or bauxite, which must be done at location.

- It is attempting to lower its production costs. For example, for many production processes (especially standardized ones) labour costs are often lower in developing countries than the multinational corporation's home country.

- The multinational corporation is attempting to benefit from slacker regulatory frameworks.

Multinational corporations do not expand indiscriminately into developing countries. A detailed examination of annual FDI inflows reveals that some developing countries receive far more FDI than others. China, Brazil and Mexico attract the majority.

So, why do some developing countries attract much more FDI than others? What factors act as 'pull factors' into a specific developing country? The following list helps to answer these questions. Note that some of these factors may also explain why companies expand and become multinational. The factors are:

- stable macroeconomic environment

- stable political environment

- public policy, including tax treatment and ease of profit repatriation

- weak regulatory systems

- environmental laws, regulations and their enforcement

- clearly defined property rights and a secure legal framework

- extent and power of labour unions

- high levels of human capital and labour productivity

- low labour costs (low wages coupled with high labour productivity)

- quality of physical infrastructure (for example roads and ports) and informational infrastructure

- proximity to a major and growing market area with high and or growing levels of income

- membership in wider free trade areas or trading blocs; avoidance of tariffs

- natural resource endowments (and their geographical distribution) including climate

- cultural similarities.

Does the presence of multinational corporations accelerate growth and development?

Arguments in support of multinational corporations'
FDI can be seen as a way of 'filling in gaps' between:

- the target level of investment spending in a country and the actual level of investments that domestic savings can finance

- the target level of foreign exchange and the actual level derived from net export earnings, foreign aid and private remittances – not only will the inflow of private foreign capital partly finance a current account deficit but if the foreign-owned enterprise generates a flow of export earnings it can also help over time

- the target tax revenues required to finance projects aimed at growth and development and the actual revenues collected.

In addition, multinational corporations may:

- create greater levels of employment, providing job opportunities to the local population

- provide training and skill creation to the local workforce

- help by providing access to management and organizational skills

- prove to be a vehicle for faster transfer and diffusion of technology.

Arguments against multinational corporations

- Multinational corporations may hurt domestic firms by eliminating competition and by importing intermediate products from overseas affiliates instead of buying these from domestic suppliers

- Repatriation of profits, payment of royalties and importation of intermediate goods may lead to problems with the balance of payments as more foreign exchange flows out of the country.

- The tax contribution of multinational corporations may be considerably less than it should be as a result of tax concessions, investment allowances and transfer pricing (which artificially reduces their income).

- The technology employed may be inappropriate if it is capital intensive and employment positions may not be generated.
- The skills of the local workforce may not improve if workers are used to fill only the low-skill positions and no training is provided.
- Multinational corporations may generate domestic incomes for higher income groups with a high propensity to buy imports and a low propensity to save domestically.
- They may worsen the imbalance between rural and urban opportunities and contribute to more unequal income distribution.
- They may use their economic power to influence government policies in directions unfavourable to the development process.

Overall

- The net effects on growth are unambiguous, at least in the short run, but the effects on the long-run development prospects of the host country are not.
- The conditions and stipulations of the contracts signed, as well as the ability of the domestic government to enforce these and to regulate the behaviour of multinational corporations, are critical in determining whether the long-run effect on the host country will be positive or negative.
- In countries where the state ensured that the multinational corporations made a direct contribution to its goals and that their activities were complementary and not at the expense of domestic production processes, the development process was accelerated.

Foreign aid

Foreign aid is the fourth major source of foreign exchange for the developing world, behind export earnings, investment inflows and migrants' remittances. Foreign aid includes any flow of capital to developing countries which is granted on concessionary terms and is non-commercial from the point of view of the donor. Foreign aid includes both outright grants (where no repayment is expected) and loans, as long as the interest rate charged on these loans is lower than that charged on commercial loans and the repayment period is longer. Such long-term loans are referred to as concessional loans and include a 25% grant element.

Aid granted by governments (public aid) is also referred to as official development assistance (ODA). Aid, especially humanitarian aid (which consists of food aid, medical relief and emergency relief aid), can also be extended by non-governmental organizations (NGOs). It is typically small (but growing) in scale.

Types of aid

Aid can be classified in many ways. It can be bilateral or multilateral. Aid is:

- bilateral when the flow is from one advanced economy to a poorer nation
- multilateral when it flows to the developing nation through an international lending agency and organization such as the UN, the World Bank or the IMF.

Aid is also distinguished into:

- tied aid, when the funds must be used to buy imports from the donor country or must be linked to a specific project (for example the donor may build a highway and be paid in oil or iron ore which form the infrastructure for commodities)
- project aid, with the funds used to finance the construction of a particular project (for example a dam, a road or a hospital) – typically project aid funds development of economic infrastructure and environmental improvement
- programme loans, in which case the funding is dependent on the recipient following specific advice and adhering to specific conditions (conditional or structural adjustment lending) and/or a loan is given to fund specific programmes, in health or education for example.

Some aid related facts

- The total annual flow of aid in 2011 amounts to 0.31% of donors' GNI. This is down from 0.34% in 1990 and significantly lower than the 0.7% target which was first set in 1970 and has been repeatedly re-endorsed.
- In 2010 the largest donors by volume were the USA, the UK, France, Germany and Japan. Denmark, Luxembourg, the Netherlands, Norway and Sweden continued to exceed the UN's ODA target of 0.7 % of GNI.
- The largest rich countries give less **per person** than smaller countries.
- Only six developed countries (Ireland, Luxemburg, the Netherlands, Sweden, Norway and the UK) provided nearly 100% untied aid. (Tying aid is considered to limit the effectiveness of aid.)
- In 2008 total official aid flows from OECD countries (including debt relief) reached a record high of $128.7 billion (OECD data) while since 1950 it has totalled $2.3 trillion 2006 dollars (Easterly and Pgutze, 2008).
- Most aid goes to those who need it least; the richer 40% of the developing world's people get twice as much aid per person than the poorer 40%.
- According to the UNDP, development aid is 'inadequate in amount and often inappropriate in form'.

Evaluating the impact of aid on development

The debate on the role of aid in the development process is highly polarized. Jeffrey Sachs, UN adviser and director of Columbia University's Earth Institute, argues that massive infusions of aid are needed to break the poverty cycle and considers aid a powerful determinant of long-term growth. Poor countries are poor because they are hot, infertile, infested with malaria and often landlocked, making it hard to increase productivity without help to deal with such endemic problems. Neither free markets nor democracy, in Sachs' opinion, will do very much for them.

On the other side of the debate, William Easterly, co-director of the Development Research Institute and Professor of Economics at New York University, argues that aid does more harm than good. It is often wasted instead of being spent productively. It may prevent people from devising their own solutions to the specific problems they face. Aid often corrupts or is granted to corrupt autocrats and undermines local institutions. It is typically fragmented among too many donor countries and is thinly spread over too many sectors with a lot of overlapping and confusion.

Some aid programmes help more than others. It is not easy to determine which ones promote development goals and which ones undermine them. One recent approach adopted by J-PAL (Poverty Action Lab) at Massachusetts Institute of Technology (MIT), under the direction of Esther Duflo and Abhijit Banerjee, is to try to find out by using 'randomized control trials', just as the effectiveness of a drug is evaluated in medicine.

The following points provide a platform for discussing the effectiveness of aid.

Effectiveness of aid

Aid can be effective:

- when it is narrowly targeted to specific pro-development projects and objectives
- when it is not tied to buying products from donor countries
- most importantly, when it is reinforced by appropriate domestic policies and institutions in a non-corrupt government environment.

Aid can be ineffective:

- when it is given to countries with corrupt governments
- when it induces countries to postpone improvements of macroeconomic conditions
- when it replaces domestic savings and trade flows as vehicles for development
- when it is given on the basis of strategic and political considerations
- when the technologies transferred and the advice given are inappropriate.

Motives for offering aid

There are three main motives for providing aid to developing countries.

- Humanitarian motives are the moral or ethical reasons for providing aid. The US response to the 2010 Haitian earthquake is an example of emergency assistance, with aid to Haiti rising in that year by 241% to US $1.1 billion.

- Political motives or strategic reasons may exist, in that aid has been used in an effort to build closer political and strategic relations with other countries. Huge amounts of development loans have been provided by several developed donor countries to secure friendly relationships. Donor countries have also used aid programmes as a bargaining chip for international negotiations. 'Aid sanctions' are used as a diplomatic instrument to produce a desirable policy shift in the aid's recipient.

- Economic motives, such as to develop markets and dispose of surpluses, may exist. Aid has often been directed to promote a country's exports of manufactured goods and imports of raw materials. Aid programmes often tied loans or grants to the purchase of the donor country's exports so that the country could expand its export market. Aid can be granted (usually as tied aid) to cover the need to import industrial raw materials, foodstuffs and other primary commodities. China's post-2000 astonishing growth of aid in Sub-Saharan Africa and elsewhere is considered to be driven by such a motive. Deals are often quasi-barter. For example, donor construction and engineering companies might design and build infrastructure facilities in a developing country and ask the recipient to repay in commodity terms, say in oil or iron ore (this would be a case of tied project aid).

Aid and NGOs

- The term NGOs usually describes an array of groups and organizations which pursue some kind of public interest or public good and aim at providing services to the public, directly or indirectly. Oxfam, Friends of the Earth and WWF are well-known NGOs but there are very many other smaller, grassroots organizations that serve similar purposes.

- NGOs have had an increasing significance in efforts toward sustainable development at the international level.

- They try to affect inter-governmental negotiations that range from the regulation of hazardous wastes and a global ban on land mines to increasing access to AIDS drugs for affected people in developing countries.

- Many NGOs work closely with the people they wish to help, which increases their effectiveness.

- NGOs have often exposed the social and environmental externalities that the practices of many multinational corporations result in. Many act as watchdogs of multinational corporations. Labour, environmental and human rights records are scrutinized and activists have in many instances forced change upon multinational corporations.

- Businesses have been forced to 'care' about the effects of their activities and not just the effects on their share price but also on workers, communities and the world at large. Many companies now allocate significant resources to environmental and social affairs.

4.7 The role of foreign debt

Foreign or external debt is usually defined as debt owed to non-residents of a country. It is the total amount of money that a country owes to foreign entities which is repaid in foreign exchange. Foreign entities include foreign governments, commercial banks and multilateral institutions.

The first debt crisis

In the mid-and late-1970s many non-oil developing countries began accumulating large trade deficits. On the other hand, oil-exporting countries were accumulating huge current account surpluses and were depositing in the banks of advanced economies the oil export earnings they could not spend. The banks then lent this money to the developing countries which had problems with their balance of payments. As a result, these countries began to accumulate huge foreign debts.

In 1982 Mexico announced that it was not able to service its debt. Mexico was not alone. Due to the factors listed below, 15 Latin-American nations and some Sub-Saharan African countries were forced to request emergency aid from the IMF.

Causes of the first debt crisis

- World interest rates increased as a result of the extremely tight monetary policy adopted by the US Federal Reserve Bank to fight off inflation. As a result, interest payments on existing loans (the outstanding debt) of these countries increased and new borrowing became more expensive.

- As a result of the higher interest rates, the USA fell into recession, dragging other countries with it. World demand for the primary exports of these developing countries therefore decreased, lowering their prices, their volumes and, consequently, the export earnings of these countries.

- The higher US interest rates led to an appreciation of the US dollar and so to an increase in the real value of the debt, as some of the export earnings of these countries were in other hard currencies.

- Worse still, the funds that had been borrowed by many governments of developing countries were often used wastefully so that the productive capacity of these economies was not enhanced.

The debt crisis inflicted tremendous pain on the people of the developing countries and led the IMF and the World Bank to assume a new role. Conditional lending programmes were initiated, with recipient countries agreeing to implement structural adjustment policies. There now seems to be a consensus that these policies usually did not advance the development cause.

Costs of high levels of indebtedness

High levels of foreign debt still burden many developing countries. High levels of indebtedness hold back the development process in many ways.

- Since foreign exchange earnings are drained to service the debt, paying for necessary imports of capital goods and food products becomes more difficult.

- The state is deprived of funds to spend on necessary infrastructure.

- The state is deprived of funds to spend on health care and education. In many Sub-Saharan countries the amount spent to service debt exceeds the amount spent on primary education and primary health care combined.

- Debt overhang adversely affects domestic and foreign investment as investors fear higher taxes and the economic instability of these economies.

- Necessary reforms are more difficult for the government to initiate. The economic problems associated with debt servicing complicate attempts to reach consensus within the population.

The Heavily Indebted Countries Initiative (HIPC)

For the poorest and most indebted countries, the accumulated debt burden obstructs any possibility for development. Debt becomes unsustainable if it exceeds the capacity of the country to service it. Viewed in this way, debt relief (that is, debt reduction) becomes necessary. This is why the HIPC and Multilateral Debt Relief Initiative (MDRI) were designed and launched in 1996 and 2006 respectively.

The goal of the HIPC was to 'ensure deep, broad and fast debt relief and thereby contribute toward growth, poverty reduction, and debt sustainability in the poorest, most heavily indebted countries'. The goal of the MDRI was to 'provide additional support to HIPCs to reach the MDGs'.

In 2010, for the 36 heavily indebted countries that have benefited from relief, the ratio of the present value of their debt to their exports declined from 457% to 78%, the present value of debt to GDP ratio decreased from 114% to 19% and the debt service to exports ratio decreased from 18% to 3%.

Development as a separate sub-discipline of economics did not exist before the 1950s. Before that little attention was paid to poor countries. The League of Nations 1938 World Economic Survey included one paragraph on South America. This was a more complete coverage than poor countries in Africa or Asia had, since there was no reference to them at all. The industrialization of the Soviet Union (through planning, forced saving and investment) changed all this.

The role of the state and of the market

The role of the state in the development process resembles a pendulum. It shifted from the heavy-handed intervention in the 1950s and 1960s when the problem of development required state planning and was reduced to the solution of a system of equations. It swung all the way to the gradual diminution of the role of the state in the 1970s and 1980s, when markets were conferred a central role (for example with privatization and trade liberalization) with increased attention paid to getting the fundamentals right (achieving, for example, low budget deficits and low inflation).

A growing consensus is now being formed which considers the role of the state and of the market complementary. As the focus has been shifting towards human development any policy, whether macroeconomic or microeconomic in nature, has to be judged with respect to its effect on the least privileged segments of society.

Markets and prices are important for these reasons.

- They provide signals for the allocation of resources.
- They create incentives.
- They permit choice.
- Profit-oriented entrepreneurs can spot opportunities and use resources efficiently.
- Competition leads to lower prices and better quality and forces firms to innovate.

On the other hand, an effective state is required to achieve development for these reasons.

- Infrastructure, which is necessary for growth and development, is a public good in the sense that the private sector will not provide it.
- An appropriate institutional environment is necessary for markets to operate. At the very least the state has to protect property rights and guarantee the rule of law.
- Basic education and health care create very significant positive externalities and would be underprovided if left to the market.
- The market cannot guarantee an equitable distribution of income between individuals, groups, regions or time.
- The market cannot guarantee effective protection of the environment.
- It is necessary to create a stable macroeconomic environment for economic activity to grow.

Markets and the state should be partners in the process of growth and development. The private sector should provide the necessary vigour and the state the framework within which economic activity can take place, rectifying market failures and augmenting the resources available.

4 Development economics: Questions

Variations on the following may be asked in questions (b) and (c) of HL/SL Paper 2

1. Distinguish between economic growth and economic development explaining that development is broader than growth.

2. Explain factors that may assist accelerating the growth process of an economy.

3. Explain why growth is typically a necessary but not a sufficient condition for a country to develop.

4. Suggest two characteristics that many developing countries share.

5. Explain the meaning of the term 'poverty trap' (or, 'poverty cycle').

6. Outline the current status of the Millennium Development Goals.

7. Explain the difference between GNI and GDP as well as between GDP (or, GNI) figures and GDP (or, GNI) at PPP dollars.

8. Explain the components of the HDI and why the later is a better indicator of development than per capita income levels.

9. Explain how (i) overspecialization, (ii) price volatility of commodities and (iii) inability to access international markets may obstruct the process of growth and development.

10. (HL only) Explain why the long term path of the terms of trade of a country may act as a barrier in its growth and development process.

11. Describe the nature of FDI and of MNC's.

12. Explain why MNC's expand into developing countries.

13. Describe the characteristics of developing countries that render FDI inflows more likely.

14. Explain the meaning of the term 'foreign aid' making reference to the various types and forms of aid that exist.

15. Describe the role of NGO's in the development process.

16. Explain reasons for which a developed country may extend aid to a developing country.

17. Outline the meaning of foreign debt and explain the constraints it may impose in the developing process.

18. Explain why good governance is considered a necessary precondition for a country to develop.

Variations on the following may be asked in part (d) of HL/SL Paper 2

1. Compare and contrast the GDP per capita figures and the GNI per capita figures for economically more developed countries and economically less developed countries.

2. Compare and contrast two health indicators for economically more developed countries and economically less developed countries.

3. Compare and contrast two education indicators for economically more developed countries and economically less developed countries.

4. Compare and contrast the HDI figures for economically more developed countries and economically less developed countries.

5. Compare and contrast the extent, nature and sources of official development assistance to two economically less developed countries.

6. Compare and contrast the roles of aid and trade in economic development.

7. Discuss the positive outcomes on development of market-oriented policies.

8. Discuss the negative outcomes on development of market-oriented strategies.

9. Discuss the strengths of interventionist policies on development.

10. Discuss the limitations of interventionist policies on development.

11. Discuss the view that economic development may best be achieved through a complementary approach, involving a balance of market oriented policies and government intervention.

12. Evaluate each of the following as a means of achieving economic growth and economic development. **a.** Import substitution **b.** Export promotion **c.** Trade liberalization **d.** The role of the WTO **e.** Bilateral and regional preferential trade agreements **f.** Diversification.

13. Evaluate the impact of foreign direct investment (FDI) for economically less developed countries.

14. Evaluate the effectiveness of foreign aid in contributing to economic development.

15. Examine, using appropriate diagrams where relevant, how the following factors contribute to economic development. **a.** Education and health **b.** The use of appropriate technology **c.** Access to credit and micro-credit **d.** The empowerment of women **e.** Income distribution.

16. Examine the current roles of the IMF and the World Bank in promoting economic development.

Remember that you are allowed to use a graphic display calculator (GDC) and this can be very useful.

1.1 Competitive markets: demand and supply

Linear demand functions

A linear demand curve has the form: $Q_d = a - bP$

This simply states that quantity demanded per period is inversely related to price reflecting the law of demand, and that the demand curve is a straight line from the northwest to the southeast on your paper.

The term a is a constant while the term $-b$ is the slope of the function.

If the term a increases, the demand curve shifts to the right, indicating that demand has increased. If the term a decreases, the demand curve shifts to the left, indicating that demand has decreased.

If the absolute value of the coefficient of price increases then the demand curve you will have plotted on the graph paper becomes flatter, whereas if the absolute value of the coefficient of price decreases the demand curve becomes steeper. If this seems surprising remember that the convention we have, since the work of Alfred Marshall, is for the independent variable (price) to be on the vertical axis.

If you are asked to plot a demand function, first find the P intercept by putting in zero for quantity demanded in your function, and then find the Q intercept by putting in zero for price. Connect the points. Initially, use a soft pencil and once you are sure you have done it right, go over the line with a black pen. The question paper will provide you with the two axes for the graph with numbers on them, so you automatically have the relevant range of values for such functions. If, for example, the horizontal axis (quantity demanded) on your exam paper goes up to 120 and you have calculated the horizontal intercept to be 500, you have probably made a mistake! Also remember that only positive numbers for price and quantities make sense.

Also keep in mind that you are allowed to use a GDC calculator. Most, for example the Casio fx–9860GII, allow you to enter the demand (or any) function and ask to plot its inverse. (Remember that the axes are inverted with P on the vertical and Q on the horizontal.) Make sure you practise using a GDC calculator a lot to avoid errors.

Linear supply functions

A linear supply curve has the form: $Q_s = c + dP$

This simply states that quantity supplied per period is directly related to price reflecting the law of supply, and that the supply curve is a straight line from the southwest to the northeast on your paper.

The term c is a constant while $+d$ is the slope of the function.

If c increases, the supply curve shifts to the right, indicating that supply has increased. If c decreases, the supply curve shifts to the left, indicating that supply has decreased.

If the coefficient of price increases, the supply curve plotted on the graph paper becomes flatter. Whereas if the coefficient of price decreases, the supply curve becomes steeper. Remember the convention to place the independent variable (price) on the vertical axis.

The question paper will provide the two axes with numbers on them. Choose any two convenient prices within the range given on the vertical axis and find the quantity supplied for each. Just substitute the values for P in the supply function. You will have determined two points on your paper which you simply connect. Use a soft pencil and then go over the line with a black ink pen. Remember that you are allowed to use a GDC calculator but plot the inverse of the linear supply function you are given. Only positive numbers for price and quantities make sense.

Equilibrium price and quantity

The equilibrium condition requires that quantity demanded per period is equal to quantity supplied per period. You will have three equations: the demand equation, the supply equation and the equilibrium condition (given below as (1), (2) and (3) respectively) and you will have three unknowns (the price, the quantity demanded and the quantity supplied):

$$(1)\ Q_d = a - bp$$
$$(2)\ Q_s = c + dp$$
$$(3)\ Q_d = Q_s$$

Put (1) and (2) into the equilibrium condition (3) and solve for price. Put the equilibrium price you find into either the demand or the supply equation to find equilibrium quantity.

For example:

$$Q_d = 60 - 2P$$
$$Q_s = 4P \text{ (here, the constant c is zero)}$$
$$Q_d = Q_s$$

Substituting the demand and the supply equations in the equilibrium condition:

$$60 - 2P = 4P$$
$$60 = 6P$$
$$P = 10$$

By putting the equilibrium price 10 into the supply equation we find that the equilibrium quantity is 40. Double check your answer by also substituting the value 10 for P into the demand equation.

If you put into the demand and supply functions any price greater than 10 (the equilibrium price), quantity supplied will be greater than quantity demanded and their difference will be the excess supply resulting at that price. For example, if you put the price 20 into the demand function, quantity demanded will equal to 20 units, whereas if you put 20 into the supply function, quantity supplied will be 80 units. Quantity supplied exceeds quantity demanded by 60 units, which is the excess supply resulting at a price of 20.

If you put into the demand and supply functions any price less than 10 (the equilibrium price), quantity demanded will be greater than quantity supplied and their difference will be the excess demand resulting at that price. For example, if you put the price 5 into the demand function, quantity demanded will equal 50 units, whereas if you put 5 into the supply function, quantity supplied will be 20 units. Quantity demanded exceeds quantity supplied by 30 units, which is the excess demand resulting at a price of 5.

Indirect taxes

An indirect tax is a tax on goods or services. For the quantitative part of the exam you need to focus only on specific taxes (that is, a specific 'dollar' amount per unit of the good). If you do not care about the logic of the problem, the easiest way to deal with such a tax is to rewrite your supply equation substituting the term P with (P − *tax*). So, if the supply equation is:

$$Q_s = 4P$$

and a \$3.00 tax per unit is imposed, rewrite it as:

$$Q_s = 4(P − 3)$$

The next step is to equate the demand with the new supply curve to find the new market price. Subtracting the tax from the new market price you just calculated will give you the new, net of tax, price that producers earn. Note that before the tax was imposed, the market price was also the average revenue earned by firms whereas after the tax is imposed, the average revenue earned is the net of tax market price found by subtracting the tax from the new market price.

If you have already plotted the original demand and supply curves on graph paper, you can just shift the supply curve vertically upwards by the amount of the tax to find the new market price and the new market quantity and to answer a lot of other related questions.

Remember that an ad valorem tax (say a 15% VAT or sales tax) will not lead to a parallel shift of the supply curve but the new supply curve will create a 'wedge' with the original one (their vertical distance will be increasing).

Here is some advice on solving indirect tax problems.

■ Solve algebraically before plotting on the graph paper to ensure that your calculations are precise.

■ Avoiding using P1 and P2. Instead adopt more meaningful symbols like Pm or Pc for the new higher market price consumers pay after the tax, and Pp for the net of tax price producers earn (their new average revenue).

■ Write down all the relevant information in a table as this will help you with any additional calculations you are asked to make.

For example, assume that demand and supply are given by:

$$Q_d = 60 − 2P$$

$$Q_s = 4P$$

Denoting the original equilibrium price by P_0 and the original equilibrium quantity by Q_0 we have already found that:

$$P_0 = 10$$

$$Q_0 = 40$$

Remembering that in the post-tax supply function we substitute (P − t) for the term P we must solve now the equations:

$$Q_d = 60 − 2P$$

$$Q_s = 4(P − 3)$$

Solving the system will yield the new market price that consumers will pay $P_c = 12$ and the new equilibrium quantity $Q' = 36$.

This is how the table might look:

P_0	10
Q_0	40
P_c	12
Q'	36
P_p	$= (P_c − tax) = 9$
Incidence on consumers	$12 − 10 = 2$ (consumers pay $\frac{2}{3}$ of the tax)
Incidence on consumers	$10 − 9 = 1$ (producers pay $\frac{1}{3}$ of the tax)
Initial revenues and expenditures TR_0	$P_0 \times Q_0 = 10 \times 40 = 400$
Post-tax producer revenues	$P_p \times Q' = 9 \times 36 = 324$
Post-tax consumer expenditures	$P_c \times Q' = 12 \times 36 = 432$
Tax revenues collected by government	$t \times Q' = 3 \times 36 = 108$
Initial consumer surplus	Area of a triangle is $\frac{1}{2}$ (base $\times$ height). Since the vertical intercept of the demand curve is 30, the height of the consumer surplus triangle is $(30 − 10) = 20$. The base is the quantity 40 so $CS = 400$.
Initial producer surplus	Similarly: $\frac{(10 \times 40)}{2} = 200$
New consumer surplus	$(30 − 12) = 18$ is the new height and 36 is the base so consumer surplus is $\frac{(18 \times 36)}{2} = 324$
New producer surplus	$\frac{(9 \times 36)}{2} = 162$
Initial social welfare	$400 + 200 = 600$
New social welfare	$324 + 162 + 108 = 594$
Welfare loss	$600 − 594 = 6$ or $(12 − 9) \times \frac{(40 − 36)}{2} = 3 \times \frac{4}{2}$ $= 6$ (the area of the triangle)

Subsidies

A subsidy is a payment to producers aimed at lowering production costs and so market price and increasing production and consumption of the good. The easiest way to deal with such a subsidy is to rewrite your supply equation substituting the term P with (P + *subsidy*). So, if the supply equation is:

$$Q_s = 4P$$

and a \$3.00 subsidy per unit is granted, rewrite it as:

$$Q_s = 4(P + 3)$$

The next step is to equate the demand with the new supply curve to find the new market price. Adding the subsidy to the new market price will give you the new price, inclusive of the subsidy, that producers earn. Note that before the subsidy was granted, the market price was also the average revenue earned by firms. Whereas after the subsidy is granted, the average revenue earned is inclusive of the subsidy market price found by adding the subsidy to the new market price consumers pay.

If you have already plotted the original demand and supply curves on graph paper, you can just shift the supply curve vertically downwards by the amount of the subsidy to find the new market price and the new market quantity and to answer a lot of other related questions.

The same advice given for indirect tax problems holds for subsidy problems, as follows.

- Solve algebraically before plotting on the graph paper to ensure that your calculations are precise.

- Avoiding using P1 and P2. Instead adopt more meaningful symbols like Pm or Pc for the new lower market price consumers pay after the subsidy, and Pp for the inclusive of subsidy price producers earn (their new average revenue).

- Write down all the relevant information in a table as this will help you with any additional calculations you are asked to make.

For example, assume that demand and supply are again given by:

$$Q_d = 60 - 2P$$

$$Q_s = 4P$$

Denoting the original equilibrium price by P_0 and the original equilibrium quantity by Q_0 we have already found that:

$$P_0 = 10$$

$$Q_0 = 40$$

Remembering that in the post-subsidy supply function we substitute (P + s) for the term *P* we must solve now the equations:

$$Q_d = 60 - 2P$$

$$Q_s = 4(P + 3)$$

Solving the system will yield the new market price that consumers will pay $P_c = 8$ and the new equilibrium quantity $Q' = 44$. This is how the table might look:

P_0	10
Q_0	40
P_c	8
Q'	44
P_p	= (P_c + subsidy) = 11

Benefit to consumers	$10 - 8 = 2$ (consumers enjoy $\frac{2}{3}$ of the subsidy)
Benefit to producers	$11 - 10 = 1$ (producers enjoy $\frac{1}{3}$ of the tax)
Initial revenues and expenditures TR_0	$P_0 \times Q_0 = 10 \times 40 = 400$
Post-subsidy producer revenues	$P_p \times Q' = 11 \times 44 = 484$
Post-subsidy consumer expenditures	$P_c \times Q' = 8 \times 44 = 352$
Total cost of subsidy to the government	$s \times Q' = 3 \times 44 = 132$
Initial consumer surplus	Area of a triangle is $\frac{1}{2}$ (base × height). Since the vertical intercept of the demand curve is 30, the height of the consumer surplus triangle is $(30 - 10) = 20$. The base is the quantity 40 so consumer surplus = 400.
Initial producer surplus	Similarly: $\frac{(10 \times 40)}{2} = 200$
New consumer surplus	$(30 - 8) = 22$ is the new height and 44 is the base, so consumer surplus is $\frac{(22 \times 44)}{2} = 484$
New producer surplus	$\frac{(11 \times 44)}{2} = 242$
Initial social welfare	$400 + 200 = 600$
New social welfare	$484 + 242 = 726$ minus the cost of the subsidy $132 = 594$
Welfare loss	$600 - 594 = 6$ or $(12 - 9) \times \frac{(40 - 36)}{2} = 3 \times \frac{4}{2} = 6$ (the area of the triangle)

Price ceilings

A price ceiling or maximum price (or rent control in the case of housing) is a price set by the government below the equilibrium price. This implies that quantity demanded is greater than quantity supplied so that excess demand, referred to in this case as a shortage, results.

You may be asked to calculate the resulting shortage. You would just have to subtract the quantity supplied from the quantity demanded at the maximum price by putting it into both the supply and then the demand equations.

Using the same demand and supply conditions:

$$Q_d = 60 - 2P$$

$$Q_s = 4P$$

with

$$P_0 = 10$$

$$Q_0 = 40$$

defining the original market equilibrium price and quantity, assume that a maximum price $\overline{P} = 7$ is imposed. Substituting this price into the demand and then into the supply functions helps us determine the quantity demanded Q_d and the quantity supplied Q_s:

$$Q_d = 46$$
$$Q_s = 28$$

so that a shortage equal to $Q_d - Q_s = 18$ units results.

You may be asked to calculate the change in consumer expenditures. Consumer expenditures are found by multiplying the price paid times the actual number of units bought. Remember that the short end of the market always prevails, so that if only 28 units were made available by firms at the maximum price set it is immaterial that consumers were demanding 46 units.

Initially consumer expenditures were $10 \times 40 = 400$ whereas after the maximum price is set they will be $7 \times 28 = 196$. The change is therefore $196 - 400 = -204$. This means that consumer expenditures decreased by 204 (for example dollars or euros) which makes sense as both the price is lower and the quantity consumed is less. Consumer expenditures in this case are equal to total revenues producers collect.

Price floors

A price floor or minimum price (or price support) is a price set by the government above the equilibrium price. This implies that quantity demanded is less than the quantity supplied so that excess supply, referred to in this case as a surplus, results.

You may be asked to calculate the resulting surplus. You would just have to subtract the quantity demanded from the quantity supplied at the minimum price by substituting it into both the supply and the demand equations.

Using the same demand and supply conditions:

$$Q_d = 60 - 2P$$
$$Q_s = 4P$$

with

$$P_0 = 10$$
$$Q_0 = 40$$

the original market equilibrium price and quantity, assume that a minimum price $\overline{P} = 14$ is imposed. Substituting this

price into the demand and then into the supply functions helps us determine the quantity demanded Q_d and the quantity supplied Q_s:

$$Q_d = 32$$
$$Q_s = 56$$

so that a surplus equal to $Q_s - Q_d = 24$ units results.

You may be asked to calculate the change in consumer expenditures. Consumer expenditures are found by multiplying the price paid times the actual number of units bought. Remember that the short end of the market always prevails, so that if only 32 units were demanded by consumers at the minimum price set it is immaterial that firms were offering in the market 56 units.

Initially, consumer expenditures were $10 \times 40 = 400$ while after the minimum price they were equal to $14 \times 32 = 448$ (for example dollars or euros). Note that these expenditures are greater than the expenditures made at the lower price. Since the price paid increased, the quantity purchased will have decreased (law of demand) so that consumer expenditures may have increased, decreased or remained the same depending on the price elasticity of demand (PED) for the good. What we have here is a movement along a demand curve. Since in this example the higher price paid resulted in higher expenditures by consumers, it implies that PED is less than one (demand is price inelastic)

In the case of a minimum price, the government must intervene and buy from producers at the promised minimum price the surplus created. It follows that producers earn not only what consumers spend on the good but also what the government spends to buy the surplus. Remember producers sell all of what they have produced, some to consumers and the rest to the government. So producers earn the product of the price set ($14 or whatever) times the total amount supplied (56 units), that is, $14 \times 56 = \$784$. The government expenditures in the case of a minimum price are the product of the surplus (24 units) purchased times the minimum price promised ($14), or $14 \times 24 = \$336$.

To double check remember that the revenues collected must equal the sum of the expenditures consumers made plus the amount of money the government spent to buy the surplus from producers or, in this example, $\$448 + \$336 = \$784$.

1.5 Theory of the firm and market structures

Total, marginal and average product

You may be asked to calculate from a table (with empty cells) or from a graph, total, marginal and average products. This is an easy task if you remember exactly what each concept means and the formula one can use.

To calculate average product (of, say, labour) you need to divide total product (TP, or in other words, Q) by the number of workers used (L) or:

$$AP_L = \frac{TP}{L} \quad (1)$$

Notice that equation (1) has three terms so if you know any two you can solve for the third. For example, if five workers can produce an average of 120 shirts per day then each worker can produce on average 24 shirts per day. Average product is $\frac{120}{5} = 24$ shirts per worker per day. Or, if you know that the average product per worker per day is 24 shirts and that the firm employs five workers you can find the total average product which is $5 \times 24 = 120$ shirts per day.

To calculate marginal product (of, say, labour) you need to remember that marginal means extra (additional) so that marginal product (MP) is the change in output induced by a change in the number of workers employed. It is equal to the ratio of the change in output produced over the change in labour employed. If the change in the number of workers is 1 (that is, you have data on the output of 0, 1, 2, 3, 4, etc. workers) then marginal product is just the change in output:

$$MP_L = \frac{\Delta TP}{\Delta L} = \frac{\Delta Q}{\Delta L},$$

and, if ΔL is always 1, then $MP = \Delta Q = Q_2 - Q_1$ (2).

Note from equation (2) that it follows that $MP + Q_1 = Q_2$, so if we know that the marginal product of, say, the fifth worker is 25 apples (per period) and that with four workers total product is 100 apples, then total product with five workers will be $25 + 100 = 125$ apples. This is very useful to remember when completing such tables.

For example, consider the table below.

Labour or number of workers (L)	Output (Q) or total product (TP)	Average product (AP)	Marginal product (MP)
0	0	–	–
1	(0 + 120) = 120	$\left(\frac{120}{1}\right) = 120$	120
2	(2 × 150) = 300	150	(300 − 120) = 180
3	(300 + 200)= 500	$\left(\frac{500}{3}\right) = 166.67$	200
4	640	$\left(\frac{640}{4}\right) = 160$	(640 − 500) = 140
5	(5 × 135) = 675	135	(675 − 640) = 35
6	(675 + 0) = 675	$\left(\frac{675}{6}\right) = 112.5$	0

Assume that the table originally contains only the cells given in black on white above and that you are asked to calculate the remaining (shaded) cells. The calculation required and the result for each cell is given in shaded cells. Note two things: if no (zero) workers are employed neither the marginal nor the average can be calculated as they are meaningless concepts; also, in each row, only one number is needed to calculate the other two. For example, for three workers you are only given that the marginal product of the third worker is 200 units of output. But since you have calculated that the total product of two workers is 300 units, you just need to add the extra output from the third worker

to the total product of two workers to calculate the total product of three workers (which is equal to $300 + 200 = 500$ units). Now that you have the total product for three workers it is easy to calculate the average product when three workers are employed by dividing total product by the number of workers, or $\frac{500}{3} = 166.67$ units per worker per period.

Total, marginal and average cost

The same logic explained above for the calculation of total product, marginal product and average product holds for calculating total, marginal and average costs (TC, MC and AC).

The definitions (formulas) to remember include:

$$TC = FC + VC \text{ (1)}$$
$$ATC = AFC + AVC \text{ (2)}$$
$$ATC = \frac{TC}{Q}, AFC = \frac{FC}{Q}, AVC = \frac{VC}{Q} \text{ (3)}$$
$$MC = \frac{\Delta TC}{\Delta Q} \text{ or, since } \Delta FC = 0 \rightarrow MC = \frac{\Delta VC}{\Delta Q} \text{ (4)}$$
if $\Delta Q = 1$ then:
$$MC = TC_2 - TC_1 \Rightarrow TC_1 + MC = TC_2 \text{ (5)}$$
$$MC = VC_2 - VC_1 \Rightarrow VC_1 + MC = VC_2 \text{ (6)}$$

These may look difficult but they are extremely easy. Equation (1) states that total costs (TC) are the sum of fixed and variable costs (FC and VC). In the long run, since there are no fixed costs total costs are variable costs.

You derive equation (2) by dividing all terms of equation (1) by Q (the level of output) to arrive at per unit of output (that is, average) costs. It states that average total cost (ATC) is the sum of average fixed costs (AFC) plus average variable costs (AVC).

The equations labelled (3) are useful as each has three terms so, if two of them are known you can solve for the third term. Remember that fixed costs are fixed as the level of output increases but average fixed costs continuously decrease as the level of output increases.

The equations labelled (4) state that marginal cost (MC) is the change in either total or variable costs divided by the change in output.

Equations (5) and (6) are most useful as they state that if we know that the total costs (or variable costs) of producing, say, eight units is $200.00 and that the marginal cost of the ninth unit is $22.00 then the total costs (or variable costs) of producing nine units is $200.00 + $22.00 = $222.00. This is most useful when asked to complete cost tables.

In the table below you are given only the total cost of production (in black on white) and you may be asked to fill in the rest of the table. The answers are in the shaded areas.

Q	TC	FC	VC	AVC	ATC	AFC	MC
0	100	100	0	–	–	–	–
1	150	100	50	$\left(\frac{50}{1}\right) = 50$	$\left(\frac{150}{1}\right) = 150$	$\left(\frac{100}{1}\right) = 100$	$(150 - 100)$ or $(50 - 0) = 50$
2	180	100	80	$\left(\frac{80}{2}\right) = 40$	$\left(\frac{180}{2}\right) = 90$	$\left(\frac{100}{2}\right) = 50$	$(180 - 150)$ or $(80 - 50) = 30$
3	190	100	90	$\left(\frac{90}{3}\right) = 30$	$\left(\frac{190}{3}\right) = 63.33$	$\left(\frac{100}{3}\right) = 33.33$	$(190 - 180)$ or $(90 - 80) = 10$
4	200	100	100	$\left(\frac{100}{4}\right) = 25$	$\left(\frac{200}{4}\right) = 50$	$\left(\frac{100}{4}\right) = 25$	$(200 - 190)$ or $(100 - 90) = 10$
5	220	100	120	$\left(\frac{120}{5}\right) = 24$	$\left(\frac{220}{5}\right) = 44$	$\left(\frac{100}{5}\right) = 20$	$(220 - 200)$ or $(120 - 100) = 20$
6	260	100	160	$\left(\frac{160}{6}\right) = 26.67$	$\left(\frac{260}{6}\right) = 43.33$	$\left(\frac{100}{6}\right) = 16.67$	$(260 - 220)$ or $(160 - 120) = 40$
7	320	100	220	$\left(\frac{220}{7}\right) = 31.43$	$\left(\frac{320}{7}\right) = 45.71$	$\left(\frac{100}{7}\right) = 14.29$	$(320 - 260)$ or $(220 - 160) = 60$
8	420	100	320	$\left(\frac{320}{8}\right) = 40$	$\left(\frac{420}{8}\right) = 52.5$	$\left(\frac{100}{8}\right) = 12.5$	$(420 - 320)$ or $(320 - 220) = 100$
9	570	100	470	$\left(\frac{470}{9}\right) = 52.22$	$\left(\frac{570}{9}\right) = 63.33$	$\left(\frac{100}{9}\right) = 11.11$	$(570 - 420)$ or $(470 - 320) = 150$
10	770	100	670	$\left(\frac{670}{10}\right) = 67$	$\left(\frac{770}{10}\right) = 77$	$\left(\frac{100}{10}\right) = 10$	$(770 - 570)$ or $(670 - 470) = 200$

Or, consider the table below where only a few entries were provided (those in the white cells). Here are a few hints to help. When output is zero, variable costs are zero as no variable factors are used. If the marginal cost of the first unit is 150 (dollars) the variable cost of producing one unit is 150 (dollars) and by dividing by 1 all average costs are found. If the average total cost when producing 2 units is 225 then the total cost is (2×225) or 450 and given that the fixed costs are 100, the variable cost of two units is 350. If the variable cost of producing two units is 350 and the variable cost of producing 1 unit is 150 then the marginal cost of producing the second unit is $(350 - 150) = 200$ (dollars) and so on.

Q	FC	VC	ATC	AFC	AVC	MC
0	100	0	–	–	–	
1	100	$(0 + 150) = 150$	$\frac{(150 + 100)}{1}$	$\frac{100}{1}$	$\frac{150}{1}$	150
2	100	$(2 \times 225) - 100 = 350$	225	$\frac{100}{2}$	$\frac{350}{2}$	$(350 - 150) = 200$
3	100	650	$\frac{(650 + 100)}{3}$	$\frac{100}{3}$	$\frac{650}{3}$	$(650 - 350) = 300$
4	100	850	$\frac{(850 + 100)}{4}$	$\frac{100}{4}$	$\frac{850}{4}$	$(850 - 650) = 200$

Total, marginal and average revenue

The logic behind the calculations of total, average and marginal revenues is once again exactly the same as the logic behind product and cost functions. The formulas are:

$$AR = \frac{TR}{Q} = \frac{P \times Q}{Q} = P \ (1)$$

$$MR = \frac{\Delta TR}{\Delta Q} \ (2)$$

And, if $\Delta Q = 1$, then:

$$MR = \Delta TR = TR_2 - TR_1, \text{ so } TR_1 + MR = TR_2$$

Equation (1) states that AR is the ratio of total revenue over output. Since TR is the product of price times output it follows that AR is always equal to price for any level of output Q independent of market structure. This is labelled on the demand curve as 'D, AR'.

For example, consider the table on the next page where the demand schedule for a product is given (that is, the quantity demanded for each price). The average revenue (AR) column as a result of equation (1) above is identical to the price column (P). The total revenue (TR) column is the product of each price times the quantity demanded. The marginal revenue (MR) is the extra revenue collected from each extra unit sold so it is the difference between successive total revenue figures (since the difference in Qs is always equal to 1). Note that since TR collected from selling zero units are zero (dollars) whereas when 1 unit is sold TR collected are 80 (dollars), it follows that MR collected from selling the first unit is 80 (dollars).

Q	P	AR	TR	MR
1	80	(80)	(1 × 80) = 80	(80 − 0) = 80
2	70	(70)	(2 × 70) = 140	(140 − 80) = 60
3	60	(60)	(3 × 60) = 180	(180 − 140) = 40
4	50	(50)	(4 × 50) = 200	(200 − 180) = 20
5	40	(40)	(5 × 40) = 200	(200 − 200) = 0
6	30	(30)	(6 × 30) = 180	(180 − 200) = −20
7	20	(20)	(7 × 20) = 140	(140 − 180) = −40
8	10	(10)	(8 × 10) = 80	(80 − 140) = −60

Remember that the revenue-maximizing level of output is that at which MR is zero. In the above case you should choose five units as for the fifth unit MR = 0. As a result of the fact that the table above does not correspond to a continuous function but is just a collection of discrete data, maximum revenues of 200 (dollars) are also collected when four units are sold. In an exercise when this happens, choose that level for which MR = 0.

Economic profits

Economic profits π for each level of output Q is given by the equation:

$$\pi(Q) = TR(Q) - TC(Q) \quad (1)$$

To maximize profits choose that level of output for which:

$$MR = MC$$

You may be given a table with cost and revenue data to complete and determine the level of output at which maximum profits are achieved. Remember that as long as MR exceeds MC, profits are rising so choose that level of output Q for which MR = MC or the largest level output Q for which MR is still greater than MC.

In a diagram, determine the level of output for which MR and MC intersect and then find TR by multiplying that output with price. Find TC by determining for the chosen level of output the corresponding ATC and multiplying the two figures.

Issues in market structures

You may be asked to calculate the short-run shut-down price and the break-even price from a set of data or a graph.

The break-even price is that price for which total revenues are equal to total costs and thus economic profits are zero (that is, normal; the minimum required for the firm to remain in business). For a perfectly competitive firm the break-even price can be found on a diagram at the minimum of the U-shaped ATC curve it faces. Remember that a perfectly competitive firm faces a horizontal demand (and so AR) curve. For all other types of firms facing a negatively sloped demand curve the break-even price is found where the negatively sloped demand (and AR curve) is tangent to the U-shaped ATC curve. If given a table with TR and TC figures (or AR and ATC figures) it is that level of output for which the two are equal.

The shut-down price and the break-even price are identical in the long run.

In the short run, when fixed costs exist and on a diagram both ATC and AVC cost curves are depicted, the shut-down price for a perfectly competitive firm is at the minimum of the AVC curve. If provided with a table with data to determine the shut-down price you just have to determine the lowest AVC figure. At any price below that price the firm will immediately shut down.

2.1 The level of overall economic activity

Measures of economic activity

You may be asked to calculate nominal GDP from sets of national income data, using the expenditure approach. In this case you just add $(C + I + G + X)$ and then subtract imports (M). Often in such exercises students are given additional data as 'smoke' to confuse them. Ignore the additional data. If asked to find the per capita GDP (or GNI) just divide GDP (or GNI) by population.

You may be asked to calculate GNP or GNI from data. GNP is GDP plus income from abroad minus factor (or property) income from abroad or plus net factor (or property) income from abroad.

Lastly, you may be asked to calculate real GDP or GNI using a price deflator. A price deflator is a price index. Divide GDP (or GNI) by the GDP deflator and multiply the result by 100. Once again, the relationship has three terms so if any two are provided you can solve for the third one.

The Keynesian multiplier

The Keynesian multiplier states that the change in income is a multiple of the change in any injection:

$$\Delta Y = k \Delta J, \text{ where } J = (G, I, X)$$

It follows that if any two terms are given you can solve for the third one.

In addition,

$$k = \frac{1}{(1 - MPC_d)}, \text{ where } MPC_d = \frac{\Delta C_d}{\Delta Y}$$

MPC_d is the additional spending on domestic goods from additional income. So, if you are told that from an extra dollar (which has 100 cents) people spend 80 cents it follows that

$$MPC_d = \frac{80}{100} = 0.8.$$

It also follows that the remaining 20 cents were paid in tax, saved and/or spent but on imports. The multiplier may therefore be written as:

$$k = \frac{1}{(MRT + MPS + MPM)} = \frac{1}{MPW}, \text{ where}$$

MRT is the marginal tax rate (the extra tax paid out of an extra dollar earned), MPS is the additional savings out of an additional dollar earned and MPM is the additional spending on imports out of an additional dollar earned:

$$MRT = \frac{\Delta T}{\Delta Y}, \ MPS = \frac{\Delta S}{\Delta Y} \text{ and } MPM = \frac{\Delta M}{\Delta Y}$$

and MPW is the marginal propensity to withdraw, or $\frac{\Delta W}{\Delta Y}$.

Continuing the previous example, if people are taxed 12 cents, save 3 cents and spend on imports 5 cents out of each additional dollar earned then:

$$MRT = 0.12, \ MPS = 0.03 \text{ and } MPM = 0.05$$

so that MPW = 0.20 (their sum).

The multiplier k is thus equal to:

$$\frac{1}{(1 - MPC_d)} = \frac{1}{(1 - 0.8)} = \frac{1}{0.2} = 5$$

or using the MPW figure directly:

$$\frac{1}{0.2} = 5$$

If the government increases spending by 150 billion, then national income will increase by $(5 \times 150) = 750$ billion. Or if, for example, the government wants national income to increase by 1.2 trillion then government expenditures should rise by $\frac{1.2}{5} = 240$ billion.

2.3 Macroeconomic objectives

The unemployment rate

You may be asked to calculate the unemployment rate from a set of data. The unemployment rate is a percentage. It is the number of unemployed expressed as a proportion of the labour force:

$$\text{Unemployment rate} = \frac{\text{number of unemployed}}{\text{labour force}} \times 100$$

Again, you have a relationship with three terms so if any two are given you can solve for the third one. The labour force is not the same thing as the population of a country. It includes the employed and the unemployed individuals, so given a total population figure, the number of those unwilling and/or unable to work are excluded. Babies, older people as well as people within the working age population who are neither working nor actively searching for a job are not part of the

denominator in the calculation of the unemployment rate as they are not included in the labour force.

The inflation rate

You may be asked to calculate the inflation rate from a set of data. The inflation rate is also a percentage. It is the percentage change in the average price level between two periods of time, usually between two years. The average price level is given by a price index.

Typical price indices include the consumer price index (CPI or retail price index) and the producer price index (PPI). If we denote by P_t the CPI at period t and by $P_{(t-1)}$ the CPI the previous period (so that if t is 2009 then $(t - 1)$ is 2008) then:

$$\text{Inflation rate in } t = \%\Delta P = \frac{P_t - P_{(t-1)}}{P_{(t-1)}} \times 100$$

So if the CPI for 2008 was calculated at 158.2 and the CPI for 2009 was at 165.6 then inflation in year-on-year inflation in 2009 was:

$$\frac{165.6 - 158.2}{158.2} \times 100 = \frac{7.4}{158.2} \times 100 = 0.0467 \times 100 = 4.68\%$$

Note that if this percentage was negative then there was deflation. Remember that if you were to calculate inflation for, say, two consecutive years and the results were positive but the rate was smaller in the second year then there was disinflation (that is, prices continued to increase but at a decreasing rate).

You may be asked to construct a weighted price index using a set of data provided. This is very easy. You will be given a limited number of goods (say, three to five), their prices in two or more periods (typically months or years) and the number of units of each good that the typical household (consumer) purchased in the base period or reference period (month or year). These are the weights of each good. Remember that goods do not carry the same weight in the calculation of the average price level or of the calculation of the cost of the 'basket' of goods purchased. The weight of each good in your simple calculation of the weighted average is the number of units of each good purchased.

So, to calculate the cost of each basket of goods in each period you just multiply the price of each good during the period times the number of units consumed by the typical consumer and add the expenditures across goods. To convert the cost (say, dollars) arrived at to a price index divide the cost of the basket in each year by its cost in the base year chosen and multiply by 100. To calculate the inflation rate of a year find the percentage between the two price indices computed. Remember it is the percentage change of the price index of one period with respect to its value in the previous period. The next example will help you understand.

The following table has the prices of three goods in some economy between 2012 and 2014.

Year	Price of X	Price of Y	Price of Z
2012	€6.00	€0.50	€3.00
2013	€6.60	€0.60	€3.10
2014	€6.80	€0.75	€3.40

We assume that the basket of the typical consumer contains 10 units of good X, 30 units of good Y and 20 units of good Z. Construct a weighted price index for all three years assuming that 2010 is the base year and calculate the inflation rate for 2013 and 2014.

First calculate the cost of the basket in each year. The cost for 2012 will be:

$$(6.00 \times 10) + (0.50 \times 30) + (3.00 \times 20)$$
$$= 60.00 + 15.00 + 60.00 = €135.00$$

The cost for 2013 will be:

$$(6.60 \times 10) + (0.60 \times 30) + (3.10 \times 20)$$
$$= 66.00 + 18.00 + 62.00 = €146.00$$

The cost for 2014 will be:

$$(6.80 \times 10) + (0.75 \times 30) + (3.40 \times 20)$$
$$= 68.00 + 22.50 + 68.00 = €158.50$$

You could calculate the inflation rate in 2013 as the percentage change in the cost of living between 2013 and 2012: $\frac{(146 - 135)}{135} \times 100 = 8.15\%$ and, similarly, the inflation rate in 2014: $\frac{(158.5 - 146)}{146} \times 100 = 8.56\%$

Or you could construct the consumer price index using 2012 as the base year:

price index for 2012 (base year) $= \frac{135}{135} \times 100 = 100$

price index for 2013 $= \frac{146}{135} \times 100 = 108.15$

price index for 2014 $= \frac{158.5}{135} \times 100 = 117.41$

and then calculate the inflation rate for 2012 as the percentage change in the price indices between 2013 and 2012: $\frac{108.15 - 100}{100} \times 100 = 8.15\%$

and then the inflation rate for 2014 as the percentage change in the price indices between 2014 and 2013: $\frac{117.41 - 108.15}{108.15} \times 100 = 8.56\%$

Growth

You may be asked to calculate the rate of economic growth between two years from a set of data. This is a straightforward percentage change calculation assuming proportional growth in discrete time. Denoting the growth rate in year t as g_t and real GDP of year t as y_t we arrive at:

$$g_t = \frac{(y_t - y_{(t-1)})}{y_t}$$

Remember that to calculate real GDP from nominal (or money) GDP or GNI data you just divide nominal GDP by the GDP deflator and multiply by 100.

Equity

The role of taxation in promoting equity

You may be asked to calculate the marginal tax rate (MRT) and the average tax rate (ATR) from a set of data. Remember that the MRT is the extra (additional) tax paid from an extra 'dollar' of income (or, from an extra dollar of the tax base; that is, whatever is taxed, for example expenditure, wealth and business profits). The ATR is the ratio of the tax paid over income (or, more generally, the tax base). Assuming the typical case of an income tax:

$$MRT = \frac{\Delta T}{\Delta Y} \text{ and, } ATR = \frac{T}{Y}$$

If the ATR is increasing as income (or, more generally, the tax base) is increasing then the tax is progressive. It follows that MRT > ATR.

If the ATR is constant as income (or, more generally, the tax base) is increasing then the tax is proportional. It follows that MRT = ATR.

If the ATR is decreasing as income (or, more generally, the tax base) is increasing then the tax is regressive. It follows that MRT < ATR.

3.1 International trade

Comparative advantage and opportunity costs

You may be asked to calculate opportunity costs from a set of data in order to identify comparative advantage. In an example featuring two goods, the opportunity cost of producing more of one good is the amount of the other good that needs to be sacrificed. The production possibilities curve (PPC) that you will be presented with will be linear. Assuming that good X is measured on the horizontal axis and good Y on the vertical then the opportunity cost of producing an extra unit of good X is given by $\frac{\Delta Y}{\Delta X}$, which of course is the slope of the PPC.

Remember that $Y = Y_2 - Y_1$.

Restrictions on trade: tariffs, quotas and subsidies

You may be asked to calculate from diagrams the effects of imposing a tariff on imported goods on different stakeholders, including domestic producers, foreign producers, consumers and the government. These can all easily be calculated from linear functions but the syllabus specifies that you will be asked to make calculations from diagrams. Beyond being able to read a diagram properly you will need to remember that

the area of a triangle is given by $\frac{base \times height}{2}$

the area of a rectangle is $a \times b$

and that the area of a trapezoid is $\frac{(B + b)}{2} \times h$.

3.2 Exchange rates

Floating exchange rates

Here you may be asked to calculate the value of one currency in terms of another currency.

Keep in mind that if the exchange rate of currency α in terms of currency β is e, then the exchange rate of currency β in terms of α will be $\frac{1}{e}$. For example if €1.00 = $1.44 then $1.00 = €0.69. You may be asked to calculate the exchange rate for linear demand and supply functions and to plot the curves. The process is identical to the determination of the equilibrium price and output for a good and the plotting of the linear demand and supply functions.

Or, you may be asked to calculate the price of a good in different currencies using exchange rates. For example, if you are given the price of an item in, say, US dollars and you want to calculate it in Indian rupees (INR) you multiply the price of the item in dollars times the $\frac{INR}{\$}$ exchange rate.

Assume that US$1.00 = INR44.69 and the item is an Abercrombie and Fitch shirt that sells for US$70.00. Its price in INR is its price in US dollars times $\frac{INR}{\$}$ or, $\$ \times \frac{INR}{\$}$ so that the $ cancels out:

the price of the shirt in US dollars = $70.00 \times 44.69 \frac{INR}{\$}$
= INR3,128.3

Lastly, you may be asked to calculate the change in the value of a currency from a set of data. Here keep in mind that if currency α depreciates by x% compared with currency β then currency β has not appreciated by x% compared with currency α. If the dollar depreciates against the euro by 10% then the euro has not appreciated against the dollar by 10%. You will need to calculate the inverse of the exchange rates given and then find the percentage change. If the euro was $1.00 and appreciated to $2.00 it appreciated by 100%. The dollar depreciated by 50% as it was €1.00 and it went down to €0.50.

3.3 The balance of payments

The structure of the balance of payments

Here you may be asked to calculate elements of the balance of payments from a set of data. You just need to remember a few things.

To find the balance on any item you must subtract payments (debits) from receipts (credits). If the result is a positive number you have a surplus in that item, while if it is negative you have a deficit.

To find the current account from its components you add net exports of goods, net exports of services, net income and net current transfers together.

To find the financial account balance from its components you add net direct investment abroad, net portfolio investment and net other investments and reserve assets together.

The sum of the capital and financial accounts must equal the current account balance.

Therefore, the sum of the capital, financial and current accounts must equal zero. If the sum is not zero it is because of errors and omissions.

3.5 Terms of trade

The meaning of terms of trade

You may be asked to calculate the terms of trade of a country. The terms of trade (TOT in the equation below) are the ratio of the average price of exports over the average price of imports of a country expressed as index numbers times 100.

$$TOT = \frac{\text{average price of exports}}{\text{average price of imports}} \times 100$$

An index number is a number that has no units of measurement and because of this it allows comparisons. You may be given the average price of exports and of imports of a country for a number of years or you may be told that a country exports only one product, say oil or coffee, and imports only one good, say tractors or computers, to make things simpler.

To convert each average exports price into an index number you will need to divide it by the average export price for the what is chosen as the base year (or reference year) and multiply the result by 100. You will do the same to convert each average imports price into an index number. Through this you are expressing the average price of exports (or of imports) for each year as a percentage of its average price in the chosen base

year. It follows that the index number value for any variable in the base year is equal to 100.

For example, assume a country that exports only coffee and imports only laptops. You are given the price of coffee and the price of laptops between 2010 and 2014 as well as the revenues in millions of US dollars from its coffee exports. You are also told that 2011 is the base year. You may be asked to calculate the terms of trade and to express export revenues as an index number (to fill in the columns in grey in the table).

First you calculate export prices as an index number by dividing the export price in each year by the export price of the base year (2011) and then multiplying by 100. Do exactly the same calculation to determine import prices as an index number. Remember that in the base year the value of an index number is 100. To find the terms of trade in each year divide the index of export prices by the index of import prices and multiply by 100. Remember that the terms of trade in the base year are equal to 100.

To express export revenues as an index number divide export revenues in each year by export revenues in the base year and multiply the result by 100.

Year	Price of coffee per ton (USD)	Average exports price as an index number	Price of a laptop (USD)	Average imports price as an index number	Terms of trade (TOT) $\frac{P_x}{P_M} \times 100$	Export revenues (USD millions)	Export revenues as an index number
2010	1500	$\frac{1500}{1650} \times 100 = 90.91$	450	$\frac{450}{500} \times 100 = 90$	$\frac{90.91}{90} \times 100 = 101$	36.5	$\frac{36.5}{35.7} \times 100 = 102.24$
2011	**1650**	$\frac{1650}{1650} \times 100 = 100$	**500**	$\frac{500}{500} \times 100 = 100$	$\frac{100}{100} \times 100 = 100$	**35.7**	$\frac{35.7}{35.7} \times 100 = 100$
2012	1770	$\frac{1770}{1650} \times 100 = 107.27$	540	$\frac{540}{500} \times 100 = 108$	$\frac{107.27}{108} \times 100 = 99.32$	34.8	$\frac{34.8}{35.7} \times 100 = 97.48$
2013	1850	$\frac{1850}{1650} \times 100 = 112.12$	575	$\frac{575}{500} \times 100 = 115$	$\frac{112.12}{115} \times 100 = 97.5$	34.3	$\frac{34.3}{35.7} \times 100 = 96.08$
2014	1920	$\frac{1920}{1650} \times 100 = 116.36$	610	$\frac{610}{500} \times 100 = 122$	$\frac{116.36}{122} \times 100 = 95.38$	33.2	$\frac{33.2}{35.7} \times 100 = 92$

Summary

If you know:

(1) that the percentage change in X is $\frac{X_2 - X_1}{X_1} \times 100$

(2) that if Total X is TX and Marginal X is MX (so that $MX = X_2 - X_1$) then $X_2 = X_1 + MX$

(3) that the area of a triangle is given by $\frac{\text{base} \times \text{height}}{2}$

the area of a rectangle is $a \times b$ and

the area of a trapezoid is $\frac{(B + b)}{2} \times h$

(4) and how to solve a system of two linear equations

you should be fully prepared for the calculations part of HL Paper 3.

Data response sample questions

HLP2 & SLP2
Question 1
Study the extract below and answer the questions that follow.

Chinese and US trade negotiators convene in Washington

1. In a US-Chinese trade dispute over tire imports the World Trade Organization (WTO) recently ruled in favour of the US. The decision concluded that the US had complied with global trade rules when last year it imposed tariffs as high as 35 percent on Chinese tires that are used in both passenger cars and light trucks. The WTO ruling relied on a special provision that the US trade negotiators had secured when China joined the WTO. Specifically, the US reserved the right to impose tariffs if it considered that US jobs were at risk as a result of a sudden and sharp increase in imports from China.

2. The WTO verdict was hailed as a major victory for the US and especially for American companies and workers. The 2009 decision to impose tariffs on tires imported from China was also a consequence of significant pressure from the United Steelworkers Union and several other US lobbying groups.

3. The ruling coincided with the preparations for a Washington meeting of US and Chinese trade officials to discuss trade and exchange rate issues. Trade frictions between the two countries include everything from steel, tires and poultry to Chinese tariffs on raw materials exports as well as concerns over the quality and safety of Chinese-made toys, foods and other products. The latter, according to Chinese manufacturers, are nothing more that an excuse for US trade protection.

4. Tension is also high as a result of the US complaint that China is maintaining its currency, the Yuan, artificially **undervalued** in order to unfairly assist its exporting firms. Since mid-2008 the Yuan had been unofficially fixed to the US dollar. In 2009 the value of US exports to China amounted to $77.4 billion whereas Chinese exports to the US, its second biggest trading partner, were significantly higher reaching $220.8 billion. The US **trade deficit** has recently narrowed as a result of the **recession** induced decrease in US demand.

5. On the other hand, the Chinese government has its own grievances over US economic policy. It claims that the loose monetary policy that the US Federal Reserve Bank (the US Central Bank) has adopted to help reflate the American economy has eroded the value of China's huge dollar reserves.

Lastly, China's massive selling of its own currency in the foreign exchange market, to help keep the Yuan low, has increased inflationary pressures at home as the money supply is increasing far too fast.

(a) (i) Define the term *recession* indicated in bold in the text (paragraph 4). **[2 marks]**

    (ii) Define the term *trade deficit* indicated in bold in the text (paragraph 4). **[2 marks]**

or:

(a) (i) Define the term *undervalued* (currency) indicated in bold in the text (paragraph 4). **[2 marks]**

    (ii) Outline two objectives of the WTO (paragraph 1). **[2 marks]**

(b) Explain using an appropriate diagram why the tariff ruling of the WTO is considered 'a major victory for the United States and particularly for American workers and businesses' (paragraph 2). **[4 marks]**

(c) Explain using an appropriate diagram how the Chinese are maintaining their currency artificially undervalued. **[4 marks]**

or:

(b) Explain how easy US monetary policy is considered responsible for decreasing the value of the dollar reserves China is holding (paragraph 6). **[4 marks]**

(c) Explain how a US recession may narrow the US trade deficit (paragraph 4). **[4 marks]**

(d) Using information from the text/data and your knowledge of economics, evaluate possible consequences of China maintaining the yuan undervalued. **[8 marks]**

or:

(d) Using information from the text/data and your knowledge of economics, examine possible economic effects on the US and China of a decision to permit the yuan to rise. **[8 marks]**

Question 2
Study the extract below and answer the questions that follow.

Brazil's current account deficit widens in 2010

1. In 2010 Brazil's **current account deficit** increased to $47.5 billion as a result of rising imports, a rapidly appreciating Real (Brazil's currency) and its adverse effect on the country's exports. Years of stable and continuous growth is responsible for higher import absorption while foreign multinational corporations with an established presence in Brazil repatriate their profits taking advantage of the higher value of the Real.

2. Rising inflows from **foreign direct investment** into Brazil fully financed the current account deficit. In 2010 multinationals invested $48.5 billion into Brazil up from $25.9 a year earlier.

3. Decreasing exports and rising imports of goods as a result of the strengthening of the currency narrowed Brazil's **trade surplus** from $25.3 billion in 2009 to $20.7 billion this year. The currency has appreciated roughly by 30% against the US dollar since the beginning of 2009.

4. In the meantime, foreign direct investment inflows continue to increase and are predicted to rise to over $50 billion in 2011. A $7.1 billion investment involving the Chinese group Sinopec and Brazil's Repsol is responsible for the increased figure this month. This trend in direct investment inflows must continue as the current account deficit is projected to further widen to $64 billion in 2011. This figure is estimated to be the equivalent of about 3% of Brazil's GDP.

5. Brazil's Central Bank announced in its quarterly report that GDP grew by 7.3 percent last year as a consequence of increased demand, cheap loans and investments. A survey of economists expects Brazil's growth to slow down to 4.5 percent this year. The Central Bank signaled that it may also start tightening monetary policy next month as inflation is projected to increase faster than originally expected.

Brazil fears international currency war

6. Brazilian Finance Minister Eduardo Mantega claimed in an interview that an international currency war has begun as governments are intervening in foreign exchange markets manipulating their currencies. Mantega considers this tactic a direct threat to Brazil as it erodes its competitiveness. Governments deliberately weaken their currencies to improve trade balances by rendering their exports more competitive and reducing the attractiveness of imported products. 'The advanced countries are seeking to devalue their currencies,' said the Finance Minister, pointing unmistakably to the United States, Japan and Europe. Such policies artificially strengthen trade competition and risk an abrupt policy reversal towards increased trade protection.

(a) (i) Define the term *current account deficit* indicated in bold in the text (paragraph 1). [2 marks]

    (ii) Describe a managed exchange rate system (paragraph 6). [2 marks]

or:

(a) (i) Define the term *foreign direct investment* indicated in bold in the text (paragraph 2). [2 marks]

    (ii) Define the term *trade surplus* indicated in bold in the text (paragraph 3). [2 marks]

(b) Using an appropriate diagram explain how a decision by Brazil's Central Bank to increase interest rates may affect the Real (paragraph 6). [4 marks]

(c) Examine the relationship described between Brazil's current and financial accounts (paragraph 2). [4 marks]

or:

(b) Explain using an exchange rate diagram how weakening currencies may boost exports and improve trade balances (paragraph 6). [4 marks]

(c) Explain the expected effect on Brazil's terms of trade of the appreciation of the Real (paragraph 3). [4 marks]

or:

(b) Explain whether each of the following is registered as a credit or a debit item in Brazil's Balance of Payments:

- greater foreign travel by Brazilians (paragraph 1)
- the $7.1 billion transaction involving the Chinese group Sinopec and Repsol Brazil (paragraph 4)
- increased overseas profits remittances by multinationals (paragraph 1)
- consumption of more imports (paragraph 1)

[4 marks]

(c) **(HL only)** Using a proper J-curve effect diagram, explain whether following the appreciation of the Real the Marshall-Lerner condition for Brazil has come into effect (paragraph 3). [4 marks]

(d) Using information from the text/data and your knowledge of economics, evaluate the possible economic consequences of the appreciation of the Real on Brazil's economy. [8 marks]

or:

(d) Using information from the text/data and your knowledge of economics, examine possible reasons for which foreign direct investment has been flowing into Brazil. [8 marks]

Question 3
Study the extract below and answer the questions that follow.

The East African Community strategy to accelerate growth

1. Burundi, Kenya, Rwanda, Tanzania and Uganda are members of the East African Community (EAC) which from July 2010 has evolved from a customs union to a common market. The total population of this regional trading bloc exceeds 125 million people while combined **GDP** is roughly $75 billion.

2. As a result of the formation of a common market, trade and investment flows inside the bloc will increase while **foreign direct investment** will also be attracted. By 2012 members also plan to establish a monetary union adopting the 'East African Shilling' as a common currency. The Common Market agreement signed at the end of 2009 has already attracted significant investments from Japan, China and India.

3. Establishing an East African Monetary Union will prove advantageous to investors who are expected to actively seek business opportunities in the region. As there will be no need to convert currencies in the foreign exchange market transaction costs will be significantly reduced. The elimination of tariffs and other trade barriers has already enhanced trade flows between the five member states. Greater transparency will permit direct price comparisons boosting competition and efficiency. Members are also expected to benefit from the greater bargaining power they will enjoy in political and economic negotiations.

4. On the other hand, doing business in the region has never been easy. Poor **infrastructure** as well as high levels of corruption burden businesses with additional costs. Sizable investments in upgrading roads and transport systems as well as in developing sufficient and reliable power generation facilities are expected to reduce production costs and thus to accelerate growth for all five member states. On the other hand, eradicating corruption may prove much more complex. For example, even though regional tariffs have been eliminated since 2005 more than 20% of current shipping costs from Rwanda to Kenya are attributed to bribes and corruption.

(a) (i) Define the term *Infrastructure* indicated in bold in the text (paragraph 4). [2 marks]

    (ii) Define the term *GDP* indicated in bold in the text (paragraph 1). [2 marks]

(b) Explain two possible reasons for which 'significant investments from Japan, China and India ' are already attracted into the EAC (paragraph 2). [4 marks]

(c) Explain using appropriate diagram(s) the possible short term and long term impact of increased and improved infrastructure in any of the EAC economies (paragraph 4). [4 marks]

(d) Using information from the text/data and your knowledge of economics, evaluate the prospect of the East African Community establishing a monetary union as a means of achieving economic growth and economic development. [8 marks]

Or:

(a) (i) Define the term *foreign direct investment* (paragraph 2). [2 marks]

    (ii) Outline the differences between a customs union and a common market (paragraph 1). [2 marks]

(b) Explain using an appropriate diagram how eliminating tariffs affects trade flows of the countries involved (paragraph 3). [4 marks]

(c) Using an appropriate diagram explain the expected effect on an economy of a decrease in the level of corruption (paragraphs 4 and 5). [2 marks]

(d) Using information from the text and your knowledge of economics discuss the possible advantages and disadvantages of signing a monetary union for the EAC member countries. [8 marks]

Question 4
Study the extract below and answer the questions that follow.

A. India: Time to rethink crutches for exports

1. India's export performance in December 2010 highlights several interesting developments. First of all, it demonstrates that the **exchange rate** is not anymore the single most important determinant of the country's export performance. Whether Indian exports penetrate foreign markets does not only depend on a cheap currency. International competitiveness relies more on increased production efficiency of Indian firms as well as on several improved non-price factors.

2. Secondly, India's export success does not anymore rely on the performance of a few **commodities** or on low value-added manufactures. Past government policies to diversify the composition of exports as well as their destination (such as the 'Look East' policy initiative or the focus on African and South America) are paying off. And even though growth in advanced economies is sluggish many emerging economies are growing fast.

3. Thirdly, rapidly increasing export revenues are narrowing India's trade and current account deficits. The gap between export revenues and import expenditures had widened during the first half of the current year to $35.4 billion or 3.7% of India's **GDP** as a result of a sharp rise in imports. The size of this deficit was then considered by many analysts as increasingly unsustainable.

4. Thus, the recently registered strong performance of export revenues which are now growing faster than import expenditures is a most welcome development. It also points to the significance of the export sector and suggests that not only should infrastructure improve to allow exporting firms but also that the government should simplify procedures and cut down on red tape. Will it move in the right direction?

B. Rupee rises on fund inflows

5. Expectations that India's economy will continue to register strong **growth** as well as relatively high interest rates have been responsible for increased foreign investment as well as for the appreciation of the Indian rupee. The Reserve Bank of India (its central bank) forecasts that the economy will grow this year by 8.5%. The interest rate has been set at 6.25% by the RBI and is the second highest after Indonesia in the region. Analysts thus expect that foreign appetite for Indian assets will remain strong as the interest rate differential will attract dollar investors.

C. Cotton prices to hit clothing exports this year

6. According to a recent report, rising cotton prices as well as the **appreciation** of the rupee could harm exports of the Indian clothing sector. As a result of these developments export revenues of clothing exporters could decrease lowering their profitability. The report adds that '...despite improving export demand in key markets – the US and Europe – rupee **appreciation** has impaired the competitive advantage previously enjoyed by the Indian clothing exporters against their Asian rivals'.

(a) (i) Define the term *exchange rate* indicated in bold in the text (paragraph 1). [2 marks]

   (ii) Define the term *growth* indicated in bold in the text (paragraph 5). [2 marks]

or:

(a) (i) Define the term *appreciation* indicated in bold in the text (paragraph 6). [2 marks]

   (ii) Outline two typical functions of a Central Bank, such as the Reserve Bank of India (paragraph 5). [2 marks]

or:

(a) (i) Define the term *commodities* indicated in bold in the text (paragraph 2). [2 marks]

   (ii) Define the term *GDP* indicated in bold in the text (paragraph 3). [2 marks]

(b) Explain using an appropriate diagram how economic recovery in the western world may affect India's aggregate demand (paragraph 2). [4 marks]

(c) Explain how greater production efficiency and improved non-price factors may increase the competitiveness of India's exports (paragraph 1). [4 marks]

or:

(b) Explain the implication for India's terms of trade of the rupee appreciation mentioned in paragraph 5. [4 marks]

(c) Distinguish the terms 'trade and current account deficits' mentioned in paragraph 3. [4 marks]

or:

(b) Explain using an appropriate diagram how India's expected growth outlook and its impact on foreign investments may have affected the Indian rupee (paragraph 5). [4 marks]

(c) With reference to the concept of price elasticity of demand, explain how India's cotton export revenues may decrease following an appreciation of the rupee (paragraph 6). [4 marks]

or:

(b) Explain using an appropriate diagram how 'relatively high interest rates' have affected the Indian rupee (paragraph 5). [4 marks]

(c) Using an appropriate diagram explain how the development in cotton prices affects the domestic (Indian) price of clothing (paragraph 6). [4 marks]

(d) Using information from the text/data and your knowledge of economics, discuss the view that economic development may best be achieved through a complementary approach involving a balance of market oriented policies and government intervention.

[8 marks]

or:

(d) Using information from the text/data and your knowledge of economics, examine diversification as a means of accelerating growth and economic development.

[8 marks]

or:

(d) Using information from the text/data and your knowledge of economics, evaluate export promotion as a means of accelerating growth and economic development.

[8 marks]

Question 5
Study the extract below and answer the questions that follow.

More Kenyans to access banking service

1. A new 'agent banking' model is soon to be introduced by the Central Bank of Kenya (CBK) which will hopefully succeed in bringing banking services closer to the population. Four **commercial banks** have been granted a license to conduct 'agent banking' business. A physical presence according to the 'agent banking' model is not required in the areas where these banks are planning to offer their services. This significantly lowers the costs of expanding.

2. The services offered by an agent bank are the same as those offered by a real bank and include, among others, cash deposits and withdrawals, transfer of funds as well as loans. Petrol station owners, village town wholesalers, supermarket owners and post offices are examples of the profiles of banking agents in this model. **Micro credit** institutions are also expected to become agents, as not only do they satisfy the requirements but they also have the experience.

3. Access to banking institutions is considered highly beneficial, especially since this model would permit a banking presence in rural and remote areas of the country. At this point only 23 percent of the country's adult population holds a bank account while 34 percent has no access to formal financial services with many forced to resort to the informal banking sector. These are exactly the individuals targeted by the proposed 'agent banking' model and by micro credit institutions. Increasing access to banking institutions will increase savings and investments. As a result, growth and development of poverty stricken, rural and remote areas will hopefully accelerate.

Philippines: Micro credit gains ground

4. The poor who need to borrow often pay extremely inflated interest rates as they are forced to resort to the informal banking system. An alternative for these people are micro credit institutions. Not only do the very poor in cases of medical or other emergencies use such institutions, but also many small household based entrepreneurs who borrow to finance short term needs of their small businesses.

5. Micro credit may help alleviate poverty but it is not a cure-all answer. Despite aiming to help the very poor, loan recipients still must satisfy some minimum requirements. For example, poor individuals hoping to set up a small business must demonstrate that they are capable to manage it.

6. In the Philippines, the market for such micro credit institutions definitely exists as about 40 percent of rural households are very poor. Success of such institutions involves significant risks since the productivity of the targeted poor largely depends on agriculture. It follows that targeted infrastructure such as farm to market roads and irrigation systems are necessary to increase their capacity to repay their loans. Micro credit and improved infrastructure thus go hand in hand: both are needed to increase agricultural productivity and incomes and the one without the other is inadequate to address the problem of rural poverty. More generally, micro credit requires complementary strategies that aim to increase the income earning capacity of the loan recipients. Only then will it become effective and sustainable in the long run.

(a) (i) Define the term *commercial bank* indicated in bold in the text (paragraph 1). [2 marks]

   (ii) Define the term *micro credit* indicated in bold in the text (paragraph 2). [2 marks]

(b) Suggest two strategies that may improve the capacities of beneficiaries to earn incomes and repay their loans (paragraph 6). [4 marks]

(c) Explain two possible problems associated with the use of informal banking systems (paragraphs 3 and 4). [4 marks]

(d) Using information from the text/data and your knowledge of economics, examine how expanded access to credit may contribute to economic development. [8 marks]

Glossary

Abnormal profits (see Supernormal profits)

Absolute advantage A country is said to have an absolute advantage in the production of a good if it can produce **more** of it with the *same* resources; or, the **same amount** using fewer resources.

Absolute poverty Measures the number of people living below the minimum income necessary to satisfy basic physical needs; the 2008 World Bank international poverty line is set at $1.25 purchasing power parity (PPP) per day. (See also Purchasing power parity (PPP) theory.)

Accounting costs Production costs for which a firm makes explicit monetary payments.

Actual and potential growth Actual growth refers to increases in real GDP through time; potential growth refers to a shift outwards of the production possibilities frontier or curve.

Ad valorem tax An indirect tax expressed as a percentage of the price of a product, for example VAT.

Administrative trade barriers (or, regulatory trade barriers) Government or administrative regulations or requirements that result in a lower level of imports into a country.

Adverse selection A problem arising when information in a market is asymmetric and the seller knows more about the characteristics of the good being sold than the buyer. The buyer would be better off trading with someone selected at random from the general population than with this seller.

Aggregate demand (AD) Total planned spending on domestic goods and services at various possible average price levels per period of time.

Aggregate supply (AS) The planned level of output at various possible price levels that firms are willing to offer per period of time.

Aid Any flow of capital (grants or loans) from developed to developing countries that is non-commercial from the point of view of the donor and for which the terms are concessional (that is, the interest rate is lower than the market rate and the repayment period longer).

Allocative efficiency Exists when 'just the right amount' from society's point of view has been produced. It requires that for the last unit produced, price is equal to its marginal cost (MC) or, more generally, that marginal social benefit (MSB) is equal to marginal social cost (MSC).

Anti-dumping duties Taxes (tariffs) that bring the import price of the good that is being dumped closer to the price charged by domestic firms in order to avoid injury to the domestic industry in the importing country.

Anti-monopoly regulation Laws and regulations that aim to restrict monopoly power and monopoly practices in markets.

Appreciation An increase in the exchange rate within a flexible (floating) exchange rate regime.

Appropriate technology Technology that employs the relatively abundant factor of production of a country.

Asymmetric information Exists when one side of a market knows more than the other side does.

Automatic stabilizers Refers to the income-induced changes of progressive income taxes and of unemployment benefits on the government's budget that tend to stabilize the business cycle.

Average fixed costs (AFC) Fixed costs on a per unit of output basis; fixed costs divided by the level of output; average fixed costs continuously decrease as output increases. (See also Fixed costs.)

Average household A fictitious household determined through surveys that possesses the average characteristics of the population and that is used in the construction of the consumer price index (CPI).

Average product (of labour) Output per worker and used as a common measure of labour productivity.

Average revenue (AR) Total revenues (TR) divided by output; AR is always equal to price and diagrammatically is identical to the demand curve a firm faces.

Average tax rate The ratio of the tax paid over the tax base, for example income or spending.

Average total costs The total costs incurred on a per unit of output basis. (See also Total costs.)

Average variable costs (AVC) Variable costs on a per unit of output basis; variable costs divided by the level of output. (See also Variable costs.)

Balance of payments (BOP) A record of all transactions of a country with the rest of the world over a period of time. It is broken down into the current account, the capital account and the financial account.

Balance of trade Refers to the difference between the value of exports and the value of imports of goods (physical merchandise) over a period of time (sometimes services are also included).

Balanced budget When government expenditures (G) are equal to government tax and other revenues/income (T)

Barrier to entry Anything that deters entry of a new firm into a market, for example a patent.

Basic economic questions The 'what', 'how' and 'for whom' questions that all economies must somehow answer.

Bilateral agreements Preferential trade agreements between two countries.

Bilateral aid Aid from one government to another through some kind of national aid agency.

Birth rate The average number of live births in a year for every 1,000 population.

Bottlenecks (in production) Used to explain the upward sloping section of the Keynesian aggregate supply (AS) curve (section 2) which refers to the fact that as aggregate demand (AD) increases, some industries being characterized by very low price elasticity of supply (PES) reach their capacity level of output before others .

Branding A type of firm-created barrier to entry which refers to the efforts firms make to establish the brand name image of their goods in order to render demand for those goods more price inelastic and deter entry of new firms.

Break-even output That level of output for which the total revenues (TR) of a firm are equal to the total costs (TC) of production so that profits are zero.

Break-even price The price at which a firm is earning zero economic profits (that is, normal profits) which for a perfectly competitive firm is the minimum of its average total costs (ATC).

Budget deficit Exists if government spending (G) exceeds government (tax) revenues (T).

Budget surplus Exists if government (tax and other) income (T) exceeds government expenditures (G) .

Business confidence The degree of optimism or pessimism characterizing businesses which affects their decisions on investment spending.

Business cycle The short-run fluctuations of real GDP around its long-run trend.

Business taxes Taxes on firms' profits.

Cap and trade schemes A solution to pollution externalities that aims at creating a market for pollution permits by limiting ('capping') the number issued (making them scarce and valuable) and then permitting firms to trade these in the open market.

Capital Produced means of production (tools, machines, equipment, factories, etc.).

Capital account of the balance of payments (BOP) An account of the BOP which records unilateral transfers of capital, such as the forgiveness of a country's debt by the government of another country as well as transfers of non-produced, non-financial assets such as natural resources, contracts, leases and licences, marketing assets (and goodwill).

Capital flight Refers to financial capital exiting a country legally or illegally and flowing into safer and more profitable financial centres.

Capital flows Investment flows per period of time into and out of a country. These include portfolio and foreign direct investments.

Capital gains tax A tax on the gains from the sale of stocks (shares).

Capital (government expenditures) Refers to public investment spending, for example spending by the government on infrastructure such as on the construction of roads, harbours, hospitals and schools.

Carbon tax A tax on polluting emissions that aims at forcing polluters to pay the cost of their action (polluter pays principle); a tax on the carbon content of fossil fuels.

Cartels Formal collusion of oligopolistic firms agreeing to behave as if they were a monopoly by restricting output in order to fix price at a higher level.

Central bank An institution responsible for monetary and exchange rate policy which provides banking services to the government and to commercial banks and which is considered the lender of last resort.

Centrally planned (command) economy Refers to an economy in which the state determines prices and output of goods and services.

Ceteris paribus All other factors remaining constant.

Circular flow model An economic model showing the major interrelationships and flows, real and monetary, between the major 'players' (decision-making units) of an economy.

Closed economy An economy that does not engage in international trade (exports and imports).

Collusive oligopoly When oligopolistic firms formally or tacitly agree to fix price or to engage in other anti-competitive practices.

Commodities Primary sector agricultural and non-agricultural products used as inputs in the manufacturing process and traded in international markets, for example coffee, cotton, tin, zinc and copper).

Commodity agreements Agreements between producers to coordinate commodity exports in order to stabilize prices. Either a production (export) quota system is operated (such as the International Coffee Agreement) where producers (exporting countries) agree to limit the amount exported, effectively forming a cartel; or a buffer stock system (for example for cocoa or rubber) may be operated. Commodity agreements usually collapse because of financing problems.

Commodity concentration of exports When one or very few products are responsible for a large percentage of the export revenues of a developing country, for example copper and nitrates for Chile.

Common-access resources Common-access (or pool) resources are resources for which it is difficult to exclude individuals from deriving benefits from their use and which are rival in consumption, for example fishing grounds and forests.

Common market A form of economic integration whereby members move forward to establish not only free trade in goods and services but also free movement of factors of production.

Common-pool resources (see Common-access resources)

Comparative advantage A country is said to have a comparative advantage in the production of good X if it can produce it at a lower opportunity cost (that is, by sacrificing fewer units of good Y) compared with another country.

Competitive supply If a firm can produce different goods with the same inputs then these goods are in competitive supply.

Complementary goods or complements Goods that are consumed jointly, for example coffee and sugar.

Composite indicators of development Indicators of development that are based on more than one economic variable, for example the Human Development Index.

Concentration ratio A measure of concentration based on ratio (CR) in an industry where typically the sales of the largest n firms are expressed as a percentage of total industry sales; for example 'the four-firm CR' expresses the sales of the largest four firms as a proportion of total industry sales.

Concessional loans Loans granted to a country usually by a multilateral institution, for example the IMF, with a longer repayment period and with an interest rate below the market rate (known as soft loans).

Constant returns to scale A production technology where a 1% increase in all inputs leads to a 1% increase in output (so that unit costs are constant).

Consumer confidence The degree of optimism or pessimism characterizing households which affects their spending decisions.

Consumer expenditures Spending by households on durable and non-durable goods and services per period of time.

Consumer price index (CPI) A weighted average of the prices of the goods and services that the typical consumer faces, expressed in index number form.

Consumer surplus The difference between how much a consumer is willing and able to pay at the most for some amount of a good and what he or she actually ends up paying.

Consumption (see Consumer expenditures)

Consumption externality When the consumption of a good imposes costs or creates benefits for third parties for which the latter do not get compensated or do not pay for.

Contractionary fiscal policy Decreases in government spending and/or increases in taxes aimed at decreasing aggregate demand (AD).

Contractionary monetary policy (see Tight monetary policy)

Core inflation A measure of inflation that excludes volatile oil and food prices.

Corporate social responsibility A possible objective of firms that aims at creating and maintaining an ethical and environmentally responsible image for them.

Corporate indebtedness The total amount of money that firms owe to banks and other holders of their debt and which is considered a factor that may affect their decision to undertake additional investment spending.

Cost-push inflation Inflation resulting from adverse supply shocks shifting aggregate supply (AS) to the left; usually, rising commodity prices are responsible, especially oil prices.

Credit item (in the BOP) Any item that leads to an inflow of money into a country, for example exports of goods and services or foreigners purchasing domestic bonds.

Cross-price elasticity of demand (XED) The responsiveness of the demand for a good to a change in the price of another good.

Crowding-out The idea that expansionary fiscal policy was not as effective as Keynesian theory claimed because deficit spending required financing which would lead to increased interest rates and so reduced private sector spending.

Current government expenditures Spending by the government on wages and salaries of public sector employees as well as spending on consumables (day-to-day items) such as stationery.

Current account (of the BOP) Records the value of exports and imports of goods and services of a country in a period of time. A current account surplus exists if the value of exports of goods and services exceeds the value of imports. This applies conversely for a deficit. More precisely, the current account includes visible trade and invisibles. The latter include trade in services and net investment income as well as net transfers.

Current account deficit When import expenditures on goods and services exceed export revenues over a period of time; more precisely, when the sum of net exports of goods and services plus net income from investments plus net transfers is negative.

Current account surplus When export revenues exceed import expenditures on goods and services over a period of time; more precisely, when the sum of net exports of goods and services plus net income from investments plus net transfers is positive.

Customs unions A form of regional economic integration whereby two or more countries abolish tariffs (and other barriers) between them and establish a common external barrier toward non-member countries.

Cyclical (demand-deficient or Keynesian) unemployment Unemployment that is a result of insufficient aggregate demand (AD) and of 'sticky' money wages. Cyclical unemployment rises as an economy moves deeper into recession.

Death rate The average number of deaths in a year for every 1,000 population.

Debit item (in BOP) Any item that leads to an outflow of money from a country, for example imports of goods and services or domestic residents purchasing foreign bonds.

Debt burden Signifies the impediment to the growth and development process of a country that a high external debt creates.

Debt rescheduling Refers to agreements between a debtor country and its creditors to defer debt service payments, to extend maturities on all outstanding debt and perhaps even to reduce debt-service obligations in order to provide the debtor with debt relief.

Debt servicing Payment of interest and principal of a debt (of a country or an individual).

Decile One of the ten equal parts of a frequency distribution.

Decreasing returns to scale A production technology where a 1% increase in all inputs leads to a smaller than 1% increase in output (so that unit costs rise; diseconomies of scale – DOS).

Deflation Refers to the case where the average level of prices is decreasing through time. Deflation implies negative inflation rates.

Deflationary gap A deflationary gap is present if equilibrium (actual) real output falls short of the level corresponding to the full employment level of output as a result of insufficient aggregate demand (AD).

Demand The relationship between various possible prices and the corresponding quantities that an individual or the market is willing and able to buy per period of time, ceteris paribus. The individual demand refers to an individual consumer whereas the market demand refers to the whole market and diagrammatically it is the horizontal summation of the individual demand curves.

Demand-pull inflation Inflation resulting from aggregate demand (AD) rising faster than aggregate supply (AS).

Demand-side policies Policies aimed at influencing the level of aggregate demand (AD) in order to affect growth, employment and inflation. They include fiscal and monetary policy.

Demerit goods Consumption of such goods creates very significant negative externalities on society so governments try to decrease or prohibit their consumption. Typical examples include alcohol, tobacco and illegal drugs.

Demographic factors Factors pertaining to the characteristics of a population in a country, for example the average age of a population.

Depreciation (of a currency) A decrease in the exchange rate within a floating (flexible) exchange rate system.

Deregulation Policies that lower or eliminate government regulations on the operation of an industry and which may have a positive supply-side effect on the economy.

Determinants of demand Factors other than the price of a good that may affect its demand and shift it, such as changes in income, tastes and prices of related goods.

Determinants of supply Factors other than the price of a good that may affect its supply and shift it, such as changes in the price of inputs or the level of technology available.

Devaluation (of a currency) A decrease in the exchange rate within a fixed exchange rate system.

Differentiated product Products which are similar but not identical across sellers in an industry. They are considered by consumers as close but not perfect substitutes.

Direct taxation Taxation on income and wealth.

Diseconomies of scale (DOS) Refers to increases in average costs (AC) as a result of increased size of the firm; see also decreasing returns to scale.

Disguised unemployment (see Hidden unemployment)

Disinflation Disinflation exists when the rate of inflation decreases which means that prices continue to rise but at a decreasing rate.

Disposable income Income after subtracting direct taxes and adding transfer payments which can be spent or saved.

Distribution of income A representation of what proportion of national income is enjoyed by different segments of a population; a frequency distribution showing groups of people classified by levels of national income.

Diversification (of exports) A policy initiative to move away from commodity concentration of exports. When a country, instead of relying on only a few commodities to export, tries to export a bigger variety of goods and services.

Dominant firm Typically the largest in size firm in an oligopoly which may set prices that other tacitly follow.

Dynamic efficiency When a firm enjoys economies of scale (EOS), leading to faster rates of innovation (new products and new processes).

Easy monetary policy When the central bank decreases interest rates (or increases the money supply) to increase aggregate demand (AD) in an economy and therefore overall economic activity.

Economic costs The value of all resources sacrificed to produce a good.

Economic development A sustainable increase in living standards that implies increased per capita income, better education and health as well as environmental protection.

Economic good Goods whose production involves the sacrifice of scarce factors of production.

Economic loss A firm is making economic losses if its revenues are insufficient to cover all economic (that is, both implicit and explicit) costs; negative economic profits.

Economic models Simplified representations of economic reality, typically but not necessarily expressed in mathematical form, aiming at facilitating comprehension of complex economic phenomena and at deriving falsifiable hypotheses.

Economic profits The reward of entrepreneurship. They are defined as the (positive) difference between total revenues (TR) and total economic costs (TC).

Economic union A form of regional economic integration where members of a customs union decide to integrate further by harmonizing taxation and other economic policies and even establishing a common currency.

Economies of scale (EOS) Economies of scale exist if average costs decrease as the size (scale) of the firm increases.

Education indicators Single variable or composite indicators that aim at summarizing an aspect or the level of education of a country, for example the adult literacy rate or primary education completion rate.

Efficiency Refers, in general, to non-wasteful use of scarce resources. (See also Allocative efficiency, Productive efficiency and Technical efficiency.)

Elasticity Generally, the responsiveness of an economic variable to a change in some other economic variable. For example, price elasticity of demand (PED).

Emergency relief aid (see Humanitarian aid)

Empowerment of women In the US definition the term has five components: women's sense of self-worth; their right to have and to determine choices; their right to have access to opportunities and resources; their right to have the power to control their own lives, both within and outside the home; and their ability to influence the direction of social change to create a more just social and economic order, nationally and internationally.

Entrepreneurship The willingness and ability of certain individuals to organize the other three factors of production and to take risks.

Equilibrium A market is considered to be in equilibrium if there is no tendency for change. This will be the case if quantity demanded per period equals quantity supplied and the market clears (that is, quantity demanded equals quantity supplied and so neither excess demand nor excess supply exist).

Equilibrium price The price at which a market clears (that is, at which quantity demanded equals quantity supplied and so neither excess demand nor excess supply exist).

Equilibrium quantity The quantity that corresponds to the equilibrium price in a market.

Equity Refers to fairness in the distribution of income.

Excess demand Excess demand exists when at some price the quantity demanded is greater than the quantity supplied, exerting pressure on the market price to increase.

Excess supply Excess supply exists when at some price the quantity supplied is greater than the quantity demanded, exerting pressure on the market price to decrease.

Exchange rate The price of a currency expressed in terms of another currency. The number of units of a foreign currency required to buy a unit of the domestic currency.

Excise tax An excise tax is an indirect tax (that is, a tax on goods or on expenditure); strictly speaking it is a tax levied on a specific commodity or group of commodities in contrast to a sales tax which is levied on all commodities (US use).

Exit (from a market) When a firm or firms shut down and cease operations in a market.

Exit barriers Costs that a firm incurs upon exit.

Expansionary fiscal policy Refers to increases in government expenditures and/or decreases in taxes aiming at increasing aggregate demand (AD) and economic activity.

Expansionary monetary policy (see Easy monetary policy)

Expectations The present perception of decision-making units concerning the future state of affairs in an economy, a market or the value of an economic variable.

Expected variables The future value of a variable as perceived presently.

Expenditure approach Refers to one of the three ways of measuring national income whereby expenditures by households, firms, foreigners and the government on domestic goods and services over a period of time are added (the other two methods are the output method and the income method).

Expenditure-changing and expenditure-switching policies Expenditure changing: demand management policies that will lower aggregate demand (AD) and therefore national income and so reduce imports and a trade deficit. Expenditure switching: policies that will try to switch expenditure away from imports and towards domestic products by making imports relatively more expensive and therefore undesirable, for example through devaluation or through the imposition of tariffs.

Expenditure flow Within the circular flow diagram of a closed economy without government it refers to the monetary flow from households to firms that reflects their spending on domestic output per period.

Explicit costs Also referred to as 'out-of-pocket' costs of production. (See also Accounting costs.)

Export promotion A growth policy that aims at using export demand as the vehicle of growth and that is often contrasted to import substitution.

Export subsidy A payment granted by a government to domestic firms to strengthen their competitiveness against foreign producers.

Export-led/outward-oriented growth A strategy stressing export markets in the belief that the resulting increase in aggregate demand (AD) and in foreign exchange earnings, together with the faster transfer and diffusion of technology and all other trade-related efficiency benefits, will accelerate the growth and development process of an economy.

Externalities When an economic activity creates benefits or imposes costs for third parties for which these do not pay for, or do not get compensated for, respectively.

Factor endowments The factors of production (land, labour, capital and entrepreneurship) of a country.

Factors of production The land (natural capital), labour, human capital, physical capital and entrepreneurship an economy has at its disposal.

Fertility rate The average number of live births per 1,000 for all women between 15 and 44 years old.

Financial account Records the portfolio and foreign direct investment (FDI) into and out of a country over a period of time as well as changes in reserve assets.

Fiscal policy Refers to the manipulation of the level of government spending (G) and of taxation (T) in order to affect aggregate demand (AD).

Fixed costs Production costs reflecting the use of fixed inputs which are independent of the level of output and exist even if output is zero; their existence signals that the firm operates in the short run.

Fixed exchange rate system A system where the exchange rate is set at a level or within a range by the government and is then maintained there through central bank intervention (specifically, through buying and selling the currency in the foreign exchange market and/or manipulating the interest rate).

Floating (flexible) exchange rate system A system where the exchange rate is determined solely through the interaction of demand and supply for the currency with no government (central bank) intervention.

Food price controls Maximum prices imposed by some governments on food items which are set below the free-market equilibrium prices and which aim at protecting the vulnerable.

Foreign debt The amount of money that a country owes to foreign entities that include foreign governments, commercial banks and multilateral institutions and which is repaid in foreign exchange.

Foreign direct investment (FDI) When multinational corporations establish a new firm or acquire controlling interest in an existing one in a foreign country. It is distinct from portfolio investment as in FDI the investor has control over the asset.

Foreign exchange reserves The value of foreign exchange holdings at the central bank of a country.

Free goods Goods that do not have an opportunity cost, for example sea water.

Free market economy Refers to an economy in which markets alone, in other words the interaction of buyers and sellers, determine prices and output.

Free rider problem A consequence of non-excludability in the case of public goods: it refers to the ability of all individuals to benefit from a good or service once it becomes available to one.

Free trade Refers to international trade that is not subject to any type of trade barriers.

Free trade area (agreement) An agreement that is formed when two or more countries abolish tariffs (and other barriers) between them while maintaining existing barriers to non-members.

Frictional unemployment Refers to people in between jobs. It is a form of unavoidable unemployment as people are constantly moving between jobs in search of better opportunities. Better and faster information concerning the labour market can lower this type of unemployment.

Full employment The term has come to refer to the situation where there is equilibrium in the labour market and so any unemployment remaining is not demand-deficient. Any increase in total output beyond the full employment level will prove inflationary and temporary.

Game theory A branch of mathematics with many applications in economics that analyses in a stylized form situations where interdependence of outcomes exists.

Gini coefficient A measure of income inequality within a population that ranges from zero (perfect equality) to 1 (or 100) in the case of absolute inequality.

Goals of firms Profit maximization is the working assumption but several other behavioural assumptions have been also proposed by theorists. Sales (revenue) maximization, growth maximization, satisficing theories, corporate social responsibility as well as managerial theories are among the alternatives.

Government budget (or national budget) An estimate of government expenditures and government (tax and other) income for a future period.

Government debt (see Public debt)

Government failure When government policies aiming at correcting a market failure fail to do so as a result of unintended consequences, measurement problems, biases, etc.

Government revenue Also referred to as government income; it includes tax and other revenues a government collects.

Grants (aid) Flows of financial aid to developing countries that do not have to be repaid to the donor country.

GDP The value of all final goods and services produced within an economy over a period of time, usually a year.

Green GDP An attempt to correct GDP by accounting for the detrimental effect of production on the environment. Green GDP is estimated by subtracting from GDP the cost of natural resource and environmental depletion.

Gross national income (GNI) (see Gross national product)

Gross national product (GNP) GNP equals GDP plus income from abroad minus income paid abroad.

Growth Refers to increases in the real GDP (the total output) of a country through time. Can be distinguished into actual and potential.

Growth maximization An alternative to the short-term revenue maximization goal where managers are assumed to seek to maximize the growth in sales revenue (that is, the growth rate of demand for the firm's output) and the capital value of the firm over time.

Health indicators Single variable or composite indicators that aim at summarizing an aspect or the level of health of a country, for example life expectancy at birth, incidence of tuberculosis per 100,000 people.

Heavily indebted countries Developing countries facing an unsustainable debt burden.

Hidden unemployment Unemployment that is not reflected in official unemployment statistics which includes, for example, discouraged workers, involuntary part-time employees and workers forced into early retirement and which causes the official unemployment statistic to understate the true level of unemployment in an economy.

Homogeneous product A product that consumers consider identical (a perfect substitute) across all firms of an industry.

Household indebtedness The amount of money households owe typically to banks from past borrowing.

Human capital The education, training and experience embodied in the labour force of an economy.

Human development Expanding people's choices and the level of wellbeing they achieve: material consumption as well as better health and better education.

Human development index A composite measure of development that focuses on three dimensions: health, education and income. It uses life expectancy; mean years of schooling of people aged 25 and older; expected years of schooling that a child of school entrance age can expect to receive if prevailing patterns of enrolment stay the same; and per capita GNP based on purchasing power parity dollars (PPP$). (See also Purchasing power parity (PPP) theory.)

Humanitarian aid Aid provided for humanitarian reasons to countries suffering from a natural disaster (for example an earthquake), famine or war.

Implicit costs Production costs for which no explicit payment is made by the firm and which include the opportunity cost of using resources the firm owns as well as normal profit, the minimum return required for the firm to remain in business.

Import substitution/inward-oriented growth A growth strategy in which domestic production is substituted for imports in an attempt to shift production away from the primary sector and industrialize.

Incentive function of prices Refers to the idea that changes in the relative price of a good will induce producers to offer more or less of it in the market as their profit margin will be affected.

Incidence (burden) of taxation Refers to who ends up paying a tax (tax shifting). An indirect tax imposed on a firm may eventually be partially or wholly paid by consumers.

Income approach Refers to one of the three ways of measuring national income whereby incomes earned by all four factors of production (namely, wages, profits, interest and rents) over a period of time are added together to arrive at an estimate of national income or GNP. The other two methods are the output method and the expenditure method.

Income elasticity of demand (XED) The responsiveness of demand to a change in income.

Income, expenditure and output method Three conceptually equivalent methods of measuring overall economic activity. The output method includes all final goods and services produced within a period of time; the income method adds all incomes that this production process generates (wages, profits, interest and rents); the expenditure method sums all the expenditures made for the purchase of these final goods and services produced.

Income flow Within the circular flow diagram of a closed economy without government it refers to the monetary flow from firms to households that reflects payments by the firms to households for the use of factors of production.

Increasing returns to scale A production technology where an increase in all inputs by 1% leads to an increase in output by more than 1%; increasing returns to scale lead to economies of scale (EOS).

Indebtedness Within a development framework the external (foreign) debt of a country. The money a developing country owes to foreigners including governments, multinational institutions and commercial banks.

Indirect taxation A tax on goods or on expenditure on a 'per unit' basis or as a percentage of the price.

Industrial policy A set of interventionist supply side policies whereby the government supports with subsidized loans, preferential tax treatment as well as other methods certain specific industries thought to exhibit high growth potential and to create significant positive spillovers for the whole economy.

Infant industry argument The argument that the only way a developing country can create a competitive domestic industrial sector is if it blocks all competing imports with prohibitive tariffs until it becomes sufficiently efficient.

Inferior goods Goods for which demand decreases following a rise in consumers' income.

Infinitely price elastic demand A limiting value of price elasticity of demand (PED) which implies that the firm is a price taker and faces a horizontal demand for its product at the going market-determined price.

Infinitely price elastic supply A limiting value of price elasticity of supply (PES) which implies that the firm is willing to offer as much as the market demands at some price and that the firm is characterized by constant returns to scale so that average costs (AC) are constant and equal to marginal costs (MC).

Inflation Refers to a sustained increase in the general price level.

Inflation rate The percentage change in the average price level, measured by some price index, between two time periods; for example if the inflation rate of a country for 2011 is 3.2% it means that prices in 2011 increased on the average by 3.2% from 2010. If it is negative it implies deflation. If it is positive but decreasing through time there is disinflation.

Inflationary gap A gap is present if equilibrium (actual) real output (temporarily) exceeds the level corresponding to the full employment level of output.

Informal markets Markets in which economic activity is not officially registered, recorded or regulated by the government. Street vendors in many cities are typically part of the informal sector of an economy.

Informal sector (see Informal markets)

Infrastructure Physical capital, typically financed by governments, which facilitates economic activity as it lowers production and transaction costs and is responsible for the creation of sizable positive externalities. The road system, the rail system, harbours, airports and telecommunications that a country has are typical examples.

Injections Within the circular flow model the term refers to spending on domestic output that is exogenous (that is, independent of the level of domestic income). It includes private investment spending, government spending and exports.

Innovations Refers to new or improved products or processes as well as new marketing and organizational methods.

Institutional factors Refers to the laws and regulations of product, labour and capital markets in a country; more generally refers to the legal and regulatory framework within which economic activity is conducted.

Interdependence In an oligopolistic setting the term refers to the fact that the outcome of any action of a firm depends on the reaction of rival firms.

Interest The reward of the factor of production capital. The payment made for using borrowed money over a period of time.

Interest rate The price paid for borrowing money over a specified period expressed as a percentage (or, the reward for lending or parting with money).

International credit rating An evaluation of a country's credit worthiness (that is, its ability to repay debt) prepared by specialized agencies such as Moody's.

Investment Spending by firms on capital goods, for example machines, tools, equipment and factories; the change in the stock of capital of an economy through time. Investment expenditures in national income accounts include not only fixed capital expenditures by firms but also inventory investment and residential housing investment.

Invisible balance Invisibles in the balance of payments include exports and imports of services, net income from investments (profits, interest and dividend receipts and payments) and net transfers (official and private remittances).

J-curve effect Following devaluation, a trade deficit will typically worsen before it starts improving (tracing the letter 'J' through time) as the Marshall-Lerner condition is not satisfied in the short run.

Joint profits The profit measure that cartel members aim at maximizing, behaving as if they were a monopoly.

Joint supply Two goods are jointly supplied if the production of one automatically is responsible for the production of the other.

Kinked demand curve An oligopolistic model developed by P. Sweezy where in a (usually non-collusive) set-up it is assumed that if one firm decreases price the rival firm will follow but if it raises price the rival will not follow. This asymmetric response gives rise to a kinked demand curve. The model shows that in an oligopoly, even if cost conditions change, prices remain 'sticky'.

Labour The human efforts used in the production of goods and services.

Labour market flexibility The ability of a labour market to adjust fast and fully to changes in labour demand and labour supply conditions.

Labour market reforms Reforms related to the operation of labour markets that aim at increasing labour force participation, lowering unemployment and improving overall flexibility of the labour market. These reforms are often but not exclusively centred around the labour unions, minimum wage laws, employment protection legislation, size and duration of unemployment benefits, etc.

Land Natural resources that an economy is endowed with.

Law of demand As the price per unit of a product rises, quantity demanded per time period decreases, ceteris paribus.

Law of diminishing marginal returns A short-run law of production which states that as more and more units of a variable factor (for example labour) are added to a fixed factor (for example capital) there is a point beyond which total output will continue to rise but at a decreasing rate or, equivalently, that marginal product will start to decrease.

Law of supply As the price per unit increases, the quantity that a firm is willing to offer per period rises, ceteris paribus.

Leakages Within the circular flow model the term refers to income not spent on domestic output but being withdrawn from the circular flow, namely savings, taxes and spending on imports.

Legal barriers (to entry) Refers to state-created barriers to entry, for example patents and licenses.

Linear demand When demand is a straight line (and not a curve) as price is raised to the first power; the general form is $Qd = a - bP$.

Long run (in macroeconomics) When money wages can fully adjust to a change in the average price level so that the real wage remains fixed at its equilibrium level.

Long run (in market structure) When not only are incumbent firms achieving their profit-maximizing goal but in addition there is no entry or exit of firms as either profits are normal or because of the existence of barriers.

Long run (in production and cost theory) When all factors of production are considered variable so no fixed factors exist. The firm can therefore change its scale of operations.

Long-run aggregate supply (LRAS) Within the monetarist or new classical perspective, the LRAS is a vertical line at the economy's potential level of output illustrating that in the long run (when money wages are assumed flexible and can fully adjust to price level changes) the level of real output is independent of prices.

Long run average cost curve (LRAC) A locus of points that show the minimum unit costs a firm will incur to produce a certain level of production when it can change all factors of production.

Long-run Phillips curve A vertical line at the non-accelerating inflation rate of unemployment suggesting the idea that there is a rate of unemployment compatible with any rate of inflation as long as this does not accelerate and that in the long run there is no trade-off between inflation and unemployment that policy makers can exploit.

Loose monetary policy (see Easy monetary policy)

Lorenz curve A diagrammatic illustration of how national income is distributed within the population of a country.

Luxury goods Usually refers to goods with a high income elasticity of demand (YED); that is, with YED greater than 1.

Managed exchange rate system Usually refers to a floating system in which authorities (central banks) intervene whenever they consider the movement of the exchange rate undesirable.

Managerial theories of the firm A collection of alternatives to the profit-maximizing behavioural assumption stemming from the separation of ownership from management in the modern corporation. Here managers are assumed to pursue their own objectives such as power and prestige, salaries, status and job security. This approach is mostly connected to Baumol, Marris and Williamson.

Marginal benefit The extra benefit enjoyed from consuming an extra unit of a good.

Marginal cost The extra cost incurred from the production of an extra unit of a good.

Marginal private benefit (MPB) The extra benefit enjoyed by the consumer from consuming an extra unit of a good.

Marginal private cost (MPC) The extra cost incurred by a firm from producing an extra unit of a good.

Marginal product (of labour) Marginal product of labour is the extra output from one more unit of labour. It is thus the change in output from a change in labour. This is the slope of the total product curve.

Marginal propensity to consume The extra consumption induced from extra income.

Marginal propensity to import The extra spending on imports induced from extra income.

Marginal propensity to save The extra savings induced from extra income.

Marginal propensity to tax (see Marginal tax rate – MTR)

Marginal revenue (MR) The extra revenue from selling one more unit of output: it is the change in total revenues (TR) from a change in output. This is the slope of the TR curve.

Marginal social benefit (MSB) The extra benefit enjoyed by society from the consumption of an extra unit of a good.

Marginal social cost (MSC) The extra cost incurred by society from the production of an extra unit of a good.

Marginal tax rate (MTR) The tax paid on the last 'dollar' of income earned.

Marginal utility The extra satisfaction a consumer derives from consuming an extra unit of a good.

Market A process or an institution through which potential buyers and sellers of a product interact.

Market clearing price That market price for which quantity demanded is equal to quantity supplied per period. No excess demand or supply exists at such a price.

Market equilibrium Exists when there is no tendency for the market price to change; it requires that neither excess demand nor excess supply exists so that quantity demanded equals quantity supplied per period.

Market failure When market forces (demand and supply conditions) alone fail to allocate scarce resources efficiently, meaning that either too much or not enough of a good is produced or consumed. Typical cases include the existence of monopoly power; of externalities and of public, merit and demerit goods.

Market success When market forces (demand and supply conditions) alone lead to socially efficient outcomes meaning that 'just the right' amount of a good is produced from society's viewpoint and so scarce resources are allocated in the best possible way.

Marshall–Lerner condition A condition stating that devaluation will improve a trade deficit if the sum of the price elasticities of demand for exports and imports exceeds unity. Since this condition is typically not satisfied in the short run the trade deficit initially worsens, giving rise to the 'J-curve' effect.

Maximum price (price ceiling) A price set by an authority (the government) below the equilibrium determined price (the market price) aiming at protecting (low-income) consumers.

Merit goods Goods whose consumption creates very significant positive externalities to society. As a result, governments often want even the poor or the ignorant to consume sufficient amounts of these goods. Typical examples include basic education, basic health care, museums, etc.

Microcredit schemes Very small loans to the very poor in developing countries that are used to help them start or grow small businesses and meet emergency expenses. Microcredit pioneer Muhammad Yunus and the Grameen Bank in Bangladesh won the 2006 Nobel Peace Prize.

Millennium development goals (MDG) Following the 2000 Millennium Summit these are eight development goals that all UN member states have agreed to achieve by 2015. The MDG are: ending extreme poverty and hunger; achieving universal primary education; promoting gender equality; reducing child mortality; improving maternal health; combating HIV/AIDS, malaria and other diseases; ensuring environmental sustainability; developing a global partnership for development.

Minimum price (price floor) A price set by an authority (the government) above the equilibrium determined price, usually in order to protect producers. Note that the expression is also used in cases of collusive oligopoly and it refers to the minimum price at which these firms have agreed to sell the product.

Minimum wage A wage set by the government above the equilibrium free market money wage that aims at protecting workers; the lowest money wage employers can legally pay.

Mixed economy Refers to an economy in which economic decisions are determined by both market forces and by the state.

Monetary policy The manipulation of interest rates in order to affect aggregate demand (AD) and so inflation, output and employment.

Monetary union An economic union where members also adopt a common currency and monetary policy conducted by a common central bank, for example the 17 eurozone countries.

Money demand A relationship showing at each interest rate how much money (non-interest bearing assets) economic agents wish to hold given the level of national income (also referred to as liquidity preference).

Money supply The total amount of money in circulation in a country; money supply includes all coins and notes plus money in current (chequing) accounts

Monopolistic competition Exists when there are very many small firms in a market, no entry or exit barriers and a differentiated product.

Monopoly Exists when there is one firm, a 'unique' product and high entry barriers.

Monopoly power The ability of a firm to raise price above marginal cost (MC): that is, the level that would prevail in competition; the Lerner index of monopoly power is given by the ratio of the difference of price charged less MC expressed as a proportion of price (P). This is equal to zero in perfect competition as in perfect competition, P = MC.

Moral hazard Moral hazard arises when economic agents, consumers or firms, as a result of asymmetric information do not bear the full cost of their actions and so become more likely to take such actions.

Movement along a curve The case in any diagrammatic representation of an economic relationship between two variables when one of these two variables changes.

Multilateral aid Aid dispensed through multilateral organizations, such as the IMF or the World Bank.

Multilateral development assistance (see Multilateral aid)

Multinational (or transnational) corporations (or enterprises) Corporations that have established a presence and manage facilities in more than one country. A result of foreign direct investment (FDI).

Multiplier effect (expenditure multiplier) The (Keynesian) idea that a rise in injections (G, I, X) will lead to a greater increase of national income. Fiscal policy is thus a powerful tool to lift an economy out of a recession.

National debt (see Public debt)

National vs. domestic (output or income) National aggregates focus on the nationality of factors independently of their location, whereas domestic aggregates focus on location independently of the nationality of the factors of production involved.

Nationalization The transfer of privately owned firms (assets) to the state.

Natural capital Refers to the resource of land but it implies that land is not a fixed endowment but that it can both increase or improve, or decrease or be destroyed by human activities and policies.

Natural monopoly A natural monopoly is said to exist if the available production technology in relation to the size of the market is such that two firms cannot profitably coexist; typically, a result of very significant economies of scale (EOS).

Natural rate of unemployment (NRU) or non-accelerating inflation rate of unemployment (NAIRU) The natural rate of unemployment is defined as the equilibrium rate of unemployment, that is, the unemployment that exists at the real wage rate that equates the number of workers that firms are willing to hire with the number of workers who are willing to accept a job offer. It is also the unemployment compatible with any rate of inflation as long as it does not accelerate. The long-run Phillips curve is vertical at this rate of unemployment.

Necessities A loose term referring to basic, day-to-day goods and services with a low income elasticity of demand (YED).

Negative externalities Arise when an economic activity, production or consumption, imposes costs on third parties for which these do not get compensated.

Net exports The difference between the value of exports and imports of goods and services over a period of time.

Net investment Gross investment minus capital consumption (depreciation).

Net national product Gross national product (GNP) minus depreciation.

Nominal variable (or value) Nominal variables are measured in monetary units and the effect of inflation has not been accounted for.

Non-collusive oligopoly When oligopolistic firms compete through price or non-price competition.

Non-excludability A characteristic of public goods which means that if a good or service becomes somehow available to one individual it automatically becomes available to all.

Non-governmental organizations (NGOs) Organizations usually independent of governments and typically aiming at designing and implementing development-related projects. An example is Oxfam which is concerned with poverty alleviation.

Non-price competition Competition typically found in oligopolistic markets that is not based on price cutting but on other methods such as advertising, provision of volume discounts or of extended guarantees.

Non-price rationing Rationing mechanisms that are not based on the use of a free market price but on other methods such as sellers' preferences or 'first come-first served'.

Non-produced non-produced assets Non-financial, non-produced assets include land, patents, leases as well as transferable contracts and Internet domains.

Non-rivalness A characteristic of public (and quasi public) goods which means that if a good or service is consumed by one, the amount available for the rest does not diminish; also a characteristic of common-access (pool) resources (non-subtractability).

Normal goods Goods for which demand increases following an increase in consumer income.

Normal profits The minimum reward required by a firm to remain in business that compensates for the risk incurred by the entrepreneur (normal profit is therefore an element of economic costs as without it the firm would not secure the factor of production entrepreneurship).

Normative (economic) statement A value judgement, an opinion; usually spotted by words such as 'ought to be', 'fair' or 'unfair'.

Official aid Aid from governments or multilateral institutions (organizations) such as the World Bank.

Official development assistance (see Official aid)

Oligopolistic interdependence Interdependence exists when the outcome of any action of an oligopolistic firm depends on the reaction of the rival firm(s).

Oligopoly Exists when there are few interdependent firms, entry barriers and either a homogeneous or a differentiated product.

Open economy An economy that engages in trade (that is, it exports and imports goods and services). The degree of openness is measured by the ration of the sum of exports and imports expressed as a proportion of GDP.

Opportunity cost (of an action) The value of the next best alternative sacrificed.

Output approach Refers to one of the three ways of measuring national income whereby production (output) is summed across all industries over a period of time. The other two methods are the expenditure method and the income method.

Output flow Within the circular flow diagram of a closed economy without government, it refers to the real flow of goods and services from firms to households over a period of time.

Overspecialization A case where a country concentrates production and exports in only one or in a very limited range of products which exposes it to higher risks.

Per capita (GDP or income) or per head The GDP (or national income) of a country divided by its population.

Perfect competition Exists when there are very many small firms, no entry or exit barriers and a homogeneous product; also, perfect information and perfect factor mobility. There are few examples, mostly found in agriculture.

Perfect resource mobility When nothing hinders the flow of factors of production from one use to another.

Perfectly inelastic demand A limiting case when price elasticity of demand (PED is equal to zero, implying that a change in price leads to no change in quantity demanded so that the demand curve is vertical at some quantity.

Perfectly inelastic supply A limiting case when price elasticity of supply (PES) is equal to zero, implying that a change in price leads to no change in quantity supplied so that the supply curve is vertical at some level of output; quantity offered is therefore independent of demand and price. Typically, this is the case for many agricultural products in the (very) short run or when a service is constrained by the amount of capital available, for example in the case of hotel services, or seating available in a sports stadium or concert hall.

Personal income taxes A direct tax levied on the income of a person.

Phases of the business (or trade) cycle The alternating periods of growth and contraction of an economy (of real GDP); usually, four phases are distinguished: the upturn (expansion or boom), the peak, the downturn (recession or contraction) and the trough. Recovery and slow down may be included as separate phases.

Phillips curve An empirically derived inverse relationship between the rate of inflation and the rate of unemployment: a decrease in unemployment will result to an increase in inflation and vice versa.

Physical capital The term is used to distinguish the term capital from the terms human capital and natural capital and refers to so-called produced means of production.

Pigovian tax Taxes levied on polluters ('polluter pays principle') equal to the external cost of pollution which not only internalize the externality but also generate revenues for the government.

Polluter pays principle The idea behind Pigovian taxes; the principle according to which polluters should pay the cost of their actions or the cost of measures to reduce pollution, according to the size of the damage inflicted on society.

Portfolio investments (in the financial account of the BOP) Refers to the acquisition of stocks and bonds and of other financial assets by foreign investors which do not provide them with ownership or management rights; international investment that covers investment in equity and debt instruments.

Positive (economic) statement An (economic) statement that can (at least in principle) be tested against data. For example, 'unemployment in Australia has decreased since 2006'.

Positive externalities A positive externality arises if an economic activity creates a benefit to a third party for which it does not pay. They can arise either in the production or in the consumption of a good.

Potential output The level of output an economy can produce in the long run when money wages are flexible and the labour market is in equilibrium so that only natural unemployment is present. At the potential level of output, the long-run aggregate supply (LRAS) is vertical. The long-term growth trend line in a business cycle diagram also illustrates potential output. It is also referred to as the full employment level of output.

Poverty (cycle) A vicious circle in which low incomes leading to poverty are responsible for low savings which are able to finance limited investments, leading to low income levels.

Price ceiling Refers to a maximum price (that is, a price usually set by the government below the free market price and above which sellers cannot charge).

Price controls Refers to both maximum and minimum prices (that is, cases where the government intervenes and sets the price because it considers the market-determined price as either too high or too low).

Price deflator A price index used to convert nominal GDP or nominal GNP/GNI to real GDP/GNI which is based on the prices of all domestically produced goods and services; more generally price deflators permit comparisons of the true change in a variable such as GDP free from the influence of price changes.

Price discrimination When a firm charges for the same product two or more different prices in two or more markets and the price difference is not a result of differences in production or provision costs.

Price elasticity of demand (PED) The responsiveness of demand to a change in price.

Price elasticity of supply (PES) The responsiveness of supply to a change in price.

Price floor (see Minimum price)

Price leadership When in oligopolistic markets tacitly colluding firms follow the price changes initiated by some industry leader (known as dominant firm or barometric price leadership).

Price maker (or price searcher) Any firm facing a negatively sloped demand curve.

Price mechanism A mechanism that impersonally and with minimum cost conveys under certain assumptions all the necessary information to market participants and allocates society's scarce resources to their best use.

Price rigidity (in oligopoly) A feature of oligopolistic markets where firms often do not change prices even if market demand or cost conditions change, preferring to adjust quantities for fear of initiating a price war.

Price support (see Minimum price)

Price taker A perfectly competitive firm which who is so small compared to the market that it cannot influence market price by its output decisions.

Price war Refers to the case where oligopolistic firms compete through successive price cuts.

Price-elastic demand Demand is considered price elastic if a change in price leads to a **proportionately** greater change in quantity demanded.

Price-inelastic demand Demand is considered price inelastic if a change in price leads to a **proportionately** smaller change in quantity demanded.

Primary products Agricultural and non-agricultural products traded in world markets and used as inputs in manufacturing.

Primary/secondary/tertiary sector The primary sector refers to agriculture, mining, forestry and fishing; the secondary sector refers to manufacturing (industry) and construction whereas the tertiary sector refers to services.

Prisoner's dilemma A simple non-cooperative game illustrating strategic interdependence and that lack of coordination leads to suboptimal solutions.

Private sector The private sector of an economy includes households and firms.

Privatization The transfer of state-owned assets (firms) to the private sector.

Producer price index (PPI) A price index that tracks the selling prices received by domestic producers for their output. These prices are also referred to as wholesale prices.

Producer surplus The difference between what a firm earns and the minimum it requires to offer a given amount of a good.

Production costs The value of resources sacrificed for the production of a good or service.

Production externalities Externalities arising in the process of production. These could be either positive or negative externalities.

Production possibilities curve (frontier or boundary) Shows the maximum amount of good Y an economy is able to produce for each amount of X it chooses to produce if it fully and efficiently employs all of its scarce resources with its given level of technology.

Productive efficiency When production takes place with minimum average (unit) costs, implying that production takes place with minimal resource waste (also technical efficiency).

Profit maximization The assumed goal of the typical firm. Firms will choose that level of output for which economic profits are maximum, which requires that marginal revenue (MR) is equal to marginal cost (MC) and that MC is rising.

Profit repatriation Profits earned by multinationals and sent back home.

Progressive, proportional and regressive taxation Progressive tax system: when a higher-income household pays proportionately more than a lower-income household. Proportional tax system: when a higher-income household pays proportionately the same as a lower-income household. Regressive tax system: when a higher-income household pays proportionately less than a lower-income household.

Project aid Flows of aid targeting the realization of specific projects, such as the construction of public infrastructure capital.

Property rights Legal ownership rights over an asset. Property rights are part of the institutional framework of an economy.

Public debt The sum of all past (accumulated) budget deficits less surpluses; the total of what a government owes.

Public goods Goods which are non-excludable and non-rival. Since they are non-excludable consumers have the incentive to conceal their preferences and behave as free riders. Public goods are a case of market failure and typical examples include national defence, law and order, traffic lights, lighthouses, etc.

Public sector The state, the government.

Purchasing power parity (PPP) theory A theory of long-run equilibrium exchange rate determination: in the absence of trade barriers, transportation costs and cross-border capital flows and if all goods were tradable then the market exchange rate would gravitate towards its PPP value (that is, it would reflect cost-of-living differences).

Quintile One of the five equal parts of a frequency distribution.

Quota A quantitative restriction of imports. The term is also used to refer to the amount of output a cartel member is assigned when joint profits are maximized.

Glossary

Rationality The assumption that all consumer behaviour is purposeful and obeys certain assumptions concerning preferences.

Rationing function of equilibrium prices The ability of free-market equilibrium prices to ration the available quantity to whoever values it the most and is willing and able to pay the price.

Rationing system A mechanism employed to allocate goods to consumers. The price mechanism is an example of a rationing system.

Real GDP GDP after adjusting for inflation. Real GDP measures the volume of output produced in an economy over a year.

Real variable An economic variable expressed in terms of goods and so adjusted for inflation.

Recession An economy is in recession if real GDP is decreasing for at least two consecutive quarters (negative growth rate); in the USA the NBER determines when the economy enters recession and its decision is based on more variables.

Reflationary fiscal policy (see Expansionary fiscal policy)

Regional economic integration When countries become members of regional trading blocs; more generally, the elimination of trade and investment barriers among a group of countries.

Regional preferential trade agreements Trade agreements among a group of often but not necessarily geographically neighbouring countries that reduce trade barriers on a reciprocal and preferential basis for only the members of the group.

Regulation Direct government intervention in the operation of markets aimed at influencing the behaviour of firms with respect to decisions on pricing, market entry and exit, competition, product standards, etc.

Regulatory framework The set of regulations within which a market, an industry or the economy as a whole operates.

Relative poverty Refers to households with income below the national average; the proportion of a population that is poor in comparison with the consumption or income level of the general population.

Rent The income for the services of a piece of land collected by its owner.

Rent control A maximum price or rent ceiling on what landlords can demand for payment on residential housing set below the free-market determined rent.

Resource allocation The appointment of scarce resources to different uses for the production of different goods and services.

Revaluation An increase in the exchange rate (the price of a currency) within a fixed exchange rate system.

Revenue maximization An alternative to profit maximization where the firm is assumed to maximize revenues (sales) choosing that rate of output for which MR = 0.

Sales maximization (see Revenue maximization)

Satisficing An alternative to profit maximization where, because of conflicting objectives of the various stakeholders within a firm and informational limitations, firms only strive to achieve at least some pre-defined minimum level of profits or revenues.

Scarcity The idea that human wants exceed the ability to produce goods and services from our limited resources to satisfy these wants; illustrated by the mere existence of a production possibilities frontier.

Seasonal unemployment Unemployment due to seasonal variations of demand, for example construction workers who are unemployed because of extremely cold weather.

Shift of a curve A curve in a diagram may shift if there is a change in a variable that is not represented in either of the two axes; for example, in a demand curve diagram with price and quantity demanded on the two axes, the curve may shift if income changes.

Short run (in macroeconomics) When money wages are assumed fixed so that a change in the average price level affects the real wage and induces a change in real output by firms.

Short run (in market structure) The time period during which the number of firms in a market is not fixed but may change as a result of supernormal profits or losses.

Short run (in production and cost theory) The time period during which some but not all adjustments are possible; in production, it is when at least one fixed factor of production exists.

Short-run aggregate supply (SRAS) Within the monetarist or new classical perspective, SRAS is an upward sloping curve illustrating that if the average price level increases firms will be offering more output because money wages are assumed fixed and so profit margins increase.

Shortage When, as a result of price being fixed by an authority below the competitive free-market equilibrium level, quantity demanded exceeds quantity supplied.

Shut-down-rule A loss-making firm in the short run will shut down and exit only if the price (average revenue, AR) is less than the average variable cost (AVC). In the long run it will shut down if it is making losses.

Signalling function of relative price changes Relative price changes within a free competitive market set-up convey information to participants concerning the existence of excess demand or supply which induces a change in their behaviour.

Slope of a demand curve Assuming a linear demand function it is the coefficient of the term P; note that if this coefficient becomes absolutely larger the curve becomes flatter as the axes in economics are reversed.

Slope of a supply curve Assuming a linear supply function it is the coefficient of the term P; note that if this coefficient becomes absolutely larger the curve becomes flatter as the axes in economics are reversed.

Social (or community) surplus The sum of the consumer surplus and the producer surplus.

Social science The set of scientific disciplines that systematically study human behaviour from different perspectives.

Soft loans Loans granted at concessionary terms. The interest rate charged is lower than market interest rates and the repayment period is longer. An example of such loans is foreign aid.

Specialization When a factor of production is employed in the production of only one good or even a part of a good. Specialization results in increased levels of output.

Specific tax An indirect tax (a tax on a good) that is set as a fixed amount per unit.

Speculation The buying and selling of foreign exchange (or more generally an asset) in order to profit from differences in its price.

Stagflation Stagnation (zero or negative growth) and rising or high unemployment at the same time.

Stagnation Stagnation exists when growth in real GDP is either negative or negligible for a number of years.

Stakeholders All parties that have a direct or indirect interest in an organization or who could be affected by its actions and decisions.

State-owned enterprises (SOE) Nationalized firms (that is, firms whose ownership rests with the state).

Strategic interdependence In a game theoretic framework, the fact that each player's welfare and pay-off depends not only on his or her actions but also on the actions of other players.

Structural unemployment Unemployment that persists way past recovery and is a result of the changing structure of an economy as well as a result of labour-market rigidities.

Subsidy A payment made by the government to firms aiming at lowering costs and price and thus raising production and consumption of the product as well as firms' revenues.

Substitute goods Two goods that can satisfy the same need for a consumer which are thus in competitive consumption and for which cross price elasticity of demand (XED) is positive.

Supernormal (abnormal) profits Anything above the minimum profit required by a firm to remain in a certain business.

Supply The quantity that a firm is willing to offer per period of time at a given price, ceteris paribus.

Supply shocks Refers to sudden changes and shifts in the short-run aggregate supply (SRAS) typically as a result of a sudden change in the price of oil (as oil is the predominant form of energy for firms) or, more generally, of commodities.

Surplus When, as a result of price being fixed by an authority above the competitive free-market equilibrium level, quantity supplied exceeds quantity demanded.

Sustainable development Development that meets the needs of the present generation without decreasing the ability of future generations to meet their own needs. Typically it implies development that does not result in environmental degradation.

Tacit collusion Tacit or informal collusion is said to exist when oligopolistic firms coordinate their behaviour (without any communication between the parties being necessary) so that it resembles that of a single dominant firm and the outcome that of explicit collusion.

Tariff A tax on imports as a result of which the domestic price of the product rises, the level of domestic production rises, the level of domestic consumption drops and the volume of imports is restricted. A tariff also generates revenues for a government.

Tax incidence (See Incidence (burden) of taxation)

Technical efficiency (see Productive efficiency)

Terms of trade The ratio of the average price of exports over the average price of imports expressed as an index number times 100. It shows the volume of imports attainable with a unit of exports.

Terms of trade: improving If the terms of trade ratio rises it shows that a greater volume of imports is now attainable by a unit of exports.

Terms of trade: worsening (or deteriorating) If the terms of trade ratio decreases it means that fewer imports can now be attained by a unit of exports.

Tied aid Aid that has to be used to buy the donor's products (often unnecessary or low priority and/or more expensive); considered a factor partially explaining the weak link between aid and development.

Tight monetary policy A central bank is employing tight monetary policy if it increases interest rates (decreases the money supply) in order to decrease (or slow down the increase in) aggregate demand

(AD) and so decrease inflationary pressures in the economy.

Time lags (in economic policy) Refers to the time that elapses from the moment a problem arises in an economy to the time a policy choice has an effect; can be distinguished into the detection lag, the administrative lag and the impact or execution lag.

Total costs The costs incurred for the production of Q units of output. Total costs are equal in the short run to fixed costs plus variable costs.

Total product Total product is the output derived from a specific combination of inputs.

Total revenues (or sales revenue) The product of the price per unit times the number of units sold by a firm in a time period.

Tradable (marketable) permits (or licences) A market-based solution to the problem of pollution-emitting firms where the government determines the maximum acceptable level of pollution and then issues to firms permits (rights to pollute a certain amount) which are tradable. Firms have the incentive to engage in active trading until a new allocation of permits emerges with the total level of pollution the same but with minimal amount of production sacrificed.

Trade balance The difference between the value of exports and imports of goods (and services) per period. If the value of exports exceeds the value of imports then a trade surplus is recorded. Conversely, a trade deficit is the case if the value of imports of goods (and services) exceeds that of exports.

Trade creation The increased trade as a result of lower trade barriers in a regional trading bloc where a less-efficient member now imports a good from a more-efficient member instead of producing it itself.

Trade cycle (see Business cycle)

Trade diversion The inefficient rise in trade within a regional trading bloc whereby a less-efficient member imports a good from another member, instead of importing it from a truly more-efficient non-member.

Trade flows Exports and imports of goods and services per period.

Trade liberalization Refers to policies aiming at decreasing or eliminating trade barriers.

Trade protection Refers to policies that aim at restricting the flow of imports into a country and/or creating an artificial advantage to exporting firms.

Trading blocs A form of economic integration where a group of countries decreases trade barriers among them while maintaining barriers to non-members. The arrangement may take the form of a free trade agreement, a customs union, a common market or an economic union.

Tragedy of the commons A term introduced in 1968 by Garrett Hardin that refers to users of a commons (a common-pool resource, for example a pasture) where in his original analysis the process inevitably leads to the destruction of the resource (for example overgrazing of the pasture) on which the users depend.

Transfer payments Payments of the government to individuals that do not reflect contribution to current production. Examples of transfer payments include unemployment benefits and pensions.

Typical consumer (see Average household)

Underemployment When individuals are employed but are working less than they would have wanted to or in positions below their skills.

Underlying inflation (see Core inflation)

Underprovision and overprovision of merit and demerit goods When market forces lead to less than the socially optimal amount being produced or consumed (in the case of merit goods) or to more than the socially optimal amount being produced or consumed (in the case of demerit goods).

Unemployment Exists when individuals who are actively searching for a job cannot find one.

Unemployment rate The number of unemployed individuals expressed as a proportion of the labour force.

Unitary price elasticity of demand When a change in price leads to a proportionally equal change in quantity demanded so that price elasticity of demand (PED) is 1. If PED is 1 throughout the length of a demand curve then the demand curve is a rectangular hyperbola.

Unitary price elasticity of supply When a change in price leads to a proportionally equal change in quantity supplied so that price elasticity of supply (PES) is 1. If PES is 1 throughout the length of a supply curve then the supply curve is linear and goes through the origin.

Variable costs Production costs that reflect the use of the variable factors of production; to produce more the firm needs more variable inputs so variable costs increase.

Voluntary export restraints A form of trade protection which is similar to a quota as it also refers to a quantitative restriction but in this case the exporting firms 'agree' to limit the volume of exports of a good, typically to avoid worse trade protection.

Wage 'stickiness' A feature of labour markets where money wages do not easily decrease because of labour unions and contracts.

Wages The reward of the factor of production labour.

Wealth The value of all assets owned by an individual minus whatever he or she owes.

Weighted average An average where each element does not carry the same significance in the calculation.

Welfare (or deadweight) loss Refers to decreases in producer and/or consumer surplus as a result of either more or less than the socially optimal level of output produced and consumed.

Withdrawals (see Leakages)

World Trade Organization (WTO) An international organization with 153 member countries which aims at further liberalizing trade through conducting multilateral trade negotiations and at regulating trade and which is the arbitrator of all trade-related disputes. It was established in 1995 and grew out of the General Agreement on Tariffs and Trade (GATT).

X-inefficiency Refers to the 'internal slackness' that often characterizes 'entrenched' monopoly firms. The term was introduced by Harvey Leibenstein.

Zero economic profits Exist when total revenues are equal to total (economic) costs. Since normal profits are included in (economic) costs, it follows that a firm earning zero economic profits is making just enough to remain in business (that is, it is making as much as it would have been making in its next best alternative).

Index